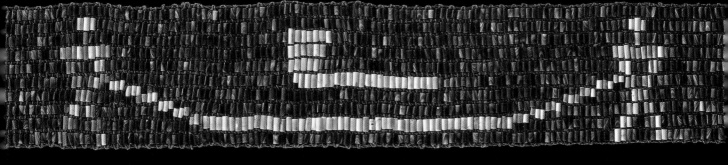

NATION TO NATION

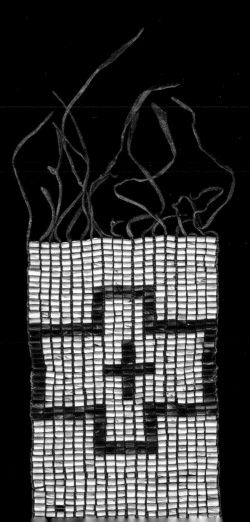

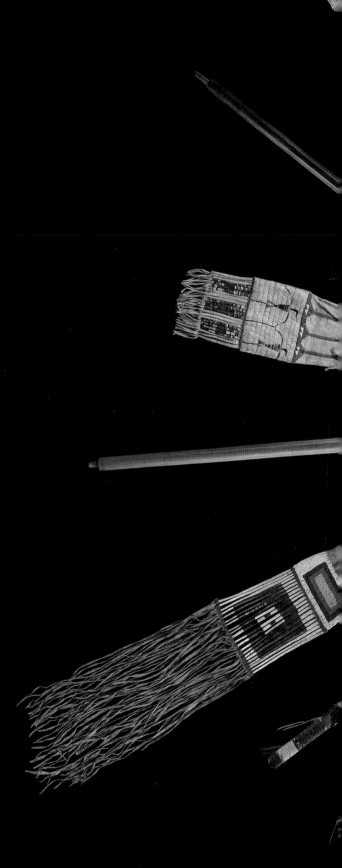

GENERAL EDITOR

Suzan Shown Harjo

PUBLISHED BY THE

National Museum of the American Indian

IN ASSOCIATION WITH

Smithsonian Books

WASHINGTON, DC, AND NEW YORK

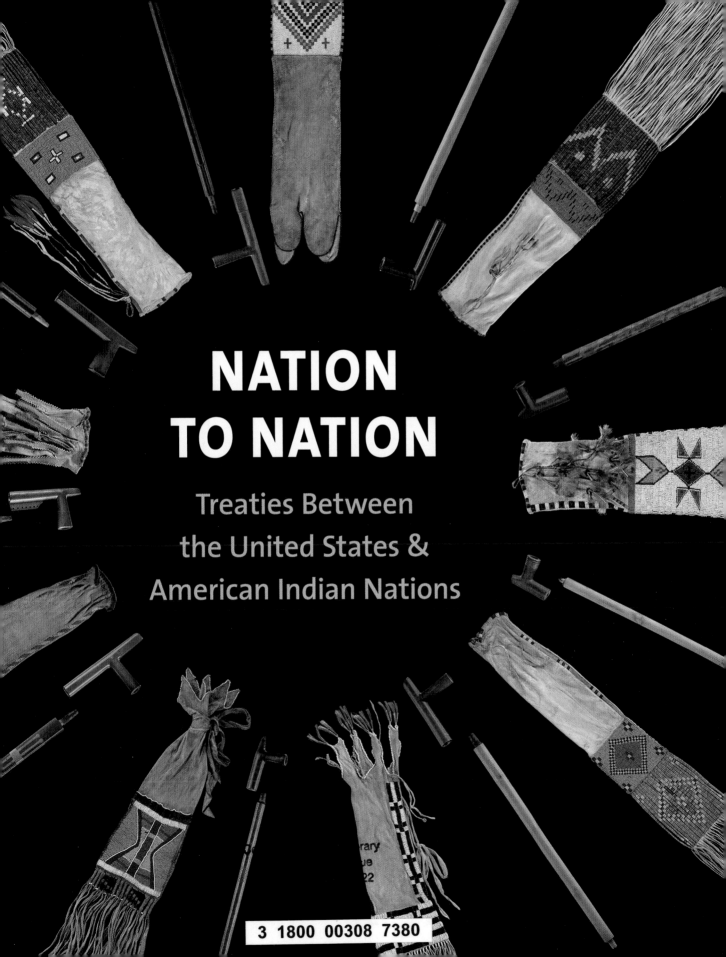

NATION TO NATION

Treaties Between
the United States &
American Indian Nations

The National Museum of the American Indian gratefully acknowledges the following for their generous leadership support of the *Nation to Nation* exhibition and publication:

Shakopee Mdewakanton Sioux Community

San Manuel Band of Mission Indians

Bank of America

Interface Media Group

This book may be purchased for educational, business, or sales promotional use. For information, please write: Smithsonian Books, Special Markets, PO Box 37012, MRC 513, Washington, DC, 20013.

The National Museum of the American Indian (NMAI), Smithsonian Institution, is committed to advancing knowledge and understanding of the Native cultures of the Western Hemisphere—past, present, and future—through partnership with Native people and others. The museum works to support the continuance of culture, traditional values, and transitions in contemporary Native life.

For more information about the Smithsonian's National Museum of the American Indian, visit the NMAI's website at www.AmericanIndian.si.edu. To support the museum by becoming a member, call 1-800-242-NMAI (6624) or click on "Support" on the website.

Director: Kevin Gover (Pawnee)
Associate Director for Museum Programs: Tim Johnson (Mohawk)
General Editor: Suzan Shown Harjo (Cheyenne and Hodulgee Muscogee)
Publications Manager: Tanya Thrasher (Cherokee Nation)
Project Editor: Sally Barrows
Editorial and Research Assistance: Erin Beasley, Cécile Ganteaume, Carolyn Gilman, Christine T. Gordon, Alexandra Harris (Cherokee), Mark G. Hirsch, Cali Martin, Jane McAllister, Arwen Nuttall (Cherokee), Edwin Schupman (Muscogee), Heather Shannon, Lindy Trolan, Christopher Lindsay Turner
Permissions: Erin Beasley, Ann Kawasaki, Bethany Montagano
Object Photography, Photo Services, and Media Group: Ernest Amoroso, Dan Davis, Katherine Fogden (Akwesasne Mohawk), Augusta Lehman, Doug McMains, R.A.Whiteside
Map Illustrations: Gene Thorp/Cartographic Concepts, Inc.
Design: Julie Allred /BW&A Books, Steve Bell
Published by Smithsonian Books
    Director: Carolyn Gleason
    Production Editor: Christina Wiginton

The essay in this book entitled "Unintended Consequences: *Johnson v. M'Intosh* and Indian Removal," was adapted by its author, Lindsay G. Robertson, from his book *Conquest by Law: How the Discovery of America Dispossessed Indigenous Peoples of Their Lands* (2007), sections of which are reprinted here with the permission of Oxford University Press, USA.

First Edition
10 9 8 7 6 5 4 3 2 1

Library of Congress Cataloging-in-Publication Data

Nation to nation : treaties between the United States and American Indian Nations / edited by Suzan Shown Harjo ; contributions by Kevin Gover [and three others].

    pages cm

Summary: "Approximately 368 treaties were negotiated and signed by U.S. commissioners and tribal leaders (and subsequently approved by the U.S. Senate) from 1777 to 1868. These treaties enshrine promises the U.S. government made to Indian people and recognize tribes as nations—a fact that distinguishes tribal citizens from other Americans, and supports contemporary Native assertions of tribal sovereignty and self-determination. Treaties are legally binding and still in effect. Beginning in the 1960s, Native activists invoked America's growing commitment to social justice to restore broken treaties. Today, the reassertion of treaty rights and tribal self-determination is evident in renewed tribal political, economic, and cultural strength, as well as in reinvigorated nation-to-nation relations with the United States"—Provided by publisher.

ISBN 978-1-58834-478-6 (hardback)—ISBN 978-1-58834-479-3 (e-book) 1. Indians of North America—Treaties—History. 2. Indians of North America—Legal status, laws, etc. 3. Indians of North America—Government relations. 4. Treaty-making power—United States—History. I. Harjo, Suzan Shown, editor.

KF8202 2014
342.7308'72—dc23   2014016031

Printed in the United States of America

Vine Deloria Jr., January 2, 2005.

*M*Y DISTINGUISHED ANCESTORS, EXTENDED FAMILY, and dear friend for forty years Vine Deloria Jr. (Standing Rock Sioux, 1933–2005) gave me the curiosity and goals to pursue the history of treaties and treaty making, to understand what went wrong, and to appreciate and wonder at those who went through the horrors of "civilization" and emerged as loving, optimistic human beings. I dedicate this book to their memory, and to the ancestors who made the treaties for all of us.

SUZAN SHOWN HARJO
(Cheyenne and Hodulgee Muscogee)

CONTENTS

Foreword   KEVIN GOVER   xi

1   **Introduction**   SUZAN SHOWN HARJO

American Indian Land and American Empire: An Interview with Philip J. Deloria
SUZAN SHOWN HARJO   12

14   **Treaties with Native Nations: Iconic Historical Relics or Modern Necessity?**
ROBERT N. CLINTON

Treaties as Recognition of the Nation-to-Nation Relationship   MATTHEW L. M. FLETCHER   34

36   **Linking Arms and Brightening the Chain: Building Relations through Treaties**
RICHARD W. HILL, SR.

The Two-Row Wampum Belt   MARK G. HIRSCH   59

William Penn's Treaty and the Shackamaxon Elm Tree   ARWEN NUTTALL   61

Illegal State Treaties   MARK G. HIRSCH   66

68   **Unintended Consequences: *Johnson v. M'Intosh* and Indian Removal**
LINDSAY G. ROBERTSON

Removal Treaties: An Interview with Carey N. Vicenti   SUZAN SHOWN HARJO   85

Avoiding Removal: The Pokagon Band of Potawatomi Indians   MATTHEW L. M. FLETCHER   86

88   **The Great Treaty Council at Horse Creek**   RAYMOND J. DEMALLIE

Language and World View at the Horse Creek Treaty   ARWEN NUTTALL   112

"The Indians Were the Spoken Word": An Interview with N. Scott Momaday
SUZAN SHOWN HARJO   114

116   **Naal Tsoos Saní: The Navajo Treaty of 1868, Nation Building, and Self-Determination**
JENNIFER NEZ DENETDALE

132   **Treaties My Ancestors Made for Me: A Family Treaty History**   SUZAN SHOWN HARJO

152   **The Betrayal of "Civilization" in United States–Native Nations Diplomacy: Pawnee Treaties and Cultural Genocide**   JAMES RIDING IN

American Indian Scouts   MARK G. HIRSCH   173

"Civilization" and the Hupa Flower Dance Ceremony   LOIS J. RISLING   175

178   **Rights Guaranteed by Solemn Treaties**

The Game and Fish Were Made for Us: Hunting and Fishing Rights in Native Nations' Treaties   HANK ADAMS   181

The Anti-Treaty Movement in the Pacific Northwest and the Great Lakes   SUZAN SHOWN HARJO   186

River by River: Treaty Rights in Washington State / An Interview with Susan Hvalsoe Komori   SUZAN SHOWN HARJO   188

"The Fish Helped to Bring People Together": An Interview with Zoltán Grossman   SUZAN SHOWN HARJO   192

Arthur Duhamel: Treaty Fisherman   MATTHEW L. M. FLETCHER   194

Rights We Always Had: An Interview with Tina Kuckkahn   SUZAN SHOWN HARJO   195

198   **From Dislocation to Self-Determination: Native Nations and the United States in the Twentieth Century**   KEVIN GOVER

The Treaty with the Lower Klamath, Upper Klamath, and Trinity River Indians— and Who We Are Today   LOIS J. RISLING   216

Treaties and the United Nations Declaration on the Rights of Indigenous Peoples   ARWEN NUTTALL   219

Modern Treaties: An Interview with Ben Nighthorse Campbell   SUZAN SHOWN HARJO   221

Treaties and Contemporary American Indian Cultures   W. RICHARD WEST, JR.   223

Notes   225   Contributors   239   Acknowledgments   243

Selected Bibliography   245   Image Credits   247   Index   249

FOREWORD

*T*HIS YEAR MARKS THE TENTH ANNIVERSARY OF THE OPENING OF THE Smithsonian's National Museum of the American Indian in Washington, DC. To commemorate the event, the museum chose to develop a publication and an exhibition about treaties between the United States and American Indian Nations.

Why treaties? Because, as this book shows, treaties matter—not only to American Indians but also to everyone who lives in the United States. For starters, the United States acquired much of its land through treaties with Indian Tribes. These negotiated, bilateral agreements are, therefore, fundamental to understanding how the United States was created, and how its citizens obtained the land and natural resources they enjoy today.

Treaties rest at the heart of Native American history as well as contemporary tribal life and identity. The approximately 368 treaties that were negotiated and signed by U.S. commissioners and tribal leaders (and subsequently approved by the U.S. Senate) from 1777 to 1868 enshrine promises our government made to Indian Nations. But they also recognize tribes as *nations*—a fact that distinguishes tribal citizens from other Americans, and supports contemporary Native assertions of tribal sovereignty and self-determination.

Far from being dusty documents of dubious relevance, treaties are legally binding and still in effect. Repeatedly recognized by the courts as sources of rights for Indian people and their Indian Nations, treaties carry the weight of the past and test the strength of our nation's commitment to honesty, good faith, and the rule of law. Promises between the leaders of nations, treaties inscribe solemn vows that cannot lightly be broken or ignored—a verity that Supreme Court justice Hugo Black recognized in 1960 when he declared, "Great nations, like great men, should keep their word."[1]

Despite the moral, legal, historical, and contemporary significance of these treaties, most Americans know little about them. That fact unsettled the late senator Daniel K. Inouye, the longtime chairman,

facing: Shan Goshorn (Eastern Band of Cherokee), b. 1957. *Pieced Treaty: Spider's Web Treaty Basket,* 2007. Paper, paint. 35 × 32 × 58.5 cm. National Museum of the American Indian 26/6080

| xi

vice chairman, and member of the Senate Committee on Indian Affairs, who lamented: "I would venture to guess that to the extent they have ever had occasion to think about them, most Americans think of treaties as ancient relics of the past that have long since been forgotten and which certainly have no relevance to modern society." Said Inouye:

> Too few Americans know that the Indian nations ceded millions of acres of lands to the United States, or that . . . the promises and commitments made by the United States were typically made in perpetuity. History has recorded, however, that our great nation did not keep its word to the Indian nations, and our pre-eminent challenge today . . . is to assure the integrity of our treaty commitments and to bring an end to the era of broken promises.[2]

The National Museum of the American Indian was established by Congress to rectify our nation's historical amnesia about the role of Native Nations in the making of modern America. Treaties are at the core of the relationship between Indian Peoples and the United States. As an educational institution, dedicated to increasing and diffusing knowledge about Native American history and culture, the museum maintains a treasure trove of objects, images, expertise, and close collaborative relationships with tribal leaders, Indigenous knowledge keepers, and Native and non-Native scholars—resources that enrich the book you now hold.

The contributors to this volume, a distinguished group of Native and non-Native historians, legal scholars, and tribal activists, have tapped a vast array of sources, including tribal oral traditions, interviews, historical documents, illustrations, newspaper articles, and Native American material culture, to recount the evolution of U.S.–Indian treaty making from the seventeenth century to the present. Each piece focuses on a different aspect of the treaty story, yet the book is unified by a consistent effort to interpret the history of U.S.–Indian treaty making from the perspective of Native people. This approach, which animates recent scholarship in American Indian history, is consistent with one of the principal canons of American law concerning treaties—that treaties must be interpreted as the Native signers understood them.

From a Native perspective, the story begins with American acceptance of tribal self-government and nation-to-nation diplomacy through treaty making. That promising start quickly morphed into disaster through broken and coercive treaties that promoted Indian removal and tribal land loss, as well as government policies that dismantled Indian Tribes as political institutions, obliterated tribal land ownership, and fostered the forced assimilation of Native people into white culture.

Happily, the story does not end there. For Native people never gave up on their treaties or the tribal sovereignty that treaties recognized. Beginning in the 1960s, Native leaders invoked America's growing commitment to social justice to restore broken treaties, to demand congressional legislation—or modern treaty amendments—that repaired the damages that had been inflicted on Native Nations by U.S. Indian policies, and to rejuvenate tribal governments long subjugated by heavy-handed federal agents. Today, the reassertion of treaty rights and tribal self-determination is evident in renewed tribal political, economic, and cultural strength, as well as in reinvigorated nation-to-nation relations with the United States.

The fundamental tenets of early treaty making—the recognition of tribal governments and Indian consent—are alive and well . . . at least for the moment. The future is untold, and ultimately the gains of Native Nations in modern times are set in fragile beads rather than carved in stone. Yet there is optimism in Indian Country that Americans will come to better understand their shared history with Indian Nations and that, as a result, they will join Native people in celebrating and upholding the rights enshrined in treaties.

We hope this book contributes to that outcome.

KEVIN GOVER *(Pawnee)*
Director, National Museum of the American Indian

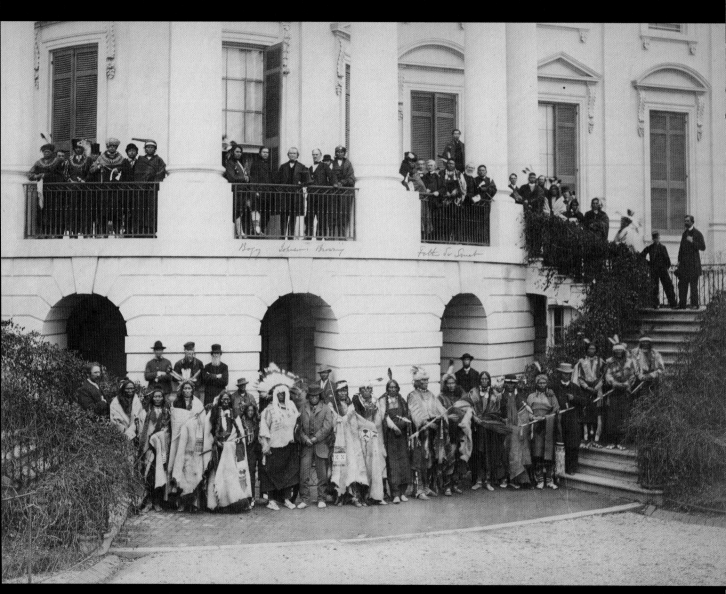

President Andrew Johnson (center, middle balcony) and delegates representing the Miami, Kickapoo, Ottawa, Ojibwe, Sac and Fox, and Sioux Nations outside the White House, February 23, 1867. Washington, DC. Photo by Alexander Gardner. National Museum of the American Indian P10142

Introduction

*T*HIS BOOK IS ABOUT NATIONS, DIPLOMACY, HONOR, PROMISES, WILL, might, territory, optimism, and survivance. It explores the diplomacy, promises, and betrayals involved in and underlying treaties and treaty making between the United States and Native Nations, as one side sought to own the riches of the so-called New World and the other struggled to hold on to traditional homelands and ways of life. These essays show how ideas of honor among nations, fair dealings, utmost good faith, rule of law, and the trust and behavior that define relationships of peace and friendship have been tested and challenged in historical and modern times.

Treaties intertwine nations at the time of their making and throughout their histories. If treaties were valued only for the paper, wampum, or hide that hold their words or meaning, they could easily become antiquated within a few generations. They set forth a relationship that begins in a particular moment, but their interpretations and emphasis may change over the years. The power dynamics and fortunes of the parties may shift and shift again, but the relationships that treaties mark, honor, and celebrate continue to bind the participating nations as long as they are kept vibrant through diplomacy and deliberate acts of renewal.

Treaties continue to link nations together unless a nation's people—town by town, family by family—decide to end the relationship. A decision to dissolve a nation-to-nation treaty relationship would be immense, larger than the original one that forged the agreement. None of the United States' treaties with Native Nations has ever been abrogated, even though most have been stretched to the breaking point, ignored, or all but forgotten.

David P. Bradley (Minnesota Chippewa, White Earth Ojibwe) b. 1954. *Treaty Dollar,* 2011. Silkscreened print on cotton cloth, acrylic on board. 61 × 121.9 cm. © David P. Bradley

The nation-to-nation relationships and dealings between Native Nations and the United States are difficult to understand and carry out in the modern era without an appreciation of the long history of Native treaty making. Many today do not know that treaties are living documents that are exercised daily, even by non-Native people, who may not know that these are their treaties, too. Treaties are possible among nations because each nation is inherently sovereign and recognizes one another's sovereign prerogatives of self-identity, self-government, and self-determination. Treaties establish a relationship, both diplomatic and familial, and they are the foundation of that relationship. Everything else is style.

When the Lenape leaders and the British Quakers came together in 1682 to negotiate the agreement that became known as the Penn Treaty, they both used silence as well as the exchange of gifts to punctuate and emphasize meaning. This, in addition to the pace of sequential translation, gave speakers, interpreters, and witnesses time to absorb, note, and record what was taking place. This style of oratory became treaty-making protocol, and it was embraced by legislative bodies and colonial and early American political oratory societies, which included some of the Founding Fathers among their membership.

In Europe, some had only dreamed of many nations united. The Founding Fathers first saw this unity in the Lenape, Haudenosaunee, and Muscogee confederacies and in the Anishinaabe, Odawa, and Potawatomi alliance as well as in other alliances. They admired these Native political systems, which were the working models for the U.S. government. Tragically, these unified confederacies were the very alliances that some later American politicians were dedicated to breaking up, taking some Native Nations to the edge of extinction.

WHAT WENT WRONG?

N. Scott Momaday (Kiowa) calls language misunderstandings within treaties a "confliction of language." He says: "Native people thought of treaties as bits of paper with this calligraphy, this print or writing on them, and that was new to them, strange to them. They did not understand that as a means of communication, as a representation of the word, as such. They dealt at the level of the human voice. The spoken word was everything to them."[1]

While differing beliefs about the relative powers of the written and spoken word contributed substantially to many treaty conflicts, myriad other misunderstandings arose in treaty making, some deliberate and some innocent. Most of the problems arose from the misperceptions and stereotypes that each side brought to the endeavor, and each thought the other duplicitous. Many Native people blamed non-Natives for bringing from Europe their diseases and blood feuds, and they believed both were intentionally inflicted. They had never seen the flu, measles, mumps, cholera, malaria, smallpox, or typhoid before being hit by the epidemics, one right after another, that eradicated or nearly eradicated whole peoples. Is it any wonder that many Native Nations wanted their treaties to guarantee that Western doctors be provided to cure the Western diseases?

Many Europeans and Euro-Americans considered Native Peoples to be beneath them—bloodthirsty, godless, and stupid. Some thought their mission was to "civilize" Indians, to turn them into English-speaking, Christian farmers. Most white settlers believed that God meant for them to have Native lands, and they behaved as if the land were exclusively theirs to use and control. Most Native leaders were fine with others, including non-Natives, living on, using, and setting boundaries on their lands, but they reserved for their people the freedom to travel in and use some areas. When Native leaders reserved territory, they also did not give up off-reservation fishing, gathering, and hunting sites, or sacred places; they did not intend to be bound by reservation borders, but they were forced into confining situations over time, which resulted in conflicts and wars.

The U.S. Supreme Court addressed this situation by developing one of the canons of federal Indian law, which is that treaties are to be interpreted as the Indians understood them at the time they were negotiated. While this did not resolve all disputes, it has helped to balance some of the inequities.

Oftentimes, federal treaty commissioners negotiated in good faith, but their agreements were overturned or not approved by the U.S. Senate. One of the worst cases of dishonor by the U.S. government in regard to its treaties took place in California, where the California legislature asked the U.S. Senate not to ratify eighteen treaties that had been made in 1851–52 between tribal representatives and federal commissioners. One of the commissioners sent impassioned pleas to the Department of the Interior, warning that many Indians would be killed in the rush for gold if the treaties were not ratified.[3] The Senate brought the treaties to the floor, then quickly withdrew and never ratified them.[4] This left the Native Peoples in California, who had every right to believe they were safe on their treaty lands, to be driven out of their homes by miners or murdered if they did not leave.

"When Indians gave their word and smoked the pipe, they sent the smoke to the Creator. It was sacred, and the treaty was good in the eyes of all. The white men had to go back and ask other white men if they could keep their promises and make good on their word."

—Vine Deloria Jr.[2]

TREATY RELATIONSHIPS OF MUTUAL RESPECT UNDERMINED BY "CIVILIZATION"

The main thing that went wrong with the treaty relationships of mutual respect was "civilization," an ever-changing policy imposed by the United States. The policy began in 1800, with congressional appropriation of a Civilization Fund, under which the War Department's Indian Office provided grants—in effect, religious franchises—to Catholic, Episcopalian, Baptist, Methodist, or other Christian denominations for the purpose of proselytizing to and converting Native people.

Over the century, the effort to impose European values became more far-reaching, all-encompassing, and punitive. Violations of the new rules brought stiff penalties of starvation and imprisonment. Native Peoples were confined to reservations, and it was a crime to leave without the Indian agent's permission, even for obligatory family events on other reservations or site-specific ceremonies at off-reservation sacred places. Treaty references to the so-called arts of civilization, or to similar phrases, were used to justify these measures. Native people understood the references to mean, for example, that they would receive the benefits of Western education and teachers to teach their children about non-Native ways, but not that the new ways would replace, or try to replace, Native values or knowledge systems.

Beginning in 1883, Secretaries of the Interior issued civilization regulations, which were enforced until they were withdrawn a half-century later, in 1935. The rules banned the Sun Dance "and all other so-called feasts assimilating thereto."[6] A 1921 Indian Affairs Commissioner's circular ordered that "a careful propaganda be undertaken [by federal agents] to educate public opinion against the dance."[7] The rules forbade give-away and other honoring ceremonies, including funerary rites. For example, an Indian defendant could not argue that his status as a mourner justified taking or destroying property according to tribal custom. To the government this was not a "sufficient or satisfactory answer to any of the offenses."[8] The civilization regulations criminalized everything that was traditional or customary in Indian life, even banning ponies. Pigs, however, were allowed, the idea being that without ponies Indians could not ride away but with pigs they would take up farming.

Native treaty signers, once respected as leaders and diplomats, were now labeled hostiles (the official term for violators of the rules), ringleaders, troublemakers, and fomenters of dissent. If they could not be brought to their knees any other way, they were controlled through their children.

In the name of civilization, many Native children were removed from their families and sent to distant places for education, which initially consisted of an English-only, Christian-only curriculum. The regulations made it a criminal act for any "so-called 'medicine man' [or parent or other hostile]" to "operat[e] as a hindrance to the civilization of a tribe . . . resor[t] to any artifice or device to keep the Indians under his influence . . . adopt any means to prevent the attendance of children at the agency schools, or . . . use [the] arts of a conjurer to prevent the Indians from abandoning their heathenish rites and customs."[9] It was a crime to "interfere with the progressive education of the children." This meant that a parent could not attempt to stop a child from being taken to boarding school.

A 1902 Indian Affairs Commissioner's circular entitled "Long Hair Prohibited" was sent to federal agents: "The wearing of long hair by the male population of your agency is not in keeping with the advancement they are making, or will soon be expected to make, in civilization. . . . The returned male student far too frequently goes back to the reservation and falls into the old custom of letting his hair grow long. He also paints profusely and adopts all the old habits and customs, which his education in our industrial schools has tried to eradicate."[10]

Carlisle Indian Industrial School was the first federal Indian boarding school; it opened in 1878 on an army base in western Pennsylvania. Carlisle's founding superintendent from 1879 to 1904 was Captain Richard Henry Pratt, who had fought Native Nations on the plains in scorched-earth campaigns under Major General Philip H. Sheridan and Lieutenant Colonel George Armstrong Custer's command. "In Indian civilization, I am a Baptist," said Pratt in an 1883 address, "because I believe in immersing the Indians in our civilization and when we get them under, holding them there until they are thoroughly soaked."[11] Carlisle employed corporal punishment and other

Unidentified Maidu leaders with U.S. treaty commissioners (front row, from left) Oliver M. Wozencraft, Redick McKee, and George W. Barbour, 1851. Photographer unknown. George Eastman House, International Museum of Photography and Film, Rochester, New York 1969:0205:0037

The boys who worked in the print shop at Carlisle Indian Industrial School, 1891. Carlisle, Pennsylvania. Photo by J. N. Choate. Back row, from left: Willie Butcher (Chippewa), Samuel Townsend (Pawnee), Yamie Leeds (Pueblo). Middle row, from left: Unidentified, Chester Cornelius (Oneida), Sergeant Major Richard Davis (Cheyenne, the author's great-grandfather), Paul Boynton (Arapaho), Benajah Miles (Arapaho). Front row, from left: Bennie Thomas (Pueblo), Dennison Wheelock (Oneida), Unidentified, Cyrus Fell Star (Sioux), Unidentified. Cumberland County Historical Society, Carlisle

abusive treatments to "civilize" the children. By the time it closed in 1918, more than ten thousand Native young people had been drenched, if not drowned, in Pratt's version of civilization.

Pratt handpicked his early classes of students from among the youngest children of the Native leaders he fought, in order to control the strongest of the reservation families. In my own Cheyenne family, he chose Chief Bull Bear's youngest daughter, Wahstah (Elsie Davis), and two youngest sons, Oscar Bull Bear and Thunderbird (Richard Davis). Thunderbird wrote that his father wanted him to go to Carlisle, as if the choice had been Bull Bear's to make. But it was not. Pratt also took Bull Bear's grandson, the son of his eldest daughter, Clouding Woman, and of the legendary Cheyenne warrior Roman Nose. Pratt took others in Bull Bear's extended family, including Matches, a prisoner-artist whom Pratt had supervised during his command of the prison at Fort Marion, Florida, in which Native fighters of the Red River War had been incarcerated.

Pratt seemed to take personal pride in Thunderbird's progress at Carlisle toward civilization. In an 1890 commissioner's report, he recounted seeing Thunderbird after a Cheyenne "Scalp Dance" at the headwaters of the Washita River, during the Red River campaign:

Among these dancers was a lad about ten or eleven [who] was induced to attend the agency school. On the opening of [Carlisle Indian Industrial School, three years later] he was one of the first pupils. He was bright and capable, advanced rapidly . . . and in time became sergeant-major of the cadet organization.

After being eight years with us he married one of our girls [in 1888] . . . found employment and went out from us to live . . . near Philadelphia. . . . During these three years neither he nor his family has cost the [United States] one cent. Both he

Clockwise from top left:

Girls at Carlisle Indian Industrial School, November 1893. Carlisle, Pennsylvania. Photo by J. N. Choate. Back row, from left: Harriet Kyocia (Pueblo), Lydia Harrington (Arapaho), Louie Cornelius (Oneida), Katie White Bird (Pine Ridge Sioux), Julia Logan (Winnebago). Front row, from left: Alice Long Pole (Osage), Jennie Black (Cheyenne), Nellie Aspenall (Pawnee), Jennie Conners (Seminole). National Anthropological Archives, Smithsonian Institution NAA INV 06855300

Nellie Aspenall, the author's great-grandmother, at Carlisle Indian Industrial School, 1879. Carlisle, Pennsylvania. Photo by J. N. Choate. National Anthropological Archives, Smithsonian Institution NAA INV 06846700

Oscar Bull Bear (left) and Thunderbird, or Richard Davis—the youngest sons of Cheyenne chief Bull Bear—at the St. Louis World's Fair, 1904. St. Louis, Missouri. Photo by Charles H. Carpenter. The Field Museum, Chicago CSA15425

Thunderbird, or Richard Davis (Cheyenne), and Nellie Aspenall (Pawnee), the author's great-grandfather and great-grandmother, with daughters Richenda Aspenall Davis (the author's grandmother) and Mary Aspenall Davis, 1891. Carlisle, Pennsylvania. Photo by J. N. Choate. Cumberland County Historical Society, Carlisle

and his wife are respected members of the church and the community. . . . He pays his taxes and votes. He desires to remain among civilized people and follow the pursuits of civilized life. He can talk of his former savage habits and the habits of his people, but he despises them and deplores the pauper condition into which his people have been forced.[12]

My mother's grandparents were Thunderbird, or Nonoma'ohtsevehahtse (Richard Davis), and Nellie Aspenall, both in the first group of hostage-students, who entered Carlisle in 1879. Thunderbird was Cheyenne and born in the Dog Men Society camp during the making of the Medicine Lodge Creek Treaty of 1867. His parents were Buffalo Wallow and Bull Bear (Buffalo Bear). Nellie Aspenall was Pawnee, born in Genoa, Nebraska, in 1868. Her older brother, Harry Sargent, became her guardian when their parents died, and she was sent to Carlisle.

They each rode the train alone across half a continent. When they arrived at Carlisle, their medicine pouches, moccasins, and comfortable clothes were confiscated. Their long hair was cut short, they were "deloused" with kerosene, even though they did not have lice, and they were given scratchy uniforms and hard shoes, which never quite fit right. They often were whipped, or their mouths were rubbed raw and blistered with lye soap, for reasons they never knew. Thus began their so-called civilization. After graduating, they married at Carlisle, had the first three of their nine children there, and lived in the dairyman's cottage behind the school's farmhouse. Beginning in February 1891, Carlisle sold their family portrait for twenty cents a copy through the *Indian Helper* and other school publications.

Thunderbird's sister, Wah-stah (Elsie Davis), still a student at Carlisle at age nineteen, died of consumption in 1893 and was buried at Carlisle. She and other Indian students were later exhumed and reburied three times before being reinterred, perhaps, in what is now the Carlisle historic cemetery, where it is doubtful that any of the 186 Native young people are buried near the tombstones etched with their names.

After his sister and father died in the same year, Thunderbird and his family moved to his Cheyenne treaty land along the Washita River for a period of intensive ceremonial life that would have been a great disappointment to Pratt. During a long and varied career, Thunderbird was the interpreter for the Cheyenne delegation at the 1898 Indian Congress in Omaha, a member of Pawnee Bill's Wild West Show, a human exhibit in the Cheyenne Village at the 1904 St. Louis World's Fair, an artist, a writer-contributor to books on the Cheyenne Sun Dance and other topics, and a performer and celebrity in the Hollywood film industry.

I observed my own parents, who were also boarding school survivors, struggle with the ongoing effects of civilization. Dad—Freeland Douglas (Muscogee, 1922–2007)— was born at home on his mother's allotment near Okemah, Oklahoma. At age nine, he was taken to Euchee Indian School, where he was beaten every time he was caught speaking Muscogee. In the lunch line or at the table, he would call out to another Muscogee boy in their language—it would have been rude not to do so—and he would be beaten and given punitive work detail. Once I asked what he was beaten with. "Boards,"

Chiefs Thunderbird, or Richard Davis (second from left), his older brother, Oscar Bull Bear (third from left), Bushyhead (second from right), and three other Cheyenne men in the Cheyenne Village exhibit at the St. Louis World's Fair, 1904. St. Louis, Missouri. Photo by Charles H. Carpenter. The Field Museum, Chicago CSA15398

he replied, "one-by-twos and two-by-twos." Think of that against a nine-year-old; it compares to being beaten with a bat. He once told *Washington Post* reporter Richard Leiby that he could guess when the civilization regulations had been lifted, even though he hadn't heard of them before. He was right in thinking they ended in the mid-1930s—that's when, he said, school disciplinarians started hitting him with leather straps instead of unforgiving boards.[13] Dad later told me, "That was a really good day."

I went with Dad to some of his Euchee Indian School reunions, where he and other men in their seventies would laugh, in the way of survivors, about their experiences there. When a boy would run away, the white bounty hunters would drive their buckboard wagons to his home and wait until the boy showed up. They would put him in a wooden cage, drive back to Euchee, and collect five dollars, which was the going rate for the capture and return of a runaway Indian boy. Dad's former schoolmates said that, of all of them, he earned the most money for the bounty hunters.

The efforts to obliterate Native languages in the federal boarding schools did not work with Dad and the other students at Chilocco Indian School (Dad's second federal

Counterclockwise from top:

Freeland Edward Douglas (Muscogee), second row, second from left, and other soldiers in Company C, 180th Infantry Regiment, Forty-Fifth Infantry "Thunderbirds" Division, 1942. Oklahoma City, Oklahoma. 45th Infantry Division Museum, Oklahoma City

Susie Rozetta Eades (Cheyenne and Pawnee) at Haskell Indian Business College, 1942. Lawrence, Kansas. Harjo Family Collection, Washington, DC

Susie Eades Douglas and Freeland Douglas with the author as a baby, 1945. Oklahoma. Harjo Family Collection, Washington, DC

boarding school), who during World War II constituted Company C of the U.S. Army's storied Forty-Fifth Infantry "Thunderbirds" Division. In the basic training camp and on the troop ship to North Africa, they made up a code from the various Native languages spoken at Chilocco, and they modeled the coordinates on those of the school's grounds and facilities. The army gave them all walkie-talkies to communicate with one another as they moved through Sicily, Anzio, Monte Cassino, and points farther north. These young men and their heritage languages helped win the war. Dad went on to be a cryptographer, and to learn many languages at the army's language school at Monterey, California. He stuttered, but only when speaking Muscogee, the language he had been beaten for speaking.

Dad met Mom at Chilocco. Susie Eades Douglas (Cheyenne and Pawnee, 1921–2003) was born in Pawnee, Oklahoma. She remembered her education at Chilocco as being punctuated by the admonition to be a "good Indian" and a "good girl," and by her fear of being a "bad Indian." While Dad was fighting in Europe, she earned her business degree at Haskell Indian Business College in Lawrence, Kansas. Throughout their fifty-nine–year marriage, they tried to sort out the origin of things, which was most instructive for their children, who were trying to keep track of what was Cheyenne and what was Muscogee, and who learned to question everything.

My brothers and I received additional education when we lived with our grandparents. But as much as I loved my older relatives' history lessons and stories, it was my parents' dialogue—about words and meaning, original instructions and law, and beans and other foods, and who first grew and cooked them just that way—that most edified and intrigued. It made me want to know so much more. Dad would ask Mom, "Is that idea Cheyenne or Chilocco?" Mom would ask Dad, "Is that Muscogee language or Euchee Indian School slang?" Some questions were meant only as a tease, while others were serious, requiring deep thought and eliciting emotions that I would not understand until I grew older and gained more experience.

For a Native person, the study of treaties leads inevitably to thoughts of what might have been. We think of how the lives of our parents and grandparents might have been different—and easier—had the United States kept its treaty promises, had the civilization regulations never been imposed, had the rightful agency of Indian Nations over the lives of their people been respected. We grieve over what was lost, not so much in land and economic resources as in the knowledge, spirit, and joy that was denied our ancestors and, for that matter, the world.

We think, too, of what still can be. The preservation and restoration of treaty rights can be the foundation of a harmonious and moral relationship between and among the Native Nations and the United States, a relationship in which each party is committed to not only the redemption of its own interests but also the well-being and progress of the other. The final chapter in this story has not been written and, it is hoped, never will be. That is how it is when great Nations keep their word.

SUZAN SHOWN HARJO
(Cheyenne and Hodulgee Muscogee)

American Indian Land and American Empire

An Interview with Philip J. Deloria

SUZAN SHOWN HARJO

PHILIP J. DELORIA: My treaty is the treaty with the Yankton Sioux of 1858. One of the reasons it's most important to me is that my ancestor Saswe was one of the signatories on this Treaty, which ceded to the American government all but four hundred thousand acres of Yankton territory.

What it does is take Indian people, as all treaties did at that period of time, crunches them down geographically into a smaller space, opens up all the surrounding land to white settlement, and then sets up the provisions for a colonial kind of structure and the reservations. So this is a reservation treaty. It creates a reservation, and it sets up all the structures that are going to go with the reservation.

This settlement is for $1.6 million over fifty years. It's got a kind of sliding scale: $50,000 a year in the first ten years, and then a lesser amount, and then a lesser amount. But what happens in this Treaty, as happens in many treaties, is a whole series of qualifiers about that money, about what happens with that money. If you don't do this, we will reduce the money. If we decide that you need an additional agent or an additional farmer, we're going to take it out of your money. If you don't send all children between seven and eighteen years of age to school to learn English, we're going to take some of your money away. If you drink alcohol, we're going to take your money away. So the Treaty goes on for many pages, laying out here's what you give up, here's the compensation for it. Oh, and by the way, we're going to fully manage that compensation; oh, and by the way, if you don't behave in all these very specific ways, we're not going to give you the compensation at all, anyway. So it's very sad in a sense to read this Treaty and read it thoroughly, because the fundamental piece of it is the land. And the next piece of

it, the majority of it, is about the money and what's going to happen with the money. Then it's about . . . altering Native behaviors in absolutely essential kinds of ways.

. . . . .

When I look at treaties and the history of treaties, what I see are four different moments. They are four moments that have everything to do with the taking of Indian land. So the first moment really is the establishment of nation-to-nation relationships. Why do we see that? Because the United States is a very small group of colonies sitting on the Atlantic seaboard, and the rest of the continent is Indian. So if we think about the British and the Proclamation of 1763, what they do is a model for thinking about these treaties. They draw an enormous line right down the middle of the Appalachians and say, "On one side is our nation; on the other side is your nation." This is where the whole sense of nation comes out of treaties. So it's a nation-to-nation relation, and it is that because Indian people possess most of the continent. Because they possess the military power to make their own claims stick, and the United States and the British Empire don't have that power. So here we see two nations negotiating a treaty over land, perhaps, but oftentimes over peace, over trade and commerce, these kinds of things. So the first moment is a nation-to-nation kind of relationship, and it produces the notion that Indian Tribes are not just village peoples but are, in fact, nations.

The second moment is an American moment. It's the moment of this Treaty, the Yankton Treaty of 1858, and many, many others. These are treaties of regional consolidation. They have everything to do with the expansion of the United States around states. So the Northwest Ordinance lays out the provisions through which colonies will become part of the American empire. For a territory to become a territory, you need five thousand people out there, five thousand white male voters. You can move five thousand people out there into a space that is still very, very Indian. If you want to cease being a territory and become a state, you have to have sixty thousand free, white, male voters; sixty thousand is a lot of people. To do it when you've got the confined boundaries of a territory, you have to take the Indian people who are disbursed within that territory and . . . shrink them down, compress them, and put them into a single space. That space is called a reservation. So once you do that, and then you open up all their other land—as happens in this Yankton Treaty in 1858—to white settlement, you can get sixty thousand people in there, because you have opened up that land for settlement.

Let's think about the third way in which land is taken from Indian people. Now we're sitting on a small reservation within a state, which has become part of the American empire. Now we think, well, what are we going to do with that? We've gone from nation-to-nation, big continental divisions, to regional divisions and states and territories, and now we've got a reservation. Let's chop it up into 160-acre parcels. Let's put a grid on it, and that grid comes straight from the Land Ordinance of 1785. So the Land Ordinance and the Northwest Ordinance are the two fundamental policies that dispossess Indian people of their land and establish the conditions for the American empire. These are things that are understudied, I think, and underappreciated: how they function in both ways. They are thought of as national policies. They are Indian policies, both of them. Let's take our reservation and split it up into 160-acre parcels. Now let's count up the Indians who are here. Oh, we have a thousand and oops, we have five thousand parcels. We're going to put one Indian on each one of our parcels, and now we're going to open up the rest of that land, too. We're going to have white settlement. So now we're talking about a neighborhood kind of relationship, where white

people and Indian people are going to be checkerboarded, perhaps, with one another. They're going to be living together. This happens only because white people believe that Indians have been pacified. They're no longer capable of being violent. The Indian wars are over. With this comes a whole set of "civilization" practices and policies. We're going to put agents here. We're going to send missionaries. We're going to name you. We're going to collect rolls so that we know who you are. We're going to identify you. We're going to put fences around the reservations. We're not going to let you leave.

So you have this moment when Indians and whites are, in effect, desegregating themselves on this land, because they have disaggregated what was once the communal landholding of Indian people into individualized parcels. This is going to hold true until 1934 and the Indian Reorganization Act, when there are some small possibilities created . . . for Indian people to start buying back land. It ends the homesteading policies. So we've gone from nation-to-nation relationships to regional consolidations to neighborhood kinds of consolidations. Then the Indian Reorganization Act sets up a different kind of structure. It's the structure that Americans carry into the rest of the world over the course of the twentieth century. We're going to have client governments that exist mostly to sign corporate deals and be the bargaining unit with the federal government or private corporations but essentially have no political power. So the story of the latter half of the twentieth century, then, is about the groups of people, the tribal councils and other groups of Indian people pushing back against this entire, long sweep of history that came out of those first treaties of land cession, peace, and commerce—to the point where they've actually forced through the American legislative and judicial systems their own claims to sovereignty and autonomy.

From an interview that took place on February 6, 2013, at the Smithsonian's National Museum of the American Indian in Washington, DC.

THE STORY OF AMERICAN INDIAN TREATIES RESEMBLES
a parabola, consisting of two peaks and a deep valley.
The first peak represents the early years of treaty making,
when powerful Indian Nations and the new United States
engaged in serious diplomacy. The descent was evident
in the nineteenth century, when a growing imbalance
of power between Indian Nations and the United States
eroded the principles of peace, friendship, good-faith bargaining, and sovereign equality that had underpinned
early treaty making. The result was a trail of broken
treaties, land loss, tribal removal, forced cultural assimilation, and a long, dark era in which the federal government largely made decisions that governed life in Indian
Country. Yet American Indians never forgot their treaties.
Strong tribal voices insisted that the United States honor
its commitments, and they reasserted a central tenet of
early treaty making: Indian tribes were sovereign nations.
From the 1960s through the 1990s, Native treaty-rights
activists, tribal citizens and leaders, and American Indian
political organizations helped reinvigorate many aspects
of the nation-to-nation diplomacy that had characterized
United States–Indian Nation treaty making more than
two hundred years before. They laid the groundwork for
the renewed political, economic, and cultural strength of
Indian Nations today.

ROBERT N. CLINTON

Treaties with Native Nations

Iconic Historical Relics or Modern Necessity?

A T ITS INCEPTION, THE UNITED STATES INHERITED FROM BRITISH COLONIAL authorities a rich tradition of bilateral negotiation and treaty making with North American Indian Nations, and throughout the nineteenth and twentieth centuries the federal government continued to negotiate its political relationships with Indian Tribes.[1] Treaties played an iconic role in tribal relations with Anglo-Americans, whose settlement on the North American continent often displaced Indigenous populations. Surprisingly, on both sides of that relationship, treaties continue to constitute important, even revered, sources of legal rights, albeit for very different reasons.

In the Anglo-American legal tradition, treaties with Native Nations are a vehicle for vindicating and rationalizing legal rights, particularly rights to land taken or otherwise appropriated from Native occupants. The famous case *Johnson v. M'Intosh* reiterates the longstanding and controversial Anglo-American colonial legal theory supporting this notion—the so-called Doctrine of Discovery.[2] From their first contact with the Indigenous occupants of North America, some European powers, most notably the British, invoked the Doctrine of Discovery to support their claims of exclusive colonial rights to "discovered" territories in the Americas, thereby claiming the right to acquire Native North American lands to the exclusion of other European powers. While the Doctrine of Discovery recognized the Indians' continued possessory rights, often called "aboriginal title," to lands they had owned from time immemorial, it also suggested that one way in which the Natives legally could be dispossessed of their aboriginal title was through voluntary cession, that is, by sale. Treaties became the central vehicle by which such sales, or land cessions, were accomplished. Further, the Doctrine of Discovery worked hand in glove with other colonial policies and practices to drive down the purchase price of such Native lands.[3]

In fact, as they pushed westward, Britain and later the United States established a common pattern in their diplomatic negotiations with Native Nations. Often the first treaty with an Indian Tribe involved merely establishing peace and friendship and, most important, the exclusive right of Great Britain or the United States to acquire lands from the Indians—a so-called preemptive right of first purchase, sometimes described by the courts as a naked fee title.[4] Later treaty negotiations generally involved demands for larger and larger cessions of the Indians' aboriginal domains, leading ultimately in many cases to the removal of the Indians to a new homeland or, later, to a small reservation within their aboriginal homeland.[5]

Sometimes the parties failed to agree on the meaning of the treaty in question. For example, in 1703, Oweneco, the son of the great Mohegan leader Uncas, petitioned the Queen in Council, claiming that a series of treaties and agreements—most notably a 1681 agreement entered into between the Mohegan, led by Uncas, and the Colony of Connecticut—had granted the colony only a preemptive right of first purchase to certain Mohegan lands. By contrast, the Colony of Connecticut claimed the agreements constituted a complete cession of the Mohegan lands, granting the colony full ownership and thereby justifying the parceling out of the lands to Connecticut settlers. This petition led the Privy Council to appoint a royal commission, which heard the dispute *Mohegan Indians v. Connecticut* from 1703 to 1773, ultimately ruling on the case only long after the Mohegan had lost most of their lands.[6] While the Colony of Connecticut objected to the handling of the treaty question through royal commission rather than the local colonial courts, the commission ruled the procedure proper. It reasoned that the treaty agreement between Connecticut Colony and the Mohegan Tribe rendered the matter of transnational, rather than local, importance, leaving it to be handled as other international issues would be. Thus, together with the Doctrine of Discovery, treaties with Indian Nations served as a Euro-American legal rationalization and ratification of the colonial dispossession of preexisting civilizations of their aboriginal homelands.

While Indian leaders and scholars have widely criticized and generally excoriated the Doctrine of Discovery, treaties—the central legal vehicle for effectuating the massive loss of Native land in North America pursuant to that doctrine[7]—generally and surprisingly are highly respected and, indeed, revered in much of Indian Country and in the academe. Some Indian people erroneously assert that treaties are the source of most, if not all, their legal rights. Even leaders and citizens of Indian Nations that never signed any formal treaties with the United States, such as most of the tribes in Arizona, frequently can be heard defending the importance of their "treaty rights." Treaties in Indian Country have become virtually synonymous with Indian rights, even though many rights held by Indian Nations, such as federally reserved water rights, often are not entirely or even substantially dependent on the existence of treaties.[8]

Given that treaties historically played such an important role in the dispossession of many Native Nations of their homelands, the iconic reverence that most Indians properly have for Indian treaties demands explanation. That explanation owes its origins to the differences between Western and Native political organization and thinking at the time of first contact. Those differences highlight the distinctive ways in which each side viewed the treaty process.

At the time of first contact, most of the European colonial powers that sought to exploit the lands and resources of North America were hierarchical, command-driven monarchies. With such organization, the European powers had developed methods of dynastic alliance and agreement that bound their various domains together politically, sometimes through formal agreement but more often through marriage.

While generalizing about the political organization of the hundreds of Native Nations that occupied North America at the time of first contact clearly is risky, since each had a distinctive culture, language, and social and political organization, suffice it to say that, compared to European societies at the time, Native Nations had distinctively different forms of political organization. While each North American Indian Tribe had leaders, some leaders were political while others were religious; some were for peacetime and others for times of war; some were for leadership in the village, while others led the hunt. Most Indian Tribes at contact valued respect and reciprocity. Preserving the honor of the extended family, clan, and/or society was paramount, and economic, social, and political responsibilities centered on such extended kinship relations. Indian Tribes generally did not conceive of authority in hierarchical, command-driven terms. Decisions emerged from consensus among the people, families, or groups constituting the tribe, and external political relationships were thought of and frequently expressed in kinship terms.

Thus, for Indian Nations, forging a treaty initially did not constitute, as in Europe, a process of forming a temporary alliance memorialized in a written document; it involved instead the formation of metaphoric, organic kinship ties. And, just as a family must periodically gather in reunion to affirm, renew, and strengthen their kinship ties, so Indian Nations viewed the treaty-making process not as a discussion aimed at producing a static document but rather as a set of discussions creating an organic and dynamic kinship between the treaty partners. The details of agreements coming out of the process were important, but maintenance of the relationship was the central goal of treaty making.

For example, the Haudenosaunee (Iroquois) Great Law of Peace, the Kayahnerenhkowah, in essence constitutes an elaborate, quasi-constitutional, multilateral treaty relationship among the five (later six) nations of the Haudenosaunee Confederacy—the Mohawk, Onondaga, Cayuga, Seneca, and Oneida—not unlike the much later series of treaties that produced the European Union. Because the confederacy lacked a formal written language, the Kayahnerenhkowah was transmitted intergenerationally through the oral tradition. Like most treaties among Native Nations, and like most kinship alliances, it required no formal, written memorialization to survive.

The Indians giving a Talk to Colonel Bouquet in a Conference at a Council Fire, near his Camp on the Banks of Muskingum in North America, in Oct.

European colonial powers fully understood the dynamic, organic, kinship nature of the treaty relationship that their Native negotiating partners sought to establish in treaty discussions. Thus, colonial negotiators employed kinship rhetoric in establishing treaty relations. In colonial New York, the Indian commissioners at Albany, who were charged with maintaining New York's relationship with the then powerful and dominant Haudenosaunee Confederacy, regularly met with leaders of the confederacy to renew and "polish the covenant chain" of friendship that bound them together.[9] That chain of friendship frequently was commemorated or symbolized by traditional wampum belts, such as the Two-Row Wampum Belt.[10] The use of wampum belts highlights the fact that the treaty relationship lay not in the specifics of a document or a wampum belt but in the kinship relationship that such memorializations commemorated. During treaty discussions between the Haudenosaunee and the British, the parties frequently employed the term *brother* to refer to one another. This use did not refer to any concept of universal human equality, as it might today; rather, it referred to the way in which

Charles Grignion (1717–1810) after Benjamin West. *The Indians giving a talk to Colonel Bouquet in a conference at a council fire ... in Oct. 1764,* 1766. Color engraving. Library of Congress, LC-USZC2-1596

At this treaty council following Pontiac's War against the British, Kiyashuta (Seneca) said, "While you hold it [a wampum belt] fast by one end, and we by the other, we shall always be able to discover any thing that may disturb our friendship."

the Covenant Chain of Friendship had allied the Haudenosaunee and the British in a kinship relationship as equal siblings. The following minutes, recording an address by the Cayuga leader Tokaaion to Teedyuscung, a Lenape leader, during negotiations over the Treaty of Easton in 1758, exemplify all these elements:

> *Cousin:* I thank you for your Openness and Honesty on this Occasion, freely to declare the Truth. We wish our *Brethren,* the English, naming the Governors of Pennsylvania, Virginia, Carolina, and Jersey, were so honest and precise.
>
> They have called us down to this Council Fire, which was kindled for Council Affairs, to *renew Treaties of Friendship, and brighten the Chain of Friendship.* But here we must hear a Dispute about Land [complaints about the infamous Walking Purchase fraud in colonial Pennsylvania], and our Time is taken up, but they don't come to the Chief point.
>
> The English first began to do Mischief. . . . They ought not thus to treat with Indians on council Affairs. . . . I fear they only speak from their Mouth, and not from their Heart.[11]

Not only are delegates from another tribe described as cousins, but the English are considered brothers. Likewise the so-called treaties of friendship are seen as an organic kinship relationship that has bound the parties together in a covenant "Chain of Friendship," which periodically must be renewed and "brightened." Complaints must be aired and settled not merely by words but also by intention of the heart and actual deeds.

While coming at the endeavor with almost diametrically opposed political concepts, European and Native ideas about treaty alliance were not so far apart at first. The monarchical and dynastic alliances of Europe, which produced frequent feuds and wars at the time of colonial contact with North America, also involved kinship alliances, though the alliances were among monarchs rather than their people. It was only after the 1648 Peace of Westphalia emerged from a series of European peace treaties that Europe's modern, treaty-driven, nation-state system began to take shape, gradually replacing the dynastic alliance systems that had preceded it. By the nineteenth century the signed treaty document had become far more important for Euro-Americans as a kind of transnational contract; the dynamic kinship relations that it symbolized, however, had been lost to them.

Not so for the Indians. Because all North American tribal cultures had oral (rather than written) traditions, their relationships, alliances, cultures, religions, and values were transmitted through oral stories rather than written words. Kinship relations of extended family and clan remained critical to both their internal political organization and the metaphoric structure of their diplomacy with other tribes and Anglo-American colonial powers.

Before contact, Native Nations traditionally operated as consensus-governed societies in which cooperation, reciprocity, and respect governed social and political behavior. This political organization greatly influenced how treaties were negotiated, approved, and perceived. While European monarchs could send their ambassadors or treaty commissioners to negotiations with apparent authority to speak for the sovereign, no such central authority existed for most Indian Nations. While the Indian Nations sometimes had political spokespersons or leaders, their power, unlike that of the European monarchs, lay in their ability to command respect for their decisions and to produce consensus among their followers. The form of approval of early American treaties indicates that this difference was well understood by American treaty negotiators. Many early American treaties with Native Nations—such as the 1785 Treaty of Hopewell with the Cherokee Nation,[12] the 1815 Treaty of Portage des Sioux with the Fox (Meskwaki) Nation,[13] or the 1817 Treaty of Ft. Meigs with the Wendat (Wyandot), Seneca, Lenni Lenape (Delaware), Shawnee, Potawatomi, Odawa, and Chippewa Nations[14]—are signed by only a limited number of federal treaty commissioners, but they include many more marks or signatures of members of the affected tribes, who are sometimes described as chiefs or warriors in the treaty document. The process of signing such treaties demonstrates that the American negotiators plainly understood the need to secure widespread consensus assent to the new relationship if it was to succeed.

The fact that Anglo-American treaty negotiators insisted on written documents signed and executed by the parties, as had become increasingly common in Europe, only confused and skewed the treaty process. Since English constituted the only written language employed by most of the negotiating parties, the documentary memorialization of Indian treaties in North America occurred in the language of only one side and, given problems of translation, too often was known only to those who spoke and read English. American law quite early recognized the unfairness of this asymmetrical relationship. In *Worcester v. Georgia* (1832), Chief Justice John Marshall developed a critical rule (or canon) for construing treaties with Indian Nations. He wrote:

> The language used in treaties with the Indians should never be construed to their prejudice. If words be made use of which are susceptible of a more extended meaning than their plain import, as connected with the tenor of the treaty, they should be considered as used only in the latter sense. . . . How the words of the treaty were understood by this unlettered people, rather than their critical meaning, should form the rule of construction.[15]

This canon, which is still enforced, has played an important role in many Indian law cases, including disputes involving the protection of Indian hunting and fishing rights[16] and Indian water rights.[17]

Indians often complain that the memorialized, signed, English version of a treaty fails to capture or misrepresents the nature of the understandings reached during the treaty negotiations. Of course, such claims often reflect disparities between the oral traditions surrounding a treaty and the written document memorialized in English. Documentary proof of this problem is hard to locate and cannot be found in North America because transliterated or other written versions of most Indian languages were developed after the treaty period.[18] In New Zealand, however, missionaries transliterated Māori into a written language that was widely employed by Māori before the negotiation of the all-important Treaty of Waitangi of 1840.

Unlike North American treaties with Native Nations, the Treaty of Waitangi simultaneously was memorialized in English and the language of the Indigenous negotiators. Thus, the memorialized English version of that Treaty can be compared to the Māori version, and the comparison plainly yields disparities. The most controversial difference can be found in the first article of the relatively short Treaty. Article 1 of the English version claims that, through the Treaty, the Māori ceded their "sovereignty" to the British Crown. The written Māori version of the Treaty, discovered later, employs language that is nowhere near as sweeping. To quote the Waitangi Tribunal, an official branch of the New Zealand government:

> In the Māori text of article 1, Māori gave the British a right of governance, *kawanatanga*, whereas in the English text, Maori ceded "sovereignty."
>   One of the problems that faced the original translators of the English draft of

the Treaty was that "sovereignty" in the British understanding of the word had no direct translation in the context of Māori society. Rangatira (chiefs) held the autonomy and authority, "rangatiratanga," over their own domains but there was no supreme ruler of the whole country. In the Māori version, the translators used the inadequate term "kawanatanga," a transliteration of the word "governance," which was then in current use. Māori understanding of this word came from familiar use in the New Testament of the Bible when referring to the likes of Pontius Pilate, and from their knowledge of the role of the Kawana, or Governor of New South Wales, whose jurisdiction then extended to British subjects in New Zealand.

As a result, in this article, Māori believe they ceded to the Queen a right of governance in return for the promise of protection, while retaining the authority they always had to manage their own affairs.[19]

Thus, in the one case where contemporaneously memorialized versions of an Indigenous treaty exist in multiple languages, the written historical record supports the claim that the texts of the treaties negotiated with Native Nations failed to accurately capture the understandings agreed to by the parties. In North America the courts' adoption of John Marshall's rule that treaties should be interpreted as the Indians would have understood them has partially ameliorated the problem. But the fact that interpretation always begins with and focuses on parsing the English text is clearly troubling if the Indian oral tradition has interpreted the treaty in a way that departs from that text.

With all these problems, it remains remarkable that treaties continue to be venerated and honored in Indian Country. Part of the reason, of course, lies in the fact that treaties create kinship alliances. Respecting family is important to Indians and non-Indians alike, and the treaty relationships that establish such metaphoric kinship relationships continue to be highly valued. Another reason for the veneration, however, can be found by contrasting the treaty period with the era that followed it.

From contact until the early twentieth century, treaties were the central vehicle for mediating relationships between Anglo-American and Indian Nations. The treaty process empowered both sides. As long as the power relationships of the parties remained relatively equal, neither side could dictate terms to the other. A good example of this balance of power can be found in the very first treaty the newly independent United States ratified with an Indian tribe, the Treaty of Fort Pitt of September 17, 1778 with the Lenni Lenape (Delaware). This Treaty was negotiated during the Revolutionary War to facilitate access for Washington's army to British encampments west of Lenape country. During the negotiations the Lenape sought to improve their political position relative to their Haudenosaunee neighbors. Knowing of former Lenape allegiance to the British, the Americans encouraged them to "hold fast the chain of friendship now entered into." More important, articles 4 and 6 clearly show how the parties employed the treaty-making process to mediate the dynamics of their political relationships with each other. Article 4 states, in part:

Probably Lenape (Delaware) shoulder bag pouch, 1760–1800. New Jersey. Deer hide, porcupine quills, deer hair, metal cones, dyes. 25 × 21 cm. National Museum of the American Indian 13/5886

For the better security of the peace and friendship now entered into by the contracting parties, against all infractions of the same by the citizens of either party, to the prejudice of the other, neither party shall proceed to the infliction of punishments on the citizens of the other, otherwise than by securing the offender or offenders by imprisonment, or any other competent means, till a fair and impartial trial can be had by judges or juries of both parties, as near as can be to the laws, customs and usages of the contracting parties and natural justice: The mode of such trials to be hereafter fixed by the wise men of the United States in Congress assembled, with the assistance of such deputies of the Delaware nation, as may be appointed to act in concert with them in adjusting this matter to their mutual liking.

Article 6 reads:

> It is further agreed on between the contracting parties should it for the future be found conducive for the mutual interest of both parties to invite any other tribes who have been friends to the interest of the United States, to join the present confederation, and *to form a state whereof the Delaware nation shall be the head, and have a representation in Congress:* Provided, nothing contained in this article to be considered as conclusive until it meets with the approbation of Congress. And it is also the intent and meaning of this article, that no protection or countenance shall be afforded to any who are at present our enemies, by which they might escape the punishment they deserve.[20]

Clearly, the American treaty-making process began with the parties continuing the colonial tradition of mediating their political relationship by discussion and negotiations as sovereign equals. Thus, active Indian participation and consent in the formation of Indian policy constituted hallmarks of the treaty process.

At this point the federal government regarded Indian affairs as akin to foreign affairs. Both involved a kind of transnational law and negotiation. This dynamic changed dramatically when the War of 1812 eliminated the possibility of Indian alliances with Britain, which had posed a threat to the stability and security of the United States. Thereafter, until 1871, the bargaining power in treaty discussions shifted greatly to the United States, and policy was increasingly dictated by the federal government, albeit still with the formal requirement of Indian consent. For example, after a decade of treaty negotiations on the subject, the southeastern states provoked a controversy over the continued presence of the Cherokee, Chickasaw, Muscogee (Creek), Choctaw, and Seminole Nations on lands within state borders. Congress decided to chart the policy unilaterally by adopting the Removal Act of 1830. The act, however, only contemplated that the United States would exchange tribal lands in the East for lands west of the Mississippi River, where, as the act reads, "The tribe or nations of Indians . . . *may choose* to exchange the lands where they now reside and remove there."[21] Thus, even the removal act retained the requirement of tribal consent for implementation.[22] The United States ultimately secured such consent by treaty.[23] Despite the increasing shift of negotiating power to the federal government, the formal requirement of tribal consent to treaties or agreements still mediated political relationships between the federal government and the tribes. That dynamic continued throughout the nineteenth century. Increasingly, however, federal treaty commissioners found themselves informing the tribes of preexisting congressional decisions or policies and seeking tribal approval through a treaty for implementing the policy on a particular tract of Indian Country.

The juxtaposition of two treaties negotiated in 1868 demonstrates how much the treaty process had changed in a half-century. While the two treaties, the Fort Laramie Treaty of 1868 with the Sioux and Arapaho Nation[24] and the Treaty of Fort Sumner of 1868 with the Navajo Nation,[25] were both negotiated in the aftermath of hostilities between the parties, the initial bargaining positions of the two Indian Nations could not have been more different. The Sioux, led by Chief Red Cloud, had just routed the

Article I From this day forward all war between the parties to this agreement shall forever cease. The Government of the United States desires peace and its honor is hereby pledged to keep it. The Indians desire peace and they now pledge their honor to maintain it

Similar wording in these two treaties suggests that by 1868 many of the clauses in the treaties negotiated with Indian Nations had become boilerplate texts, drafted in Washington.

top: Treaty with the Sioux and Arapaho, page 1. April 29, 1868. Fort Laramie, Wyoming Territory. Calendar paper, ink. 27.9 × 21.6 cm. National Archives and Records Administration, Washington, DC

bottom: Treaty with the Navajo, page 1. June 1, 1868. Fort Sumner, New Mexico. Ledger book paper, ink. 30.5 × 20.3 cm. National Archives and Records Administration, Washington, DC

Article 1

From this day forward all war between the parties to this agreement shall for ever cease. The Government of the United States desires peace, and its honor is hereby pledged to keep it. The Indians desire peace and they now pledge their honor to keep it.

American army, forced the closure of forts intended to protect the overland trail to Oregon, and driven the Americans out of Sioux country. In the Fort Laramie negotiations, the United States essentially was suing for peace. By contrast, the Fort Sumner negotiations occurred after Kit Carson had raided Dinétah (Navajo lands), terrorized the Diné (Navajo), rendered most of them military prisoners, and marched them three hundred miles to the barren lands of Bosque Redondo in southeastern New Mexico, where they were interned for four years. Vanquished Diné were seeking mercy and permission to return to their sacred lands in Dinétah.

Given this difference in negotiating leverage, one would think that the contents of the two treaties would look very different. In reality, however, the treaties' commonalities—including government provision of land parcels, seed, farm implements, and education—suggest that by 1868 many of the clauses in negotiated treaties had become boilerplate texts, drafted in Washington, for which federal Indian commissioners merely sought Indian consent. If one looks closely enough at the two treaties, a few isolated clauses suggest the vast differences in the two parties' negotiating leverage: article 16 of the Fort Laramie Treaty, for example, pledges to keep white persons from settling in or occupying areas north of the Platte River and east of the summit of the Big Horn Mountains, and it requires the United States to remove from that

Cheyenne and Arapaho leaders meeting with members of the U.S. Indian Peace Commission, 1868. Fort Laramie, Wyoming Territory. Photo by Alexander Gardner. The commissioners (at center, from left) include Samuel F. Tappan, Major General William S. Harney, Lieutenant General William T. Sherman, John B. Sanborn, Major General Christopher C. Augur, and Major General Alfred H. Terry. National Anthropological Archives, Smithsonian Institution NAA INV 00514500

Mila Hanska Tashunke Icu, or American Horse (Oglala Lakota), giving information to allotment officer Charles Bates (center), with Billy Garnett, an interpreter (left), 1907. Pine Ridge, South Dakota. Photo by Edward Truman. The Denver Public Library, Western History Collection, X-31717

territory the military forts it had erected. Despite the differences in the tribes' negotiating leverage, however, the two 1868 treaties are far more similar than they are different. Although Indian consent was still thought necessary for the implementation of federal Indian policies, Indian agency in the initial formation of policies for Indian Country had all but disappeared.

It was therefore not surprising that Congress enacted a statute in 1871 that purported to end treaty making with Indian Nations but in reality did no such thing. That statute remains in the *United States Code* to this day as 25 U.S.C. § 71, which reads:

> [N]o Indian nation or tribe within the territory of the United States shall be acknowledged or recognized as an independent nation, tribe, or power with whom the United States may contract by treaty: *Provided, further,* That nothing herein contained shall be construed to invalidate or impair the obligation of any treaty therefore lawfully made and ratified with any such Indian nation or tribe.[26]

The history surrounding the adoption of this statute shows that its formal language was far broader than anyone ever intended and that it was never fully enforced. The basic dispute that produced the statute did not primarily focus on the status of Indian Tribes but rather centered on a conflict between two important features of American constitutional government. Article 2, section 2, of the Constitution grants the president the power "*by and with the Advice and Consent of the Senate,* to make treaties, *provided two thirds of the Senators present concur.*" Thus, while they were nego-

tiated initially under presidential authority, treaties with Indian Tribes traditionally had to be ratified by the Senate. The problem was that the annuity payments as well as the agricultural, educational, and, in some cases, health assistance promised in treaties with Native Nations often were quite expensive. By precedent, all appropriations bills generally originate in the House of Representatives. In the aftermath of the Civil War and the conflicts between the House and President Andrew Johnson, the House of Representatives repeatedly balked at appropriating money to fund treaties in which it had no say. In its first effort to wrest control of Indian policy from the president and the Senate, the House in 1867 added a provision to an appropriations bill:

> [A]ll laws allowing the President, the Secretary of the Interior, or the Commissioner of Indian Affairs to enter into treaties with any Indian tribe are hereby repealed, and no expense shall hereafter be incurred in negotiating a treaty with any Indian tribe *until an appropriation authorizing such expense shall first be made by law.*[27]

Column of cavalry, artillery, and wagons commanded by Lieutenant Colonel George A. Custer, crossing the Dakota plains during the U.S. Army expedition that would lead to the confiscation of the Black Hills, 1874. Black Hills, Dakota Territory. Photo by W. H. Illingworth. National Archives and Records Administration 77-HQ-264-854

This provision was repealed a few months later, almost simultaneously with Congress' appointment of a peace commission to negotiate new federal-tribal treaties.[28] The issue was rejuvenated when the House debated the 1871 Department of the Interior appropriations bill.[29] Congressman William Armstrong of Pennsylvania introduced and added to the bill Joint Resolution 502, which read:

> That hereafter no Indian nation or tribe within the territory of the United States shall be acknowledged or recognized as an independent nation, tribe, or power, with whom the United States may contract by treaty; and *all treaties and agreements hereafter made by and between them, or any of them, and the United States shall be subject to the approval of Congress*: Provided, That nothing herein contained shall be construed to invalidate or impair the obligation of any treaty heretofore lawfully made and ratified with any such Indian nation or tribe.[30]

As the italicized language demonstrates, the proposal plainly was not meant to end treaty making per se, but rather to ensure that any treaties thereafter made would be subject to the approval of the full Congress, not merely the Senate. The statement that no Indian Tribe thereafter should be "acknowledged or recognized as an independent nation, tribe, or power, with whom the United States may contract by treaty" merely constituted a means of distinguishing the ratification procedure for Indian treaties from that followed for foreign treaties. The Senate ultimately did not agree to the limitation, and the Interior appropriations bill was sent to a conference committee to reconcile the differences. On the treaty question, the Senate receded, and the ultimate approval of the reconciliation report for the Interior appropriations bill produced an extensive debate in the House on treaties with Indian Nations and the necessity for full congressional approval. The outcome, of course, was the enactment of the final provision, quoted above. While various scholars have questioned the constitutionality of this statutory limitation of treaty negotiating power,[31] the courts have never had occasion to address the issue.

Whatever the final language of section 71, history clearly demonstrates that the intent and effect of its enactment did not immediately end federal-tribal treaty making, as many wrongly believe. As the original language of Joint Resolution 502 makes clear, Congress did not mean to end treaty making; it meant to end exclusive Senate ratification. Unfortunately, perhaps owing to the awkwardness of the language of the original proposal, the italicized portion was ultimately deleted, thereby obscuring the resolution's true meaning and the original intent of Congress.

Nevertheless, on the ground little changed after 1871. Congress continued to send federal commissioners to Indian Country to negotiate agreements, which were then brought back to Washington for approval. Instead of being ratified by the Senate as treaties, however, the agreements were submitted to both houses of Congress for passage as statutes. From the Indian perspective, section 71 therefore produced absolutely no changes—treaties were still being negotiated with federal commissioners and sent back to Washington. Thus, when Congress adopted the General Allotment Act of 1887, notwithstanding section 71, it still sent out federal commissioners to negotiate allot-

ment agreements with each affected tribe. The allotment agreements were then enacted by Congress as statutes, later to be commonly called surplus lands acts. Despite section 71, the formality of tribal consent through agreement/treaty remained and continued well into the twentieth century.

Nevertheless, as the congressional procedure for approving treaties moved from Senate ratification to enactment as a statute, Congress, not surprisingly, assumed greater and greater authority over Indian affairs with less and less concern for actual, formal tribal agreement. Thus, some of the agreements carefully negotiated with Indian Tribes to implement land allotments were unilaterally amended by Congress during the enactment process.[32] Perhaps the most egregious example of this problem occurred when Congress sent a federal commission out to Lakota (Teton Sioux) country to secure for the United States a treaty to relinquish the Lakota's sacred Paha Sapa (Black Hills). The Fort Laramie Treaty of 1868 required that any further cession of Lakota land could take place only if a treaty was signed by three-quarters of adult, male Lakota. The federal treaty commissioners had trouble securing approval of the document from even 10 percent of the adult males, but Congress nevertheless enacted the alleged "agreement" as a statute, thereby confiscating the Black Hills under the pretense of Lakota consent.

left: Chief Lone Wolf (Kiowa), 1872. Washington, DC. Photo by Alexander Gardner. National Museum of the American Indian P02657

Lone Wolf sued to resist allotment of his reservation, arguing that it violated the Medicine Lodge Creek Treaty of 1867. The lawsuit backfired when the Supreme Court ruled in 1903 that Congress had the power to abrogate Indian treaties without tribal consent.

right: Delos Lone Wolf (Kiowa), ca. 1888–96. Rev. George W. Hicks Collection, Oklahoma Historical Society Research Division, 2117.28

Delos, a nephew of Chief Lone Wolf, used his boarding school education to help with his uncle's lawsuit.

The General Allotment
Act of 1887 gave the fed-
eral government the
power, after negotiating
agreements with Native
Nations, to break up res-
ervations and allot the
land to private owners.
After each Indian received
an individual parcel, the
"surplus" was sold to
non-Indians. This map
of an allotted reserva-
tion in Oklahoma shows
the "checkerboarding"
of Indian and non-Indian
lands.

What really ended formal Indian treaty making—or, more accurately, set it back for a half-century—was not the enactment of section 71 but rather a decision of the United States Supreme Court. In 1903 the court decided *Lone Wolf v. Hitchcock*,[33] a case that one federal judge later called the "Indian's *Dred Scott*."[34] In *Lone Wolf*, Kiowa and Comanche leaders sought to invalidate one of the agreements (enacted as a statute) to implement allotment on their reservation, claiming that Indian signatures on the agreement had been procured by fraud, and that the signatures also failed to meet the 1867 Medicine Lodge Creek Treaty requirement that three-quarters of all adult male tribal members approve any land cession. Additionally, they claimed that the allotment agreement/statute violated the Fifth Amendment takings clause, which requires that "just compensation" be paid if private property is taken by the government.

The U.S. Supreme Court summarily rejected the Indian claims, holding that Congress had plenary power to legislate for Indians, including the power to unilaterally abrogate treaties without tribal consent. The ruling came to be known as the Plenary Power Doctrine. Until this 1903 decision, the federal government generally believed that it needed tribal consent through treaty or agreement to implement federal Indian policy with respect to any particular tribe. That approach certainly constituted the unwavering tradition before 1871 and continued to be followed after 1871, even during the allotment period, until the Supreme Court decided *Lone Wolf*. After 1903, however, while the federal government occasionally resorted to agreements with affected tribes, Congress increasingly dispensed with tribal consultation or consent, thereby unilaterally imposing its will through the Plenary Power Doctrine.[35]

Since unilateral congressional and executive action in Indian affairs characterized much of Indian policy making in the twentieth century, it is not surprising that Indians long for and often romanticize the treaty-making period. During the early period of treaty making, consultation with Indian Tribes constituted an integral part of federal Indian policy formation, and tribal consent was seen as necessary for implementing federal Indian policy with respect to any particular tribe. While tribal agency in form-ing and shaping Indian policy became far more attenuated during the latter portion of the treaty period as the tribal geopolitical position became more attenuated, formal tribal consent was still deemed essential throughout most of the nineteenth century. The post–*Lone Wolf* reliance on the Plenary Power Doctrine to unilaterally impose federal policies on Indian tribes without consultation or consent clearly explains the veneration of treaties in Indian Country, even though many of the treaties constituted vehicles for the dispossession of Indian lands. At least with treaties, the Indian voice was at the negotiating council, and the formal protocols of tribal consent were fol-lowed, approaches that disappeared completely during much of the twentieth century. Modern Indians also revere treaties because they constitute a clear federal acknowl-edgment of Native Nations' sovereign status, a critical feature of their survival struggle that the federal government increasingly suppressed during the twentieth century as it departed from reliance on tribal agency, consultation, and consent. After *Lone Wolf*, Congress based more and more of its Indian policies on the federal unilateralism of the Plenary Power Doctrine.

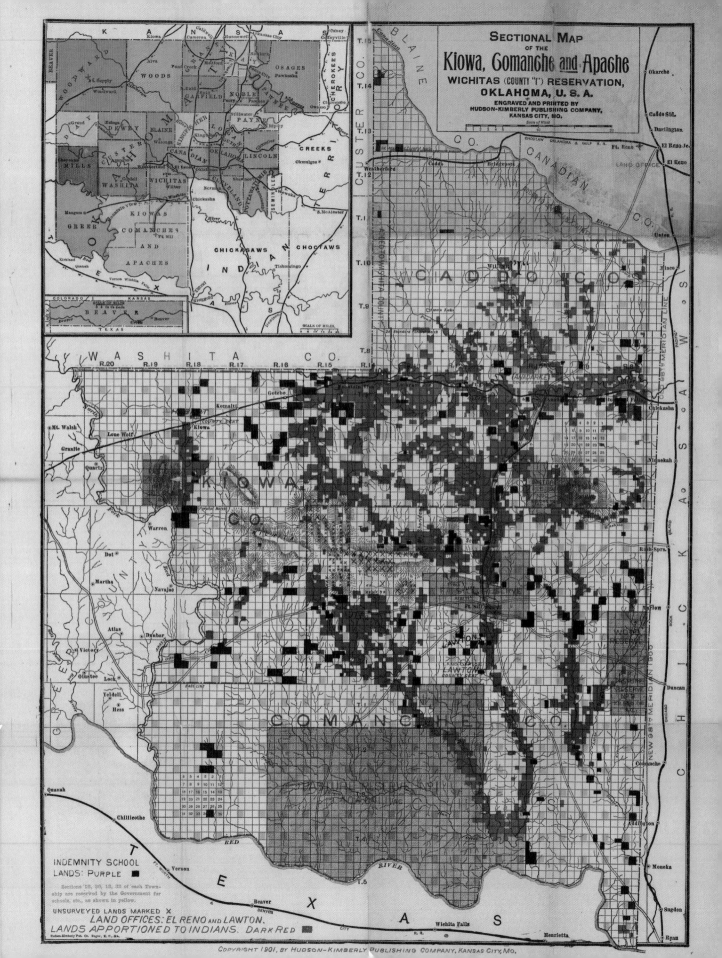

SECTIONAL MAP
OF THE
Kiowa, Comanche and Apache
WICHITAS (COUNTY "I") RESERVATION,
OKLAHOMA, U. S. A.
ENGRAVED AND PRINTED BY
HUDSON-KIMBERLY PUBLISHING COMPANY,
KANSAS CITY, MO.

INDEMNITY SCHOOL
LANDS: PURPLE ■

Sections 16, 20, 18, 33 of each Township are reserved by the Government for schools, etc., as shown in yellow.

UNSURVEYED LANDS MARKED X
LAND OFFICES: EL RENO AND LAWTON.
LANDS APPORTIONED TO INDIANS. DARK RED ■

While many believe that 1871 marks the end of the treaty-making period, in reality a persistent, sometimes successful effort has been made to rejuvenate the elements of tribal consultation/agency and tribal consent in forming and implementing federal Indian policy. This effort probably first began with a proposal by the federal Indian Commissioner, John Collier, during the New Deal era, as part of his initial draft of the Indian Reorganization Act, to contract with Indian Tribes for the delivery of federal Indian services.[36] While Congress balked at reinstituting such contractual/treaty relations with Indian tribes in the final, enacted version of the Indian Reorganization Act of 1934, Collier's initial proposal finally came to fruition in the contract relationships called for by the Indian Self-Determination and Education Assistance Act of 1975.[37] The so-called Public Law 638 contracts authorized by that statute permit any Indian Tribe to enter into agreements with the Secretary of the Interior and the Secretary of Health and Human Services. Under these agreements, tribes receive federal funding to assume and implement any of the federal service programs provided for Indians by the Bureau of Indian Affairs or the Indian Health Service.[38] Many tribes have entered into such Public Law 638 contracts for law enforcement, land management, health, education, and various other services. These agreements in essence constitute modern federal-tribal treaties that provide for the funding and implementation of Indian services.

In another re-creation of treaty making, the Indian Gaming Regulatory Act (IGRA) of 1988 requires a federally approved, tribal-state compact as a precondition for any tribe engaging in casino-style gaming under that statute.[39] While some tribal leaders have criticized this compacting requirement as an infringement on what they regard as an inherent tribal sovereign right to conduct gaming operations, in reality all that IGRA does is create a new form of federally supported treaty, the compact, as a precondition for exercising such sovereign rights. Indians supporting the treaty-making process should recognize the gaming compacts as a new, modern form of treaty.

Since most sovereigns need to interact and cooperate with their neighbors, modern Indian tribal governments, not surprisingly, often enter into formal agreements with neighboring counties or cities, and sometimes with states, over matters of mutual governmental concern. Everything from garbage collection to hunting, fishing, and resource conservation has been the subject of such intergovernmental agreements. Sometimes, the agreements are simply labeled agreements, memorandums of understanding, leases, or the like. Some tribes have entered into tax agreements with the states in which their reservations are located.[40] Some of the agreements, such as those dealing with child welfare, are expressly authorized by federal law,[41] while others have been implemented without any federal statutory sanction. Whatever the label or authority, however, these modern, contractual, intergovernmental agreements constitute another effort at rejuvenating the treaty-making process, albeit at a more local level. Indeed, since the 1970s, tribal relations both with the federal government and with state and local governments increasingly have been affected by such intergovernmental agreements. Thus, while seldom discussing the change, Indian Country has quietly witnessed during the last quarter-century an attenuation of the Plenary

Power Doctrine and an increased reliance on Indian treaty substitutes in the form of various intergovernmental agreements to harmonize relationships between Native Nations and the federal, state, and local governments with which they must interact on a daily basis.

As the great Indian scholar Vine Deloria Jr. noted, a strange fascination has long existed for calculating the exact number of treaties with Native Nations. While some scholars have advanced estimates of around four hundred, based on the collection of treaty texts first assembled by Charles J. Kappler in 1904, others have demonstrated that the Kappler collection is incomplete. Not only does Kappler's compilation omit most colonial agreements and treaties not ratified by the Senate but it also missed many others. More important, the Kappler catalog arbitrarily ends with treaties negotiated in 1868, despite the fact that the federal government and Native Nations continued to make agreements in the style of treaties well into the twentieth century. In their important two-volume work, published in 1999, Vine Deloria Jr. and his coeditor Raymond J. DeMallie try to document these omissions.[42]

Nevertheless, as this essay makes clear, treaty making with Native Nations continues. The only difference is that tribal intergovernmental agreements no longer are labeled treaties. They are instead called gaming compacts, tax agreements, memorandums of understanding, water law settlements, or the like. Treaty making therefore has undergone a resurgence, and the process continues. The names of the documents have changed, but their functions remain the same: working out intergovernmental relations and issues through tribal consultation and consent. Cataloging and counting the myriad number of such useful intergovernmental agreements constitutes an absolute impossibility. What is more important is that treaties with Native Nations are not merely historical relics of a colonial relationship. Modern treaty making in the form of intergovernmental agreements of various sorts continues to play an important role in ensuring tribal consultation and consent on issues affecting Indian Country.

Treaties as Recognition of a Nation-to-Nation Relationship

MATTHEW L. M. FLETCHER

OBSERVERS HAVE OFTEN WONDERED, AS PRESIDENT George W. Bush did in 2004, why the United States "gave" Indian Nations their sovereignty. The United States did not give anything to Indian Tribes. American Indian leaders guaranteed their nations' sovereign status through the treaty process with the United States. Indian Tribes negotiated and agreed to more than four hundred treaties with the United States. More than half of them remain in force, and they recognize the status of Indian Tribes as nations.

Consider the following four treaties between the United States and Indian Tribes:

In 1778, during the height of the American Revolution, the nascent United States executed a treaty with the Lenape (Delaware) Nation known as the Treaty of Fort Pitt. The American military needed a clear path from their bases on the Atlantic coast to the Great Lakes, from which it intended to attack the British in Detroit. The American treaty negotiators expressly recognized Lenape nationhood and even held out to them the possibility of American statehood in the aftermath of an American victory in the war.

In 1785 the United States executed a treaty with the Cherokee Nation known as the Treaty of Hopewell. In that treaty, the tribe and the federal government established boundaries between the two nations. The United States further recognized the authority of the Cherokee to punish any American citizen who illegally strayed onto tribal lands.

In 1868, after the Great Sioux Nation had fought the American military to a standoff, the parties entered into the Treaty of Fort Laramie. The treaty recognized the Great Sioux Reservation—as well as tribal land rights beyond the reservation that encompassed the western half of South Dakota and parts of Montana, Nebraska, North Dakota, and Wyoming.

Like the Sioux treaty, the 1868 Treaty of Fort Sumner, involving the Navajo Nation, incorporated a "bad men" clause, recognizing tribal authority to deal with lawbreakers within its territories. This authority is a strong claim to governance and sovereignty.

With the exception of the first treaty (which came before the Constitution), the U.S. Senate ratified and the president declared these documents. Article 6 of the Constitution pronounces ratified treaties the supreme law of the land. Under foundational American law, no president and no Senate may enter into or ratify a treaty with a group that is not a nation. In short, each treaty is an explicit recognition of the sovereign governmental status of an Indian Tribe. Hundreds of Indian tribes continue to share treaty relationships with the United States. These Indian *Tribes* are actually Indian *Nations*.

One might wonder how a tribal sovereign could exist in America, where we have state and federal governments. The treaties answer that question, too. For example, the Cherokee treaty acknowledges their status as a nation under the "protection" of the stronger sovereign, the United States. *Protection,* as the United States Supreme Court would later find in *Worcester v. Georgia* (1832), was a term of art under international law, meaning that a domestic sovereign might continue to exercise dominion over its lands within the borders of a larger sovereign, much as Monaco or Vatican City does.

Indian Tribes didn't always enjoy the benefits of their status as a domestic sovereign. Federal Indian policy usually worked against the tribal governments until the 1970s, with Indian children being forced into often oppressive boarding schools, and reservation Indians living under the thumb of racist or paternalistic federal bureaucrats. Indian treaties often were the only law preventing assimilation and ethnocide. Indian treaty negotiators smartly sought and received federal guarantees to education and sometimes health care as well as access to hunting, fishing, and gathering areas.

Today, Indian Tribes operate their own government services such as public safety, health care, social services, and judicial systems, and they have worked hard to function seamlessly with federal, state, and local governments. The core purposes of tribal governance are to protect tribal cultures and languages, and to make a home for Indian families. All this is made possible by treaties and Indian tribal sovereignty.

IN THE MID-EIGHTEENTH CENTURY, THE SIX NATIONS (also known as the Haudenosaunee or Iroquois) Confederacy included, as it does today, the Mohawk, Oneida, Tuscarora, Onondaga, Cayuga, and Seneca Nations— the latter constituting in the 1760s about half of the ten-thousand-strong Haudenosaunee population. Their homeland stretched westward in present-day New York State from the Hudson Valley to Lake Erie, and from Lake Ontario and the Adirondack Mountains south into Pennsylvania. Formidable warriors and scouts, the Haudenosaunee were coveted as allies by British colonial officials, who recruited them to provide a military buffer against attacks by Indian Nations allied with the French. After the French and Indian War ended in 1763, Anglo-American officials continued to value their alliance with the Six Nations, wooing tribal leaders with gifts and employing time-honored Haudenosaunee diplomatic protocols at treaty council meetings. Nevertheless, settlers and speculators in New York coveted the fertile lands of "Iroquoia," and they pressed for land cessions. By the 1760s, the Mohawk had lost most of their land, and the Oneida had relinquished some of theirs.[1]

RICHARD W. HILL, SR.

Linking Arms and Brightening the Chain

Building Relations through Treaties

Brothers! We live upon the same ground with you. The same island is our common birth-place. We desire to sit down under the same tree of peace with you: let us water its roots and cherish its growth, till the large leaves and flourishing branches shall extend to the setting sun, and reach the skies.

—Commissioners of Indian Affairs for the Continental Congress,
   from a treaty renewal speech at Albany, New York, August 28, 1775[2]

ORIGINS OF TREATY MAKING

In 1775, as war clouds gathered on the horizon, the Continental Congress was eager to make peace with the Six Nations. More specifically, the American rebels did not want the English to seduce the Six Nations into fighting on their behalf, so the Americans developed a treaty strategy that would use older political protocols employed by the British to swing Native support toward the Twelve United Colonies. As expressed in the speech above, the strategy depended on an emotional appeal for peace, but it also included pragmatic steps to ensure that the Americans would better address the needs of the Six Nations than the British had.

The carefully worded speech in August 1775, which had been pre-pared months in advance, contained metaphorical phrases that had been a part of treaty making with Native Nations for several generations. The Tree of Peace, with its long branches sheltering those who seek peace, was an ancient symbol of the Six Nations. The Haudenosaunee perceived a treaty as the mutual planting of this tree, the burying of war weapons underneath it, and the provision of goods and services to treaty allies.

It sounds like a simple matter to make a peace treaty. Say the right words, give the right wampum belts, placate the chiefs, bestow gifts upon them, and walk away with a peace treaty. No treaty, however, was that

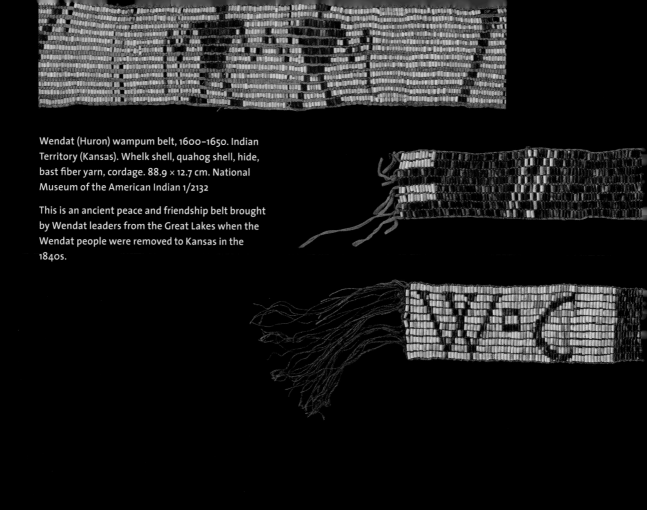

Wendat (Huron) wampum belt, 1600–1650. Indian Territory (Kansas). Whelk shell, quahog shell, hide, bast fiber yarn, cordage. 88.9 × 12.7 cm. National Museum of the American Indian 1/2132

This is an ancient peace and friendship belt brought by Wendat leaders from the Great Lakes when the Wendat people were removed to Kansas in the 1840s.

simple. A treaty is not solely words of agreement on parchment but rather an ongoing relationship in which both parties continue to have their concerns openly discussed and considered. The excerpt (above) from the commissioners' speech also informs us about how the colonial governments expressed respect for the intellects and cultures of the Native leaders they courted.

As proof of their sincerity, the commissioners, like the British before them, picked up on an older tribal tradition of giving wampum—long belts made of marine shell— during treaty negotiations. By using wampum belts, including a Union Belt and what they called the Large Belt of Intelligence and Declaration, the Americans showed respect for Native protocol and sought to arrive at one mind with Native leaders on important matters. Herein lies the birth of American treaty making.[3]

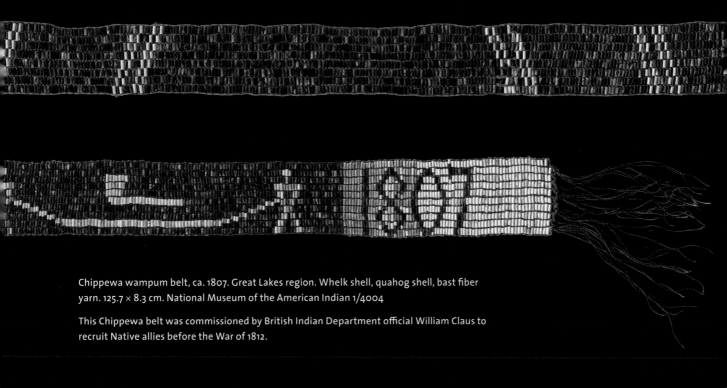

The diagonal lines on this wampum belt have been referred to as braces or strengtheners and represent two nations that have established a peaceful relationship. In doing so, they are strengthening the rafters of the great longhouse.

Chippewa wampum belt, ca. 1807. Great Lakes region. Whelk shell, quahog shell, bast fiber yarn. 125.7 × 8.3 cm. National Museum of the American Indian 1/4004

This Chippewa belt was commissioned by British Indian Department official William Claus to recruit Native allies before the War of 1812.

THE CULTURE OF TREATY MAKING

At the 1775 council the commissioners explained the meaning of the Union Belt:

> By this belt, we, the Twelve United Colonies, renew the old covenant chain by which our forefathers, in their great wisdom, thought proper to bind us and you, our brothers of the Six Nations, together, when they first landed at this place; and if any of the links of this great chain should have received any rust, we now brighten it, and make it shine like silver. As God has put it into our hearts to love the Six Nations and their allies, we now make the chain of friendship so strong, that nothing but an evil spirit can or will attempt to break it. But we hope, through the favor and mercy of the Great Spirit, that it will remain strong and bright while the sun shines and the water runs.[4]

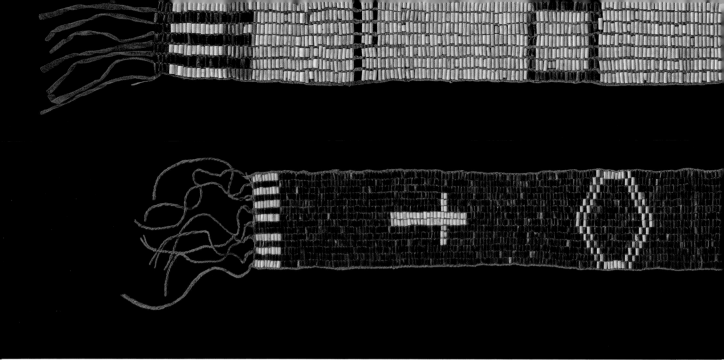

One of the cultural metaphors at the center of early American treaty making was the Covenant Chain of Peace. The concept behind this metaphor is of an unbreakable chain that unites treaty partners. The chain is made of three links—representing respect, trust, and friendship—that create a wide path of peace uniting the treaty partners and allowing for open, honest communication. Symbolically, the leaders of each treaty nation hold the Covenant Chain.

To firmly hold the chain means that treaty nations do not let minor difficulties interfere with the larger peace. In fact, when such difficulties are overcome, the culture of the Covenant Chain requires that the chain be strengthened by "polishing" it with pledges to reaffirm or restore peace and friendship, provide just compensation for any harm that may have been inflicted, and keep citizens in line to avoid future infractions. The chain is the mechanism by which the treaty is made real.

For the Six Nations and many other northeastern Native Nations, the linking of arms by making a treaty was a way to bring peace and prosperity to all parties. The Mohawk name for the Covenant Chain of Peace is *tehontatenentsonterontahkhwa,* or

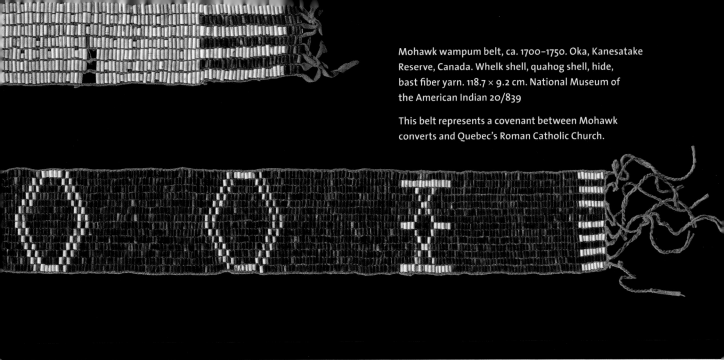

Mohawk wampum belt, ca. 1700–1750. Oka, Kanesatake Reserve, Canada. Whelk shell, quahog shell, hide, bast fiber yarn. 118.7 × 9.2 cm. National Museum of the American Indian 20/839

This belt represents a covenant between Mohawk converts and Quebec's Roman Catholic Church.

"the thing by which they link their arms." In the Onondaga language, the term *dehudadnetsháus* means "they link arms." In the Cayuga language, *tehonane:tosho:t* means "they have joined hands/arms."

The conceptual premise of Haudenosaunee treaty-making protocols is that mutual respect will allow trust to develop, and that such trustworthiness will result in ongoing friendship between treaty partners. The trust is symbolized in wampum belts and treaty council rhetoric as the physical interlocking of the arms, a sign of unity and strength. This linkage also will create mental, emotional, and spiritual well-being if the treaty partners are earnest in not letting human frailties destroy the treaty. This is very different than seeing treaties as only legal, political documents. It represents the Native intent of treaty making.

Two great diplomatic traditions came into play as America sought to shape its destiny as a new republic. By the late eighteenth century, both sides had become expert at negotiating treaty relationships. The roots of American treaty making can be found in Indian relations with Dutch traders and British colonists in the early seventeenth cen-

I think we could learn from the Iroquois Confederacy, just as our Founding Fathers did when they laid the groundwork for our democracy. The Iroquois called their network of alliances with other tribes and European nations a "covenant chain." Each link represented a bond of peace and friendship. But that covenant chain didn't sustain itself. It needed constant care, so that it would stay strong. And that's what we're called to do, to keep the covenant between us for this generation and for future generations.

—President Barack Obama, November 13, 2013

tury. For the Six Nations, treaty making goes back much further, to the era of their confederacy's formation. Their intellectual, political, and cultural treaty-making principles had been created under Kayahnerenhkowah, or the Great Law of Peace.

In the Native mind, when the American rebels defeated the British army during the Revolutionary War, the king symbolically dropped the Covenant Chain, and the Americans picked it up. Therefore, this required forging a new Covenant Chain relationship. Early American attitudes toward treaty making varied, but many American diplomats heartily embraced the custom of negotiating treaties with Native Nations. Secretary of War Henry Knox wrote to the newly elected president of the United States on May 23, 1789, reminding him of the treaty-making traditions that the Americans had inherited: "That the practice of the late English colonies and government, in purchasing the Indian claims, has firmly established the habit in this respect, so that it cannot be violated but with difficulty, and [at] an expense greatly exceeding the value of the object."[5] In many ways Indian protocols had become an American inheritance from the English.

For northeastern Native Nations, wampum strings and belts were the main diplomatic tools for negotiating and recording treaties. Wampum are small, cylindrical beads made of shell; the beads are woven in contrasting designs of purple and white. Invitations, messages, and commitments were recorded in wampum strings. Major treaty issues and the confirmation of the agreements were recorded in woven "belts," long bands of beads that were not worn but rather held upright when their message was recited.

Wampum was so critical to a successful treaty that American officials at times put off treaty councils until a proper number (fifty- to a hundred-thousand) of wampum beads could be acquired and woven into proper belts. An old treaty agreement could be remembered by displaying the wampum belt that was associated with it. The historical record refers to hundreds of different wampum belts, but it is difficult to associate a particular belt with a specific treaty unless the written and oral history of it has been kept clear. At the same time, written notes and paper treaties do not always reflect the memories attached to wampum belts.

Perhaps the most important person at a treaty council was the interpreter who translated the Native and European languages so that the treaty partners could understand one another. Interpreters often had conflicting loyalties. Being raised within a Native society creates cultural bonds that at times clash with loyalties to outsiders. The Native delegates had to trust the interpreter and believe that that he would translate faithfully. This could be a difficult task, as some concepts in English are hard to translate well. A corrupt translator could change the meaning of words to hide the real intent of the written documents. Unfortunately, political intrigue, spying, and double

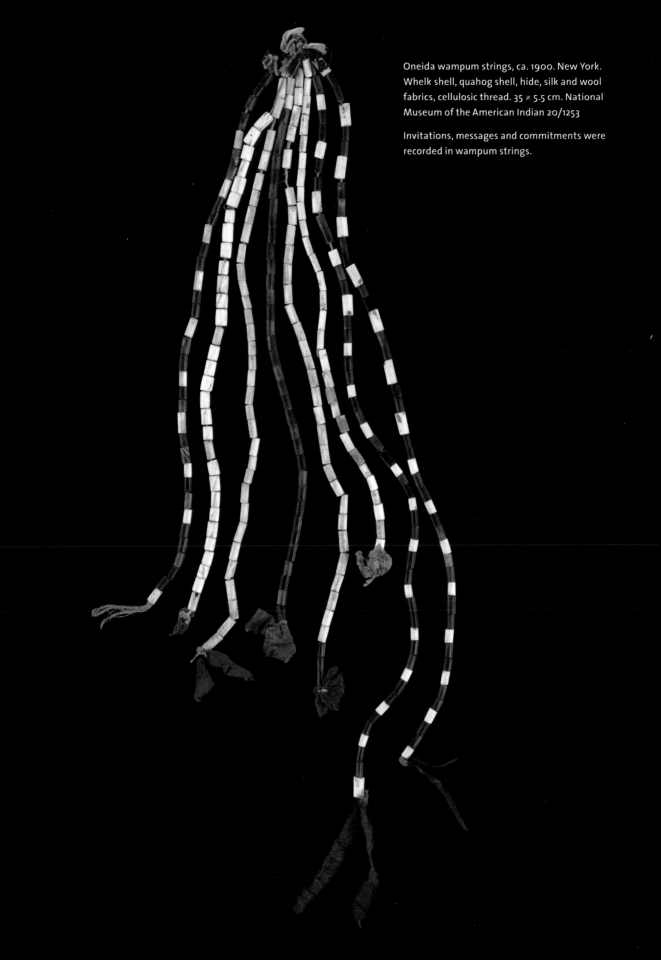

Oneida wampum strings, ca. 1900. New York.
Whelk shell, quahog shell, hide, silk and wool
fabrics, cellulosic thread. 35 × 5.5 cm. National
Museum of the American Indian 20/1253

Invitations, messages and commitments were
recorded in wampum strings.

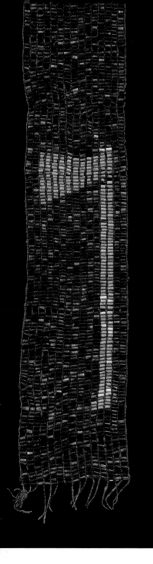

Algonquin wampum belt, ca. 1671. Quebec, Canada. Whelk shell, quahog shell, bast fiber yarn, hide, pigment. 128 × 11 cm. National Museum of the American Indian 9776

This belt, which the Haudenosaunee are said to have presented to the Algonquin at the end of a protracted war, is of a type often exchanged to form military alliances. Generally, belts with purple backgrounds and tomahawk motifs were associated with warfare.

talk also were traditions of treaty making.[6] When the Haudenosaunee became suspicious of mistranslations, they asked the Society of Friends (Quakers) to witness the treaty negotiations and affirm the truth of what was being said. Quaker records show that they took their role seriously.[7]

NATIVE INTENT

In the Haudenosaunee language a treaty is called a "completed matter." But this does not reflect how deeply people felt about the agreements. For the Six Nations, treaty making was a relationship-building process that had begun with the United Colonies in August 1775. There was spiritual underpinning to treaty making. Both sides made numerous references to the One Above, or Great Spirit, who allowed the delegates to assemble, to make sense out of what they were doing and reach one mind on the matters at hand. Many Native leaders considered treaties to be sacred agreements. The kindling of the council fire also had spiritual overtones, as the fire was thought to have the power to purify the words spoken over it.

The treaty council was part ritual, part political diplomacy, and part cultural performance. To truly understand the meaning of a treaty, one needs to study what led up to it; what was discussed and agreed to along the way; and what oral history is associated with the council or any wampum belts attached to it. One also needs to review any written minutes, journals, and subsequent reflections. The printed version of the treaty by itself cannot convey what it meant to the people who completed the matter.

Treaty making, from a Haudenosaunee point of view, was a way in which cultural principles of peace were extended to the newcomers. Within the Great Law of the Haudenosaunee, adding new people to its protection and safety is called "adding to the rafters," meaning, metaphorically, adding to the roof elements that provide protection and shelter to the people. Treaties extended those metaphorical rafters over the newcomers.

A treaty council also could be a form of healing, a way to renew and refresh friendships and help hearts and minds recover from losses that had been suffered since the parties had last met. It was important that all sides be able to actively participate in treaty making with uncluttered minds, without any distracting emotions or lingering animosities. In a 1783 council at Lower Sandusky, in present-day Ohio, the famous Mohawk leader Joseph Brant offered a wampum belt as he stated:

> We the chief warriors of the Six Nations with this belt clear your Ears, that you may listen with attention and without interruption to what we have to say. . . . We now conform to the ancient custom of our Fore Fathers, to condole with you for the Losses you have sustained in the war, and we hope your minds will now be eased from all trouble, since we have gathered the bones of all your dear departed Friends and covered them over, so that all is smooth and even.[8]

Once the delegates were "healed" they could proceed to think clearly and make good decisions. Haudenosaunee delegates saw justice as a form of "medicine." If one of the treaty partners seriously transgressed against another, that injustice had to be dealt

Haudenosaunee wampum belt, ca. 1775. New York. Whelk shell, quahog shell, bast fiber yarn. 98 × 7 cm. National Museum of the American Indian 11/1829

This wampum belt belonged to an American commissioner at the 1775 council named Volckert Petrus Douw (1720–1801), who was well-liked by the Six Nations. His daughter, Catherine Hoffman, died on October 26, 1775. Following an ancient protocol, the Six Nations, wanting to uplift his mind and remove the grief, performed a Condolence Ceremony for Douw in December 1775, during which they presented this belt to Douw.

Artist unknown. *Volckert Petrus Douw*. Engraving (from a wax medallion) in Cuyler Reynolds, *Albany Chronicles: A History of the City Arranged Chronologically* (Albany, NY: J. B. Lyon, 1906), 257.

with in the council, and the injured party had to feel that his concerns had been adequately addressed. The process could result in apologies and pledges to prevent such abuses in the future or in some form of compensation (usually wampum beads) to make amends for any emotional or physical harm. In this way the treaty ensured ongoing peace, because no wounds would be left to fester.

In a 1783 message to the governor of Quebec, Brant reminded him of the longstanding alliance between Britain and the Six Nations, describing the purpose and benefits of treaty making:

> You renewed your assurances of protecting and defending ourselves, lands, and possessions against any encroachment whatsoever, procuring for us the enjoyment of fair and plentiful trade of your people, and [we] sat contented under the shade of the Tree of Peace, tasting the favour and friendship of a great Nation bound to us by Treaty, and able to protect us against all the world.[9]

AMERICAN INTENT

The Founding Fathers were immersed in Native peace protocols and sincerely believed that their future rested upon their ability to maintain peace through a series of treaties. Benjamin Franklin, one of the original Indian affairs commissioners for the Continental Congress, advocated for peace with and respect for Native Nations. Foremost, treaties were required because after the Revolutionary War ended in 1783, Great Britain maintained treaty relationships with many Native Nations on American borderlands. The United States could ill afford to lose the alliance of these nations. Tensions between Great Britain and the United States remained high, with the British holding on to many of their forts on U.S. soil. Native Nations were claiming much of the western lands—encompassing the present-day states of Ohio, Indiana, Michigan, Wisconsin, Illinois Kentucky, West Virginia, and most of Alabama and Mississippi—that Britain had ceded to the United States, and war with these Native Nations, and with the Haudenosaunee, was a very real threat at this time. The newly formed United States had to make peace with Britain's former allies.

Some Iroquois Confederacy citizens and nations had supported the British and some had supported the Americans. As a result of the devastating Sullivan-Clinton Expedition of 1779—a systematic, scorched-earth, American military campaign against the Native inhabitants of western New York—the Six Nations had lost whatever bargaining power they may previously have had. But during the 1780s the Americans, not wanting to face another war with the confederacy, labored to create a new Covenant Chain. The new chain, to be effective, had to address some new matters—specifically, protecting Haudenosaunee land from individual speculators and state officials.

Congress was competing, however, with the New York state government, which not only claimed the power to make its own treaties with Native Nations but also wanted to remove the Six Nations entirely. The federal government claimed that only it could make treaties. But under the Articles of Confederation—the fledgling nation's first constitution—the lines of authority were not clear. New York took full advantage of the void to negotiate a series of alarming land cession treaties with the Oneida, Onondaga, and Cayuga Nations.

Reflecting the federal-state conflict, two treaty councils were held at Fort Stanwix in 1784. The first was arranged by New York State, which had its own Indian commissioners, "to renew the ancient Covenant which subsisted between us"; the second, a month later, was convened by federal commissioners. At the state council, New York's governor, George Clinton, said:

> Brothers! We now conclude with the fullest Confidence that our Chain of Friendship will not contract any Rust, but that it will always remain bright throughout every Part of the State, that our Posterity may see their Faces in it, and that it will be their Object, as it has been ours, to promote each other's Happiness and as a Pledge therefore We now give You this [wampum] Belt.[10]

facing: Map showing Haudenosaunee (Six Nations) land loss between 1768 and 1794, and the land that was restored to the Seneca Nation by the 1794 Treaty of Canandaigua. Map by Gene Thorp/Cartographic Concepts, Inc. © Smithsonian Institution

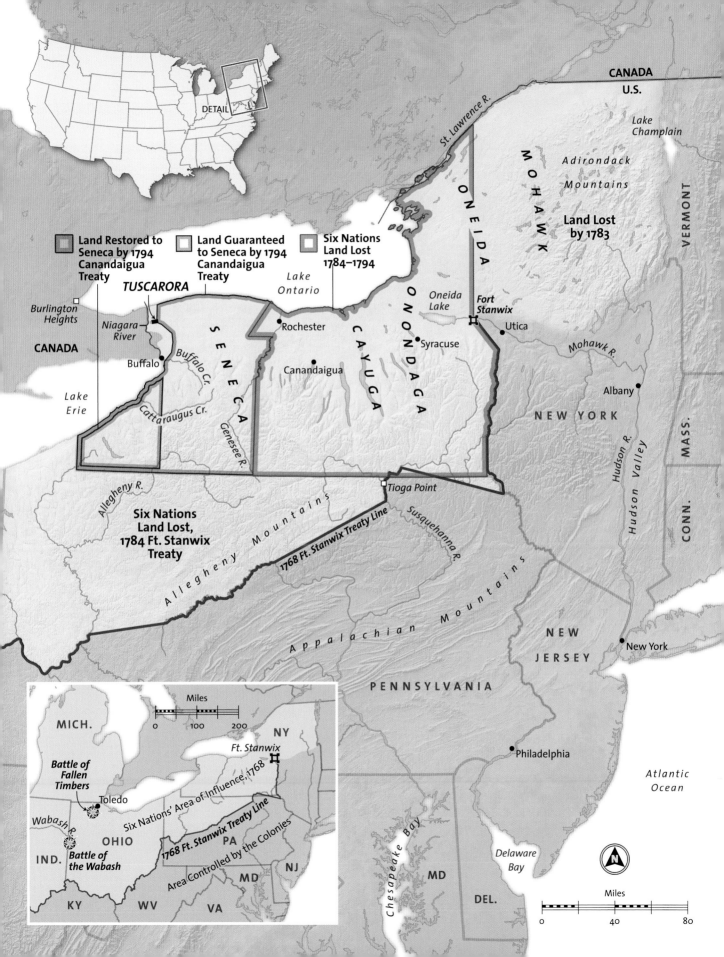

CANADA
U.S.

Lake
Champlain

Adirondack
Mountains

MOHAWK

VERMONT

Land Lost
by 1783

St. Lawrence R.

ONEIDA

Land Restored to
Seneca by 1794
Canandaigua
Treaty

Land Guaranteed
to Seneca by 1794
Canandaigua
Treaty

Six Nations
Land Lost
1784–1794

TUSCARORA

Lake
Ontario

ONONDAGA

Oneida
Lake

Fort
Stanwix

Utica

Burlington
Heights

Niagara
River

Rochester

Syracuse

Mohawk R.

MASS.

Buffalo

S E N E C A

Buffalo Cr.

CAYUGA

Canandaigua

Albany

NEW YORK

CANADA

Lake
Erie

Cattaraugus Cr.

Genesee R.

Hudson R.

Hudson Valley

CONN.

Allegheny R.

Six Nations
Land Lost,
1784 Ft. Stanwix
Treaty

Allegheny Mountains

Tioga Point

1768 Ft. Stanwix Treaty Line

Susquehanna R.

NEW
JERSEY

New York

Appalachian Mountains

PENNSYLVANIA

Philadelphia

Atlantic
Ocean

MICH.

Miles

0   100   200

NY

Ft. Stanwix

Battle of
Fallen
Timbers

Toledo

Six Nations' Area of Influence, 1768

Wabash R.

OHIO

1768 Ft. Stanwix Treaty Line

PA

Area Controlled by the Colonies

IND.

Battle of
the Wabash

NJ

MD

Chesapeake Bay

MD

Delaware
Bay

DEL.

KY

WV

VA

Miles

0   40   80

At the federal Fort Stanwix treaty council, Kenwendeshon (Captain Aaron Hill) expressed the Haudenosaunee position on the federal-state struggle for treaty-making authority:

> We are free, and independent, and at present under no influence. . . . You directed us not to attend to what any particular state might say to us on public business, and [stated] that the commissioners of Congress alone were adequate to that purpose. We of the Six Nations are fully sensible of the truth of this, and we think that no particular State can have any right to treat separately, but that it belongs only to the United States. In consequence of this when the Governor of New York sent a message to us to assemble here in order to treat with that State, we requested that it might be a continental treaty, as we conceived that the United States formed one general system, or plan.[11]

The federal negotiators acted with fierce determination at the council to make the Six Nations pay further for their support of the British: the Treaty of Fort Stanwix required the confederacy to relinquish all its lands in the Ohio Valley and Pennsylvania, as well as lands along the Niagara River and south and west of the mouth of Buffalo Creek in western New York. Throughout the 1780s the Six Nations denounced the coercive treaty and pressed for the restoration of two of the tracts that had been ceded.

From 1785 to 1788, New York state commissioners, intent on taking more and more land, continued to make separate agreements with individual Haudenosaunee Nations.[12] Federal officials tried to dissuade New York from making the agreements, and they informed the Native Nations that any treaties negotiated without federal oversight would be invalid. In the great contest over who had the legal powers to make treaties, the Haudenosaunee were caught in the middle. Ultimately, state officials, settlers, and land speculators used coercion, fraud, and deceit to pressure tribal leaders into signing treaties that ceded land to New York State.[13]

In the meantime, on July 13, 1787, Congress passed the Northwest Ordinance, which required that:

> The utmost good faith shall always be observed towards the Indians; their lands and property shall never be taken from them without their consent; and, in their property, rights and liberty, they never shall be invaded or disturbed, unless in just and lawful wars authorized by Congress; but laws founded in justice and humanity shall, from time to time, be made, for preventing wrongs being done to them and for preserving peace and friendship with them.[14]

In 1788 the State of New York nevertheless formally commissioned a group to extinguish Haudenosaunee land titles by any means necessary. To counter the move, President Washington promised that the "principles of justice and humanity"[15] would be the hallmark of the relationship between the Haudenosaunee and the United States. By 1788, however, New York had acquired most of the Six Nations' aboriginal lands.[16]

Soon after recommending in 1789 that the United States continue to follow British treaty-making protocols, Henry Knox, the Secretary of War, stated in a report to Washington the general principles upon which U.S. relations with Native Nations should be conducted:

> The Indians, being the prior occupants, possess the right of the soil. It cannot be taken from them unless by their free consent, or by the right of conquest in case of a just war. To dispossess them on any other principle, would be a gross violation of the fundamental laws of nature, and of that distributive justice which is the glory of a nation. . . . The time has arrived, when it is highly expedient that a liberal system of justice should be adopted for the various Indian tribes within the limits of the United States.[17]

At that time, Indian affairs were under Knox's jurisdiction. Land was the issue then, as it is today. Knox saw his mission as convincing Indian Nations to relinquish their lands, but he wanted the land cession treaties to be carried out legally and fairly: "The principle of the Indian right to the lands they possess being thus conceded, the dignity and interest of the nation will be advanced by making it the basis of the future administration of justice towards the Indian tribes."[18] Thus, one of the first proposals made by President Washington to the Congress under the new Constitution was that treaties with Native Nations should be submitted to the Senate for ratification in the same manner as treaties with European nations.[19]

Charles Willson Peale (1741–1827). *Henry Knox*, ca. 1784. Oil on canvas. 58.4 × 48.2 cm. Independence National Historical Park, Philadelphia INDE 14081

Knox and Washington faced, however, the very real prospect of an Indian war in the Old Northwest—the present-day states of Ohio, Indiana, Illinois, Michigan, Wisconsin, and the northeast part of Minnesota—so they launched a strategy to pull the Six Nations eastward, away from the more hostile western Indians. The Six Nations, for their part, were seeking relief from the punitive Treaty of Fort Stanwix, and from New York State's aggressive efforts to acquire tribal lands. In December 1790, President Washington addressed the latter issue in a statement to Seneca delegates, who had come to Philadelphia to meet with him:

> The general Government only has the power, to treat with the Indian Nations, and any treaty formed and held without its authority will not be binding. Here then is the security for the remainder of your lands. No State nor person can purchase your lands, unless at some public treaty held under the authority of the United States. The general government will never consent to your being defrauded. But it will protect you in all your just rights.[20]

In 1790 what has been called Harmar's Defeat sent chills into the hearts of the Americans. Six years after its victory over Great Britain, the American army was defeated soundly by the western confederacy of united Indian Nations in the Old Northwest. The killing of fifteen hundred civilians along the Ohio River had prompted Washington and Knox to order General Josiah Harmar to launch a campaign against the Shawnee and Miami Nations and their allies. The resulting conflicts led to three defeats and the deaths of more than two hundred soldiers and militia. Of this setback Washington wrote: "My mind . . . is prepared for the worst; that is, for expence without honor or profit."[21]

The war in the Old Northwest was caused by treaty violations. The British had negotiated a treaty at Fort Stanwix in 1768 that recognized Indian sovereignty over a vast tract of land extending westward from present-day Utica, New York, including the Ohio Valley. The United States claimed, however, that Britain had surrendered all that territory to them in the 1783 Treaty of Paris—in which no Native Nations had participated. This was a fatal assumption. The Indian Nations had never agreed to relinquish their lands, and when white settlers moved in to stake their claims, the nations resisted vigorously.

In 1791 an even greater defeat was suffered by General Arthur St. Clair at the Battle of the Wabash in present-day western Ohio. About six hundred soldiers were killed in the great victory of Little Turtle (Miami), Blue Jacket (Shawnee), and their warriors, which resulted in the first congressional investigation of the executive branch. The president refused to provide the War Department with documents requested by the House of Representatives.[22] While Congress did not issue a final report, serious questions arose about the president's Indian policy. Congress did authorize the creation of more military units and the use of those units, rather than militia soldiers, to fight Indians.

In written instructions from the Secretary of War, St. Clair had been told that an Indian war should be avoided. "It is considered that the sacrifices of blood and treasure in such a war far exceed any advantages which can possibly be reaped by it. The great policy, therefore, of the General Government, is to establish a just and liberal peace with all the Indian tribes within the limits and in the vicinity of the territory of the United States."[23] It is hard to imagine such a just and liberal peace without a treaty that guaranteed Indian Nations title to and jurisdiction over their lands.

During the early 1790s, Washington twice selected Colonel Timothy Pickering to negotiate treaties with the Six Nations in New York, and Pickering generally was respected by Haudenosaunee leaders as an honest broker. In a meeting with the Seneca at Tioga Point in 1790, for example, he listened carefully to delegates' grievances, presented wampum and gifts according to protocol, and promised to research the Seneca Nation's charges of fraud at the hands of land speculators. Pickering's job during this period was to convince the Six Nations that the president's 1790 pledge to Seneca leaders to protect their land holdings was real.

Washington also commissioned artist John Trumbull to design a series of peace medallions to be given to Indian leaders. The medals featured images of farmers, seed sowers, shepherds, and women spinning yarn—people engaged in so-called civilized pursuits—to represent his intentions for his treaty allies. Pickering advocated that the Six Nations emulate their white neighbors. In this regard, treaty making for Americans was a way of socializing potential enemies into a friendlier mind-set. According to federal reasoning, the Indian Nations could move away from hunting and develop a pioneer lifestyle by turning to the cultivation of the soil. Their white neighbors would then be safer.

By 1794, Washington had been trying for more than ten years to end what he saw as the dangerous antics of the "land jobbers, speculators, and monopolisers," who were cheating Indians out of their land.[24] Although he wanted to acquire tribal lands for the United States, Washington also thought that national expansion could be achieved in a fair and orderly way through federal

Charles Willson Peale (1741–1827). *Timothy Pickering,* ca. 1792. Oil on canvas. 58.4 × 48.3 cm. Independence National Historical Park, Philadelphia INDE 14131

treaty making. Washington had sought to prevent white settlers from trespassing on Indian lands, but during the early 1790s they continued to pour into the Old Northwest, provoking retaliation from Indian Nations intent on keeping them out.

Washington knew that white encroachment was the source of not only tensions in the west but also Haudenosaunee hostility. He continued to pursue diplomacy with the Six Nations through treaty making, but he kept his army ready to quell opposition if diplomacy failed. He feared that citizen reprisals would make the Six Nations the enemy of the United States, so he ordered the military to ensure the safe passage of any Six Nations diplomat.

After a series of treaty councils, continuing unrest in Ohio persuaded Washington to dispatch Major General "Mad Anthony" Wayne to quash Indian resistance to white settlement there. This resulted in an August "victory" at Fallen Timbers, near present-day Toledo, which many felt ended the Indian Wars in the Northwest Territories and secured the region for non-Native settlers.

In the meantime, Pickering, once again in the role of Washington's envoy, convened a treaty council at Canandaigua, New York, to negotiate land matters and affirm peace between the United States and the Six Nations. At the council the Seneca spokesman, Sagoyewatha (Red Jacket), explained that lingering issues over land had created rust on the Covenant Chain, potentially weakening the alliance with the Americans. Such

GEORGE WASHINGTON

PRESIDENT.

1792.

facing: This large silver medal depicts George Washington offering a pipe to a chief. In the background, a white man plows his fields with a yoke of oxen. On the reverse is an image of an eagle and the words, "E Pluribus Unum." For years, Red Jacket wore the medal with pride, but he advocated for neutrality in disputes between Britain and the United States.

Artist unknown. Medal presented by George Washington to Red Jacket, 1792. Silver. 18 × 13.2 cm. The Buffalo History Museum, New York

Charles Bird King (1785–1862). *Red Jacket, A Distinguished Seneca Chief*, 1833. Oil on wood. 44.8 × 32.9 cm. Colby College Museum of Art, Waterville, Maine, The Lunder Collection 2013.172

rust could break the chain. Ignoring the rust was equivalent to letting go of the chain, thereby disregarding the peace it was intended to preserve.

> We told you before of the two rusty places on the chain of friendship. . . . We thought you had a sharp file to take off the rust, but we believe it must have been dull, or else you let it slip out of your hands. . . . You are cutting off our land piece by piece. You are a kind-hearted people seeking your own advantages. . . . We have told you of the rusty part which the file passed over without brightening, and we wish you to take up the file again and rub it very hard.[25]

Pickering was successful in getting the Six Nations to agree to the treaty's terms. He was helped by the defeat of the western confederacy at Fallen Timbers, the news of which arrived during the treaty council. The situation affected the Indian bargaining position to a degree (the Americans gained the friendship of a powerful Indian Nation to the north, the right to build a road from Lake Ontario to Lake Erie, and free passage for American citizens through Indian lands), yet the Treaty of Canandaigua was one of the first to restore land that had been relinquished by previous treaty. More than one million acres of territory that had been ceded under the Fort Stanwix Treaty of 1784 were restored to the Seneca. The United States also agreed not to claim any Indian land until the Indian Nations chose to sell it.[26] The agreement put an end to Seneca hostility

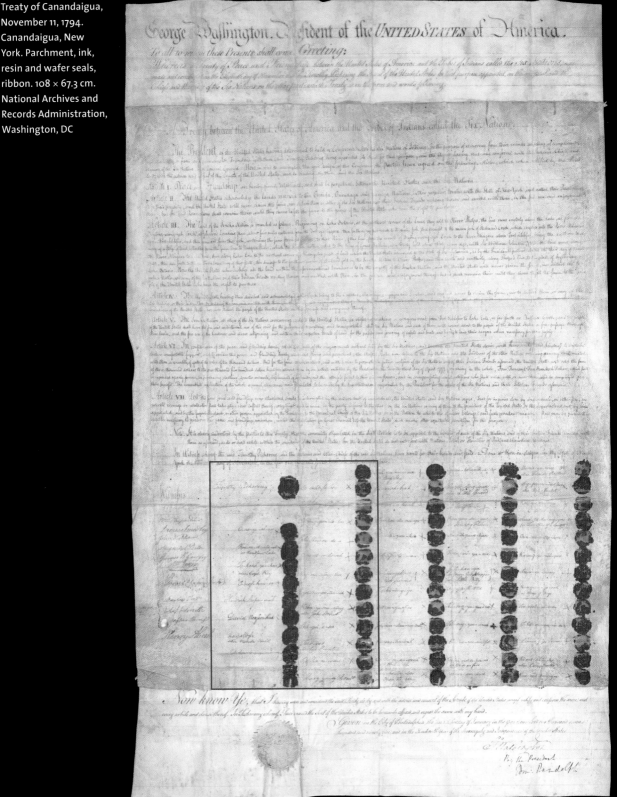

Treaty of Canandaigua, November 11, 1794. Canandaigua, New York. Parchment, ink, resin and wafer seals, ribbon. 108 × 67.3 cm. National Archives and Records Administration, Washington, DC

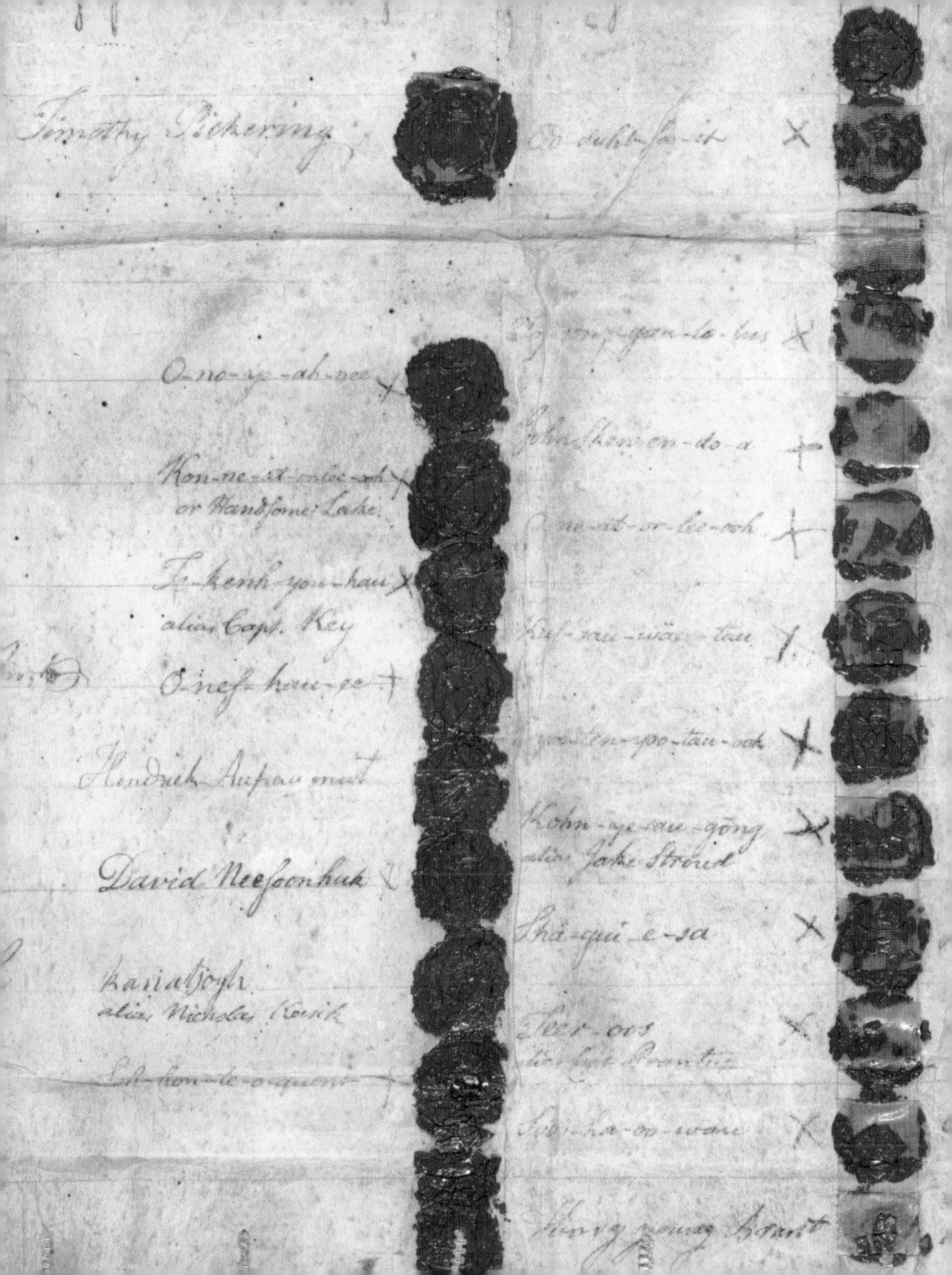

Timothy Pickering [seal] Oo-ndeh-fa-it ✗

Oij-nnj-gan-la-tees ✗

O-no-ye-ah-nee ✗ John Shen-en-do-a ✗

Kon-ne-it-nlee-xh O-ne-at-or-lee-ooh ✗
or Handsome Lake

Te-kenh-you-hau Kaf-nau-nau-tau ✗
alias Capt. Key

O-nesh-hau-ee gwedon-ypo-tau-uh ✗

Hendrick Aupaumut Kohn-ye-nau-gong ✗
alias Jake Stroud

David Neesoonhuk ✗ Sha-que-e-sa ✗

Kanatiogh Teer-oos ✗
alias Nicholas Kasik alias Capt. Prantie

Sh-hon-te-oquent Nun-ha-oo-ware ✗

Kung young heart

Tadodaho Sid Hill (left) and faithkeeper Oren Lyons, both of the Onondaga Nation, hold a full-size replica of the George Washington Covenant Chain wampum belt, which ratified the 1794 Canandaigua Treaty, February 2012. Onondaga Lake, New York. Photo by Michelle Gabel. *Post-Standard.*

but also spoiled relations between the Haudenosaunee and their western allies. Many western Native Nations afterward viewed the Six Nations with suspicion.

A huge parchment treaty was made and signed by the lead delegates. Wax seals were attached to it, and several copies were made. A separate parchment with Washington's signature was added to one copy after the treaty was proclaimed by Congress.

Washington also asked Congress to authorize the making of a massive wampum belt to ratify the Treaty of Canandaigua and symbolize his new attachment to the Six Nations. Called the George Washington Covenant Chain Belt, the belt is one of largest ever made by the United States, and its symbolism best embodies treaty relationships. The two central figures stand under the roof of the longhouse, holding the Covenant Chain between them. Their arms are linked to those of thirteen other figures, which represent the original thirteen states. They stand together in peace and unity, forming a bond that is nearly unbreakable.

MAKING PEACE IN 1815

While many Native Nations on both sides of the U.S.-Canadian border participated in the War of 1812 as allies of either Britain or the United States, none were at the overseas negotiation of the Treaty of Ghent, which ended that war. Article 9 of the treaty, however, states that all the rights, privileges, and possessions held by Native Nations before the war would be recognized. Nothing would be lost. While subsequent events may have raised questions about whether the United States intended to keep its pledge, the Treaty of Ghent—the two hundredth anniversary of which will be celebrated in 2015— still raises the issue of Indian treaty rights.

Another, lesser known treaty took place in 1815. At the British stronghold at Burlington Heights, near present-day Hamilton, Ontario, Britain, Canada, the United States, the Six Nations, and other Native Nations made peace. Colonel William Claus, named Kora Shotsitsyowanen (Superintendent, His Flower Is Great), as the imperial superintendent of Indian affairs, declared the war over and read article 9 to show that no Indian lands would be relinquished. The Grand River warriors (pro-British Mohawks who had settled in Canada) returned the ceremonial tomahawk they had received from the British king at the start of the war, and the peace chiefs replanted the Tree of Peace that had nearly toppled when Haudenosaunee warriors had faced off against one another during the American Revolution, in violation of the Great Law.

Colonel Claus then presented a wampum belt to the Grand River chiefs to formally acknowledge their assistance in the war. He pledged that the Crown, as their ally, would never interfere in their culture or government. He then asked that the Six Nations leaders take the belt, along with other belts he presented, around to all of the communities that had participated in the war, to let them know that it had ended.[27] Today the belt, with its unusual design, represents the hope of the Grand River Haudenosaunee that the Covenant Chain still exists and that they continue to have a treaty relationship with the Crown.

Six Nations chiefs—including John Smoke Johnson, or Sakayenkwaraton (Mohawk), keeper of the Pledge of the Crown Belt—explaining their wampum belts, September 14, 1871. Brantford, Ontario, Canada. Photo by James N. Edy. National Anthropological Archives, Smithsonian Institution NAA Photo Lot 86-58

Tadodaho Leon Shenandoah (Onondaga) holds some of the treaty cloth the United States government delivers each year to the Six Nations to maintain the Treaty of Canandaigua, 1994. New York. Photo by David Lassman. *Post-Standard*

Yet, they still face an uphill struggle: the Canadian government, while negotiating in 2009 on Grand River land rights, stated: "Canada does not believe that a protracted debate over the historical significance of the Covenant Chain or the Two Row Wampum would be constructive, since the historical record suggests that it would be difficult, if not impossible, for the parties to reach a common understanding of these symbols."[28]

Each fall, hundreds of people gather at the Treaty Rock in Canandaigua, New York, to celebrate the 1794 Treaty. The terms of the Treaty are read and one of the originals is shown publicly. Each year the president is invited to attend, but he never does. Presidents Clinton and Obama have, however, sent letters of support to the Treaty commemoration. The letters were a small sign of hope. Every few years the U.S. government sends bundles of cloth to the Six Nations in fulfillment of one of its Treaty obligations—another sign that the Treaty is still alive.

Experience shows us that no matter how long the history of wampum and treaty making, a treaty relationship has to be regularly renewed so that the rust on the chain does not break the spirit of the relationship. We have learned that treaties have withstood great stress, even war, but rational people will always gravitate toward peace. Treaties can be the springboard to that peace.

The Two-Row Wampum Belt

MARK G. HIRSCH

HAUDENOSAUNEE ORAL TRADITION TELLS OF A treaty circa 1613 in which Mohawk chiefs and Dutch traders agreed to live in peace, friendship, and equality as politically and culturally distinct peoples. The principles of their agreement were recorded for future generations in the Guswenta, or Two-Row Wampum—a long beaded belt consisting of two parallel rows of purple beads and three rows of white beads. One row of purple wampum represents the Haudenosaunee in their canoes; the other represents the Europeans in their ships. Each vessel carries its people's way of life, culture, and government. "In the Two Row, we agreed that we will travel the river of life together, side by side," observed Onondaga chief Jake Edwards. "We will not try to steer each other's boats, but travel side by side linked by peace, friendship, and forever."[1] For Oren Lyons, faithkeeper of the Onondaga Nation, the Two-Row treaty was the "Grandfather of all treaties," establishing the foundation "for all of our ensuing treaties."[2]

In 2013 the Onondaga Nation partnered with an organization of non-Native supporters of Haudenosaunee treaty rights and environmental stewardship to commemorate the four hundredth anniversary of the original Two-Row Treaty with the Dutch. To raise awareness of the principles and contemporary relevance of the Guswenta, organizers of the Two Row Renewal Campaign planned an extensive educational outreach program as well as a slate of cultural events throughout New York State. The events would culminate in a symbolic "enactment" of the 1613 treaty, with canoes (representing the Haudenosaunee) and ships (representing Europeans) sailing side by side down the Hudson River from a launching point near Albany, New York, to New York City.

The four hundredth anniversary commemoration was blindsided in August 2012, when the *Syracuse* (New York) *Post-Standard* revealed that organizers of the Two Row Renewal Campaign had been contacted by scholars who asserted that the 1613 Dutch-Iroquois treaty was a "forgery," and that the anniversary commemoration was based on a nonevent.[3] Drawing on research published in 1987, anthropologist William Starna and linguist Charles Gehring charged that the 1613 treaty—a two-page, handwritten transcript collected, translated, and published by Lawrence Gwyn Van Loon (1903–1985), a retired physician and amateur historian of Dutch exploration and settlement in seventeenth-century North America—was forged. After scrutinizing the Dutch-language text of the treaty transcript, the scholars discovered "problematical linguistic and orthographic anomalies" that they said made it impossible for the treaty to have originated in 1613.[4] Their conclusion: the 1613 treaty was "a fake."[5]

The allegations sparked a firestorm of controversy. Arguments for the authenticity of the 1613 treaty were posted on the Two Row Renewal Campaign's website, while other critics branded the academics "anti-Iroquois" for questioning the integrity of Haudenosaunee oral history. For their part, Starna and Gehring reaffirmed their assertions in "Revisiting the Fake Tawagonshi Treaty of 1613," published in the journal *New York History* (2012). Cooler academic heads also recently entered the fray in the pages of the *Journal of Early American History* (2013). The historians noted that the written historical evidence failed to corroborate claims that 2013 was the four hundredth anniversary of the Two-Row Treaty. They insisted, however, that their findings in no way

| 59

Tadodaho Sid Hill (Onondaga) stands on the shore of Onondaga Lake, holding a replica of the Two-Row Wampum Belt, 2006. Onondaga Lake, New York. Photo by John Berry. *Post-Standard*

discredited Haudenosaunee oral traditions regarding the Guswenta and the irrefutable influence of its principles on European-Iroquois diplomacy from the seventeenth century forward. The historical record contains "substantial documentation in support of Iroquois oral tradition concerning the Guswenta," concluded Cornell University historian Jon Parmenter, which "attests to its deeply rooted character in Haudenosaunee cultural understandings of the past."[6]

Ultimately, the Two Row Renewal Campaign went forward, culminating on August 9, when Iroquois and non-Native paddlers completed a ten-day, two-row canoe and kayak journey down the Hudson River to Pier 96 in Manhattan. There, tribal leaders and supporters exchanged greetings with Dutch consul-general Rob De Vos, and then marched to the United Nations, where Secretary General Ban

Ki-moon acknowledged the contingent at an event marking the International Day of the World's Indigenous Peoples.[7]

If anything, the controversy surrounding the Two Row Renewal Campaign bolstered Haudenosaunee faith in tribal oral traditions. "While a specific, uncontested, historical document has not been found to affirm the date of the first meeting [between the Haudenosaunee and the Dutch], an agreement resulted from this first encounter, according to our oral history and wampum memory," said Richard W. Hill, Sr. (Tuscarora) of the Deyohahá:ge: Indigenous Knowledge Centre, in Ohsweken, Ontario, Canada. "It is our understanding that we have inherited from our ancestors, which is not subject for debate, [but something] to be shared with those who are willing to consider our side of the story."[8]

William Penn's Treaty and the Shackamaxon Elm Tree

ARWEN NUTTALL

TREES ARE SYMBOLS OF STRENGTH AND LONGEVITY; their roots show the interconnectedness of all living beings, and their fruit, leaves, limbs, and shade provide food, domicile, and protection to all creatures. It is under and among these great symbols of natural beauty and permanence that Native Nations came together to make treaties with one another as well as with the newly arrived European nations.

In 1682, meeting beneath a sturdy, aged elm located in the Lenape village of Shackamaxon ("place where the chiefs meet"), William Penn, a Quaker entrepreneur who established the Pennsylvania Colony, and Tamanend, Turtle Clan chief of the Lenni Lenape Nation, forged a Treaty of Amity and Friend-ship. Other Native Nations in attendance included the Six Nations, the Shawnese, the Gawanese, and the Conestoga. Also known as the Great Treaty or Penn's Treaty, this agreement set forth the terms of a reciprocal relationship whereby Penn was granted lands for his Quaker colonists in exchange for an alliance with the Lenape for purposes of trade and relations with other nations. The Lenape retained "meander rights," or the freedom to travel, hunt, fish, and gather on the granted lands.

Seeking refuge from religious persecution in England, Penn had appealed to King Charles II for help. In 1681, to assist Penn and help satisfy a significant debt he owed the Quaker leader's father,

Francis Place (1647–1728). *Portrait of William Penn*, ca. 1698. Pastel on paper. 30 × 21 cm. Historical Society of Pennsylvania, Philadelphia 270

Raymond Sandoval. Tamanend statue (detail), 1996. Philadelphia, Pennsylvania. Bronze. Length 670.6 cm. Photo by J. J. Prats.

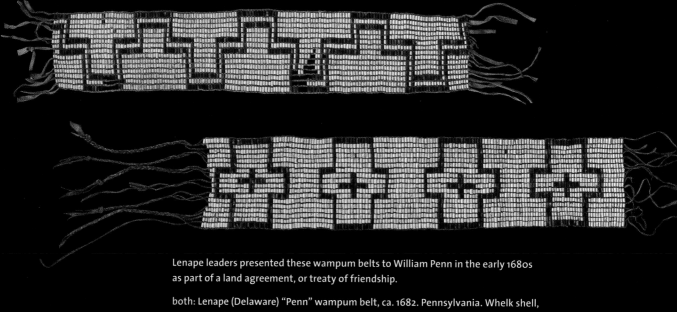

Lenape leaders presented these wampum belts to William Penn in the early 1680s as part of a land agreement, or treaty of friendship.

both: Lenape (Delaware) "Penn" wampum belt, ca. 1682. Pennsylvania. Whelk shell, quahog shell, hide, bast fiber yarn, ochre.
top: 78 × 12 cm. National Museum of the American Indian 5/3151
bottom: 103 × 13.5 cm. National Museum of the American Indian 5/3150

the king had granted Penn a generous charter that included lands west of New Jersey and north of Maryland, lands traditionally belonging to the Lenape people. Penn sought to make this new colony his "holy experiment." It was to be a safe haven, where people of many different backgrounds and religions could live together in peace. To Penn, this group also included his Native neighbors. He refused to settle in any part of the new colony until he had acquired it through fair means from the Native residents. And his "Concessions to the Province of Pennsylvania" mandated that all Native people be treated fairly:

No person shall harm or mistreat an Indian in any way. If a person breaks the law he or she would be punished as if the harm had been done to any white settler. If any Indian, in any way, harms a settler, the settler may not take the law into his or her own hands but must present a case before an officer of the district. The district officer or judge will take the case to the local Indian chief who has

the power to determine how the dispute should be settled.[1]

The Penn Treaty is unique in that it was never written down. Only four wampum belts exchanged between Penn and Tamanend recorded the events that took place under the great elm that day in 1682. Dating to a time when colonial relations with Native communities were marked with strife and sometimes bloodshed, the Penn Treaty is also recognized as a treaty that was never violated. Described as "not been sworn to, and which has not been broken" by the French historian and philosopher Voltaire, the Penn Treaty represents an idealized relationship between European colonists and Native Nations. Penn's relations with the Lenape and other neighboring nations were colored by his Quaker principles. He was a pacifist who spoke out against the enslavement of Native Peoples (though his opinions on Negro slavery followed popular thought), and he treated them virtually as equals.

The peaceful relations and mutual respect that

THE GREAT ELM TREE OF SHACKAMAXON NOW KENSINGTON
Under which William Penn concluded his Treaty with the Indians in 1682 it fell during a storm in 1810.
This block of marble was placed by the Penn Treaty in 1827 to mark the site of the Elm Tree an
Treaty Ground of William Penn & the Indian Nations in 1682 & bears the inscription "Treaton Kensington The Bond of Peace"

Penn maintained between his colony and the Lenape people did not last after his death. Penn's heirs did not uphold his principles. His sons John and Thomas rejected Quakerism and fell into debt. To reduce that debt they began selling land to the increasing numbers of European immigrants pouring into the region before purchasing it from the Native inhabitants. In addition, German immigrants began settling on the upper Schuylkill River and further northeast without permission from either the Lenape or the proprietors (colonial governors) of Pennsylvania. Pennsylvania officials felt it was necessary to gain clear title from the Lenape to extend governance over these new settlements.

Whereas William Penn believed in fair trade with his Native neighbors, his sons and land agent, James Logan, did not. The result was the fraudu-

George Lehman (ca. 1800–1870). *The Great Elm Tree of Shackamaxon (Now Kensington)*, ca. 1829. Philadelphia, Pennsylvania. Aquatint with watercolor. 36.8 × 45.7 cm. State Museum of Pennsylvania, Pennsylvania Historical and Museum Commission, Harrisburg 95.75.19

lent 1737 Walking Purchase, an agreement based on a fabricated 1686 treaty in which the Lenape had allegedly agreed to sell land west of the Delaware River to William Penn. The number of acres would be demarcated by what a man could walk in a day and a half. When the walkers began their journey to measure the land, however, they walked far more briskly—almost running—than the Lenape felt was fair. The walk also did not begin at the agreed-upon boundary. As a result, the Pennsylvania government received an area slightly smaller than Rhode Island, far more land than the Lenape had thought they

Elm Treaty Chair, ca 1810. Philadelphia, Pennsylvania. Elm wood. 92.7 × 53.3 × 48.3 cm. State Museum of Pennsylvania, Pennsylvania Historical and Museum Commission, Harrisburg

One of two surviving chairs made from pieces of the Shackamaxon treaty elm.

would be giving up. The Lenape's claim against the deceitful agreement has continued into the twenty-first century. The Walking Purchase destroyed the trust between the Lenape people and the Pennsylvania colonists. They, along with other Native Nations in the Delaware Valley, were eventually driven westward. The purchase is cited as one of the major reasons the Lenape sided with the French during the French and Indian War two decades later.

Like the peace between the Lenape and their European neighbors, the elm tree at Shackamaxon also did not survive. It was felled by a violent storm in 1810, but its legacy was not forgotten. Roberts Vaux, a founder of the Penn Society, was one of the first to advocate for a memorial to commemorate Penn's Treaty. He commissioned at least eight small boxes to be made from its wooden remnants, which he gifted to various friends and associates, including Supreme Court justice John Marshall. President John Quincy Adams also received a box, though it is unclear if it was Vaux who gave it to him. Today the place where Penn first met with his new Native neighbors is marked by a descendant of the Treaty Elm. The tree, planted in 2000, is a reminder to the people of Pennsylvania and the Lenni Lenape Nation of their connection and historical legacy.

Probably Lenape (Delaware) knife and sheath, ca. 1760.
New Jersey. Iron, hide, wood, porcupine quills, horsehair,
dye, metal cones. 42 × 8.7 × 2.5 cm. National Museum of
the American Indian 4/901

Illegal State Treaties

MARK G. HIRSCH

AFTER THE ADOPTION OF THE CONSTITUTION, treaties and federal statutes became the principal instruments of United States Indian policy. In 1790 the first federal Congress enacted the Indian Trade and Intercourse Act, which prohibited the sale of tribal lands without the consent of the federal government. By protecting Indian Tribes from shady property transactions with land-hungry settlers, speculators, and states, Congress hoped to alleviate a major source of Indian unrest and establish an orderly system for acquiring lands for western expansion.[1]

The original thirteen states violated the new federal law with impunity. Accustomed to dealing with the Indian Nations within their borders, states along the eastern seaboard continued to negotiate land cession treaties with them long after 1790. Increasingly, Native Nations on the East Coast found themselves coerced into ceding their lands. The illegal treaties withered the landholdings of the Penobscot, Passamaquoddy, and Maliseet in Maine; the Wampanoag in Massachusetts; the Narragansett in Rhode Island; the Pequot in Connecticut; the Haudenosaunee in New York; and the Catawba in South Carolina.[2] Dispossessed of most of their vast estate, the eastern Indians survived as fishermen, fishing-boat hands, peddlers, and laborers on farms and in logging camps.[3]

Despite poverty and dislocation, the Native Nations continued to press for restoration of—or compensation for—their illegally appropriated homelands. Demands for redress gained traction in the late 1960s, when the United States recognized the tribal right to bring suit in federal courts to litigate questions of federal law. With the assistance of Native legal action organizations, eastern Indian tribes began to file lawsuits in the 1970s, seeking restitution of or damages for territories lost in violation of the 1790 trade and intercourse act.[4]

The Narragansett was the first eastern nation to win a settlement of their land claims. In the 1978 agreement, the Narragansett relinquished all claims to aboriginal lands in Rhode Island in exchange for eighteen hundred acres, half donated by the state and half purchased from private landowners with $3.5 million in federal funds.[5] Two years later, Congress enacted a settlement of the Penobscot, Passamaquoddy, and Maliseet claims, in which the tribes demanded restoration of twelve million acres that had been acquired through illegal treaties and transactions with Massachusetts and Maine between 1794 and 1833. Under the Maine Indian Claims Settlement Act of 1980, which the *Christian Science Monitor* described as the "biggest Indian victory since Little Big Horn,"[6] the nations acquired $54 million to purchase three hundred thousand acres from private landowners, a $27 million tribal trust fund, and restoration of tribal recognition from the federal government. In return, the Maine Indians agreed to relinquish title to their aboriginal landholdings, a decision many Native critics considered a surrender of tribal sovereignty.[7]

From 1974 to 2005, approximately two dozen tribes—from New England down the eastern seaboard and west to Alabama, Louisiana, and Texas—filed land claims based on illegal treaties with states. Nearly all were settled by congressional statutes that extinguished the tribes' aboriginal title, approved the historic land transfers that had violated the 1790 law, and provided the tribes with federal recogni-

66

tion, parcels of other, publicly owned lands, and/or money to purchase property from private landowners.[8] But not all tribes were successful in recovering or obtaining compensation for their lands. From 1974 to 2005, Haudenosaunee Nations, including the Oneida, Cayuga, Mohawk, Seneca, and Onondaga, initiated lawsuits to recover approximately 330,000 acres taken through illegal treaties and land transactions with New York State after 1790.[9] Although the lawsuits won favorable decisions in the lower courts, increasingly conservative land claims decisions in the federal appeals courts reversed earlier rulings and stymied Haudenosaunee litigation against New York State.[10]

Although the future of Indian land claims cases is unclear, there is little doubt that the past forty years of litigation has strengthened Indian Nations that once faced bleak circumstances. When they received federal recognition and fourteen hundred acres of land in a 1983 land-claims settlement, the Mashantucket Pequot Nation in Connecticut established a successful gaming operation, which has enabled the tribe to reconstitute itself, expand its land base, and develop a tribal museum that celebrates Pequot history and culture.[11] The Mashantucket Pequot are hardly alone. Land-claim settlements and federal recognition have transformed once marginalized eastern Indian tribes, such as the Aquinnah Wampanoag on Martha's Vineyard, Massachusetts, the Mashpee Wampanoag Tribe in Massachusetts, and the Catawba Indian Nation in South Carolina into modern, resilient Indian Nations.[12]

IN THE 1600S, EUROPEANS INVOKED THE DOCTRINE of Discovery to claim that Christian nations that "discovered" lands in North America gained property rights over those territories. According to the doctrine, the discovering nation also could exercise sovereignty over Indigenous Peoples, and it held an exclusive right to transfer colonial lands to other European powers without consulting the Indian owners.[1]

The hubris of discovery collided on contact with powerful North American Indian Nations that claimed and stoutly defended proprietorship of their sacred homelands. To ensure the peaceful acquisition of land and obtain legally valid titles for white settlers, Europeans were forced to recognize Indian property rights, and began purchasing tribal land rather than simply taking it. The practice of acquiring Indian land through purchase and treaties became customary for American colonial governments and, later, for the new U.S. government.[2]

As the nineteenth century progressed, however, the rapid growth of the non-Native population and burgeoning hunger for Indian land severely weakened tribal bargaining power and eroded American respect for tribal property rights. To promote the rapid acquisition of the Native estate, to realize the nation's "manifest destiny," Americans needed a powerful legal justification for removing Indians from—and dispossessing them of—their traditional homelands. Ultimately, Americans found legal sanction in Chief Justice John Marshall's pivotal Supreme Court opinion in the case of *Johnson v. M'Intosh* (1823).

Drawing on the discovery doctrine, Marshall declared that Indians had a right to occupy their territories but were not full owners of their land. Instead, Native Peoples were basically tenants who lived on land owned by the discovering sovereign. After the Revolutionary War, Marshall opined, title to Indian land passed from the British Crown to the United States, making the new nation the landlord of a vast continent. The logic of Marshall's opinion did not escape states and settlers who coveted tribal lands. After *Johnson v. M'Intosh*, land-hungry Americans and state officials had a powerful legal justification for evicting and dispossessing the Indian Nations.[3]

Marshall's opinion in *Johnson v. M'Intosh* did not end treaty making with Indian tribes. Indeed, about 90 percent of the land in the forty-eight contiguous states was acquired from Indian Tribes through treaties or the agreements that replaced them in 1871.[4] The opinion, however, provided states and the federal government with a powerful coercive weapon for evicting Indians from the eastern half of the country and for rounding up and resettling western tribes on Indian reservations.[5]

LINDSAY G. ROBERTSON

Unintended Consequences

Johnson v. M'Intosh and Indian Removal

O
N A COLD FEBRUARY DAY IN 1823, IN THEIR COURTROOM BENEATH THE Old Senate Chamber in the U.S. Capitol, Chief Justice John Marshall and five colleagues on the Supreme Court of the United States opened argument in the case of *Johnson v. M'Intosh*. The case raised a fundamental question: what rights did Europeans acquire, and Indigenous peoples lose, by virtue of the European "discovery" of America? To answer it, Chief Justice Marshall, writing for the court, introduced into U.S. law the "discovery doctrine." According to this doctrine (as formulated in *Johnson*), upon European discovery of North America, the continent's Indigenous Peoples lost to the discovering European sovereign the underlying title to their lands, retaining only a right to occupy those lands. This occupancy right might be transferred, but only to the same discovering sovereign. Throughout the United States the American political descendants of the discovering sovereigns overnight became owners of lands that had previously belonged to Native Americans, while Native Americans became their tenants. This formulation of the discovery doctrine is the law today.

The case arose as a last-ditch effort to save a failed late-colonial land speculation. In 1773 and 1775 the United Illinois and Wabash Land Companies purchased four enormous tracts of land from the Piankashaw and Illinois Indian Nations in what would become the states of Indiana and Illinois. The purchases were illegal under King George III's proclamation of October 7, 1763, which forbade individuals to purchase Indian lands west of the Allegheny Mountains without Crown consent. To get around the prohibition, the speculators prepared and circulated an edited draft of an old British legal opinion—the Camden-Yorke opinion—that seemed to suggest that the Proclamation of 1763 had been repealed. Unrest in the

Artist unknown. *Robert Goodloe Harper,* 1810–1820. Oil on canvas. 76.4 × 63.3 cm. Maryland Historical Society, Baltimore 1986.24

eastern colonies (including the Boston Tea Party and the Battles of Lexington and Concord) proved sufficiently distracting to British authorities that no decisive action was taken to stop the speculators, and as British power dissolved in the face of the American Revolution, the speculators eagerly set about lobbying a succession of new American governments to recognize their title to the purchased lands. In the end, the Illinois and Wabash Land Companies would devote nearly fifty years to pleading its case before various American legislatures, until finally, in 1820, they were positioned to commence a lawsuit for title in the federal district court for the District of Illinois.[6]

The history of the *Johnson* litigation is troubling, particularly given the impact of the case on Indigenous rights. The litigation was orchestrated by the companies' chief counsel, Robert Goodloe Harper, a leading Baltimore attorney and one-time Federalist congressman (perhaps best remembered for coining the phrase, "Millions for defense, not one cent for tribute"). An unsuccessful

Old Supreme Court Chamber, below the Old Senate Chamber in the U.S. Capitol. Washington, DC. Photo by Franz Jantzen. Franz Jantzen, Collection of the Supreme Court of the United States

The Supreme Court heard cases, including *Johnson v. M'Intosh,* in this room from 1819 to 1860.

The following is the Opinion of the late Lord Chancellor Cambden & Lord Chancellor York on Titles derived by the Kings Subjects from the Indians or Natives

"In respect to such places as have been or shall be acquired by Treaty or Grant from any of the Indian Princes or Governments, your Majestys Letters Patents are not necessary, the Property of the Soil vesting in the Grantee, by the Indian Grants, subject only to your Majestys Right of Sovereignty over the Settlements as English Settlements and over the Inhabitants as English Subjects, who carry with them your Majestys Laws, wherever they form Colonys and receive your Majestys Protection, by Virtue of your Royal Charters

The above is a true Copy compared in London the first day of April 1772

Taken from the Original in the Hands of Samuel Wharton

"The opinion of the late Lord Chancellor Cambden & Lord Chancellor York on Titles derived by the King's Subjects from the Indians or Natives," April 1, 1772. United Illinois and Wabash Land Companies Digital Collection, Courtesy of Jasper Brinton and the Donald E. Pray Law Library, University of Oklahoma College of Law, Norman

The Camden-Yorke opinion provided a way for the Illinois and Wabash Land Companies to purchase Indian land without a license, an activity that had been prohibited by the Proclamation of 1863.

land speculator, Harper had been hired by the Illinois and Wabash Land Companies after his marriage to the daughter of a companies' shareholder, Charles Carroll of Carrollton, who was at the time the richest person in the United States. Once the decision had been made to sue, Harper's first job was to arrange parties. As defendant, Harper selected William M'Intosh, former treasurer of the Indiana Territory. M'Intosh had purchased lands in the companies' claim area from the United States, which had purchased them from the Piankashaw Nation after the Revolution. He was a social outcast. His wife, Lydia, was alleged to be an escaped slave, and after charging that the territorial governor, William Henry Harrison, had cheated the Lenape (Delaware), Potawatomi, Miami, and Eel River Miami Nations in treaty negotiations, he himself was successfully sued for slander. After losing the slander suit, M'Intosh and his family left Indiana's territorial capital of Vincennes and settled on the opposite side of

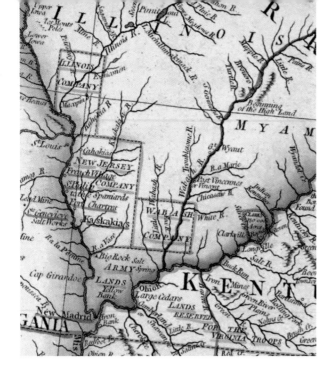

William Faden (1749–1836). *The United States of North America, with the British Territories* (detail), 1793. Library of Congress

This map shows two of the tracts, labeled "Illinois Company" and "Wabash Company," respectively, that the United Illinois and Wabash Land Companies claimed they purchased legally from Indian Nations in the 1770s. The map also shows the lands in western Kentucky that John Marshall, in the *Johnson v. M'Intosh* ruling, decided were Virginia's to grant to its Revolutionary War veterans.

the Wabash River, twenty miles south of the town. When Harper's agents found him, he was prepared to cooperate. As plaintiff, Harper selected companies' shareholder Thomas Johnson, who had served as Maryland's governor during the Revolution and briefly as an associate justice of the U.S. Supreme Court. Johnson's death in 1819 delayed the suit, and his place was eventually taken by his heirs, Joshua Johnson and Thomas Grahame. The companies' claim had been denied by numerous congressional committees over the years, on a variety of factual grounds: for example, that the companies had purchased the lands from the wrong Indians, or that they hadn't paid enough. To prevent the court's finding against him for any of these reasons, Harper prepared a stipulation of facts eliminating as possible grounds for denying the Illinois and Wabash claims all the factual objections ever raised against them by legislative bodies. M'Intosh's lawyer agreed, and the case went forward confined to one issue: whether the purchases were invalid under the Proclamation of 1763. After a pro forma trial, with M'Intosh's agreement, the case was taken to the Supreme Court for a final determination of whether the proclamation was constitutional under the British Constitution. If it was not, the speculators believed, the Supreme Court would have to recognize their claim to title, and with a decision of the Supreme Court in hand, they might force Congress to compensate them for lands in their claim area purchased after 1775 by the United States.

The case was argued for the speculators by Harper and Daniel Webster, then widely agreed to be the best lawyer in the United States. "For effect," Harper had arranged that M'Intosh's case would be argued by his friends, Maryland lawyers William Winder and Henry Murray, with their fees to be paid by the United Illinois and Wabash Land Companies.

The argument lasted three days, but the decision of the Supreme Court was not long in coming: the court ruled against the speculators. The court held, in a paragraph, that the Proclamation of 1763 was constitutional. Then, for reasons not argued, the court devoted more than twenty pages to announcing and justifying the incorporation of the discovery doctrine into U.S. law. Because the underlying title to the purchased lands belonged to the British Crown, the court announced, the tribes could not sell it to the speculators. Moreover, in 1775, the occupancy right was transferable only to British Crown, and the tribes lacked the power to convey that to the speculators as well. The claims of the Illinois and Wabash Companies were denied, and the discovery doctrine was now a part of United States law. Where did this rule come from? Why did Marshall adopt it in the *Johnson* opinion? The answers to these questions are as troubling as the litigation history.

As for the source of the rule, Marshall stated in his opinion that it was the law in the colonial era and that he was therefore bound by it. His authority for this view is questionable: it was drawn from Marshall's own *Life of George Washington* (1804), written (by his own admission) without his having had the opportunity to consult primary materials. As for motive, the court appears to have grafted the discovery doctrine onto the *Johnson v. M'Intosh* holding to accommodate Marshall's desire to resolve a contemporaneous (and unrelated) dispute involving title to lands in western Kentucky. Virginia had granted these lands to its Revolutionary War militia veterans; after it became a separate state in 1792, Kentucky wanted them for its citizens. A major problem with the veterans' claims was that at the time of the militia grants the lands were owned by the Chickasaw: for this reason, Kentucky argued, Virginia had nothing to grant. By retroactively vesting title to the lands in Virginia (as the successor to the British Crown), Marshall eliminated this objection to the militia claims. Three months after the opinion, Thomas Jefferson complained to Justice William Johnson: "This practice of Judge Marshall, of travelling out of his case to prescribe what the law would be in a moot case not before the court, is very irregular and very censurable." It also sometimes had unintended consequences.

To Marshall's evident surprise, after the publication of the opinion, *Johnson v. M'Intosh* was seized upon by Georgians to provide a legal mechanism for ousting the Cherokee from their lands in northwest Georgia. Georgia had ceded its western land claims (including most of Alabama and Mississippi) to the United States in 1802 on the condition that the United States promise to enter into a treaty with the Cherokee Nation to transfer Cherokee lands to Georgia. The Cherokee being unwilling to sell, the United States had done nothing. In the wake of *Johnson*, Georgia claimed that Georgia had succeeded to the British Crown's right of ownership of the underlying title to the Cherokee lands. As the owner—effectively, the landlord—Georgia had a right to impose its own laws on the Cherokee, which it did by statute in 1828. The Cherokee were free to remain, Georgia offered, but they would be subject to state law. Mississippi and Alabama followed suit, legislating the imposition of their laws on the Choctaw, Chickasaw, and Muscogee (Creek) Nations. In the Indian Removal Act of 1830, President Andrew Jackson's government volunteered that, if the Cherokee and other similarly threatened tribes in these states did decide to move, the United States would make available to them land in what would become Oklahoma.

John Marshall was riding circuit in Virginia and North Carolina during the debate on the Indian removal bill. Newspaper coverage, however, was widespread, and key opponents of removal, including Senator Theodore Frelinghuysen of New Jersey and Congressman Edward Everett of Massachusetts, forwarded to Marshall copies of their speeches.[7] Marshall was distressed at Congress's cooperation in completing "the coercive measures begun by the states" of Georgia, Alabama and Mississippi,[8] and he privately denounced the removal act in a letter to Virginia judge Dabney Carr, lamenting, "Humanity must bewail the course which is pursued." His distress was no doubt enhanced by feelings of culpability. The degree to which he had developed in *Johnson v. M'Intosh* the legal theory on which the "coercive measures" were grounded was

Young & Delleker. *Georgia*, 1829. Hargrett Rare Book and Manuscript Library/University of Georgia Libraries, Athens

Georgians were eager to acquire the Cherokee lands to their northwest and, in the wake of the *Johnson v. M'Intosh* decision, claimed that the state was the effective owner-landlord of the Cherokee Nation's territory. This map is a reissue of an earlier one; by 1829 the Muscogee (Creek) Nation had ceded all its land in Georgia.

apparent in the public record. Four months after the enactment of the removal bill the source of these measures became even more obvious—and no doubt more painful—when a convention of Georgia's circuit judges used *Johnson v. M'Intosh* to uphold a state court death sentence imposed on a Cherokee man, George Tassel, accused of killing another Cherokee man within the borders of the Cherokee Nation.

On December 20, 1830, four days before Tassel's slated Christmas Eve execution, Cherokee principal chief John Ross informed Georgia governor George Gilmer that the Cherokee Nation itself, by counsel, would ask the Supreme Court to enjoin the enforcement of any Georgia law within Cherokee territory.[9] Georgia nevertheless proceeded with Tassel's hanging, and the Cherokee Nation filed suit.[10]

If the Supreme Court invalidated the purported assertion of state laws, it would remove the

Alfred M. Hoffy (ca. 1790–1860), after a painting by Charles Bird King (1785–1862). *John Ross, A Cherokee Chief,* 1843. Hand-colored lithograph on paper, published in Thomas McKenney and James Hall, *History of the Indian Tribes of North America.* 50.6 × 36 cm. National Portrait Gallery, Smithsonian Institution; gift of Betty A. and Lloyd G. Schermer NPG 99.169.23

teeth from the Indian Removal Act: if the states could not validly impose their laws on Native Nations within their limits, the nations would have no incentive to move. The problem was that the Cherokee Nation lacked clear capacity to file suit in the Supreme Court. Under the Constitution, the court could try lawsuits "between two or more States" and "between a State . . . and foreign states."[11] The Cherokee Nation clearly was not a state within the union. Was it a foreign state?

When the case was called for argument, Georgia failed to appear. Attorneys John Sergeant and William Wirt argued valiantly for the Cherokee in a doomed cause. Marshall delivered his opinion on March 3, 1831. "Though the Indians," he declared, "are acknowledged to have an unquestionable and, heretofore, unquestioned right to the lands they occupy until that right shall be extinguished by a voluntary cession to our government, yet it may well be doubted whether those tribes which reside within the acknowledged boundaries of the United States can, with strict accuracy, be denominated foreign nations." Instead, he found, "they may, more correctly, perhaps, be denominated domestic dependent nations."[12] The Supreme Court of the United States had no jurisdiction to entertain original actions brought by domestic dependent nations. The suit thus invited the resolution of questions beyond the court's capacity, "at least in the form in which those matters are presented." That said, these questions "might," Marshall noted, "perhaps be decided by [the] court in a proper case with proper parties."[13] The motion for an injunction was denied, but the Cherokee were invited to try again.

Two relatively new Jackson appointees sat on the court during the 1831 term. One—John McLean of Ohio—joined Marshall's opinion. The other—Henry Baldwin of

ᏣᎳᎩ · ᏧᎾᏓᏘᏓᏍᏗ

CHEROKEE PHŒNIX.

EDITED BY ELIAS BOUDINOTT.

PRINTED WEEKLY BY

ISAAC H. HARRIS,

FOR THE CHEROKEE NATION.

At $2 50 if paid in advance, $3 in six months, or $3 50 if paid at the end of the year.

To subscribers who can read only the Cherokee language the price will be $2,00 in advance, or $2,50 to be paid within the year.

Every subscription will be considered as continued unless subscribers give notice to the contrary before the commencement of a new year.

The Phœnix will be printed on a Super-Royal sheet, with type entirely new procured for the purpose. Any person procuring six subscribers, and becoming responsible for the payment, shall receive a seventh gratis.

Advertisements will be inserted at seventy-five cents per square for the first insertion, and thirty-seven and a half cents for each continuance; longer ones in proportion.

☞ All letters addressed to the Editor, post paid, will receive due attention.

[Cherokee syllabary paragraph.]

A GOOD CONSCIENCE.

What is there, in all the pomp of the world, the enjoyments of luxury, the gratification of passion, comparable to the tranquillity of a good conscience? It is the health of the mind. It is a sweet perfume, that diffuses its fragrance over every thing near it without exhausting its store. Unaccompanied with this, the gay pleasures of the world are like brilliants to a diseased eye, music to a deaf ear, wine in an ardent fever, or dainties in the languor of an ague. To lie down on the pillow, after a day spent in temperance in beneficence, and piety, how sweet is it! How different from that state of him, who reclines, at an unnatural hour, with his blood inflamed, his head throbbing with wine and gluttony, his heart aching with rancorous malice, his thoughts totally estranged from Him who has protected him in the day and will watch over him, ungrateful as he is, in the night season! A good conscience is, indeed, the peace of God. Passions lulled to sleep, clear thoughts, cheerful temper, a disposition to be pleased with every obvious and innocent object around; these are the effects of a good conscience; these are the things which constitute happiness; and these condescend to dwell with the poor man, in his humble cottage in the vale of obscurity. In the magnificent mansion of the proud and vain, glitter the exteriors of his p... ness, the gliding, the trapping, the pride and the pomp; but in the decent habitation of piety is oftener found the downy nest of heavenly peace; that solid good, of which the parade of the vain, the frivolous and voluptuous, is but a shadowy semblance.

Christian Philosophy.

Flattery.—Few things are more universally condemned than flattery; yet there are few men, who are above its influence, and still fewer, who have courage sufficient to repel it with a faithful rebuke. The following anecdote is recommended, as affording a specimen of a good answer to flatterers. A certain clergyman in New England, eminent both for talents and humility, was one day accosted by a parishioner, who highly commended some of his performances, of which the clergyman himself had a very low opinion. After patiently hearing him a few moments, the clergyman replied; "My Friend, if I that you say gives me no better opinion of myself than I had before, but gives me a much worse opinion of you."

CONSTITUTION OF THE CHEROKEE NATION,

Formed by a Convention of Delegates from the several Districts, at New Echota, July 1827.

WE, THE REPRESENTATIVES of the people of the Cherokee Nation in Convention assembled, in order to establish justice, ensure tranquillity, promote our common welfare, and secure to ourselves and our posterity the blessings of liberty; acknowledging with humility and gratitude the goodness of the sovereign Ruler of the Universe, in offering us an opportunity so favorable to the design, and imploring his aid and direction in its accomplishment, do ordain and establish this Constitution for the Government of the Cherokee Nation.

ARTICLE I.

Sec. 1. THE BOUNDARIES of this nation, embracing the lands solemnly guarantied and reserved forever to the Cherokee Nation by the Treaties concluded with the United States, are as follows; and shall forever hereafter remain unalterably the same—to wit—Beginning on the North Bank of Tennessee River at the upper part of the Chickasaw old fields; thence along the main channel of said river, including all the islands therein, to the mouth of the Hiwassee river, thence up the main channel of said river, including Islands, to the first hill which closes in on said river, about two miles above Hiwassee old Town; thence along the ridge which divides the waters of the Hiwassee and little Telico, to the Tennessee river at Tallassee; thence along the main channel, including Islands, to the junction of the Cowee and Nanteyalee; thence along the ridge in the fork of said river, to the top of the blue ridge; thence along the blue ridge to the Unicoy Turnpike road; thence by a straight line to the main source of the Chestatee; thence along its main channel, including Islands, to the Chattahoochy; and thence down the same to the Creek boundary at Buzzard Roost; thence along the boundary line which separates this and the Creek Nation, to a point on the Coosa river opposite the mouth of Wills Creek; thence down along the South bank of the same to a point opposite to Fort Strother; thence up the river to the mouth of Wills Creek; thence up along the East bank of said creek, to the West branch thereof, and up the same to its source; and thence along the ridge which separates the Tombechee and Tennessee waters, to a point on the top of said ridge; thence due North to Camp Coffee on Tennessee river, which is opposite the Chickasaw Island; and thence to the place of beginning.

Sec. 2. The Sovereignty and Jurisdiction of this Government shall extend over the Country within the boundaries above described, and the lands therein are, and shall remain, the common property of the Nation; but the improvements made thereon, and in the possession of the citizens of the Nation, are the exclusive and indefeasible property of the citizens respectively who made, or may rightfully be in possession of them; Provided, That the citizens of the Nation, possessing exclusive and indefeasible right to their respective improvements, as expressed in this article, shall possess no right nor power to dispose of their improvements in any manner whatever to the United States, individual States, nor to individual citizens thereof; and that, whenever any such citizen or citizens shall remove with their effects out of the limits of this Nation, and become citizens of any other Government, all their right and privileges as citizens of this Nation shall cease; Provided nevertheless, That the Legislature shall have power to re-admit by law to all the rights of citizenship, any such person or persons, who may at any time desire to return to the Nation and become members of, by memorializing the General Council for such

readmission. Moreover, the Legislature shall have power to adopt such laws and regulations, as its wisdom may deem expedient and proper, to prevent the citizens from monopolizing improvements with the view of speculation.

ARTICLE II.

Sec. 1. THE Power of this Government shall be divided into three distinct departments;—the Legislative, the Executive, and the Judicial.

Sec. 2. No person or persons, belonging to one of these Departments, shall exercise any of the powers properly belonging to either of the others, except in the cases hereinafter expressly directed or permitted.

ARTICLE III.

Sec. 1. THE LEGISLATIVE POWER shall be vested in two distinct branches; a Committee, and a Council; each to have a negative on the other, and both to be styled, the General Council of the Cherokee Nation; and the style of their acts and laws shall be,

"Resolved by the Committee and Council in General Council convened."

Sec. 2. The Cherokee Nation, as laid off into eight Districts, shall so remain.

Sec. 3. The Committee shall consist of two members from each District, and the Council shall consist of three members from each District, to be chosen by the qualified electors of their respective Districts for two years; and the elections to be held in every District on the first Monday in August for the year 1828, and every succeeding two years thereafter; and the General Council shall be held once a year, to be convened on the second Monday of October in each year, at New Echota.

Sec. 4. No person shall be eligible to a seat in the General Council, but a free Cherokee Male citizen, who shall have attained to the age of twenty-five years. The descendants of Cherokee men by all free women, except the African race, whose parents may be or have been living together as man and wife, according to the customs and laws of this Nation, shall be entitled to, all the rights and privileges of this Nation, as well as the posterity of Cherokee women by all free men. No person who is of negro or mulatto parentage, either by the father or mother side, shall be eligible to hold any office of profit, honor or trust, under this Government.

Sec. 5. The Electors, and members of the General Council shall, in all cases except those of treason, felony, or breach of the peace, be privileged from arrest during their attendance at election, and at the General Council, and in going to, and returning from, the same.

Sec. 6. In all elections by the people, the electors shall vote *viva voce.* Electors for members to the General Council for 1828, shall be held at the places of holding the several courts, and at the other two precincts in each District which are designated by the law under which the members of this Convention were elected; and the District Judges shall superintend the elections within the precincts of their respective Court Houses, and the Marshals & Sheriffs shall superintend within the precincts which may be assigned them by the Circuit Judges of their respective Districts, together with one other person, who shall be appointed by the Circuit Judges for each precinct within their respective Districts; and the Circuit Judges shall also appoint a clerk to each precinct. The superintendents and clerks shall, on the Wednesday morning succeeding the election, assemble at their respective Court Houses and proceed to examine and ascertain the true state of the polls, and shall issue to each member, duly elected, a certificate; and also make an official return of the state of the polls of election to the principal Chief, and it shall be the du-

[Columns of Cherokee syllabary text corresponding to the Constitution.]

Pennsylvania—concurred, pointedly concluding, however, that *Johnson v. M'Intosh*, to which Marshall had avoided all reference in his opinion, justified Georgia's acts.

The Jackson administration had not been idle during the months after the passage of the Indian Removal Act. After Congress adjourned, Jackson himself went to Tennessee with his Secretary of War, John Eaton, and General John Coffee, then dispatched Eaton and Coffee to Mississippi, where they negotiated a cession treaty with the Choctaw. The Treaty of Dancing Rabbit Creek, signed on September 27, 1830, made clear that both parties understood the incentive to remove: "Whereas the General Assembly of the State of Mississippi," it began, "has extended the laws of the said State to persons and property within the chartered limits of the same, and the President of the United States has said that he cannot protect the Choctaw people from the operation of these laws; Now therefore that the Choctaw may live under their own laws in peace with the United States and the State of Mississippi they have determined to sell their lands east of the Mississippi."[14] To protect against future loss of sovereignty to a surrounding state, and in accordance with the terms of the Indian Removal Act, the Choctaw received two guarantees: first, that they would receive in exchange for the eastern lands "a tract of country west of the Mississippi River, *in fee simple*"—thus not subject to a discovery doctrine claim that they were tenants to a successor of the discovering European sovereign—and second, that "no Territory or State shall ever have a right to pass laws for the government of the Choctaw Nation."[15] The Treaty was ratified by the Senate and proclaimed by the president on February 24, 1831, a week before Marshall delivered the *Cherokee Nation v. Georgia* decision.[16] Four days later, on February 28, leaders of a Seneca band living on the Sandusky River in Ohio signed a treaty exchanging their lands for fee lands west of the Mississippi; over the summer, other Ohio bands, including Seneca, Shawnee, and Ottawa, did the same, as did the Ohio Wendat (Wyandot) the following January.[17] Removal was proceeding as planned.

All this activity reinforced Marshall's commitment to arrest the process when, during the Supreme Court's February 1832 term, a "proper case with proper parties"— *Worcester v. Georgia* —again brought before the court the question of the legitimacy of Georgia's acts. The case arose when New England missionaries Samuel Worcester and Elizur Butler challenged being sentenced to hard labor by the Gwinnett County, Georgia, court for residing in Cherokee country without a state license.[18] *Worcester* would become celebrated among Indian rights proponents for holding the state's act imposing Georgia laws on the Cherokee invalid under the Supremacy Clause of the U.S. Constitution because the act conflicted with federal treaty guarantees. Of greater contemporaneous significance, however, were the implications of *Worcester* for the discovery doctrine.

The discovery doctrine had given Georgia and other eastern states a claim to the underlying fee title to the Indian lands within their borders. The claim offered the states a basis for asserting jurisdiction over the lands. The assertion—or threat of assertion— of state jurisdiction gave coercive force to the federal removal program. To frustrate the removal program, Marshall would have to return to the source. In *Worcester*, therefore, he would dismantle the discovery doctrine by overruling that part of the doctrine

facing: *Cherokee Phoenix*, February 21, 1828. New Echota, Georgia. 52 × 34 cm. Courtesy of American Antiquarian Society, Worcester, Massachusetts

This inaugural issue of the first Native newspaper in the United States features the opening articles of the Cherokee Constitution of 1827, which established the three main branches of the tribal government and defined the borders of the Cherokee Nation. The newspaper, written partly in English and partly in Cherokee, is still being published.

assigning fee title to the discovering sovereign. *Worcester* was intended to prove *Johnson*'s undoing.

As noted, Marshall in *Worcester* held that Georgia's imposition of its laws on the Cherokee Nation violated federal treaty guarantees and was therefore invalid under the Supremacy Clause of the U.S. Constitution. The Georgia court's condemnation of Worcester and Butler, therefore, the Supreme Court said, should be "reversed and annulled."[19] But more was at stake. A Supremacy Clause ruling would only protect from coercion those tribes with treaty protections (including boundary recognitions and guarantees) similar to those in the 1785 Cherokee Treaty of Hopewell. Many tribes did not have such guarantees and so would continue to be vulnerable to the extension of state law on the authority of Georgia's construction of the *Johnson* ruling. Returning to the source, Marshall now held that the discovery doctrine construction on which Georgia relied was wrong. Discovery, Marshall now wrote, "gave to the nation making the discovery, as its inevitable consequence, [only] the sole right of acquiring the soil and of making settlements on it"—a preemption right. And while it "shut out the right of competition among those who had agreed to it," it could not "annul the previous rights of those who had not agreed to it." While it "regulated the right given by discovery among the European discoverers," it "could not affect the rights of those already in possession, either as aboriginal occupants, or as occupants by virtue of a discovery made before the memory of man." The discovery right was not dependent on and did not result in the diminishment of tribal sovereignty. "It gave the exclusive right to purchase, but did not found that right on a denial of the right of the possessor to sell."[20] It limited the rights of individuals and states but not the rights of tribes. It did not convey fee title.

To support this reformulation, Marshall reintroduced and (rather brazenly) discarded the lengthy historical defense of the rule he had imported in *Johnson* from his *Life of George Washington*. "Soon after Great Britain determined on planting colonies in America," he wrote in *Worcester*, "the king granted charters to companies of his subjects, who associated for the purpose of carrying the views of the crown into effect, and of enriching themselves. The first of these charters was made before possession was taken of any part of the country. They purport, generally, to convey the soil, from the Atlantic to the South Sea," which was then "occupied by numerous and warlike nations, equally willing and able to defend their possessions." What was the intended legal consequence of these charters? Certainly not the "extravagant and absurd idea" entertained by Georgia, "that the feeble settlements made on the sea-coast, or the companies under whom they were made, acquired legitimate power by [the royal charters] to govern the people, or occupy the lands from sea to sea." This idea "did not enter the mind of any man," Marshall declared. Instead, he stated, "[The charters] were well understood to convey the title which, according to the common law of European sovereigns respecting America, they might rightfully convey, *and no more. This was the exclusive right of purchasing such lands as the natives were willing to sell.*" To repeat: all discovery brought was a preemption right. Any other construction was ahistorical. "The crown could not be understood to grant what the crown did not affect to claim,

Edward F. Peticolas (1793–1853). *John Marshall*, 1824. Oil on canvas. 91.4 × 76.2 cm. Kirby Collection of Historical Paintings, Lafayette College, Easton, Pennsylvania

nor was it so understood. . . . [T]hese grants asserted a title against Europeans only, and were considered as blank paper so far as the rights of the natives were concerned."[21] Under the discovery doctrine as reformulated, Georgia had no claim either to title to the Cherokee lands or to sovereignty over them. Georgia's purported assertion of jurisdiction was invalid. The Indian Removal Act had no coercive force.

It was at this juncture that Andrew Jackson allegedly said, "John Marshall has made his opinion; now let him enforce it." Worcester and Butler remained in prison, and the Georgia governor declared publicly that he would not allow their release on the authority of the expected Supreme Court mandate. Issuance of that mandate would not be possible until the Supreme Court reconvened in January, and throughout the country there was much anxious speculation as to the possible consequences of Georgia's refusal to obey. If Jackson refused to enforce the mandate, Georgia's refusal to release the missionaries threatened to shake the entire federal system.[22]

That the system did not crack at this juncture owes, ironically, to the precipitous actions of South Carolinians evidently hopeful that it would. On November 24, 1832, while the nation awaited the issuance of the mandate, a convention called by the South Carolina legislature took advantage of Georgia's so-far successful resistance to the federal government and issued an ordinance by which the state claimed the authority to nullify federal statutes within its borders. This proved too much for Andrew Jackson, who, while prepared to look the other way while Georgia ousted the Cherokee, was not about to preside over the dissolution of the United States.[23] Jackson immediately put a stop to the Georgia problem, pressuring Governor Wilson Lumpkin to release Worcester and Butler, which he did on condition that they leave Georgia. No mandate was therefore required from the Supreme Court, and the Georgia crisis eased. Jackson then turned his attention to the South Carolina nullifiers and they, now isolated, were also returned to line.

While the threat to the Union had been averted, the threat to the removal policy remained. *Worcester* had taken the teeth out of removal by denying that discovery had given the states anything more than a preemption right. For removal to proceed on a surer legal footing, the *Johnson* formulation providing that discovery gave the discoverer fee title to discovered lands, on which the eastern states based their claims to jurisdiction over Indian lands, had to be restored. It was at this point that John Marshall lost control of his court.

Two Jackson appointees—John McLean and Henry Baldwin—had joined the high court during the 1830 term. In the winter of 1832 Andrew Jackson was reelected to the presidency. In 1834, Justice William Johnson died, and on January 9, 1835, Jackson appointed in his place James M. Wayne, a former member of the Georgia Supreme Court and, from 1829 to 1835, a member of the state's congressional delegation.[24] Wayne, who took his seat on January 14, was a vigorous supporter of removal. Within hours of Wayne's swearing in, Justice Gabriel Duvall resigned, and the balance of power on the court shifted.[25] Of the six justices, three—McLean, Baldwin, and Wayne—were Jackson appointees. Of the remaining three—Marshall, Joseph Story, and Smith Thompson—only two were in good health. Marshall was dying. "He still possesses his intellectual powers in very high vigor," Story wrote, "but his physical strength is manifestly on the decline."[26] It was to be his last term on the Supreme Court.[27] He died on July 6.

The 1835 term—Marshall's last—offered the Jackson appointees a chance to restore the *Johnson* formulation of the discovery doctrine. The vehicle was *Mitchel v. United States* (*Mitchel I*), which involved a title claim to a vast tract in Florida held under an evidently publicly sanctioned Indian deed. Baldwin was assigned authorship of the court's opinion. "As Florida was for twenty years under the dominion of Great Britain," he wrote, "the laws of that country were in force as the rule by which lands were held and sold. . . . One uniform rule seems to have prevailed from their first settlement, as appears by their laws," he continued: "that friendly Indians were protected in the possession of the lands they occupied," but that "[s]ubject to this right of possession, the ultimate fee was in the crown and its grantees, which could be granted by the crown or colonial legislatures while the lands remained in possession of the Indians, though possession could not be taken without their consent." [28]

Only five justices sat during the 1836 term. With Marshall dead, the majority were Jackson appointees—a circumstance that would persist for the next eight years. Baldwin again reintroduced the *Johnson* rule in *United States v. Fernandez*, another Florida case. At issue in *Fernandez* was the validity of a grant of lands to which the Indian title had not been extinguished. "This subject was so fully and ably considered in *M'Intosh v. Johnson* [*sic*]," Baldwin wrote, "that we have only to refer to the language of the court to show that every European government claimed and exercised the right of granting lands, while in the occupation of the Indians."[29]

In 1836, Jackson appointed Philip P. Barbour of Virginia and Roger B. Taney of Maryland to the seats vacated by Duvall and Marshall. Barbour had served as a member of the House in the Thirtieth Congress and voted for removal. Taney had opined in favor of removal while serving as Jackson's attorney general. In 1837 the court was enlarged to consist of nine members, and Jackson nominated fellow Tennesseean John Catron to the first of the two new seats.[30] Catron had established his political orthodoxy on the Indian question as Tennessee's chief justice, in *State v. Foreman*, decided in 1835.[31] Jackson's term expired before he had the opportunity to name a ninth justice to the high court, but his vice president and chosen successor, Martin Van Buren, no doubt had his approbation in elevating to that position John McKinley, a former representative and senator from Alabama and a veteran of the Senate Indian Affairs committee.[32] After 1837 the court thus included seven Jacksonians. Only two members, Story and Thompson, remained from the old Marshall court. *Worcester* was, for the foreseeable future, dead beyond redemption.

No case argued during the 1838 term offered the Jackson appointees a vehicle for reiterating *Johnson*. The following term, however, the court finally received the case for which John Marshall evidently had been looking. To John Catron fell the ironic task of applying the *Johnson* rule to the claim of a Virginia militia warrant holder to lands west of the Tennessee River. In *Clark v. Smith* he denied that a patent was void because it was issued for "lands lying within a country claimed by Indians." According to Catron, "the colonial charters, a great portion of the individual grants by the proprietary and royal governments, and a still greater portion by the States of this Union after the Revolution, were made for lands within the Indian hunting grounds." Indeed, "North Carolina and Virginia, to a great extent, paid their officers and soldiers of the revolutionary war by such grants. . . . It was one of the great resources that sustained the war, not only by these States, but others." The *Johnson* discovery doctrine settled the question of the

George Catlin (1796–1872). *U. States' Indian Frontier in 1840, Shewing the Positions of the Tribes That Have Been Removed West of the Mississippi*, 1841. Hand-colored map published in George Catlin, *Letters and Notes on the Manners, Customs, and Condition of the North American Indians, Vol. 2.* (1841) Length 26 cm. Yale Collection of Western Americana, Beinecke Rare Book and Manuscript Library, Yale University, New Haven, Connecticut 2000314

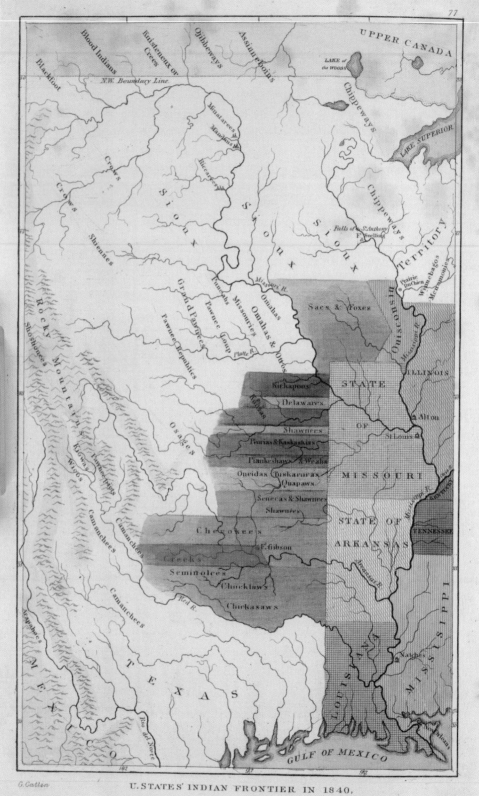

U. STATES' INDIAN FRONTIER IN 1840,

Shewing the Positions of the Tribes that have been removed west of the Missisipi.

grants' legitimacy. According to this doctrine: "The ultimate fee (encumbered with the Indian right of occupancy) was in the crown previous to the Revolution, and in the States of the Union afterwards, and subject to grant. This right of occupancy was protected by the political power and respected by the courts until extinguished; when the patentee took the unencumbered fee. So this court and the State courts have uniformly and often holden."[33]

Mitchel returned to the Supreme Court in 1841. In *Mitchel v. United States* (*Mitchel II*), Justice Wayne wrote for the court: "We will not enter into the question how far the appropriation of the land for a fortress, by order of the government, extinguished the Indian title. It might be done successfully, upon the position taken by this court in respect to the rights of European monarchs to Indian lands in North America, in *Johnson v. M'Intosh* (8 Wheat.)."[34] The following year, in *Martin v. Lessee of Waddell*, Chief Justice Taney took one last opportunity to reinforce the rule, stating, "The English possessions in America were not claimed by right of conquest, but by right of discovery. . . . The Indian tribes in the new world were regarded as mere temporary occupants of the soil, and the absolute rights of property and dominion were held to belong to the European nation by which any particular portion of the country was first discovered." In consequence, "whatever forbearance may have been sometimes practiced towards the unfortunate aborigines, wither from humanity or policy, yet the territory they occupied was disposed of by the governments of Europe at their pleasure, as if it had been found without inhabitants."[35]

In five decisions issued between 1836 and 1842—*Mitchel I, Fernandez, Clark, Mitchel II*, and *Martin*—the Jackson-appointed members of the Supreme Court thus hammered the *Johnson* formulation of the discovery doctrine into constitutional law. Three of these cases arose from the acquisition of Florida, one from conflicting claims to a New Jersey riverbed, and one from the militia grants. All were issued against a backdrop of ongoing federal efforts to coerce Indian removal. The court's repeated citations to *Johnson* provided ongoing legitimization of these efforts. Only after the removal of the southern tribes was concluded in 1842 with the defeat of resistant Seminoles in the Second Seminole War did reiteration of the *Johnson* formulation temporarily cease.

The appearance of a Jacksonian majority on the court made possible the reintroduction of the *Johnson* formulation of the discovery doctrine. When American courts cite to the doctrine, they cite not to a well-reasoned opinion of the Great Chief Justice, but to the politically motivated resurrection of a doctrine Marshall himself had buried.

Moreover, the decision has had an impact beyond the United States. *Johnson v. M'Intosh* has been cited to support British-derived claims to fee title to Indigenous lands in other parts of the world. In its 1984 decision in *Guerin v. The Queen*, for example, the Supreme Court of Canada, after citing *Johnson*, held "Indians have a legal right to occupy and possess certain lands, the ultimate fee to which is in the Crown." Under Canadian law, as under U.S. law, Native Nations lost ownership of their lands by virtue of discovery. Subsequently, the High Court of Australia, in a remarkable opinion (*Mabo v. Queensland*) recognizing for the first time the title claims of Indigenous

Australians, cited *Johnson* to support nevertheless limiting those claims under a variation of the discovery doctrine. There too, the discovering European sovereign was held to be the owner of the underlying fee.

In 2007 the United Nations General Assembly adopted the United Nations Declaration on the Rights of Indigenous Peoples. Article 26 of the declaration provides, in part, that "Indigenous Peoples have the right to own, use, develop and control the lands, territories and resources that they possess by reason of traditional ownership or other traditional occupation or use, as well as those which they have otherwise acquired." This article arguably provides a basis for making a claim for recognition of Indigenous title to traditionally held lands not covered by statute or treaty. In the United States and elsewhere, the discovery doctrine articulated in *Johnson v. M'Intosh* remains at the center of the debate over Indigenous rights.

Removal Treaties

An Interview with Carey N. Vicenti

SUZAN SHOWN HARJO

SUZAN SHOWN HARJO: Judge Vicenti, could you talk about removal treaties and what their intent was, and about what you have seen of their consequences today in places where you've judged or even just visited?

CAREY N. VICENTI: Removal treaties obviously were intended to fulfill the anger faction's racist vision of this newly emerging country, in which the land was going to be yielded up to them, and the Natives were going to be sequestered, removed, and placed in an entirely different setting—so that there would be no way that the non-Indians would have to comingle with them. They were originally suggested by Thomas Jefferson. He was really the first person to come up with the idea of removal. And—actually it's kind of a funny thing—but what happens is that at the end of the War of 1812, you see a major psychological shift in the country. If you can imagine, these revolutionaries twice beat one of the most powerful countries in the world, and now they saw themselves as being militarily unstoppable. Not only were Indian Tribes not as militarily powerful as they had been a century before, but they had also been fighting on behalf of the British in many instances. So ultimately the removal treaties seemed a necessary next step for the United States government.

It didn't help that the notorious Indian fighter, Andrew Jackson, moved up into the presidency. Andrew Jackson, I think, had been governor of Florida for a period of time, and he dealt with the Seminoles, so he was bent on just getting rid of the Indians. To Natives, he has become pretty much the equivalent of Hitler, and he removed many, many tribes. The various treaties were not really negotiated in an evenhanded way. They were negotiated at the point of a bayonet.

The treaty that I'm familiar with, down at Mississippi Choctaw, is the Treaty of Dancing Rabbit Creek. That treaty was really . . . intended—in fact he was going to hold women and children hostage until that treaty was negotiated. And so the people were removed as a result. It usually happened in two phases. The first phase was to find a group among the tribe who were willing to leave. The second phase was just to send in the military. We're most familiar with the movement of the Cherokee to Oklahoma on the Trail of Tears. But the removals that eventually took place were forced removals—of Seminoles, of Creeks, of Choctaws—to Oklahoma, which became sort of like an Indian dumping ground. It was a place they thought that they'd never need, and they just left the people there.

To me, probably the most powerful and significant social consequence of those kinds of treaties was that they had a tendency to drive a wedge into tribal society and create two different political factions, which somewhat survive to this day. One of the factions was like the Major Ridge party of Cherokee, which negotiated the Treaty of New Echota and voluntarily removed to Oklahoma. And then you have the other party, the John Ross party, which was forced to move to Oklahoma. . . . Ross lost his wife and his children along the way. It was a brutal, a really brutal removal that came in successive waves and [took place during] one of the coldest winters in recorded history. So of course when Ross gets to Oklahoma, the people of his party begin assassinating people of the Ridge party. So you get this lingering dichotomy in tribal politics, in which you have people who engage in concessions with the federal government and people who resist. And to this very day, when you look at tribal society, what you see are just those exact kinds of factions. You see people of resistance and people of concession.

From an interview that took place on August 15, 2005, at the School of Advanced Research in Santa Fe, New Mexico.

Avoiding Removal

The Pokagon Band of Potawatomi Indians

MATTHEW L. M. FLETCHER

IN 1838 THE U.S. MILITARY, UNDER AN ORDER from War Secretary Lewis Cass, force-marched more than eight hundred Potawatomi Indians from southwestern Michigan and northern Indiana through Springfield, Illinois, and on to lands west of the Mississippi River. More than a hundred died along the way, about half of them children. The march is now called the Potawatomi Trail of Death.

The Pokagon Band of Potawatomi Indians living near Dowagiac, Michigan, avoided the Trail of Death through a combination of negotiating skill, strategic foresight, bravura, and luck. The Pokegnek Bodewadmik community is named after Leopold Pokagon, the Potawatomi *wkema* (boss) who served as their primary leader from 1826 to 1841, when he walked on to the next world. Pokagon, who was born in a northern Michigan Odawa community, married into the family of Topinabee, a Potawatomi wkema in the St. Joseph (Michigan) River Valley. Pokagon assumed leadership of the band after Topinabee's death; his leadership would effectively prevent the band's removal.

In 1830, the same year Congress approved the Indian Removal Act, Pokagon, seeking a political alliance useful in resisting pressures to move, asked Father Gabriel Richard of the Detroit Diocese to establish a mission to serve his band. He also consented to baptism, and the diocese sent a priest that August.

By the time the Americans sought to treat with the Potawatomi Nations for removal purposes in 1833, Pokagon was ready. Initially, Pokagon's people threatened to kill any wkema who signed a treaty consenting to the sale of land, but eventually they backed down. The Treaty of Chicago provided for the removal of all Potawatomi Nations to western lands beyond the Mississippi River, with one exception—the Pokegnek Bodewadmik. Pokagon negotiated an amendment that effectively authorized his band to remain near the St. Joseph River Valley. Supposedly, Pokagon refrained from the alcohol that American treaty negotiators provided to the Potawatomi leaders for the purpose of cajoling concessions from them. During the negotiations, Pokagon also emphasized his community's conversion to Catholicism.

One by one the Potawatomi *wkemuk* entered a tent with American treaty negotiators to make their marks expressing consent to removal on American terms. Tribal legends suggest that the Americans in the tent threatened the wkemuk with violent death if they refused to sign the treaty. Pokagon allegedly went into the tent armed with a knife and came out armed with treaty annuities and an implicit right to remain in Michigan. To be sure, what Pokagon acquired under the terms of the treaty was $2,000—perhaps equivalent to more than $500,000 today—which was enough to purchase a large amount of land in fee simple under federal and state law.

Removal was not immediate: all the Potawatomi villages remained in Michigan and Indiana until War Secretary Cass ordered the American military to remove them in accordance with the Indian Removal Act. Another Potawatomi band, led by Menominee, a wkema who had refused to sign the 1833 treaty, was not lucky enough to avoid removal. American soldiers imprisoned Menominee in a wood cage before capturing his community members and forcing them west. In 1838, when they swept all the remaining Potawatomi people from their homelands, the Americans bypassed the citizens of Pokegnek Bodewadmik, who were residing on land purchased with treaty annuities, probably paying taxes, and had long ago converted to Catholicism.

Even so, in 1841 American military personnel, at the urging of Michigan officials, informed Pokagon that they would commence the removal of the Pokagon Band. Pokagon, in a last act of powerful leadership, persuaded Michigan Supreme Court Associate Justice Epaphroditus Ransom to issue a legal opinion that the 1833 Treaty guaranteed the Pokagon Band protection from removal to the west. Pokagon walked on later that year. While the Pokegnek Bodewadmik did not escape incredible hardship over the next two centuries, including administrative termination by the Department of the Interior in the 1870s, their federal recognition status was confirmed by Congress in 1994, and they remain in Michigan and Indiana.

Plains Nations, the Great Treaty Council at Horse Creek, occupies a prominent place in the history of U.S.–Indian treaty making. In September 1851 some ten thousand Plains Indians—including Teton and Yankton Sioux,[1] Cheyenne, Arapaho, Crow, Shoshone, Assiniboine, Mandan, Hidatsa, and Arikara—met with U.S. treaty commissioners along the Platte River at the mouth of Horse Creek, in present-day western Nebraska, about thirty-six miles east of Fort Laramie.[2] Many of the Indian Nations brought to the council ground long histories of bitter intertribal warfare. But for three weeks at Horse Creek they met, smoked, talked, held dances and horse races, and lived peacefully in vast tipi encampments that encompassed a population nearly equal to that of 1850s Nashville, Tennessee.[3]

The resulting treaty not only provided for peace between the United States and Indian Nations and among warring Indian Tribes but also granted the United States the rights to build roads and forts on tribal lands, which facilitated the emigration of—and secured safe passage for—Americans travelling through Indian Country to the Pacific along overland trails. The treaty also protected Indians on tribal lands from the "depredations" of wayward whites, and it assigned for the first time territorial boundaries to the tribes. The United States also pledged to pay the tribes $50,000 per year for fifty years in provisions—compensation for the buffalo and other natural resources that American travelers destroyed en route to the west.[4]

Hopes for lasting peace, friendship, and good faith were short-lived. In 1854 a cow owned by a Mormon emigrant strayed from the Oregon Trail and wandered into a Teton Sioux camp near Fort Laramie. When a young warrior shot the animal for food, the cow's owner complained that the Sioux had stolen his property. A patrol of twenty-nine mounted soldiers from the U.S. Sixth Infantry Regiment, under the command of second lieutenant John Lawrence Grattan, was quickly dispatched to apprehend the Indian "thief." Arriving at the village, the soldiers met with Chief Frightening Bear, who had been selected to represent the entire Sioux Nation at the Horse Creek treaty council. Grattan summarily demanded the surrender of the "cow killer." When Frightening Bear was unable to compel the man to surrender, the soldiers opened fire, killing the chief. The Sioux quickly returned fire, killing all but one of the bluecoats.[5]

The "Grattan Fight" precipitated twenty-five years of war against the northern Plains Nations and helped etch the names Sand Creek and Little Bighorn into American memory. By the 1870s few Americans remembered the Horse Creek Treaty or its vision of peace and good-faith diplomacy. But Indians remembered it well. "At the mouth of the Horse Creek . . . the Great Father made a treaty with us by which we agreed to let all that country open . . . for the transit of those who were going through," Red Cloud recalled in a speech at the Cooper Union in New York in 1870. "We kept this treaty; we never treated any man wrong; we never committed any murder or depredation until afterward the troops . . . killed our people and ill-treated them, and thus war and trouble arose; but before the troops were sent there we were quiet and peaceable, and there was no disturbance."[6]

RAYMOND J. DEMALLIE

The Great Treaty Council at Horse Creek

*T*HE PLAINS OF THE AMERICAN WEST, FROM TEXAS NORTH TO CANADA and from the Missouri River to the Rocky Mountains, is the homeland of many Native American Peoples who spoke a variety of languages and have diverse histories. Some, like the Pawnee, Arikara, and Mandan along the Missouri River and its tributaries, and the Shoshone, Kiowa, and Plains Apache on the western plains, were likely ancient inhabitants of the region. Others, including the Hidatsa and their close relatives the Crow, as well as the Arapaho, Cheyenne, and Sioux and their close relatives, the Assiniboine, were more recent migrants to the plains, having come from farther east. The Comanche, close relatives of the Shoshone, were more recent arrivals, too, but they came from the west. Beginning in the early 1700s and continuing to the beginning of the 1800s, horses were introduced to the plains from the south and west, spreading from tribe to tribe. It was during this period that the tribes developed their distinctive way of life, based on mounted buffalo hunting. The abundance of buffalo, and the relative ease with which they could be killed and the meat transported using horses, brought about population increases and cultural innovation. Religious beliefs and ceremonies such as the Sun Dance; communal hunts using the mounted surround as a technique for maximizing the number of buffalo killed; tall buffalo-hide tipis; the camp circle; men's societies; and patterns of intertribal warfare all developed during this period.[7]

At the same time, the Plains Peoples met and interacted with the first white people to visit them. A few were explorers or missionaries, but most of them were traders. At first they were French, Spanish, or British; after the Louisiana Purchase, Americans began to arrive, in greater numbers than any of the others. To protect U.S. trade interests after the War of 1812, the government entered into treaties with some

George Catlin (1796–1872). *Buffalo Chase with Bows and Lances*, 1832–33. Oil on canvas. 60.9 × 73.7 cm. Smithsonian American Art Museum; gift of Mrs. Joseph Harrison, Jr. 1985.66.410

of the Sioux and other tribes of the Midwest and eastern plains (1815–17). These promised "perpetual peace and friendship" with the United States but also specified that the Indians were "under the protection of the United States of America, and of no other nation, power, or sovereign."[8] Subsequently, into the 1840s, the government signed more treaties with the Plains Nations, promising peace not only with the United States but also among the various tribes. In return, government officials presented medals and flags to the chiefs and gave them varying quantities of presents to distribute to their people. A treaty only became law, however, after it was taken back to Washington and ratified by the Senate.

The rationale for these treaties from the government's point of view was simple. Indian warfare, against American citizens or other Indians, disrupted travel across what was popularly called the Great American Desert. Following what became known as the Oregon Trail, trappers and fur traders traveled annually to the mountains in search of beaver furs and, later, to trade with Indians for buffalo hides. Entrepreneurs also blazed a trail from Missouri to Santa Fe to obtain horses and exchange manufactured goods. They considered the plains empty space that needed to be crossed as expeditiously as possible.[9]

There is little direct evidence of how Plains Indians understood the actual content of the treaties to which they affixed their signatures. From the proceedings of councils throughout the second half of the nineteenth century, it is clear that many individuals believed that in signing they were validating what they had said during the council, not agreeing to the provisions as set forth on paper.[10] Although the concept of writing was foreign and poorly understood, the concepts of peace and alliance were familiar. The Cheyenne and Arapaho had a bond of alliance between them as far back as either nation remembered, though fights periodically broke out. In the early 1800s the Lakota also established peace with the Cheyenne and Arapaho. The Comanche, Kiowa, and Plains Apache Nations were similarly allied. The Mandan and Hidatsa, joined later by the Arikara, also were allied with one another. But stealing horses from the enemy and performing brave deeds in battle were integral to Plains cultures as the essential means for men to establish themselves as responsible adults and rise to positions of prestige in the tribe. Just as some tribes were linked in alliances, others were linked in relationships of enmity based on generations of warfare. These were somewhat complicated patterns. The Cheyenne and Lakota, for example, warred with the Crow, but the Arapaho did not. Some, but not all, of the Lakota warred with the Arikara. Warring tribes not infrequently met, smoked a pipe together, and established a temporary peace for the purpose of trade. Lakota bands, for example, would approach Arikara villages in peace to trade for horses and corn. Soon after the Lakota left, warfare would resume.[11]

Throughout the first half of the 1800s relations between the Plains Nations and white men—mostly trappers, traders, and small parties passing through the country—remained largely peaceful. The whites brought welcome manufactured goods, including guns, ammunition, and metal tools, and traded them for furs and buffalo robes. But conditions rapidly changed in the 1840s. In 1846, after war was declared with Mexico, American troops captured Santa Fe and ultimately occupied Mexico City; in 1848, Mexico surrendered New Mexico and California to the United States. In 1847 the Mormons, headed by Brigham Young, began the trek that would take them to their new home in Utah. The discovery of gold in California in 1849 unleashed a flood of fortune seekers and emigrants who crowded the California and Oregon Trails, starting in Westport, Missouri (part of present-day Kansas City), and following the North Platte River through the heart of the central plains. Each summer wagon trains cut through the territories of the Sioux, Cheyenne, Arapaho, and Shoshone: gold seekers heading for California, settlers destined for Oregon, and Mormons on their way to join their brethren in Utah. All these travelers depended on buffalo hunting to provide meat, which took a toll on the herds and drove them away from the North Platte River. Their campfires decimated wood resources along the trail. Even worse, they brought with them cholera, smallpox, and measles, which spread to devastating effect among

overleaf: A composite map of the homelands of the northern Plains Native Nations throughout the early nineteenth century. Shifting boundaries and areas of shared use are shown by indistinct borders among the tribal territories. The inset map of the council grounds, based on available sources, shows the estimated locations of some of the negotiators' camps. Map by Gene Thorp/Cartographic Concepts, Inc, with research assistance from Jacob Goldstein. © Smithsonian Institution.

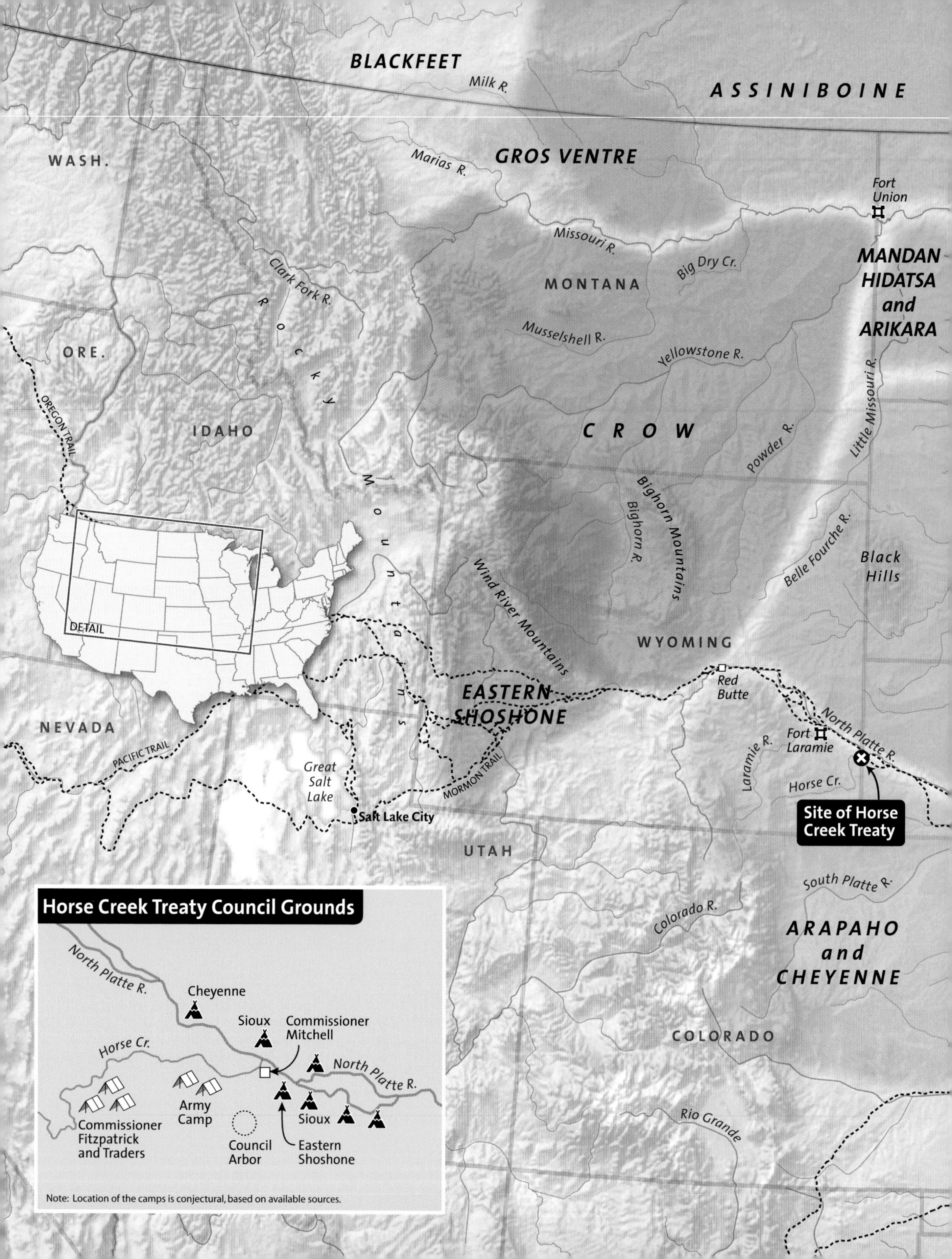

BLACKFEET

Milk R.

ASSINIBOINE

WASH.

Marias R.

GROS VENTRE

Fort
Union ⊞

Missouri R.

Big Dry Cr.

MANDAN
HIDATSA
and
ARIKARA

MONTANA

Musselshell R.

Yellowstone R.

Little Missouri R.

ORE.

Clark Fork R.

R
O
C
K
Y

OREGON TRAIL

IDAHO

C R O W

Powder R.

Bighorn Mountains

Bighorn R.

Belle Fourche R.

Black
Hills

M
o
u
n
t
a
i
n
s

Wind River Mountains

WYOMING

Red
Butte

North Platte R.

NEVADA

PACIFIC TRAIL

EASTERN
SHOSHONE

Laramie R.

Fort
Laramie ⊞

⊗

MORMON TRAIL

Site of Horse
Creek Treaty

Great
Salt
Lake

Horse Cr.

● Salt Lake City

UTAH

South Platte R.

ARAPAHO
and
CHEYENNE

Colorado R.

COLORADO

Rio Grande

DETAIL

Horse Creek Treaty Council Grounds

North Platte R.

Cheyenne

Sioux

Commissioner
Mitchell

□

North Platte R.

Horse Cr.

Army
Camp

Council
Arbor

Sioux

Commissioner
Fitzpatrick
and Traders

Eastern
Shoshone

Note: Location of the camps is conjectural, based on available sources.

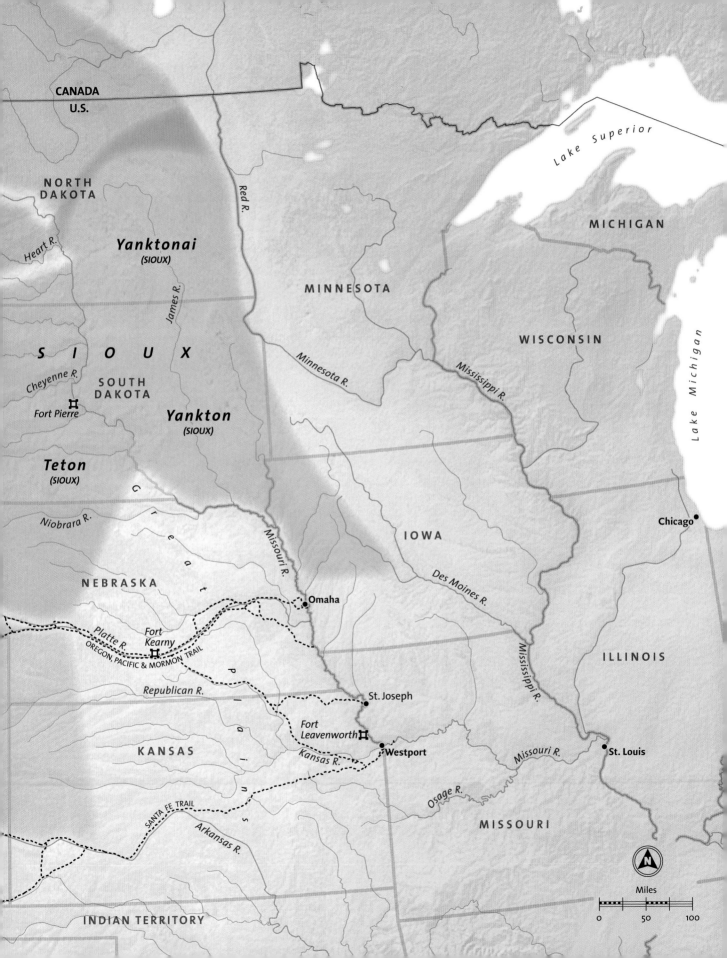

Charles Waldo Love (1881–1967), after a ca. 1850 drawing. *Thomas Fitzpatrick*, 1935. Oil on canvas. History Colorado, Denver 10027099

the Lakota and other tribes who came into contact with them. As early as May 1846 a group of Brule and Oglala Lakota chiefs sent a petition through the federal Indian agent to the U.S. president, asking for compensation for the damage done by emigrants in driving away the buffalo.[12]

By 1850, when California was admitted to the Union as the thirty-first state, the federal government foresaw the necessity of building a railroad to link the east and west coasts. The route was long a subject of debate, but no matter which one ultimately was chosen, it would be essential for the Plains Indians to be at peace so as not to impede railroad survey and construction. To accomplish this goal Congress authorized $100,000 in February 1851 to hold a great council with the Plains Nations and bring a delegation of their leaders to Washington.[13]

The responsibility of arranging the council fell jointly to two men in the Indian service. The first was David D. Mitchell, the superintendent of Indian affairs for the Central Superintendency. Although his headquarters were in St. Louis, his jurisdiction included the entire plains region. The second was Thomas Fitzpatrick, the Indian agent for the Upper Platte Agency, which embraced the central plains from Nebraska to Wyoming and Kansas to Colorado. Both had begun their careers in the fur trade, and each had extensive experience throughout the West as well as personal familiarity with the land and the Native Peoples.[14]

In 1849 the United States had purchased Fort John, on the Laramie River near its juncture with the Platte, renamed it Fort Laramie, and garrisoned it to serve as a way stop on the road to California and Oregon. Mitchell and Fitzpatrick decided to hold the great council there. Mitchell contracted with the St. Louis firm R & W Campbell to supply $60,000 worth of trade goods and food and transport them to Fort Laramie. To spread word of the council to the Indians, he had a circular printed, which he began sending up the Missouri by steamboat in April to be distributed to traders and government agents, requesting them to encourage the tribes to assemble at Fort Laramie on September 1. Meanwhile, on April 22, Fitzpatrick left Westport on the Santa Fe Trail, following the Arkansas River and then heading north through the southern plains to carry the invitation to the tribes of that region.[15]

The treaty invitation met with mixed results. Many of the tribes were at war with one another and had longstanding enmity. Those who warred with the Sioux were reluctant to go to Fort Laramie, in the midst of their enemy's country. When Fitzpatrick met with Comanche, Kiowa, and Kiowa Apache leaders, they refused to consider attending. They asked that a council be held in their territory—then they would gladly meet with the government representatives. The Cheyenne and Arapaho, however, as allies of the Sioux, agreed to go to Laramie.

When the circular reached Fort Kearny, Nebraska, Captain H. W. Wharton, the commanding officer, visited the Pawnee villages and extracted from them a promise to send a delegation to the council. They failed to do so, however, and when he visited them again in mid-September to ask why they had broken their promise, they said they had decided that while the Sioux, Cheyenne, and Arapaho might meet with them in peace at Fort Laramie, they feared the three nations would attack them on their way home.[16]

The task of distributing circulars on the upper Missouri and persuading the tribes there to come to the council was assigned to Father Pierre-Jean De Smet, the Jesuit missionary whose numerous trips from St. Louis upriver and over the Rockies to Oregon had made him a familiar and much respected figure among many tribes.[17] He left St. Louis on the steamboat *St. Ange* on June 7. When the boat reached the Big Bend of the Missouri, De Smet found the Yankton Sioux, with whom he

Father Pierre-Jean De Smet, ca. 1863. Washington, DC. Photo by L. C. Handy Studio. Brady-Handy Collection, Library of Congress, LC-BH824-5343

had long established close relations, afflicted with smallpox. He spent the night in their camp, baptizing children; farther upriver he continued his religious duties by baptizing children in the Sioux camp at Fort Pierre, a post of the American Fur Company. De Smet wrote that the Sioux, witnessing his apparent immunity to the disease and appreciating his prayers and rituals for the dying, were prepared to hear his request that they attend the upcoming peace council. Continuing upriver, De Smet arrived at Fort Union on July 14, where he was met by his friend and benefactor Alexander Culbertson, the American Fur Company superintendent of the trading posts on the upper Missouri.

Mitchell and his party left St. Louis on July 24. He brought with him A. B. Chambers, the editor of the *Missouri Republican,* a St. Louis newspaper, and Benjamin Gratz Brown, a lawyer, both of whom would serve as secretaries for the treaty commission.[18] When they reached Westport on July 29 they learned that the twenty-seven wagons carrying treaty presents, which should have been well on their way to Laramie, had not yet even been loaded. At Fort Leavenworth, Mitchell discovered that the troops under Major Roger Chilton who were to serve as his military escort had already left for Laramie. Mitchell followed on August 10 and caught up with the dragoons the next day. Finally, on Saturday, August 30, they arrived at Fort Laramie, where they found that

Jim Bridger, ca. 1860s. Photographer unknown. Kansas State Historical Society, 209200

According to one of his descendants, Bobby Bridger, Jim Bridger was already an experienced mountain man, fur trader, and scout—and was married to a Shoshone woman—when he accompanied Shoshone chief Washakie to the Horse Creek treaty council in 1851. Bridger's fluency in the Native sign language and his knowledge of plains topography would have been invaluable assets to both Native and non-Native negotiators—and to Father Pierre-Jean De Smet in creating the first map of Plains Indian lands. During his last years, Bridger lived on his farm in Missouri with his Shoshone daughter, Virginia.

Fitzpatrick, with the Cheyenne and Arapaho delegations, had already arrived. Large numbers of Sioux also were camped near the fort. Unanticipated by Mitchell, a delegation of Shoshone arrived, accompanied by their agent, Jacob A. Holeman of the Utah Superintendency, and by James Bridger, the famous mountain man, who served as their interpreter. Their arrival presented a dilemma for Mitchell, who believed that he was authorized to sign a treaty only with Indian Tribes belonging to the Central Superintendency.[19]

Chambers reported in considerable detail on the daily activities of the treaty council in articles later printed in the *Missouri Republican*.[20] Mitchell's party made camp near the fort and prepared for the opening of the council, as scheduled, on September 1. The troops under Major Chilton positioned themselves by Mitchell's tent as a signal for the Indians to assemble. As they rode up, Mitchell presented the chiefs and leading men with tobacco. After the ceremonial smoking of the pipe Mitchell "instructed the interpreters to interpret truly what he said." This seemingly routine instruction points to a crucial aspect of the treaty council: its success depended entirely upon the ability of the interpreters, who were either mixed-bloods or white men married to Indian women, to translate intelligibly and honestly what one side said to the other. The problem was compounded by the fact that each tribe spoke a different language.

The commissioner paused after each sentence to allow the interpreters time to repeat his words. It is easy to imagine the cacophony of voices speaking loudly in the various languages. Huge crowds of spectators attended the council meetings, and there is no doubt that most of them were not able to hear what was said; the winds so characteristic of the plains make hearing over even short distances difficult. For this very reason Plains Indian oratory always involved the simultaneous use of sign language. Shared among all the tribes, this language of gestures enabled speakers to say silently what they were also saying in words. For both the interpreters and the Indian leaders who spoke at the councils, this dual system of communication helped ensure that meaning was communicated.

On the first day the only business was to decide on a suitable location for the council. There was not adequate grass for the horses or wood for the fires in the immediate vicinity of Fort Laramie. Moreover, Mitchell was worried about how long it would take for the presents to arrive, so he proposed moving farther down the Platte to save the wagon train some days of travel. After much discussion, Blue Earth, the oldest and most respected of the Teton Sioux chiefs, suggested a site at the mouth of Horse Creek, some thirty miles downstream, and all agreed.

The next few days were occupied with the move to the council grounds, which were just below the Oregon Trail. Chambers reported that the commissioners arrived there on September 5; Mitchell erected his tent on the point of land formed by the junction of the creek with the river, while Fitzpatrick camped with some of the traders farther up Horse Creek.[21] The military detachment camped nearby on higher ground. Some of the Sioux camped on the north side of the Platte and some on the south, near the commissioners. The Cheyenne, probably with the Arapaho, camped on the Platte, west of the Sioux, and the Shoshone camped to the east of the commissioners.

On Saturday, September 6, nearly a thousand mounted Sioux made a formal entry on horseback, "in solid column, about four abreast, shouting and singing." They carried an American flag that had been given them by William Clark many years earlier, when he was the superintendent of Indian affairs. That afternoon several hundred Cheyennes made their formal entry. The commissioners gave the Indians token presents of tobacco and vermillion, and Mitchell informed them that because the next day was the "White Man's Medicine Day," the council would not begin until Monday.[22]

Also on that Saturday, the delegation of tribal leaders from the upper Missouri, representing the Assiniboine, Arikara, Hidatsa, and Mandan as well as a few Crows, arrived at Fort Laramie, having left Fort Union on July 31 with an escort that included Culbertson and De Smet. The next day they moved on to the treaty grounds, St. Louis fur trader Robert Campbell giving De Smet a ride in his carriage.

On Sunday morning the commissioners tied three long poles together in the form of a tripod to serve as a flagstaff. Chambers commented, "Notwithstanding the paucity of materials, our staff made a fine appearance, and the American flag floated gracefully to the breeze." That day the Sioux and Cheyenne women used lodge poles and tipi covers to construct a circular arbor, its eastern third left open. Feasts and dances were held in the Indian camps until late in the night, with much visiting back and forth. Chambers estimated that ten thousand Indians were present.

Starting at dawn on Monday, September 8, groups of Indians began making their way to the council grounds.[23] At nine o'clock, when the cannon was fired and the flag raised as a signal for the Indian delegates to assemble, each tribal group approached the arbor, some on foot and others on horseback. All were dressed in their finest regalia, with faces painted, each group singing in its own language. Only the chiefs and head-men were invited into the council area. Starting at the entrance, the Sioux leaders were seated to the north and west, followed by the Cheyenne, Assiniboine, Shoshone, Ari-kara, Hidatsa,[24] Mandan, and Arapaho. Behind each tribal delegation crowds of men, women, and children stood watching. Under the arbor in the center sat the government officials, including Commissioners Mitchell and Fitzpatrick, the military officers, and Father De Smet, together with the interpreters.

Mitchell opened the council by stating that he had come to discuss important business, but—acknowledging his familiarity with Indian etiquette—before doing so he wanted the tribal representatives to smoke a pipe with him, as an oath that they would speak truly and sincerely and fulfill their promises, just as white men take an oath when "they lay their hands on the Bible, the book of the Great Spirit—their Great Medicine." Taking a large catlinite pipe with a three-foot-long decorated stem, the Sioux interpreter filled it with tobacco and *kinnikinnick,* lighted it, and held it while Mitchell, then Fitzpatrick, smoked. After that it made the rounds of the Sioux leaders. Each man offered the pipe to the four directions, then up to the sky and down toward earth. Chambers reported:

> Another ceremony was observed by nearly every one. When the Indian took the pipe, the interpreter holding the other end, he would extend his right hand to the bowl, and draw it back along the stem to his breast. Some of them would repeat this action several times. It is understood to be the most solemn and sacred attes-tation of truth they can give.[25]

The ceremony of smoking was repeated for each tribe in turn. During this time the wife of Lieutenant W. L. Elliott, an officer of the Mounted Rifles who was present, arrived and was seated within the arbor, a sign of the white men's trust that the gath-ering would be a peaceful one. Then the proceedings were suddenly interrupted when a Cheyenne woman led a horse on which rode her ten- to twelve-year-old son. Her husband had been killed in battle by one of the Shoshone chiefs and she intended to present the boy to the man who killed his father, to be raised by him as Shoshone. The Cheyenne chiefs intervened and postponed this private matter for another time.

Pipes and pipe bags representing the nine Native Nations present at the 1851 Horse Creek treaty council. Counterclockwise from top (pipes to the left of each bag originated in the same Native Nation): Assiniboine, Minitari (Hidatsa), Numakiki (Mandan), Shoshone, Apsáalooke (Crow), Tsistsistas (Cheyenne), Sahnish (Arikara), Northern Inunaina (Arapaho), Yankton Sioux bag and Lakota Sioux pipe, ca. 1851–80. Bags: Hide, glass beads, porcupine quills, dye, pigment sinew, horsehair, cotton thread, wool yarn, wool cloth, metal cones, copper alloy disks, feathers, tobacco. Pipes: wood, pipestone, stone, lead, lead alloy, feathers, horsehair, porcupine quills, dye, cotton yarn, bird skin. Lengths: pipe bowls 8.4 to 24.2 cm; pipe stems 30.9 to 73.2 cm; pipe bags 58 to 106.7 cm. National Museum of the American Indian (bags) 12/7393, 8/8088, 2/3294, 14/828, 8/8037, 20/1400, 23/1176, 16/7255; (pipes) 11/392, 11/393, 8/8030, 20/3667, 1/2599, 11/3150, 14/5105, 1/389, 8/8028. Hidatsa pipe bag courtesy of the Division of Anthropology, American Museum of Natural History 50.1/5350B

When all the leaders had smoked with the commissioners, Mitchell made a formal speech to the delegates. Chambers's report emphasizes the importance placed on accurate translation:

> His expressions were short, in simple language, such as they could readily understand, in many cases adopting various forms and employing their own hyperbolical mode of thought. Between sentences, he paused to see that the interpreters understood him correctly and to allow time for them to communicate it to their respective tribes. As many of the Indians understand the dialect of other tribes, the interpreters announced their interpretation in a loud voice, that all might hear, and mistakes in conveying the correct meaning be corrected. Whenever the Indian understands, or thinks he understands, what has been said to him, he signifies it by a guttural exclamation, "how."

Mitchell began by emphasizing that the commissioners had been sent by "your Great Father at Washington . . . to make peaceful arrangements with you for your own benefit." He made it clear that, unlike most white men who visited them, they were not traders who had come to buy and sell: "We have nothing to sell you, and do not want to buy anything from you. We do not want your lands, horses, robes, nor anything you have; but we come to advise with you, and make a treaty with you for your own good."

He asserted that the "white children" of the Great Father had the right to open roads and travel through the Indians' country, but, at the same time, the Great Father wished to compensate them for the damages done by driving away the buffalo and depleting grass and timber along the routes. He asked the Indians to recognize the Great Father's right to construct military and other posts there for the protection of both whites and Indians. To insure peace, boundaries would be drawn around the lands that belonged to each Indian Nation. These boundaries were not intended to restrict the movements of the tribes, but whenever a "depredation" was committed, the tribe within whose territory the act occurred would be held responsible. "When a horse is stolen, or a scalp taken, or a woman or child carried off, or any other wrong done, [the Great Father] wants to find out who did it and punish the bad man or nation; and the nation will be held responsible for the acts of its people."

Mitchell emphasized that the Indians' way of life must change. Now that the white men had settled west of their country, warfare among the tribes must cease. Although each tribe or nation was divided into various bands that were at times hostile to one another, they must now unite. "Your Great Father will not recognize any such divisions," he told them. "Your Great Father will only treat with the whole nation or tribe when united, not with any band, however large or powerful." Each nation must select one man to be "'chief of the whole nation,' who shall be recognized as the head of the nation or tribe and through whom your Great Father will transact all government business." The Great Father, Mitchell told them, would support the head chiefs as long as they acted properly, and the chiefs and leaders were asked "to pledge yourselves to respect, obey, and maintain him in the exercise of his just authority."

If the Indians agreed to these propositions the Great Father would give them

$50,000 worth of goods annually for fifty years, to be divided proportionally among the nations. In the future, when the buffalo were gone, they would receive cattle, horses, sheep, agricultural implements, and seed, with which they would sustain themselves. Mitchell asked each nation to hold councils to discuss these matters, and to meet and make peace with one another. The council would resume in two days. Meanwhile, if there was anything they did not understand, he invited them to come to his tent, where he and Fitzpatrick would explain it to them.

Chambers reported that, before adjourning, three chiefs—Blue Earth (Teton Sioux), Wahata-uh ("Elk's Tongue," Arikara), and Washakie (Shoshone)—made brief replies affirming that they would return to their camps and discuss what they had heard. The speech of Wahata-uh suggests that as yet the Indians did not all fully understand Mitchell's message; he ended his speech, saying, "We will do the best we can to satisfy our Great Father. We hope he will send us more buffalo."

Charles B. Chambers (1882–1964), after a portrait by Manuel Joachim de Franca (1808–1865). *Col. David Dawson Mitchell*, ca. 1900. Oil on canvas. 76.2 × 63.5 cm. Missouri History Museum, St. Louis 1904 003 0001

Mitchell's speech presented formidable problems for translation. The tribal delegates recognized, of course, that the United States had opened roads and built posts without consulting the Indian Nations. Now the commissioners were asking the Indians to acknowledge that the government had the right to do so. Implicit was the issue of sovereignty. On the one hand, the U.S. government was treating the Indian Tribes as sovereign nations by signing a treaty with them; on the other hand, the government was asking the Indians to acknowledge that their lands were subordinate to the sovereignty of the United States. Neither the commissioners nor the Indians would have phrased the issue in this way, but from a historical perspective it is clear that ever since the federal government bought the Louisiana Territory from France in 1803, it has considered that vast region its own, despite the Native inhabitants.

The issue of "driving away the buffalo" was understood in completely different ways by the two sides. Men like Mitchell and Fitzpatrick, who had lived for decades in the West, recognized that the herds were fast diminishing and would eventually become extinct. They thought fifty years would be sufficient to see the end of the hunting way of life and the establishment of those Indians who would survive the difficult transition as independent farmers and ranchers. In contrast, the Indians perceived the buffalo as part of the natural world guaranteed to them by the Creator, a spiritual gift that, if properly respected, would endure. The concept of species extinction was foreign to

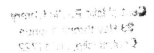

them, and, unlike American culture, Native cultures were built on an ethos of stability, not change. Progress was uniquely a white man's concept, virtually impossible to translate into Indian languages.[26]

The "depredations" of which Mitchell spoke were the acts of warfare that brought honor and prestige to young men and allowed them to make names for themselves in the social hierarchy. No other activity could substitute for war honors. Peace was highly valued, but peace—which the tribes conceptualized as alliance—was limited. Some Indian Nations were related as allies, others as enemies. By demanding a general alliance among all the nations, the United States was asking for a complete transformation of the very foundation of Plains Indian society.

The issue of selecting a chief for each nation was equally challenging. Plains Indian chiefs were respected leaders and elder kinsmen who guided their people. Much of the year the tribes lived dispersed in small bands, to maximize access to game and forage. Each band had its own chiefs. When they came together in great encampments during the summer, the nation was represented by a council of chiefs, with no single man claiming precedence. Moreover, chiefs were advisors and peacemakers, but they had no authority to command their people. The white and Indian conceptions of chief were totally at odds. By asking each nation to choose a single head chief, the commissioners were essentially asking the Indians to reorganize their political system to reflect that of the United States.

Another huge issue that was clearly puzzling was the identity of the Great Father. Who was he? For decades, traders had told the Indians about their Great Father across the ocean—some spoke of their Spanish Father, others of a British Father. Now there was an American Great Father. Was he a man or a spirit? Perhaps Wahata-uh's request that the Great Father send them more buffalo could be interpreted to mean that at least some of the Indians at the council thought Mitchell was talking about the white men's God.

After the council broke up there was much activity in the Indian camps. The Cheyenne invited the Shoshone for what Chambers called a "Scalp Peace."[27] On the way to the council a Cheyenne war party had killed and scalped two Shoshones; no celebration had been performed over the scalps, however, and the Cheyenne were returning them to the Shoshone, together with lavish gifts, to establish peace with them.

The next day, September 9, some one hundred Cheyennes performed a mock battle, together with dances and the recitation of coups, for the edification of the commissioners. That evening the Sioux invited the commissioners and their party to a Dog Feast. Dog was considered the appropriate food for ritual and special occasions, and, moreover, buffalo meat was in short supply, since the enormous camp had driven the herds far off.[28]

Just as the cannon was fired and the flag raised on the morning of September 10 to call the Indian delegates to the council ground, the Crow delegation arrived, riding in procession and wearing their finest regalia. They were assigned a campsite near Mitchell's tent, and their chiefs were invited to join the other leaders in the council arbor.

Mathó sap'íc'iye, or Bear That Paints Itself Black, more often translated as Painted Bear or Smutty Bear (Yankton), 1858. Washington, DC. Copy by A. Zeno Shindler of a photo by James E. McClees. National Anthropological Archives, Smithsonian Institution NAA INV 06597800

The day's meeting began with Mitchell asking the Sioux to report their deliberations. The elderly Teton Sioux chief, Blue Earth, spoke first. His people wanted to be at peace, he said. But they could not agree with the demand to choose a single chief for their nation. Addressing Mitchell as "Father," he requested that one or two chiefs be recognized for each band. They would appoint young men as soldiers who would be responsible for the welfare of the people, including whites who were in their territory.

Painted Bear,[29] one of the Yankton Sioux chiefs, was less conciliatory: "Father, this is the third time I have met the whites. We don't understand their manners, nor their words. . . . We suppose the half breeds understand it, and we leave them to speak for us." The "half breeds," children of white men and Indian women, served as interpreters at the council; because some of them spoke English and were literate, the Indians necessarily depended on them. This is an acknowledgment of what would become a major theme in Plains Indian history: the mixed bloods were assigned an intermediary role between the two cultures their parents represented.

Perhaps disheartened, Mitchell once again explained each of the propositions he had made, "stating each one separately and distinctly." Afterward, other Sioux leaders spoke, but Chambers characterized them as "mere begging speeches" and did not record them.

Next, Mitchell called on the Cheyenne. Bark, or The Bear's Feather, gave a speech in which he reported that his people were in agreement with the U.S. government propositions. Then the Arapaho chief, Beka-chebotha, or Cut Nose, made a similar speech, emphasizing his satisfaction that all would be at peace. When he finished, Authonish-ah, "an old, gray-headed Arapaho chief," addressed his people rather than the commissioners. He also spoke of peace as the "pleasantest thing in the world," then said, "Let our ears be open to the advice of our Great Father, and no lies in our hearts in what we promise him."

More speeches followed that, again, Chambers did not record. At the end of the day the Cheyenne presented the man they had selected as head chief, Wan-ne-sah-tah, or Who Walks With His Toes Turned Out, the Southern Cheyenne chief who was keeper of the Sacred Arrows, one of the tribe's two great sacred bundles. Then the Arapaho presented Biah-at-sah-ah-kah-che, or Little Owl, as their choice for head chief.

On the morning of September 11 the commissioners met separately with the Crow delegation to explain the treaty terms.[30] Chambers reported that Robert Meldrum, the Crow interpreter, "understands their language perfectly, and is capable of comprehending the extent, effect, and importance of the propositions submitted." Both he and the trader Alexander Culbertson, who was also present, were respected and trusted by the Crow.

While the Crow leaders met to discuss the treaty, the flag was again hoisted and the general council assembled. Chiefs of a number of different Sioux bands made speeches explaining why they could not select a single head chief and putting forward chiefs for their individual bands. Frustrated, Mitchell insisted that they must choose one man, and asked them to try again.

Then the Crow delegates came into the council. The Crow chief Arra-tu-resash, or Big Robber, addressed the commissioners. His people were willing to make peace if the other tribes agreed to it. "Father, all nations have a big chief—my people have theirs. . . . Hereafter, if any wrongs are done on any person in his country, he will see that the guilty are punished." He ended with a solemn oath: "The Sun, Moon, and Earth are all witnesses of the truth I have spoken, and that all I have promised will be fulfilled." When he finished, Mountain Tail spoke and told the commissioners that it was Big Robber himself who was the choice of the Crow Nation to be their chief. Chambers wrote: "The commissioners saluted him as the chief of the Crows, and presented him with the usual presents to distribute among his people."

The next day, September 12, Mitchell met with representatives of each nation to delineate territorial boundaries. He invited the interpreters, traders, and others famil-

 iar with the Indian Country—among whom James Bridger and Father De Smet were acknowledged as having, based on their travels, the most extensive geographical knowledge—to participate in the deliberations. Both Mitchell and Fitzpatrick themselves had decades of experience in the fur trade. Unfortunately, Chambers made no record of those important discussions, which defined tribal boundaries for the first time. De Smet took on the task of preparing a map to represent them.[31]

When the council met on September 13 the issue of tribal boundaries and what they meant was the main topic. A number of the Sioux leaders were angry to learn that the boundary between their territory and that of the Cheyenne and Arapaho had been set at the Platte River. Chambers summarized their objection: "They did not contend that the south side of the Platte belonged to them, but as they had always hunted on the south side, as far as the Republican Fork of the Kansas and the waters of the Arkansas, they claimed the same right now, and therefore objected to the line." Given that the concept of land ownership separate from using the land made no sense in Indian cultures and must have been almost impossible to translate into any of the languages,

Pierre-Jean De Smet (1801–1873). *Map of the Upper Great Plains and Rocky Mountains Region,* 1851. Brown ink and watercolor on paper. 82 × 131 cm. Library of Congress G4050 1851 .S6

This map defined for the first time the territorial boundaries of the Native Nations that signed the Horse Creek Treaty. It parcels out 1.1 million square miles of land.

Horse Creek Treaty, September 17, 1851. Fort Laramie, Wyoming Territory. 125.1 × 45.1cm. Animal hide, ink, silk ribbon. National Archives and Records Administration, Washington, DC

it is little wonder that the Indians were perplexed. The Oglala Sioux leader Black Hawk expressed this concern when he told Mitchell, "You have split the country, and I don't like it."

Although Chambers's report is terse, it seems that Mitchell glossed over the main point, which was that boundaries were necessary for the purpose of knowing which tribe to blame should depredations occur. Instead, he explained that the territorial boundaries were not intended to prevent them from hunting in the territory of other tribes, as long as peace was maintained. Doubtless he considered that the imminent extermination of the buffalo would make the matter moot.

September 14 was a Sunday, so no council was held. In the mixed-blood camp a large tipi had the covers pulled back to form a sanctuary in which Father De Smet said Mass. Speaking in French, he addressed an attentive crowd, urging them to remain at peace and to accept Christianity.

On September 15 the Indians were again called into council.[32] Mitchell asked if all understood the treaty and agreed with it. Chambers reported that, after some discussion, all seemed satisfactory. The only unfinished business was selecting a head chief of the Sioux. Each band put forward a number of chiefs in proportion to its population. The twenty-four men who were chosen were seated on the ground in a semicircle, and each one was given a short stick. Mitchell announced that he would propose a candidate for head chief and those who wished to support him should give him their stick. He then raised up Mah-toe-wah-yu-whey, or Frightening Bear, who was one of the electors. A younger man, between thirty and forty, he came from an influential family was well thought of by the traders. Frightening Bear seemed stunned by his selection and protested that he had no desire to be head chief, but if he must, he would have to be a strong chief. After an hour's discussion among themselves one of the Yankton chiefs stood up and gave Frightening Bear his stick; the others followed one by one. One of the oldest chiefs made a speech to the assembled Sioux, exhorting them to listen to Frightening Bear: "Hereafter, this chief was to be the voice of their Great Father." Following this, Mitchell gave Frightening Bear presents, which he then distributed to others, keeping nothing for himself.

At last, on September 17, the general council was again called for the purpose of signing the Treaty.[33] Mitchell read the document sentence by sentence, sometimes repeating at the request of the chiefs to insure the articles were understood. In addition to the propositions made on the first day of the council, the Treaty now included the agreed-upon boundaries for each of the tribes.

When the reading was finished Mitchell and Fitzpatrick signed the Treaty. Twenty-one chiefs touched the end of the pen while the secretary who held it wrote an X. Finally, fifteen military officers, interpreters, traders, and others signed as witnesses. Afterward, several chiefs made speeches to their people, addressing especially the young men, urging them to keep the peace with the whites and with other tribes as the chiefs had promised.

The record of speeches by the leaders of the tribes attending the great council makes it clear that they understood their pledge to remain at peace with the whites and with

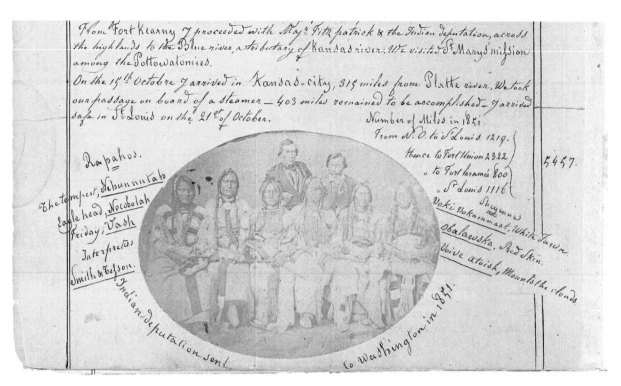

From Fort Kearny I proceeded with Maj.^r Fitzpatrick & the Indian deputation, across the highlands to the Blue river, a tributary of Kansas river. We visited St Marys mission among the Pottowatomies.

On the 15th Octobre I arrived in Kansas-city, 315 miles from Platte river. We took our passage on board of a steamer — 403 miles remained to be accomplished — I arrived safe in St Louis on the 21st of October.

Rapahos.
The tempest, Nebunnutab
Eagle head, Nocobolah
Friday, Vash
    Interpretas
Smith & Gefson.

Indian deputation sent
to Washington in 1851.

Number of Miles in 1851.
From N. O. to St Louis 1219.
Hence to Fort Union 2322
" to Fort laramie 800
" St Louis 1116

5457.

Voki Nokainmast, White Fawn
Sheyennes
Obalawska, Red Skin.
Voive atoish, Mounts the clouds.

Arapaho, Cheyenne, and Sioux leaders—and their interpreters—who traveled to Washington as members of a delegation after the signing of the Horse Creek Treaty, 1851. St. Louis, Missouri. Photographer unknown. On October 24, they were the honored guests of the Jesuits at St. Louis University. Back row, from left: interpreters John S. Smith and Joseph Tesson Honoré. Front row, from left: Friday (Arapaho), Alights on a Cloud (Cheyenne), possibly One Horned Elk (Oglala Dakota); possibly White Antelope (Cheyenne), possibly Little Chief (Cheyenne), and possibly Red Plume (Blackfoot Sioux). Page reproduced from the Moses Linton Album, De Smetiana Collection, Midwest Jesuit Archives, St. Louis, Missouri

one another. Yet they also recognized, as the Crow chief Big Robber said to Mitchell, "Our young men, Father, will go to war sometimes, in defiance of the wish and orders of the old men, and they commit wrongs; but we hope we will be able to restrain them hereafter." Since going to war to steal horses, take scalps, and count coups was necessary for young men to prove themselves and advance their status, it must have been obvious to all that a permanent peace among the tribes was an impossibility.

Although the official business was over, the great camp had to remain on Horse Creek to wait for the promised presents. The Shoshone stayed, too; even though they had not been asked to sign the Treaty, they were offered a share of the presents. At last the wagon train arrived on the evening of September 20. The unloading and distribution of the goods was not finished until September 23, after which the Indians headed off to the South Platte, where there was a report of buffalo herds, and the commissioners began their return to St. Louis. In Sioux winter counts for 1851–52 the Treaty is designated by a pile of trade goods, topped with blankets, and is called the Winter of the Big Distribution.[34]

Battiste Good, or Wapostangi, or Brown Hat (Brule Lakota) 1821–1908. *First issue of goods winter,* pictograph for winter of 1851–52, detail from sketchbook copy of artist's cloth winter count, 1880. Rosebud Reservation, South Dakota. Graphite, ink, and watercolor on paper. 27 × 19 cm. National Anthropological Archives, Smithsonian Institution NAA INV 08746800

The colored patches inside the circle represent blankets issued, and the circle the people sitting. According to one interpretation, fifty-five years was the amount of time the Sioux understood would elapse before they would be required to take up farming.

Recorded in these two winter counts, a peace agreement between the Sioux and Crow Nations was concluded at the Horse Creek treaty council.

Lone Dog, or Shunka Ishnala (Yankton). *Peace with the Crows.* Pictograph for winter of 1851–52, detail from winter count, 1800–1870. Plains. Buffalo hide, paint. 259 × 207 cm. National Museum of the American Indian 1/617

Long Soldier (Hunkpapa Lakota) ca. 1847–ca. 1925, interpreter of the winter count. Artist unknown. *Year Sitting Bull was made chief because he made peace with the Crows.* Pictograph for winter of 1851–52, detail from winter count, 1798–1902. Cotton cloth, paint. 181 × 88 cm. National Museum of the American Indian 11/6720

Blackfeet

Milk R.

Assiniboine and Gros Ventre
Fort Belknap

Assiniboine and Sioux
Fort Peck

Mandan, Hidatsa and Arikara
Fort Berthold

CANADA
U.S.

2

Grand Forks

29

Red R.

Marias R.

15

Great Falls

Missouri R.

Big Dry Cr.

MONTANA

Sioux
Spirit Lake

NORTH DAKOTA

2

Bismarck

94

Fargo

2

MINNESOTA

35

Heart R.

Helena

90

Musselshell R.

Yellowstone R.

94

Butte

Bozeman

Billings

Northern Cheyenne

Crow

Powder R.

Little Missouri R.

Missouri R.

SOUTH DAKOTA

Sioux
Standing Rock

Sioux
Lake Traverse

St. Cloud

94

Saint Paul

Minneapolis

Minnesota R.

Sioux
Cheyenne River

IDAHO

84

Rocky

Bighorn R.

Bighorn Mtns.

90

Belle Fourche R.

Rapid City

Cheyenne R.

Black Hills

90

Sioux
Crow Creek

Sioux
Lower Brule

James R.

Sioux Falls

IOWA

35

Idaho Falls

Snake R.

WYOMING

Eastern Shoshone and Northern Arapaho
Wind River

Mountains

Casper

25

Red Butte

Sioux
Pine Ridge

Sioux
Rosebud

Sioux
Yankton

Sioux City

Des Moines

80

Fort Laramie

Laramie R.

Horse Cr.

Site of Horse Creek Treaty

Scottsbluff

Niobrara R.

Missouri R.

Omaha

Council Bluffs

Great Salt Lake

Salt Lake City

Laramie

Cheyenne

North Platte R.

NEBRASKA

North Platte

Platte R.

Kearney

80

Lincoln

35

29

St. Joseph

UTAH

Green R.

70

Denver

South Platte R.

Republican R.

Topeka

Kansas City

Salina

Kansas R.

MO.

Colorado R.

Grand Junction

COLORADO

Colorado Springs

Pueblo

70

KANSAS

Wichita

Joplin

44

Rio Grande

25

Arkansas R.

35

Tulsa

ARIZONA

Santa Fe

OKLAHOMA

40

Amarillo

40

Oklahoma City

DETAIL

NEW MEXICO

Red R.

TEXAS

Miles

0   100   200

When the commissioners began their long trip home they took with them not only the signed Treaty but also a delegation of younger Indian leaders—Sioux, Cheyenne, and Arapaho–whom they would escort to Washington to meet the Great Father. They arrived in Washington on November 15, having first visited St. Mary's Roman Catholic mission school for the Potawatomi, located north of Kansas City, then St. Louis, Louisville, and Baltimore. They remained in the capital until January 11, returning west by way of Philadelphia.[35]

Shortly after the delegation left Washington the Treaty was submitted to the Senate for ratification. The legislators, however, considered the terms too generous and insisted that the number of years during which annuities would be provided be reduced from fifty to ten, with a possible five-year extension at the will of the president. It was therefore necessary once again to obtain the signatures of the chiefs of each of the tribes concerned, a task that was assigned to the Indian agents. Chiefs representing each tribe signed the amendment in August and September 1853, except for the Crow chief, who did not receive the amendment until September 1854.[36] Meanwhile, the government provided annuities for the tribes according to the provisions of the treaty. When the copies of the amendment signed by the chiefs finally reached Washington, they were filed away in the Office of Indian Affairs. For reasons now unknown, the Treaty was never brought back to the Senate floor for ratification, but it remained in effect for fifteen years, as though it had been ratified.

Northern Plains Native Nations' reservations, 2014. Map by Gene Thorp/ Cartographic Concepts, Inc. © Smithsonian Institution

Language and World View at the Horse Creek Treaty

ARWEN NUTTALL

THE ANSWER TO THE QUESTION OF WHY NATIVE Nations made treaties that took away their land and resources is often influenced by the misconception that they were not politically savvy or that their forms of government, which differed from tribe to tribe, were far simpler than that of the United States. When discussing treaties, however, and why Native Nations agreed to terms that in the end hurt them, Kevin Gover (Pawnee), director of the National Museum of the American Indian (NMAI), said during the museum's special symposium on the Horse Creek Treaty of 1851, "It is important to acknowledge . . . that while the United States may have had a particular way of memorializing and negotiating and talking about the treaties, the Indians had ways too. And they had specific understandings. They had specific protocols. They had ways of solemnizing and memorializing the treaties."

Held at the National Museum of the American Indian on June 28, 2012, the roundtable brought together heritage language speakers from the Native Nations present at the Horse Creek treaty council: Lakota (Sioux), Cheyenne, Arapaho, Shoshone, Assiniboine, Arikara, Hidatsa, Mandan, and Apsáalooke (Crow). The meeting at the museum was the first time that speakers of these languages had gathered since 1851. The participants agreed that the differences in languages and world views among individual Native Nations and the U.S. government had very real effects on treaty negotiations, as exemplified during the parley between federal agents and the nine tribes who came together at the mouth of Horse Creek on the North Platte River. The meeting resulted in the first treaty between the U.S. government and northern Plains Tribes as a group. The main purpose of the Treaty was to create geographical boundaries around each of the Plains Indian Nations and ensure smooth passage across the plains for non-Native emigrants moving west.

Plains Nations were familiar with coming together in council to discuss tribal issues, and informal peace agreements were already established among many of them; however, they did not employ formal written documents that relied on legal concepts. According to treaty scholar and anthropologist, Raymond DeMallie:

> There were so many different concepts that seem obvious on the surface, but when you start to look at them, you realize there is no simple way of translating that into a Native language, because it depends on a whole Western epistemology that is not shared by the Indians. So just think about things like the word *treaty*. What is a treaty? Well, I've argued that it's a relationship. It's a drawing of kinship. What that requires is faith on each side, each side being honest with the other and supporting the other. If you stop supporting the other, the treaty stops. There's no longer any treaty. So it's not something that's seen as a political legal agreement. It's a moral agreement, because the whole concept of a political, legal agreement . . . did not exist among American Indians.

Bernadine Young Bird (Hidatsa), another guest speaker at the NMAI's symposium, highlighted the impact world view had on the Plains Peoples' understanding of the Treaty: "One of the things we have to talk about and think about is the many different world views we have. Very obviously, the Europeans who came into our land had a completely different world view from ours. How they have said and interpreted things calls into question, 'How did they say these things to our people at that time?' Obviously they were not accurate." Young Bird also emphasized the foreignness of a written contract to her people who, like the other Plains Nations, relied on oral tradition: "It was a white concept, the treaty. Basically, what everyone shared was oral tradition, nothing in writing. The word was considered sacred once you said it. It was your bond. That was held sacred. So you were careful what you said, because you were held to it. That was the sacredness of our language and our words. That's what we went by." Reba Terran made a similar comment about her nation, the Shoshone of Wyoming: "Our Shoshone people didn't do written treaties with other Indian people. We agreed with our words. We didn't write."

To make treaty negotiations even more convoluted, each of the groups representing the nine Native Nations at the treaty council spoke its own language, and few of them understood English. DeMallie points out,

> Translation is not only difficult from English into any one of the Indian languages [spoken at Horse Creek], but it's also difficult . . . because the peoples there spoke such vastly different languages. If you look at Cheyenne and Arapaho, for example, which are Algonquian languages, and then compare them with Lakota or Hidatsa, which are Siouan languages . . . the structure is completely different; the whole way in which things are—which sentences and words are put together—is different. So you know that there have to have been multiple understandings throughout that entire group.

Some of the Native people spoke several Native languages.

Native and non-Native interpreters translated the federal agents' speeches into each of the languages represented at the council. DeMallie notes,

The record says that [Indian commissioner] David D. Mitchell, as he was delivering his speeches to the Indians, repeated each sentence slowly and carefully, and then the interpreters for each tribe interpreted what he had to say into that Native language and announced it loudly. One can imagine this cacophony of nine languages being spoken at the same time. . . . There was a back-and-forth correction of what it was that was being said.

DeMallie goes on to point out,

> What we don't see referred to in the record, and I think it's important to realize, is that traditionally when Plains Indians spoke in council, they said everything that they had to say in speech also simultaneously in sign. The sign language was universal throughout the plains, and it was tremendously valuable. . . . So I think probably the substance of what the white commissioners had to say was very well communicated. The meaning is another question.

Brown Owl Woman (Lakota) also stressed the difficulty of language and translation during the treaty-making process: "There are many words that we cannot translate from English into Lakota and Lakota into English."

When discussing the Horse Creek Treaty, and treaties in general, it is imperative to recognize the forces of language and world view at play and not simplify the whole process as one government being more advanced and politically astute than the other. DeMallie acknowledges the uniquely difficult situation in which Native Nations found themselves when faced with treaty negotiations and the very real ways in which they tried to do what they thought was best for their people: "I think they were politically very sophisticated and tried in their own ways within the context of their own cultures to outwit the white people."

"The Indians Were the Spoken Word"

An Interview with N. Scott Momaday

SUZAN SHOWN HARJO

SUZAN SHOWN HARJO: What comes to mind when you think of the U.S.–Indian treaties and their immediacy, their antiquity, the impetus behind them?

N. SCOTT MOMADAY: The people who composed the treaties, the federal government, thought of language in one way and the Indian thought about it quite another. And so you have, right at the outset, every chance for misunderstanding. It's a matter of looking at language in a certain way, and the treaties were the written word. The Indians were the spoken word, represented the spoken word. The two things are very different, and we have a reflection of that difference in the treaties.

SUZAN SHOWN HARJO: What illustrates that difference? How did the Native people think of treaties and how did the non-Native people think of treaties?

N. SCOTT MOMADAY: Language is sacred to the Native American. It once was sacred to the white man as well, but that has been lost in the shuffle. We've lost our respect for the word. We tend to take it for granted, and the Indian didn't, couldn't, didn't dare.

SUZAN SHOWN HARJO: Before Native people entered into a treaty camp, what did they do to prepare that was different from what non-Native people did?

N. SCOTT MOMADAY: I think they thought of it as they do now, as ceremony. We are gathering. This is good. We're going to have a good time. We're going to feast. We're going to have giveaways. We're going to laugh and talk, and it's going to be wonderful. So they thought of it as a celebration, whereas proba-

bly those who composed the treaties thought of it in very different terms. Well, this is not fun; this is business. We've got to come to an agreement. We've got to pin things down. We do that through this piece of paper and the ink on it.

I remember hearing about a treaty in Kansas. I've forgotten just which one it was, but the Kiowa, and I think the Arapaho, and maybe the Cheyenne met. The purpose was to bring peace among the three tribes. They didn't have a problem at that time with the troops, but they were fighting each other. The government decided that they had to agree not to fight any longer. So they came together, and the Indians were looking at it as a ceremony. . . . We can stop fighting. We can have a feast. There was a famous Kiowa chief named Sitting Bear present at this particular treaty, and the Kiowa at that time owned more horses per capita than any other tribe. So he went among the Cheyenne and the Arapaho, and he said to their chiefs, "Look, we have to do this, this thing today, this paper, but tomorrow, tomorrow we dance, we eat. There will be a giveaway. It's going to be wonderful. But do not give us horses. Do not give the Kiowa horses. We will give you horses." And he gave away 250 horses from his own herd. Now I think that's wonderful. It says something about the idea of a treaty, and it says something about wealth among the Native Peoples, and the love of coming together.

SUZAN SHOWN HARJO: What would you say are the main ideas behind treaties, from a Native perspective and from a non-Native perspective? What are the main goals? Why did the people on all sides want to have treaties?

N. SCOTT MOMADAY: I think the idea of giving one's word is ancient among the Native Peoples. Nothing is more important. The treaty represented to the Native American the giving of one's word and the accepting of someone else's word; these were taken very seriously and thought to be sacred. When someone gave his word, it was to be kept. That was just a simple understanding. I don't think it was even spelled out. It was not like the Ten Commandments. It was not like, if you don't keep your word, this and this and this will happen to you. It was just understood that you didn't do anything but keep your word.

On the other side, I think it was legislation. The people who composed the treaties thought of it in a different way. They thought, yes, we are going to agree with these people that this and this will happen, or that these pronouncements will be observed and kept, and if they are broken, there will be punitive measures. So it was more of a law-giving kind of thing with the non-Natives. And so you come together, and the idea is to keep the word. But the whites thought nothing of breaking the word. There was nothing sacred about it, and that was the crucial difference.

SUZAN SHOWN HARJO: Could you talk a bit about honor?

N. SCOTT MOMADAY: The warrior ideal, which was the ideal of the Plains culture, the Sun Dance cultures, had four principles to be observed by the warrior and by the society. They were bravery, steadfastness, generosity, and virtue. Virtue meant appropriate behavior, which incorporated the idea of honor. We do things in a proper way. We do things in an honorable way. Honor was tied up with the sacredness of the word. One demonstrated his honor by speaking honorably and behaving honorably, probably in that order. The word comes first. So honor is a way of life. It's not something that you aspire to and go out and try to achieve.

It wasn't looked at that way on the other side. Honor was a wonderful thing, but it had to do with chivalry and combat. It was a different idea of honor . . . apart from the Indian view. For Native Peoples honor was something so intrinsic that you demonstrated it in your daily life without thinking about it. It was the water you drank and the food you ate. It was just who you were. I am what I say.

SUZAN SHOWN HARJO: Could you talk a bit about your Pueblo side and how these questions of honor and fair dealings affected the Pueblo people and what they encountered?

N. SCOTT MOMADAY: One of the first impressions I had of [Jemez] Pueblo when I went there was that, again, language is sacred here. I remember listening on winter evenings to the town crier. You could hear his voice coming from the village up to the day school, floating on that cold winter air, and it was magical. I couldn't understand what was being said, but I understood that the language, the utterance, the voice was sacred. When you hear the singing at the dances and the sound of the drums, you understand that this language—which consists not only of spoken words but also of song and dance and drums—it's somehow connected to the center of the earth. It's not anything superficial. It's deep and real.

From an interview that took place on August 15, 2005, at the School for Advanced Research, Santa Fe, New Mexico.

THE NINETEENTH CENTURY WAS A TIME OF DISPOSSES-sion and dislocation for many Native nations.[1] Yet not all tribal groups lost or were banished from their homelands. Though wrenched from their aboriginal territories, the Navajo managed in 1868 to return to and regain a significant portion of their tribal estate in the Four Corners area of the Southwest, and they continued to expand their nation's boundaries in the late nineteenth and twentieth centuries.

The Navajo paid dearly for their territories. Beginning in late 1863, the United States uprooted about 10,500 Navajo men, women, and children from their homes and force-marched them 450 miles to Bosque Redondo, an internment camp on the Pecos River in southeastern New Mexico. After four years of suffering, starvation, disease, and death, the exiles convinced U.S. officials to allow them to return to their "beloved country" in 1868.[2] In the Treaty they signed that year, the Navajo accepted a 3.4 million-acre reservation in what is now northeastern Arizona and northwestern New Mexico. Although it included only about one-fourth of the Navajo's traditional territories,[3] the reservation provided a haven in which to regroup and repopulate— and from which to reclaim additional homelands.

As they returned from Bosque Redondo, the Navajo began to spread across and beyond the reservation. Farmers planted new fields and peach orchards. Herders tended the government-issued fourteen thousand sheep and one thousand goats they received in 1869, and they gladly accepted ten thousand more sheep three years later. By the 1880s, Navajo stockmen boasted a herd of one million sheep and goats, some fifty animals for every Navajo man, woman, and child.[4] More confident about their future, the Navajo started new families, and the population surged from approximately twelve thousand in 1868 to twenty thousand by 1890.[5]

As their population swelled and their sheep multiplied, the Navajo began to find their 3.3 million-acre reservation inadequate, and they demanded more land from the government. That their demands were met had less to do with U.S. altruism and more to do with nature. Arid, isolated, and seemingly bereft of mineral wealth, the deserts and mesas of Navajo country were not yet coveted by non-Indians. Consequently, from 1876 to 1901, the size of the Navajo Reservation tripled through federal executive orders.[6] Navajo land holdings were further supplemented in the twentieth century by executive orders, acts of Congress, and court decisions.[7] Today, the Navajo Nation is the largest Indian reservation in the United States, encompassing about twenty-five thousand square miles across Arizona, New Mexico, and Utah.[8]

During an era when many Native Nations in the Great Plains and the West were being whittled into oblivion, facing removal to Indian Territory (present-day Oklahoma), and confronting diminished opportunities, the Navajo managed to find peace and relative security in their ancestral homelands. Living within the boundaries of their four sacred mountains, they drew spiritual strength from their lands as well as the inspiration to demand the expansion of their treaty-established reservation. The choices and actions of people who had experienced the terrible ordeal at Bosque Redondo established the foundation for the flowering of Navajo life, culture, and nationhood in the twentieth century.[9]

Naal Tsoos Sani

The Navajo Treaty of 1868, Nation Building, and Self-Determination

O N JUNE 1, 1868 NAVAJO (DINÉ) LEADERS SIGNED A FINAL TREATY WITH THE United States.[10] At the Bosque Redondo reservation to which they had been exiled four years earlier, Diné leaders successfully persuaded General William Tecumseh Sherman to allow their people to return to their homeland. Of their return the Diné leader Manuelito said, "The days and nights were long before it came time for us to go to our homes. . . . When we saw the top of the mountain from Albuquerque we wondered if it was our mountain, and we felt like talking to the ground, we loved it so, and some of the old men and women cried with joy when they reached their homes."[11] Naal Tsoos Sani, or the Old Paper, as the Navajo have named the 1868 treaty, marks a shift in Navajo history, the point at which the Navajo people lost their freedom and autonomy and came under American colonial rule. Since the treaty, Navajo history has been one of ongoing efforts to reclaim their former independence, sovereignty, and self-determination.

The treaty evokes memories of Navajo resistance to colonial powers and a strong sense of ongoing injustices wrought by the United States. On the one hand, the people (an English translation of Diné) retain a deep sense of the deprivation that their ancestors suffered; on the other, they remember their ancestors' successful struggle to regain a land base, sustain cultural traditions, and keep alive the Diné language. Naal Tsoos Sani also represents the birth of the modern Navajo Nation, for in coming to an agreement with Navajo leaders, the United States acknowledged the Diné as sovereign. Finally, as the Navajo people face the challenges of life in the twenty-first century, they often have conversations about what it means to move beyond a relationship with the United States in which their nation is cast as a "domestic dependent."[12]

Diné (Navajo) serape, ca. 1868. New Mexico. Commercial wool yarn, dyes. 152.4 × 76.2 cm. National Museum of the American Indian 20/5235

This serape belonged to General William T. Sherman. The most likely time for him to have acquired it was at the treaty council of 1868.

In these visions of a Navajo Nation, the Diné emphasize the importance of their way of life, founded in the concept of *sa'ah nagháí bik'eh hózhóón,* which can be translated as "the path to beauty and old age."

Sovereignty and self-determination for the Diné mean their concrete rights to self-government, territorial integrity, and cultural autonomy under international law.[13] Between 1706 and 1819, Spain and Mexico signed treaties with Navajo leaders, thereby recognizing Navajo sovereignty.[14] Laying claims to territory long before any Spaniard ever set foot in the Southwest, the peoples who would become the Diné emerged from the lower worlds in a region still known as Dinétah, or "among the People." Dinétah is the place where earth people and Holy People interacted; their relationships form the foundation of practices and teachings that underlie Navajo life today. The Holy People

facing: This map shows the approximate area of the original Navajo homelands; the six mountains named as the leaders of the Diné; the three main routes along which the Navajo were forced to walk to Bosque Redondo; and the reservation to which they negotiated their return in the 1868 treaty. Map by Gene Thorp/ Cartographic Concepts, Inc. © Smithsonian Institution

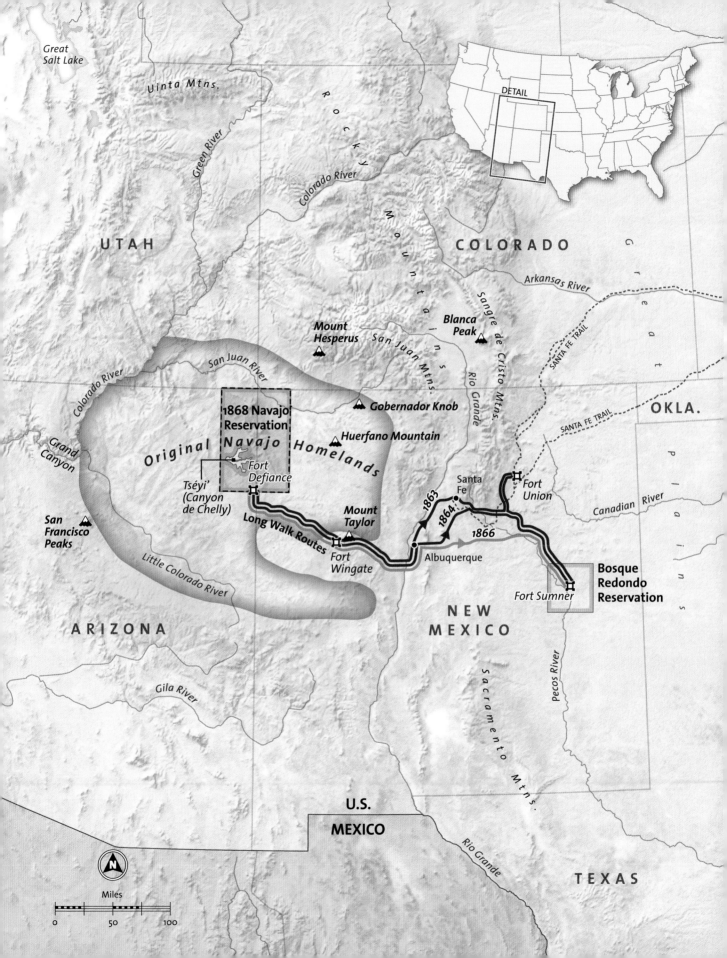

Great
Salt Lake

Uinta Mtns.

R O C K Y

Green River

Colorado River

M o u n t a i n s

UTAH

COLORADO

Arkansas River

G r e a t

SANTA FE TRAIL

Mount
Hesperus

Blanca
Peak

Sangre de Cristo Mtns.

San Juan River

San Juan Mtns.

Rio Grande

Colorado River

Gobernador Knob

1868 Navajo
Reservation

SANTA FE TRAIL

OKLA.

Navajo   Homelands

Grand
Canyon

Original

Huerfano Mountain

Fort
Defiance

Tséyi'
(Canyon
de Chelly)

Santa Fe

Fort
Union

P

Long Walk Routes

Mount
Taylor

1863

1864

Canadian River

l

San
Francisco
Peaks

Fort
Wingate

Albuquerque

1866

Bosque
Redondo
Reservation

a

Little Colorado River

i

ARIZONA

Fort Sumner

n

NEW
MEXICO

s

Sacramento Mtns.

Gila River

Pecos River

U.S.

MEXICO

Rio Grande

TEXAS

N

Miles

0   50   100

DETAIL

set the Diné homeland's boundaries with soil brought from the lower world, placing the soil as mountains in each of the four directions. Diné Bikéyah refers to the lands that lie within the four sacred mountains, which are named Sis Naajiní, or Blanca Peak, in the east; Tsoodził, or Mount Taylor, in the south; Dook'ooslííd, or the San Francisco Peaks, in the west; and Dibé Nitsaa, or Mount Hesperus, in the north. The soil brought from the world below also formed two other mountains: Dził Na'oodiłii, or Huerfano Mountain—east of the center, and Ch'ool'í'í, or Gobernador Knob—the center. These last two mountains are within Dinétah and central to events that occurred when the progenitors of the Diné emerged into the world we inhabit today, which is known as the Glittering World. Traditional Navajo philosophy names these six mountains as the leaders of the Diné. It is in this place that the philosophy sa'ah naghái bik'eh hózhóón was established through actions and words. Navajo leaders and citizens declare that traditional teachings form the foundation of the sovereignty that the United States recognized in the Treaty of 1868.

Under cycles of foreign invasion, the Diné saw vast transformations in their way of life, transformations that proved to be both beneficial and destructive. The introduction of horses, sheep, and goats by the Spaniards in the sixteenth century led the Navajo people to become pastoral and more effective in countering Spanish and then Mexican efforts to colonize them. Under Spanish and Mexican rule, however, slave raiding escalated, targeting Navajo women and children. With the signing of the Treaty of Guadalupe Hidalgo in 1848, Americans claimed the Southwest. As white settlers flooded in from the East, an influx the federal government claimed it could not control, the United States sought to end its expensive Indian wars. Historian Robert M. Utley notes that U.S. policy toward Indians vacillated between the war and peace: because war proved costly, the federal government sought ways to pacify Indians who stood in the way of white settlement, so it continued the policy it had established in 1830 of "removing" Indians to reservations away from, or within a portion of, their original homelands.[15]

Treaties signed by Navajo leaders and the United States did not cease hostilities; relationships moved between conflict and peace among the Navajo, other Native Peoples, and the New Mexicans. The conflicts escalated in 1851, when the Americans established Fort Defiance in the heart of Navajo country. Based on continued hostilities and reports of potentially valuable minerals in Navajo territory, and to clear any obstacles that might impede a trail from the East to California, Major General James H. Carleton in the late fall of 1863 ordered Kit Carson to quash Navajo resistance. Carleton declared that force against the Navajo was necessary, for they could, he said, "no more be trusted than you can trust the wolves that run through their mountains." If the army placed the Navajo on a reserve far "from the haunts and hills and hiding places of their country, and there be kind to them," they would "acquire new habits, new ideas, new modes of life." Carleton claimed that "civilizing" the Navajo could be achieved through their children: "The young ones will take their places without these longings: and thus, little by little, they will become a happy and contented people."[16] Carson conducted a scorched-earth campaign to defeat the Navajo. He and his men slaughtered livestock,

Navajo captives under
guard, 1864–66. Fort
Sumner, New Mexico.
Photo by U.S. Army Signal
Corps. Palace of the Gov-
ernors Photo Archives,
Santa Fe, New Mexico
NMHM/DCA 028534

burned hogans, slashed cornfields, and destroyed water sources, thereby reducing the
Navajo to starvation. Thoroughly demoralized by Carson's brutal methods, thousands
of Navajos surrendered at Forts Wingate and Defiance beginning in late 1863.

From 1863 to 1866, more than ten thousand Navajo prisoners were force-marched to
the Bosque Redondo reservation at Fort Sumner, in present-day eastern New Mexico.
Known as the Long Walk, the removal actually consisted of no fewer than fifty-three
marches, during which the captives walked anywhere from 250 to 450 miles, depending
upon the route taken.[17] Official military reports on the Long Walk can appear objective and do not provide a sense of what the Navajo experienced. Oral history, however,
illuminates Navajo perspectives. Stories passed down from those who lived through
the attacks describe the terror that the Navajo felt as they tried to escape Carson's men.
In the stronghold of Tséyi' (Canyon de Chelly), they desperately sought refuge. One
man named Preparing a Warrior escaped by jumping into the canyon. He landed on
some bushes and ran to safety. In the melee a baby girl strapped in a cradle was left
behind; the cradle saved her from harm. One man was wounded and taken captive. He
was warned that if he and others did not immediately surrender, Carson's men would
kill them. With that message, sixteen Navajos surrendered.[18] In another story a couple struggled during the forced marches to keep up with the group because their infant
was growing weaker. In desperation the husband entreated his wife to abandon their
child. When she refused, he said angrily, "All right, stay there if you like, but I'm going
on. The baby is going to die anyway." As the man hurried to catch up with the rest, he
had an idea. Breaking off some cactus stalks, which were oozing juice, he took them
back to his wife and fed the liquid to the newborn. The infant stirred, the father broke

Navajo captives waiting for ration tickets, 1866. Fort Sumner, New Mexico. Photo by U.S. Army Signal Corps. Palace of the Governors Photo Archives, Santa Fe, New Mexico NMHM/DCA 044516

off more cactus stalks and, with his family, hurried to join the slow-moving caravan.[19] When the people became exhausted and entreated the soldiers to slow down, the soldiers became harsh. If a prisoner persisted, he was shot to death. The persistence of these stories is evident in the testimony of John Daw to the Land Claims Commission in 1951. Daw recounted, "These soldiers did not have any regard for the women folks. They took unto themselves for wives somebody else's wife, and many times the Navajo man whose wife was being taken tried to ward off the soldiers, but immediately he was shot and killed and they took his wife."[20]

From the start, the plan to turn the Navajo into white men was destined for failure. The Bosque Redondo reservation was ill-suited for farming, and after the first year the Navajo prisoners refused to plant because the heat and the cutworms destroyed their fields. On a daily basis the prisoners faced deprivation, starvation, disease, and death. By November 1864, approximately 8,570 men, women, and children were interned at Hwéeldi—the Navajo word for the Bosque Redondo.[21] At the reservation, the prisoners were expected to embrace American cultural values. The policy was often called the federal Indian assimilation policy. It is better described as "ethnic cleansing" and a violation of international laws regarding human rights.[22]

The first photographs ever taken of the Navajo depict them on ration day at the Bosque Redondo reservation. As they huddle together, some wrapped in blankets, soldiers stand guard with bayoneted rifles. An Indian agent reported on his wards' misery, "They eat their rations in two days, and during the other three days they suffer, eating hides, and begging wherever they can."[23] Of the first months at the reservation, historian Gerald Thompson has observed, "It was clear that many Navajos would be buried that winter, in the cold strange Pecos country, for want of food and clothing."[24]

The names of the Navajo leaders who led the resistance against the American invasion of their homeland and then signed the Treaty of 1868 with their X-marks come to us through both non-Indian written documentation and through Navajo oral history. Two leaders in particular, Manuelito and Barboncito, are well remembered for their efforts to protect the land and the people. Manuelito is best known for resisting the Americans until September 1866, when he and around fifty people from his band finally surrendered and were taken to Bosque Redondo. His advocacy for Navajo sovereignty persisted beyond the removal and into the late nineteenth century. The peace leader Barboncito had surrendered in 1864 and made the Long Walk to Fort Sumner, but he escaped and took his people to live among Apache allies in their mountains. The Diné leader surrendered once again, however, arriving back at Fort Sumner in November 1866. Like other leaders, he yielded because he realized that the Americans would stop at nothing to force Navajo surrender and because his fellow Navajo required his spiritual guidance and encouragement while he worked to secure their beloved homeland. Barboncito is best known for his oratory, and he was selected to negotiate what became the last treaty on behalf of his people.

By 1866, Carleton ordered that no more prisoners were to be sent to the Bosque Redondo, for he did not have the resources to care for them. The efforts to force the Navajo to adopt American ways had failed. Whenever federal officials visited the fort, Navajo men and women besieged them and pleaded to be allowed to return home. Many Diné have retained stories of the Long Walk through oral history and continue to tell them to their relatives. One storyteller, Fred Descheene, for example, quoted the incarcerated Diné as saying, "We are lonesome for our land. How can we return to it?"[25] He has shared a story, which many other Diné also know, about a ceremony that was performed to prophesy the future of the Diné as a people: would they return

Barboncito, 1868. Fort Sumner, New Mexico. Photo by Valentine Wolfenstein, National Museum of the American Indian P20816

Navajo women and children, 1864–68. Fort Sumner, New Mexico. Photographer unknown. Palace of the Governors Photo Archives, Santa Fe, New Mexico NMHM/DCA 038207

to their homeland? Or would they be condemned to more years at the hateful Hweéldi? Suffering greatly and longing for home, the medicine men conducted Ma'ii' Bizéé'nast'á by capturing a coyote and placing a bead in its mouth. The medicine men then interpreted the coyote's actions, predicting that the people would return to Diné Bikéyah before too long.[26]

THE RETURN HOME

After four long years, on May 28, 1868, peace commissioners General Sherman and Samuel F. Tappan met with Navajo leaders to discuss the future of the Navajo. Barboncito described to Sherman and Tappan the harsh realities of exile and captivity as well as his people's hopes for a future of peace and prosperity. The Navajo people had endeavored to make the best of their situation, but the land at Bosque Redondo "did not know them." Of his people's poverty, Barboncito said, "The Commissioners can see themselves that we have hardly any sheep or horses, nearly all that we brought here have died, and that has left us so poor that we have no means wherewith to buy others."[27]

Major General William Tecumseh Sherman, 1865. Probably Washington, DC. Photo by Mathew Brady. National Archives and Records Administration, Washington, DC ARC 525970

General Sherman attempted to persuade the leaders that their people should move to Indian Territory (now Oklahoma). Barboncito's response is legendary: "I hope to God you will not ask me to go to any other country except my own."[28] Navajo oral history sheds light on how the people tried to influence the negotiations in their favor. Pete Price, a local leader and medicine man from the Tuba City, Arizona, region, shared stories passed down from his kin. "But they heard, instead of returning to their ancient homes, they were to be taken still farther east. They were displeased with the idea, so the wise men of the tribe got together and planned for a meeting with the white man." Price continued, "After the men of the tribe had failed, the women went to the white men, cried and pleaded to be allowed to go back to their home in the west. The women were successful, and the people returned to their country.[29]

In relenting, General Sherman said, "You are right, the world is big enough for all the people it contains and all should live at peace with their neighbors."[30] Historian John Kessell remarked about Navajo determination to return to their homeland: "In fact, the will of more than seven thousand discontented Navajos did amount to something—the difference between removal to the Indian Territory and going home. The will of the Navajo—personified in the intense resolve of Barboncito, their wily little, mustached spokesman—changed General Sherman's mind."[31] Once the Navajo leaders had accomplished their goal of being allowed to return home, Barboncito declared, "After we get back to our country, it will brighten up again and Navajos will be as happy as the land. Black clouds will rise and there will be plenty of rain. Corn will grow in abundance and everything will look happy."[32] On May 30 the Treaty was drawn up.

On June 28, more than seven thousand Diné began the journey home. Fifty-six wagons carried the elders, the ill, and the young, while the able walked. Although they had only 940 sheep, 1,025 goats, and 1, 550 horses among them, it would not be long before their herds would prosper. Once they passed Albuquerque and the Rio Grande River, they spied their sacred Tsoodził, Mount Taylor, and thanked the Holy People for answering their prayers. They were going home.

THE TREATY OF 1868

Treaties signed between the United States and tribal leaders on behalf of their people in the latter half of the nineteenth century are often seen as the beginning of Native dependency on the United States and an erosion of tribal autonomy and freedom. American negotiators clearly sought the conversion of Native Peoples and their cultures to something resembling Euro-American social, political, and economic systems, and, for the Navajo people, the Treaty they signed in 1868 with the Americans was no different.[33] The Navajo Nation, like many other Native Nations, was established as a "domestic dependent" of the United States. As Native scholars Wallace Coffey and Rebecca Tsosie write, "In a world where tribal political sovereignty is dependent upon federal acknowledgement, Indian nations will always be vulnerable to restrictions on their sovereignty, and perhaps even to the total annihilation of their sovereignty."[34]

In affixing their X-marks to paper, Diné leaders both affirmed Diné sovereignty and acknowledged the authority of the United States to limit tribal sovereignty. They did what they had to do in an impossible situation to allow their people to have a future.[35] This future, according to Native scholar Scott Lyons, meant "adopting new ways of living, thinking, and being that do not necessarily emanate from a traditional cultural source (or, for that matter, 'time immemorial'), and sometimes it means appropriating the new and changing it to feel like the old."[36] Further, the document remains an important symbol of Navajo sovereignty and all the possibilities for living once again under Diné philosophy.

Thus, the Navajo Treaty of 1868 resonates as a document that has historical, legal, and cultural meaning. For the Navajo people, the Treaty term that allowed them to return to their ancestral territories was paramount, even though their domain was substantially less than what it had formerly been. In addition, as political scientist David Wilkins points out, treaties "have an ongoing symbolic and substantive significance and are still the most important device for creating and maintaining the unique political relationship between tribes and the United States."[37] From the Navajo perspective the Treaty reflects the foundation of the U.S.–Navajo relationship. The Navajo people trust that the United States will fulfill its legal and moral obligations under the Treaty.[38] Even though the Treaty anticipated the eventual assimilation of the Navajo, it also created the physical space and opportunity for the Navajo to define and exercise sovereignty and self-government. Navajo leaders and community activists have used this opportunity to develop a cultural dimension of Navajo sovereignty, one that links the Navajo Nation to "its territory, its environment, its neighbors, and entails the people's right to think and act freely and to meet their own needs as they see fit."[39]

Under the Treaty, the Navajo agreed to cease war against the United States and allow structures and buildings where federal authorities could oversee their obligations to the Navajo. The United States agreed to provide annuities for ten years. Federal agents thought that ten years of annuities would be enough to move the nation to self-sufficiency. Other provisions allowed for the allotment of the land for farming (a provision that was largely not implemented), and the Navajo agreed not to oppose the construction of railroads through their country. Perhaps one provision that remains contentious is the stipulation that Navajo children would be afforded an American education. Indeed, Manuelito sent his own sons to the Carlisle Indian Industrial School in Pennsylvania because he believed education could be a tool for protecting sovereignty. At Fort Sumner, Manuelito had said, "Life does not end. It goes on."[40] In 1874, together with his wife, son, and other Navajo leaders, he led a delegation to Washington, DC, to affirm Navajo land rights.[41]

The Treaty confirms the Navajo Nation's rights and powers to regulate its own affairs without undue interference. These rights and powers include the ability to make laws, execute and apply them, and impose and collect taxes.[42] In particular, in the 1959 case *Williams v. Lee* the U.S. Supreme Court affirmed the Navajo Nation's right to regulate non-Indian companies that do business on Navajo land. The case involved a non-Indian trader bringing suit against a Navajo couple and confiscating their livestock to settle their debt to him. In its ruling, the Supreme Court held that, without congressional authorization, state courts have no jurisdiction in a civil case brought by a non-Indian doing business on a reservation against tribal citizens who live there, and that the case should have been filed in the tribal court.[43] In the 1985 case *Kerr McGee*

Treaty with the Navajo, page 18. June 1, 1868. Fort Sumner, New Mexico. Ledger book paper, ink. 30.5 × 20.3 cm. National Archives and Records Administration, Washington, DC

The list of signatures on this page of the 1868 treaty includes the marks of Barboncito and Manuelito.

Manuelito, ca. 1882. Photographer unknown. Probably New Mexico. Palace of the Governors Photo Archives, Santa Fe, New Mexico NMHM/DCA 134484

Juanita, or Asdzáá Tł'ógi (Diné [Navajo]), the wife of the Navajo leader Manuelito, 1874. Washington, DC. Photo by Charles M. Bell. National Museum of the American Indian P02723

Corp. v. Navajo Tribe of Indians, the Supreme Court once again affirmed Navajo tribal sovereignty when it ruled that the Secretary of the Interior's approval was not required for the Navajo Nation to pass laws imposing taxes on companies conducting business on Navajo land.[44]

The cultural dimension of sovereignty is just as important as its legal and historical aspects. On numerous occasions Navajo leaders and their allies have commemorated the meaning of the 1868 Treaty. In 1968 the Navajo people celebrated the hundredth anniversary of their return from the Bosque Redondo. In 2005, after years of planning, the Navajo and their allies dedicated the Bosque Redondo Memorial at the site of the old reservation in Fort Sumner, New Mexico. Gregory Scott Smith, a manager of the memorial, acknowledged its importance: "It will honor the memory of thousands of Navajo and Mescalero Apache people who suffered and died as a result of the forced relocation and internment. Moreover, it will celebrate the official birth of a sovereign nation born of the tragedy of Bosque Redondo."[45] These commemorations reflect Navajo leaders' and their citizens' sense of accomplishment for having retained cultural values and controlled their government in the decades since the Treaty was made.

Juanita, or Asdzáá Tł'ogi (Diné [Navajo]), posing with Indian agent William F. M. Arny and her weaving during her trip to Washington, DC, as part of a delegation led by her husband, Manuelito, 1874. Washington, DC. Photo by Charles M. Bell. National Anthropological Archives, Smithsonian Institution NAA INV 06396900

Weaving on a loom that was acquired by Indian agent William F. M. Arny from Juanita (Asdzáá Tł'ogi), the wife of the Navajo leader Manuelito, during their trip to Washington, DC, as part of a delegation, 1874. Made by Juanita, (1845–1910), Diné (Navajo). New Mexico. Wool yarn, wooden rods. 90.2 × 45.1 cm. Department of Anthropology, National Museum of Natural History, Smithsonian Institution E16494-0

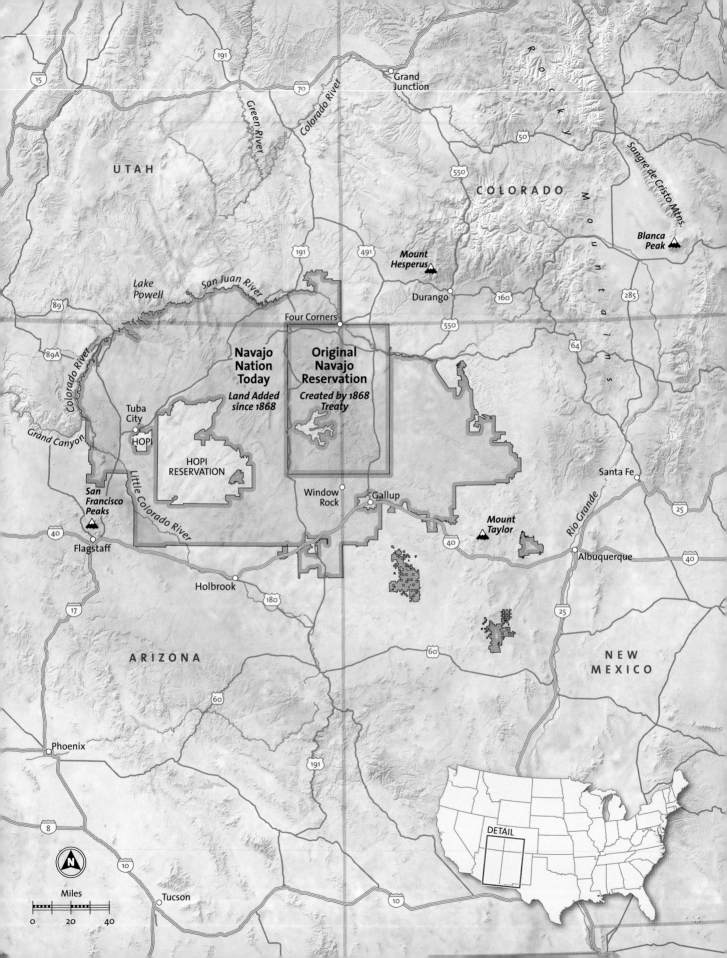

15

191

70

Grand
Junction

191

Green River

Colorado River

50

U T A H

R
O
C
K
Y

50

C O L O R A D O

550

M
o
u
n
t
a
i
n
s

Sangre de Cristo Mtns.

Blanca
Peak

89

Lake
Powell

San Juan River

191

491

550

Mount
Hesperus

Durango

160

550

285

Four Corners

64

89A

Colorado River

Navajo
Nation
Today

**Land Added
since 1868**

Original
Navajo
Reservation

**Created by 1868
Treaty**

Tuba
City

HOPI

Santa Fe

Grand Canyon

Little Colorado River

HOPI
RESERVATION

25

San
Francisco
Peaks

Window
Rock

Gallup

Mount
Taylor

Rio Grande

40

Flagstaff

40

Albuquerque

40

Holbrook

180

25

17

A R I Z O N A

N E W
M E X I C O

60

191

Phoenix

60

8

10

DETAIL

Miles

10

0   20   40

Tucson

The meaning of the 1868 Treaty remains integral to Navajo efforts to determine what sovereignty and self-determination mean to them. As Navajo scholar Lloyd Lee notes, a number of Indigenous intellectuals express the desire of Native Nations to return to health and prosperity based upon Native methods of governance.[46] The Navajo people must decide if and how they will create a nation based upon their own Diné laws, and they must decide what kind of relationship they wish to have with the United States. Lee writes, "One future goal is reclaiming true Navajo nationhood. Prior to colonization, Navajo society had true self-sufficiency. The People could direct their way of life without outside intrusion." In Navajo formulations of sovereignty and self-determination, revaluing the Navajo philosophy of sa'ah nagháí bik'eh hózhóón is key.[47] Certainly, the Navajo Nation's establishment of a Navajo Nation Human Rights Commission shows the desire to pursue a vision of belonging to the international community of nations on an equal basis with other nations.[48]

Every year Navajo citizens celebrate Navajo Treaty Day. Integral to the celebrations are the memories and stories about leaders such as Manuelito, his wife, Juanita (her public Navajo name was Asdzáá Tł'ógi), Barboncito, and others who claimed the rights of their people to live within the four sacred mountains and in a manner of their own choosing. They sacrificed much to ensure the future of their nation and people. That sacrifice has made it possible for the Navajo to maintain and revitalize their culture, assert their sovereignty, and continually negotiate their relationship with the United States.

facing: The Navajo Nation in 2014, including lands that have been added to the reservation created by the 1868 Treaty. Map by Gene Thorp/Cartographic Concepts, Inc. © Smithsonian Institution

Diné (Navajo) concho belt, 1870s–90s. New Mexico. Silver, leather. 113 × 7.5 cm. National Museum of the American Indian 18/2190

The Diné began making silver concho belts like this one right after their release from Bosque Redondo.

IT IS A COMMONPLACE THAT TREATIES WITH INDIAN Nations enabled Americans to wrest a continent from Indigenous Peoples. In about 230 of the roughly four hundred treaties negotiated between 1777 and 1871, Native Nations relinquished large portions of their homelands. Yet a preoccupation with treaties as instruments of colonialism and dispossession obscures the fact that contemporary Native Americans venerate their treaties with the United States and have taken umbrage at non-Natives who would disregard, break, or negate what they consider the inviolable promises their leaders wrung from American representatives at nineteenth-century treaty councils.[1]

Even as they were forced to cede their homelands, forward-thinking Indian leaders insisted on treaty provisions that ensured their people's survival and secured the welfare of future generations. In many treaties, tribal leaders retained their people's right to hunt, fish, and gather natural resources on lands that were being ceded to the United States. Tribal leaders also bargained for their people's right to reserve a diminished portion of their once-vast homelands—territories non-Natives know as Indian reservations. In other treaty provisions, American officials promised to supply tribes with teachers, blacksmiths, manufactured goods, vaccines, and money, sometimes forever.[2]

Yet tribal reverence for treaties transcends government promises of cash, goods, and services; it flows from the fact that treaties recognize Indian Tribes as sovereign nations that have a unique relationship with the federal government. Their status as citizens of distinct nations provides tribal members with a range of unique legal rights, preferences, and immunities that fundamentally distinguish them from other segments of American society, and it provides the political basis of American Indian cultural autonomy.[3]

Long after they were negotiated, treaties are inscribed in Native American communal memory and remain the law of the land. They define tribes as self-governing nations; protect many Indian social, economic, and political rights; and shape relations with state and federal governments. For these and many other reasons, American Indians consider treaties gifts from their ancestors.

Treaties My Ancestors Made for Me

A Family Treaty History

TREATIES ARE, FIRST, A FAMILY MATTER. THE TREATY RELATIONSHIP—OF citizen to nation and of nation to nation—is one of kinship, and the agreed-upon duties and rights are recognized as both familial and national. Treaties represent the people's values and ideals that nations have agreed to uphold and strive toward. They are the hopes and prayers of those who must provide for their people far into the future. The Haudenosaunee instruct their leaders to consider the consequences of their actions unto the seventh generation. On the Plains, leaders of Native Nations are directed to take actions with respect to three generations f ancestors, three generations to come, and their own generation.

My own Cheyenne and Muscogee ancestors made treaties with the United States for all their coming generations. For the Muscogee Confederacy, the treaty making began in 1790; for the Cheyenne Nation it began in 1825. Muscogee and Cheyenne treaty negotiators provided for not only their Indigenous descendants but also all the non-Native people who came from other parts of the world and live on our original lands or within the borders set by our treaties. Our treaty relationships and rights are exercised regularly, and we honor the treaties today. What follows is a brief history of treaties in my family. I am Tsistsistas (Cheyenne) on my mother's side—a Cheyenne citizen of the Cheyenne and Arapaho Tribes in Oklahoma—and Hodulgee Muscogee (Wind Clan Creek), Nuyakv Ground, on my father's side.

MUSCOGEE NATIONS' TREATIES WITH THE UNITED STATES

Before encountering Europeans, an alliance of mostly Muscogee Peoples (Creek Nations) had been created in the Southeast by treaties among numerous smaller nations such as the Alabama, Euchee, Koasati, and

Miccosukee. The alliance had also negotiated treaties with the Choctaw, Chickasaw, Cherokee, Haudenosaunee, Shawnee, and other Native Nations and confederations. By the time its leaders first met with representatives of the fledgling United States, the Muscogee Confederacy had forged treaties or trade agreements with Britain, France, and Spain.

The Muscogee Confederacy's treaty relationship with the U.S. government began in 1790. President George Washington sent letters to a Muscogee leader, Alexander McGillivray, inviting the Muscogee (Creek) to send a delegation to New York for treaty making. McGillivray (1750–1793) was Hodulgee (Wind Clan) on his Muscogee mother's side and Clann Mhic Gillebrath on his Scottish father's side. Raised in the Muscogee town of Little Tallassee, along the Coosa River in present-day Alabama, and in Charleston, South Carolina, he spoke the many Muscogee dialects as well as English, Greek, and Latin. He had been the lead negotiator of the 1784 Treaty of Pensacola with Spain.

Known as an eloquent speaker and writer, McGillivray wrote a letter in 1787 to the congressionally appointed superintendent of the Muscogee, James White, describing his experiences in attempting to treat with Americans the previous year.

We warned the Georgians of the dangerous consequences that would certainly attend the settling of the lands in question. Our just remonstrances were treated with contempt, and these lands were soon filled with settlers. The nation, justly alarmed at the encroachments, resolved to use force to maintain their rights; yet, being averse to the shedding of the blood of a people whom we would rather consider as friends, we made another effort to awaken in them a sense of justice and equity. But we found, from experience, that entreaty could not prevail, and parties of warriors were sent to drive off the intruders, but were instructed to shed blood only where self-preservation made it necessary. . . .

[Five months later] we were invited by Commissioners of the State of Georgia to meet them. . . . [They professed] a sincere desire for an amicable adjustment of our disputes, and pledg[ed] their sacred honors for the safety and good treatment of all those that should attend and meet them. It not being convenient for many of us to go . . . a few, from motives of curiosity, attended. They were surprised to find an armed body of men, prepared for and professing hostile intentions. Apprehensions for personal safety induced those chiefs to subscribe to every demand that was asked by the army and the Commissioners. Lands were again demanded, and the lives of some of our chiefs were required, as well as those of some innocent traders, as a sacrifice, to appease their anger. Assassins have been employed to effect some part of their atrocious purposes. If I fall by the hand of such, I shall fall the victim of the noblest of causes, that of maintaining the just rights of my country. I aspire to the honest ambition of meriting the appellation of the preserver of my country, equally with the chiefs among you, whom, from acting on such principles, you have exalted to the highest pitch of glory. And if, after every peaceable mode of obtaining a redress of grievances proved fruitless, a recourse to arms to obtain it be a mark of the savage, and not of the soldier, what savages must the Americans be.[4]

John Trumbull (1756–1843). *Hopothle Mico, or the Talassee King of the Creeks*, 1790. Pencil, paper. 12.7 × 9.8 cm. Charles Allen Munn Collection, Fordham University Library, Bronx, New York

John Trumbull (1756–1843). *Hysac, or the Woman's Man*, 1790. Pencil, paper. 12.7 × 9.8 cm. Charles Allen Munn Collection, Fordham University Library, Bronx, New York

The Muscogee delegation to New York comprised at least twenty-four men. They traveled overland to Savannah and then mostly by water to Washington's home in Virginia before landing at Wall Street on the south end of Manhattan. Entering the city, they received an extraordinary welcome as diplomats. Gunboats in the harbor fired salutes, and some three hundred cheering members of the Tammany Society, all dressed as "Indians," escorted the Muscogee leaders to Washington's New York residence.

Artist John Trumbull, who had painted the now-iconic portrait of Washington in his dress military uniform, also sketched "by stealth" five of the Muscogee delegates as Washington dined with them during their visit. Trumbull wrote in his autobiography that the Muscogee men "possessed a dignity of manner, form, countenance and expression, worthy of Roman senators."

Trumbull recounted the president's practical joke, which had made the Muscogee leaders wary of the painter's art. Washington opened a door for them on his full-length painting, which hung on the other side. "I had been desirous of obtaining portraits of some of these principal men," wrote Trumbull, "but after this I found it impracticable; they had received the impression, that there must be magic in an art which could render a smooth flat surface so like to a real man."[5]

In seeking an alliance with the Muscogee Confederacy, Washington was trying to left to right:

John Trumbull (1756–1843). *Fuskatche Mico, or The Birdtail King of the Cusitahs*, 1790. Engraving from the artist's original drawing, published in John Trumbull, *Autobiography, Reminiscences, and Letters of John Trumbull from 1756 to 1841* (1841). Length 23 cm. General Collection, Beinecke Rare Book and Manuscript Library, Yale University, New Haven, Connecticut 1391003

John Trumbull (1756–1843). *John—A Creek*, 1790. Engraving from the artist's original drawing, published in John Trumbull, *Autobiography, Reminiscences, and Letters of John Trumbull from 1756 to 1841* (1841). Length 23 cm. General Collection, Beinecke Rare Book and Manuscript Library, Yale University, New Haven, Connecticut 1391001

John Trumbull (1756–1843). *Stimafutchki, or Good-Humor—of the Coosades, Creeks.* Engraving from the artist's original drawing, published in John Trumbull, *Autobiography, Reminiscences, and Letters of John Trumbull from 1756 to 1841* (1841). Length 23 cm. General Collection, Beinecke Rare Book and Manuscript Library, Yale University, New Haven, Connecticut 1391002

expand and secure the southwestern boundaries of the United States; to guard against threats by the English, French, and Spanish; and to appease the escalating demands for Indian lands by Georgia and other powerful states. The Muscogee Nations wanted to ally with the United States for protection against further threats and encroachments by Georgia and Euro-American settlers.

On July 22, 1790, the new United States had just enacted the first federal Indian law, P.L. 1-33, which was intended to regulate trade and intercourse with Indian tribes. Section 4 reads, "And be it enacted and declared, That no sale of lands made by any Indians, or any nation or tribe of Indians within the United States, shall be valid to any person or persons, or to any state, whether having the right of pre-emption to such lands or not, unless the same shall be made and duly executed at some public treaty, held under the authority of the United States."[6] Washington explained the new law in this way to the Seneca Nation on December 29, 1790: "Here, then, is the security for the remainder of your lands. No State, nor person, can purchase your lands, unless at some public treaty held under the authority of the United States. The General Government will never consent to your being defrauded, but it will protect you in all your just rights."[7]

The Treaty of New York of August 7, 1790, was the first treaty with a Native Nation ratified under the U.S. Constitution and the last action of the Senate while New York City was the U.S. capital. In the Treaty the Muscogee Confederacy and the United States pledged peace and friendship forever. McGillivray and Secretary of War Henry Knox drafted much of the language. The Treaty contains an agreement, secret at the

Daggett, Hinman & Co. Sc.

time, for Muscogee abrogation of its Treaty with Spain, which had granted to Spain exclusive trade privileges with Muscogee Peoples. Only the signatories and the Senate knew of this provision until the Muscogee delegates had time to return home and inform their people that breaking the Treaty could mean retaliation or war with Spain, neither of which came to pass. In the Treaty of New York the Muscogee relinquished certain disputed land along the Oconee River that Georgia had previously given to immigrants, and were provided an annual payment. Additionally, as part of a "civilization" plan for all Indians to become full-time farmers, the United States provided farm animals, agricultural tools, and four farm advisor-interpreters.

The Treaty of New York limited British as well as Spanish influence on the southwestern frontier. It also sought to end Georgia's unilateral actions, laws, and jurisdiction regarding Muscogee people and territory. It specified that Muscogee people traveling in federal territory and Americans traveling in Muscogee territory would be under U.S. law rather than state law. It specified that Americans settling in Muscogee territory would be under Muscogee laws: "If any citizen of the United States, or other person not being an Indian, shall attempt to settle on any of the Creek lands, such person shall forfeit the protection of the United States, and the Creeks may punish him or not, as they please."[8] As Knox wrote to Washington on the same day the Treaty was signed, Georgia asserted that it had acquired Muscogee lands through what it called valid treaties, while the Muscogee argued "against the validity of the said treaties."[9] The Treaty of New York and the Indian Trade and Intercourse Act of 1790 did not validate

George Washington President of the United States of America.

To all to whom these Presents shall come, Greeting: Whereas a treaty of peace and friendship between the United States of America and the Creek nation of Indians was made and concluded on the seventh day of the present month of August by Henry Knox, Secretary for the department of war...

Article 1st...

Article 2nd...

Article 3rd...

Article 4th...

Article 5th...

Article 6th...

Article 7th...

Article 8th...

Article 9th...

Article 10th...

Article 11th...

Article 12th...

Article 13th...

Article 14th...

Given at the city of New York the thirteenth day of August in the year of our Lord One thousand seven hundred and ninety and in the fifteenth year of the Sovereignty and Independence of the United States.

G. Washington
By the President

state transactions as treaties. Because the 1790 Treaty affirmed that the disposition of Muscogee lands within Georgia was under federal rather than state jurisdiction, it reduced the size of Georgia and led indirectly to the establishment of Alabama and Mississippi.

After treaty making was concluded, the Muscogee delegates conducted a private ceremony in New York to consecrate the Treaty. Upon returning to their towns and ceremonial grounds, they related the history and provisions of the treaty and their experiences in New York. There were two tribal towns/ceremonial grounds with the same name, Tvpafkv, or Heart of the Fire. One town/ground decided to commemorate the Treaty with a new name: Nuyakv, pronounced "nu-yaw-kah," which is what the delegates heard when many English-speaking people in New York said, "New Yorker." Nuyakv remains the only ground that starts its fire with the center of the oak, the Heart of the Fire. The Muscogee delegates to the 1790 Treaty gathering truly are the founding fathers of Nuyakv. My father's and his mother's family traces back through Faulena and Yaha Fixico, and Silwar and Louie Mikey, all of Nuyakv.

In 1790, Nuyakv was in territory that would become Alabama. Indian tribes fought against militant encroachment on their territories, mostly by American citizens, and were forced to fight for or against the United States in its 1812 war with the British. In present-day eastern Alabama, near Nuyakv, Muscogee soldiers fought on both sides of

facing and details: Treaty of New York. August 7, 1790. New York. 143.5 × 76.2 cm. Parchment, ink, wafer, fabric ribbon fragments. National Archives and Records Administration, Washington, DC

The signatures of the Muscogee delegates, grouped by town, are at lower right. Alexander McGillivray signed first, and the rest made marks by their names. George Washington, Thomas Jefferson, and Henry Knox signed at the bottom of the document.

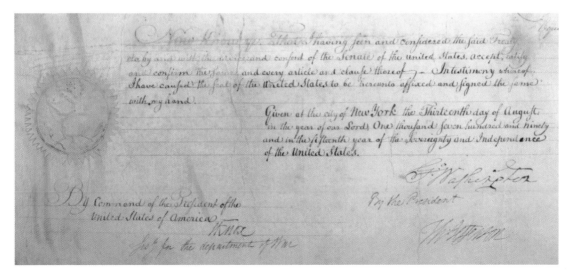

the Battle of Horseshoe Bend on March 27, 1814. In the battle, General Andrew Jackson fought a thousand Muscogee Red Sticks—the faction that sided with the British and Spanish in the War of 1812—killing more than eight hundred of them with the help of Muscogee, Cherokee, Chickasaw, and Choctaw allies. Jackson and his troops skinned and severed body parts from Red Sticks on the field, using the cut-off noses to count 557 dead. Approximately three hundred more Red Stick fighters had died trying to escape across the Tallapoosa River. The Red Sticks had opposed the United States for its failure to fulfill its Treaty promises. They had joined the treaty resistance led by the Shawnee leader Tecumseh and his brother, known as the Prophet. The Muscogee who fought against the United States were fighting for treaty rights that Americans had ignored, while the Muscogee on the U.S. side were upholding their obligations under the 1790 Treaty.

Jackson's victories in the Battle of Horseshoe Bend and the Battle of New Orleans propelled him to the Senate and White House. In the Senate Committee on Indian Affairs, he, his former aide-de-camp, and other former Indian fighters developed the Indian Removal Act, which he signed into law in 1830, a year after becoming president.

On August 9, 1814, Jackson forced the Muscogee Nation, including those who had been his allies at Horseshoe Bend four months earlier, to sign the Treaty of Fort Jackson, which ceded to the United States 23 million acres of land in Alabama and Georgia. This coerced treaty was signed near Wetumka, Alabama, at Hickory Ground (Oce Vpofv), the mother ground to Nuyakv and the capital of the Muscogee Confederacy. Jackson signed for the United States. The treaty reads more like a heavy-handed scold than a document of diplomacy. It punishes "hostile Creeks" and Creek allies alike, berating those leaders who, "disregarding the genuine spirit of existing treaties, suffered themselves to be instigated to violations of their national honor, and the respect due to a part of their own nation faithful to the United States and the principles of humanity, by impostures [impostors] denominating themselves as Prophets, and by the duplicity and misrepresentations of foreign emissaries, whose governments are at war, open or understood, with the United States."[10]

Britain and the United States signed the Treaty of Ghent four months later, ending the War of 1812. The United States agreed "forthwith to restore to such Tribes or Nations respectively all the possessions, rights, and privileges which they may have enjoyed or been entitled to in one thousand eight hundred and eleven previous to such hostilities."[11] The Muscogee lands taken in the Treaty of Fort Jackson, however, were not restored. Twenty years later—following the Georgia gold rush of 1829, the clamor of the southern states for Indian removal, and Jackson's 1830 Indian Removal Act—most Muscogee were marched to Indian Territory (present-day Oklahoma) at bayonet point.

Even though they had not signed a removal treaty, as had been mandated by the Indian Removal Act, the Muscogee were wrenched from their homelands, property, sacred places, and ancestors, and funneled into unfamiliar territory 750 miles away. The fracturing of the Muscogee Confederacy accomplished one of Jackson's goals: to break apart large Native Nations' social and military alliances. Muscogee Peoples and other removed nations still suffer the collective and individual effects of being forced

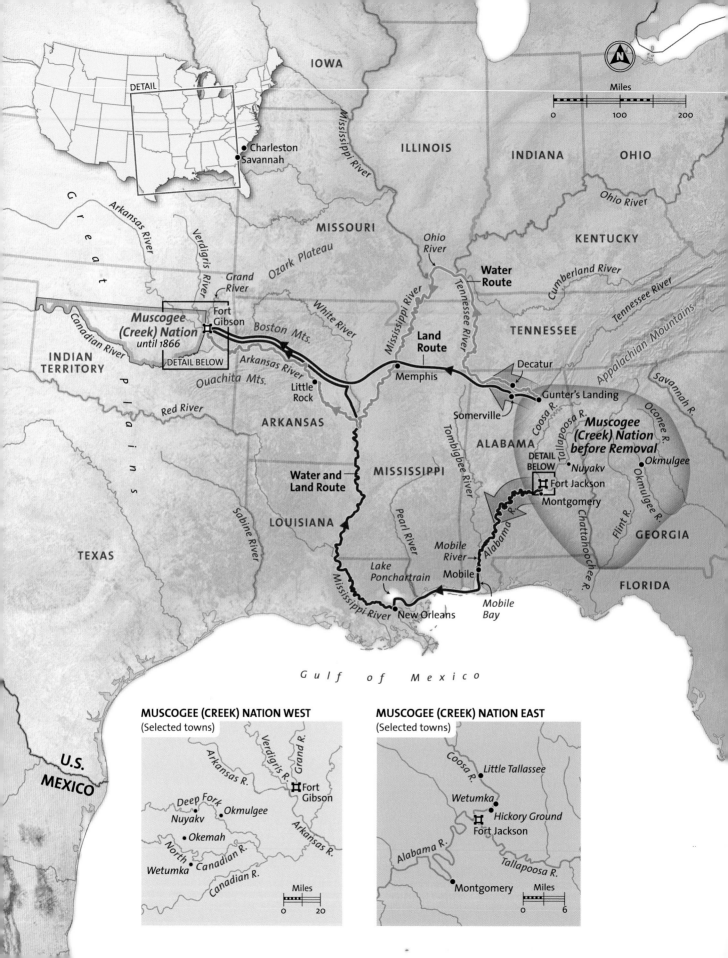

DETAIL

Charleston
Savannah

IOWA

ILLINOIS

INDIANA

OHIO

Miles

0   100   200

Mississippi River

Arkansas River

Great

Verdigris River

Grand
River

Ozark Plateau

MISSOURI

Ohio River

*Ohio
River*

**Water
Route**

KENTUCKY

Cumberland River

Tennessee River

Tennessee River

Muscogee
(Creek) Nation
until 1866

Fort
Gibson

Boston Mts.

White River

Mississippi River

Tennessee River

TENNESSEE

Appalachian Mountains

INDIAN
TERRITORY

Canadian River

Arkansas River

DETAIL BELOW

Ouachita Mts.

Little
Rock

Memphis

**Land
Route**

Decatur

Gunter's Landing

Somerville

Coosa R.

Savannah R.

**Muscogee
(Creek) Nation
before Removal**

Red River

ARKANSAS

Tallapoosa R.

Oconee R.

Okmulgee

P
l
a
i
n
s

Tombigbee River

ALABAMA

DETAIL
BELOW

Nuyakv

Fort Jackson

Okmulgee R.

**Water and
Land Route**

MISSISSIPPI

Montgomery

Chattahoochee R.

Flint R.

GEORGIA

Sabine River

LOUISIANA

Pearl River

Alabama R.

FLORIDA

TEXAS

Lake
Ponchartrain

*Mobile
River*

Mobile

Mississippi River

New Orleans

*Mobile
Bay*

U.S.
MEXICO

Gulf   of   Mexico

MUSCOGEE (CREEK) NATION WEST
(Selected towns)

Arkansas R.

Verdigris R.

Grand R.

Fort
Gibson

Deep Fork

Okmulgee

Nuyakv

Arkansas R.

Okemah

North Canadian R.

Wetumka

Canadian R.

Miles

0   20

MUSCOGEE (CREEK) NATION EAST
(Selected towns)

Coosa R.

Little Tallassee

Wetumka

Hickory Ground

Fort Jackson

Alabama R.

Montgomery

Tallapoosa R.

Miles

0   6

against their will to move from their homelands and walk for months to unfamiliar lands. Some say that the reason most of the people of removed nations in Oklahoma today are Republican is that Jackson was a Democrat.

Muscogee ceremonial leaders recite the history that their ancestors "carried the Fires on [their] backs" to Indian Territory and arranged the ceremonial grounds there in the same proximity to one another as they had been in the Old Fields. The Nuyakv Ground, named in honor of the Treaty of New York, was reestablished in Indian Territory, near Okemah and Okmulgee, the new capital of the Muscogee (Creek) Nation.

THE CHEYENNE NATION'S TREATIES WITH THE UNITED STATES

The Tsistsistas (Cheyenne) Nation made treaties with many Native Nations—including the Anishinaabe, Apache, Arapaho, Assiniboine, Blackfeet, Caddo, Comanche, Crow, Dakota, Fox, Kickapoo, Kiowa, Lakota, Nakota, Pawnee, Sak, Shoshone, Sutaio and Ute—before ever meeting Europeans or Americans. The Cheyenne Nation made treaties with the United States in 1825, 1851, 1863, 1867, and 1868. My ancestors helped make all these treaties.

The Treaty of July 6, 1825, was a first-contact treaty of peace and friendship. The Cheyenne Nation agreed to trade exclusively with the Americans. The Treaty contained "deliver the bad men" provisions, stating that the Cheyenne would apprehend any foreigner who attempted to trade or treat with the Cheyenne Nation and deliver that person to federal officials to be dealt with according to federal law. Bad Americans and bad Cheyenne would be delivered to their respective nations for punishment or restitution.

The Treaty of September 17, 1851, was made by the Native Nations of the Plains and the United States. Known as the Treaty of Long Meadows and the Fort Laramie Treaty, it also was called the Great Horse Creek Treaty, because the vast gathering of more than ten thousand people camped on the meadowlands where the Horse Creek met the North Platte River, in present-day western Nebraska. Native people called it the Great Smoke because of the extraordinary number of pipe carriers and medicine makers who conducted ceremonies and consecrated treaty agreements by smoking and burning sacred cedar, tobacco, sage, sweetgrass, and other medicines.

The Treaty pledged lasting peace among the United States and the Arapaho, Arikara, Assiniboine, Cheyenne, Crow, Hidatsa, Mandan, and Sioux (Lakota and Dakota) Nations. As much as this was a treaty with the United States, it was even more a treaty among the Native Nations, some of which had been making treaties with one another for centuries. In this Treaty, the Native Nations set and confirmed territories and boundaries, agreed on joint-use areas, and reserved rights to hunt, fish, gather, and travel in their traditional and treaty places on the Plains. The Native Peoples who made and celebrated the Horse Creek Treaty understood that everyone promised to live in peace and respect one another's territory and security forever, and that they would resolve differences in a friendly and good way.

The Great Horse Creek Treaty covered 1.1 million square miles of Native Nations' lands. Today, these lands are home to much smaller reservations surrounded by such states in the American west as Colorado, Montana, Nebraska, North Dakota, South

facing: This map shows the approximate locations of the Muscogee (Creek) Nation before and after its population was removed from the Southeast to Indian Territory (present-day Oklahoma), and it traces the three primary routes along which the removal took place. Between 1827 and 1838, about nineteen thousand Muscogee people were forced to leave their homeland. Four thousand more left voluntarily or were transported as prisoners. Adapted from Christopher D. Haveman, "The Removal of the Creek Indians, 1825–1838," PhD diss., Auburn University, 2009. Map by Gene Thorp/Cartographic Concepts, Inc. © Smithsonian Institution

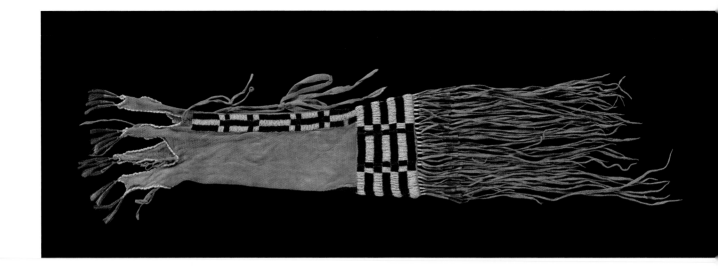

Dakota, and Wyoming. The U.S. treaty commissioners wanted to establish safe passage on trails only the width of a Conestoga wagon for Americans rushing across the
plains toward gold on the West Coast; they also wanted safety for the planned transcontinental railroad, but they did not explain this. The Native Nations' leaders considered these roads to be tiny tracks across an endless land and a small price to pay for
protection against American encroachment, so they granted the United States the right
to establish roads and build military posts in their territories. Even though it had been
foretold—by the Tsistsistas prophet Sweet Medicine, for one—few Native treaty makers
could have imagined the dramatic and tragic impact of the railroads, gold fever, buffalo
slaughter, foreign diseases, and the myriad settlers who would cross and invade tribal
and treaty lands.

Each Native Nation at the Great Smoke spoke a distinct language. The non-Native
military officers, scribes, clergymen, and mountain men spoke English, French, and/
or German. The mountain men and missionaries also could converse in a few tribal
languages. While many Indian and non-Indian people spoke two, three, four, or more
languages, it is unlikely that any one person could know all the languages spoken in
the treaty camps. Native Peoples on the Plains had communicated with one another
for a very long time with the aid of sign language. Native sign-language experts as well
as the mountain men and missionary interpreters relied heavily on sign language to
translate, ask questions, and arrive at consensus.

Under the 1851 Treaty, the Cheyenne and Arapaho Nations together reserved 51.2
million acres of land in present-day Colorado, Kansas, Nebraska, and Wyoming, to
the south of Crow and Sioux lands. After the Pike's Peak gold rush of 1858, Denver City
and other mining camps were settled illegally on the treaty lands. Over the next four
decades of land division, land seizures, and nearly successful genocide, the Cheyenne
and Arapaho lands were reduced to five hundred thousand acres in Indian Territory,
which have been further pared down to fewer than twenty thousand acres in Oklahoma today.

White Antelope, Alights on a Cloud, and Little Chief (all Cheyenne), 1852. St. Louis, Missouri. Copies by A. Zeno Shindler of a daguerreotype by John H. Fitzgibbon. National Anthropological Archives, Smithsonian Institution NAA INV 06105400

This photograph of three Cheyenne leaders who were present at the Horse Creek Treaty likely was taken as they were returning home after having participated in a post-treaty delegation that visited the East in 1851–52.

As the United States was being torn apart by the Civil War, President Abraham Lincoln and his military and civilian officials were searching far and wide for Union allies, or for those who would pledge their neutrality. The Confederate states had reached out to Native Nations and signed treaties with some. As a sign of peace and friendship, Lincoln sent emissaries to the Native Nations on the southern Plains—Apache, Arapaho, Caddo, Cheyenne, Comanche, and Kiowa—inviting tribal leaders to meet with him at the White House. He had peace medals struck for them in the event that they could reach an agreement. Washington's *Daily Morning Chronicle* reported, "The Indians are fine-looking men. They have all the hard and cruel lines in their faces which we might expect in savages, but they are evidently men of intelligence and force of character. They were both dignified and cordial in their manner, and listened to everything with great interest."[12]

The unwritten Treaty of March 27, 1863, was made in the White House by President Lincoln and chiefs of the southern Plains Nations. The chiefs had chosen Cheyenne chief Starving Bear, or Lean Bear (Awoninahku), and Comanche chief Ten Bears to represent them as heads of the delegation. Starving Bear was the older brother of Chief Bull Bear, my mother's great-grandfather. As young men, they had been witnesses at the Great Smoke, with young men of other nations, such as Sitting Bull (Hunkpapa Lakota) and Crazy Horse (Oglala Lakota). The brothers were very tall—newspapers reported that Bull Bear was between six feet seven and seven feet tall—and suffered from vertigo, a continuing family ailment. Starving Bear had an attack of vertigo during the meeting with Lincoln and had to speak while seated on a chair rather than standing up, as is customary among Cheyenne people.

Imp. Ch. Chardon aine __ Paris.

Ferd. Delannoy sc.

LINCOLN RECEVANT LES INDIENS COMANCHES.

Ferdinand Delanoy (act. 1850). *Lincoln Recevant Les Indiens Comanches,* 1863. Hand-colored engraving. 33.7 × 39.4 cm. Indiana Historical Society P0406

This French print depicts Abraham Lincoln welcoming a delegation of Plains Indians to the East Room of the White House on March 27, 1863.

Starving Bear spoke for the delegation, reaffirming its friendship. However, he said, there were many *veho* (spiders/white men) in their countries, where they were not supposed to be, and they were not peaceful people. "It is the object of the government to be at peace with you," Lincoln said, "and with all our red brethren. We constantly endeavor to be so. We make treaties with you, and will try to observe them; and if our children should sometimes behave badly, and violate these treaties, it is against our wish. You know it is not always possible for any father to have his children do precisely as he wishes them to do." Lincoln described the great numbers, land, and wealth of the world's "pale-faced" people. Smithsonian secretary Joseph Henry rolled out a large globe and told the chiefs that the world was covered with white people, who were coming to this land. To become as rich as their "pale-faced brethren," said Lincoln, Native people would have to give up their ways, such as hunting and eating wild game,

and take up farming. They would need to become more peaceful, like his people, who "are not, as a race, so much disposed to fight and kill one another as our red brethren." Apparently, he did not see the irony of his assertion, in light of the bluecoats and gray-coats who were waging war all around Washington.[13]

The president asked for the southern Plains Nations' neutrality in the War Between the States, and he received it. The chiefs promised they would not join with the Confederacy and would uphold their treaties of peace and friendship with the United States. The chiefs asked for relief from the white buffalo hunters, gold miners, and settlers who were swarming their treaty lands in greater numbers every day.[14] Lincoln promised new treaties and lands away from the growing population of immigrants. These were the terms of the unwritten Treaty they struck that day, according to oral history handed down in each of the Native Nations, including the Cheyenne, and in the descendant families, including mine.

Starving Bear returned home and was hunting buffalo with another Cheyenne chief, Black Kettle, in Kansas in May 1864, when he was accosted by a Colorado Volunteers militia that was under orders from its commander, Colonel John M. Chivington, to "kill Cheyennes whenever and wherever found."[15] They murdered Starving Bear as he was wearing his peace medal and showing them a letter of safe transit from Lincoln.

The southern Plains delegation in the White House conservatory, March 27, 1863. Washington, DC. Photo attributed to Mathew Brady Studio. The delegation included (front row, from left) Cheyenne chiefs War Bonnet, Standing in the Water, and Starving Bear, and Yellow Wolf (Kiowa). Standing, at left, is William Simpson Smith, an interpreter, and Samuel G. Colley, an Indian agent. The identities of the others are unknown. Library of Congress LC-DIG-ppmsca-19914

In November of that year, the Colorado Volunteers executed the Sand Creek Massacre, killing the other Cheyenne chiefs who had met with Lincoln. Cheyenne chief White Antelope also was murdered and mutilated at Sand Creek; he was the eldest chief in the peace camp and had signed the 1851 Horse Creek Treaty. Five months later, Lincoln was murdered, as well. Little more than a year after they had negotiated the unwritten Treaty, the president and all the Cheyenne chiefs had been killed.

The Sand Creek Massacre was the subject of numerous military and congressional investigations, but no one was ever punished for it. The report of the 1865 joint Senate-House Committee on the Conduct of the War described the events this way: "And then the scene of murder and barbarity began—men, women, and children were indiscriminately slaughtered. In a few minutes all the Indians were flying over the plain in terror and confusion. . . . From the sucking babe to the old warrior, all who were overtaken were deliberately murdered. . . . The soldiers indulged in acts of barbarity of the most revolting character, such, it is to be hoped, as never before disgraced the acts of men claiming to be civilized."

The Treaty of October 28, 1867, was signed at the Medicine Lodge Creek in Kansas. As leader of the Hotamétaneo'o, or Dog Men Society, which comprised more than half of Cheyenne families, Chief Bull Bear (Ho-Dooh-Nocco, or O-to-ah-nacco) was the first signatory. No one would sign before Bull Bear did, because they knew that no treaty would be binding without the support of the Dog Men. The Dog Men camp was separate from the main treaty camp; and newspapers reported that the Dog Men warriors made a dramatic entrance into the camp each morning, riding in full regalia, their horses galloping at full speed and raising great clouds of dust.

The Cheyenne and Arapaho Nations wanted the new treaty territory promised by Lincoln, so they would not have to live with the constant encroachment of gold rushers and other Americans in Colorado. They were among the very few nations that actually wanted to move to Indian Territory, and the Treaty established the Cheyenne and Arapaho Reservation there.[16] The Cheyenne and Arapaho Nations also entered into a Treaty signed at Fort Laramie on May 10, 1868, which provided Cheyenne and Arapaho citizens with the choice between lands within the reservation borders established by the Medicine Lodge Creek Treaty (in present-day Oklahoma) and lands in the north (in present-day Montana for the Cheyenne and Wyoming for the Arapaho). Like many other treaties, the Fort Laramie Treaty also included a civilization plan.[17]

No sooner had the ink dried on the 1867 and 1868 Treaties than Chief Black Kettle's camp on the Washita River was attacked at dawn in November 1868, killing many Cheyenne people, including Black Kettle, who had escaped the Sand Creek Massacre four years earlier. The attack was part of the overall campaign against Plains Indians, which was conducted under the scorched-earth policies of Major General Philip H. Sheridan (who spawned the phrase, "The only good Indian is a dead one," by saying, "The only good Indians I ever saw were dead") and the notorious Lieutenant Colonel George Armstrong Custer. Their soldiers chased Native people, including my family, around the plains, killing most of them and giving away or burning their tipis, sacred objects, clothing, and anything else they left behind while trying to save their children,

On the part of the Cheyennes

O-to-ah-nac-co.	Bull Bear	his	+ mark	seal
Mokie-tav-a-to.	Black Kettle	his	+ mark	seal
Nac-co-hah-ket.	Little Bear	his	+ mark	seal
Mo-a-vo-va-ast	Spotted Elk	his	+ mark	seal
Is-se-sa-von-ne-be	Buffalo Chief	his	+ mark	seal
Vip-po-nah	Slim Face	his	+ mark	seal
Wo-pah-ah	Grey Head	his	+ mark	seal
O-ni-hah-Ket	Little Rock	his	+ mark	seal
Ma-mo-ki, or	Curly Hair	his	+ mark	seal
O-to-ah-has-tis.	Tall Bull	his	+ mark	seal
Wo-po-ham. or	White Horse	his	+ mark	seal
Hah-Ket-home-mah,	Little Robe	his	+ mark	seal
Min-nin-ne-wah	Whirlwind	his	+ mark	seal
Mo-yan-histe-histow	Heap of Birds	his	+ mark	seal

On the part of the Arapahoes

Little Raven	his	+ mark	(seal)
Yellow Bear	his	+ mark	(seal)
Storm	his	+ mark	(seal)
White Rabbit	his	+ mark	(seal)
Spotted Wolf	his	+ mark	(seal)
Little Big Mouth	his	+ mark	(seal)
Young Colt	his	+ mark	(seal)
Tall Bear	his	+ mark	(seal)

21

Treaty with the Cheyenne and Arapaho, page 21. October 28, 1867. Medicine Lodge Creek, Kansas. Calendar paper, ink. 27.9 × 21.6 cm. National Archives and Records Administration, Washington, DC

The first signature on this page of the treaty is Bull Bear's.

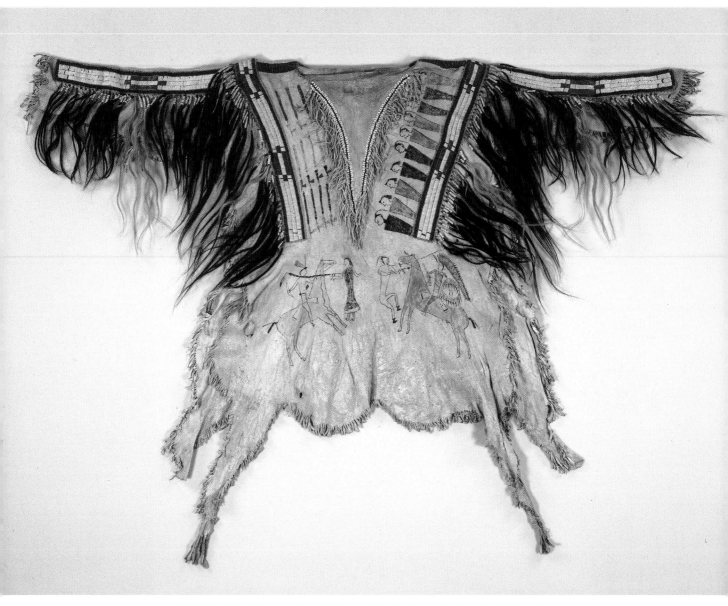

Tsistsistas/Suhai (Cheyenne) man's shirt, ca. 1860. Fort Laramie, Wyoming? Hide, quills,
glass pony beads, human hair, horsehair, sinew, tree pitch/gum, paint. 102 × 150 cm.
National Museum of the American Indian 8/8034

elders, and themselves. After the attack at Washita, Custer shot all the ponies, burned the village, and delivered the scalps of Black Kettle and others to Sheridan "as trophies of the Battle of the Washita." Sheridan later reported it as a great triumph over the "savage butchers" and "cruel marauders."[18]

The Cheyenne and Arapaho signatories to the 1867 Medicine Lodge Creek Treaty believed that, in addition to establishing the reservation in Indian Territory, they also had secured the freedom to hunt, fish, and travel in their original territory. Contemporaneous news reports documented the same agreement, but that information does not appear in the written Treaty. The omission was at the core of the conflict that occurred when the people were starving on the reservation and Cheyenne hunters went off-reservation in search of buffalo. As white buffalo hunters were slaughtering New Mexico and Texas herds, Sheridan's reaction was, "Let them kill, skin, and sell until the buffalo is exterminated, as it is the only way to bring lasting peace and allow civilization to advance." According to army estimates, 7.5 million buffalo were killed between 1872 and 1874.[19]

Eventually, the desperate situation led the Cheyenne, together with the Apache, Arapaho, Comanche, and Kiowa Nations, to strike out for the Good Buffalo Road, Palo Duro Canyon, in the Staked Plain of northern Texas. This was the start of the Red River War of 1874–75, which ended in the killing of a thousand ponies and a surrender procession of Cheyenne chiefs in order from the eldest to the youngest: Stone Calf, Bull Bear, Eagle Head, Gray Beard, Little Wolf, Many Magpies, and others.

These deplorable conditions, plus white miners digging for gold in the sacred Black Hills, also led to the Battle of the Little Bighorn on June 25–26, 1876. Bull Bear; his wives, Buffalo Wallow and Pipe Woman; and many of our Cheyenne, Lakota, and Arapaho relatives were in the north for ceremonies and fought Custer's Seventh Cavalry at the Greasy Grass (Little Bighorn) River. They believed then and we believe now that the Americans broke the treaties by swarming the Black Hills and that the Native alliance won the day for treaty rights.

In the Cheyenne and Muscogee Nations, our Treaties are part of our identities. They are family and national histories and futures. They are blood spilled on the plains and etched in the trails of the Southeast. Americans owe a great debt of gratitude to our peoples and the Treaties for the United States we know today. I and my next generations owe a great debt to our ancestors and the Treaties they made for us.

to tribal sovereignty, though guaranteed by treaties with the United States, seemed incongruous with the unified nation-state that emerged after the Civil War.[1] Government officials, missionaries, and even those who considered themselves to be "friends of the Indian" shared the conviction that tribal governments and cultures had no place in modern America. That consensus underpinned the federal government's "civilization" program—a vast, multifaceted initiative to forcibly assimilate Native Americans into mainstream American culture. By consolidating Native people on reservations, government agents and religious missionaries attempted to coerce Indians into exchanging their tribal religions and cultures as well as their communal form of property holding for Christian worship and farming on individually owned lands.[2] The assault on tribalism took special aim at Native children, many of whom were wrenched from their families and sent to far-away boarding schools, where educators attempted to eradicate all traces of tribal culture and identity and replace them with the values of white society.[3]

Few Indian Tribes escaped the juggernaut of forced cultural assimilation, removal, land loss, and consolidation that upended tribal communities during the nineteenth century.[4] Even the Pawnee, longtime allies of the United States, found themselves driven into dependency and deprived of control over much of their own lives and land. The toll on Native populations and cultures was widespread and staggering. In 1890 the U.S. Census Bureau counted fewer than three hundred thousand Native Americans—roughly half the population that had inhabited the continental United States a century earlier, and perhaps one-tenth of those who had lived there in 1492. By 1900 the precipitous decline of the American Indian population helped promote the myth of the "vanishing" Indian: U.S. expansion, it was thought, had largely eradicated Indian people and consigned tribal cultures to the trash heap of history.[5]

Yet the emergence of modern America fell short of wiping out Indigenous Peoples or their cultures.[6] During the twentieth century, tribal leaders, wisdom keepers, clan mothers, and activists—many of whom, as children, had attended Indian boarding schools that sought to detribalize them—embraced tribal cultures that had been targeted for destruction. Rejecting the ethos of assimilation, many tribal citizens worked against all odds to retain Indigenous values and traditions, maintain and strengthen their communities, and secure a future for themselves as a distinct people in modern America. In so doing, these tribal stalwarts made cultural survival a central theme of American Indian life in the twentieth century.[7]

The Betrayal of "Civilization" in United States–Native Nations Diplomacy

A Case Study of Pawnee Treaties and Cultural Genocide

EVEN BEFORE SO-CALLED CIVILIZATION REGULATIONS BEGAN IN THE 1880S to subject American Indians to cultural genocide, U.S. government agents and missionaries on the Great Plains endeavored with varying degrees of success to carry out a massive campaign of assimilation. With settler society poised to devour them, the nineteenth-century Pawnee, like other Native Nations, had tough choices to make regarding their physical and cultural survival. Confronted by foreigners convinced of their own cultural and intellectual superiority, they could fight, take flight, or yield— or a combination thereof—to maintain their culture, independence, and sovereignty. Pawnee leaders initially hoped that diplomacy and treaties, legally binding agreements between nations, might mitigate the harm. Although they rejected the false premise of white American supremacy, they faced economic hardships: in 1833 and 1857 they reluctantly accepted, in exchange for their land, government promises to teach them the arts of "civilized" life. They did not, however, consent to the eradication of their traditional ways of living or agree to being colonized. Then too, they entered into a long-term military alliance with the United States, sending hundreds of their finest men to fight common enemies from 1864 to 1877.

Yet U.S. officials betrayed the loyal Pawnee. They devised policies that violated the treaties and considered them conquered enemies. They increasingly dealt with the Pawnee as dependent, inferior, and incompetent people who lacked the ability to manage their affairs and futures. Even before the U.S. government began to impose civilization regulations, it had subjected the Pawnee to colonization and assimilation, endangering their sovereignty, landholdings, world view, political structure, health, economy, ceremonies, language, identity, and physical existence.

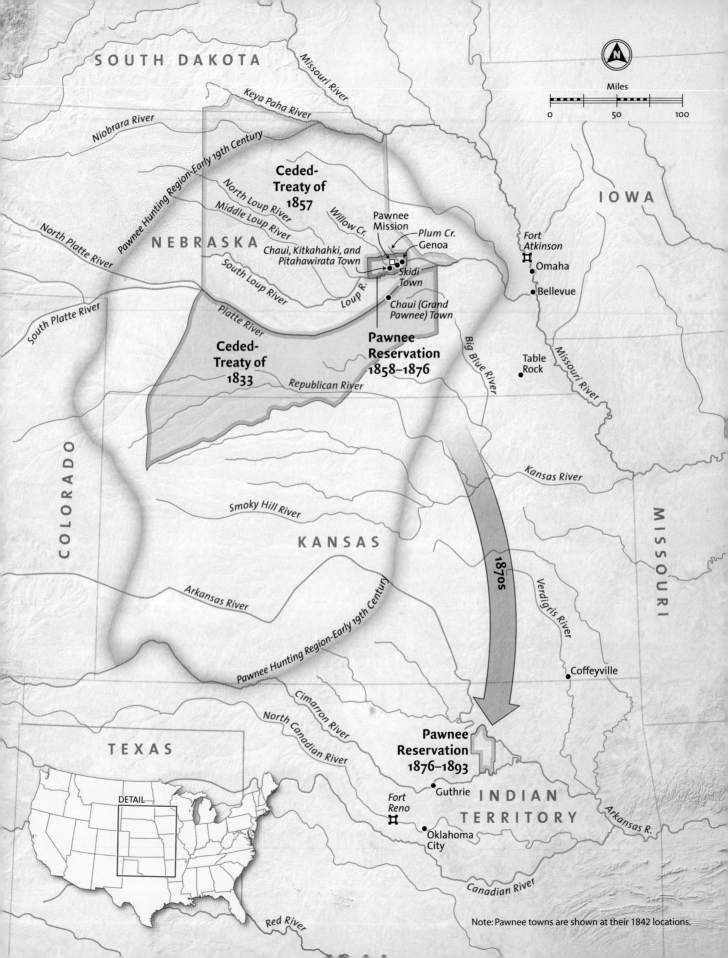

SOUTH DAKOTA

Missouri River

Keya Paha River

Niobrara River

Ceded-
Treaty of
1857

Pawnee Hunting Region–Early 19th Century

North Platte River

North Loup River

Middle Loup River

Willow Cr.

NEBRASKA

South Loup River

South Platte River

Chaui, Kitkahahki, and
Pitahawirata Town

Pawnee
Mission

Plum Cr.
Genoa

Loup R.

Skidi
Town

*Chaui (Grand
Pawnee) Town*

IOWA

Miles

0   50   100

Fort
Atkinson

Omaha

Bellevue

Pawnee
Reservation
1858–1876

Big Blue River

Table
Rock

Missouri River

Platte River

Ceded-
Treaty of
1833

Republican River

COLORADO

Smoky Hill River

KANSAS

Kansas River

Arkansas River

Pawnee Hunting Region–Early 19th Century

Verdigris River

1870s

Coffeyville

MISSOURI

Cimarron River

North Canadian River

TEXAS

DETAIL

Pawnee
Reservation
1876–1893

Guthrie

Fort
Reno

Oklahoma
City

INDIAN
TERRITORY

Arkansas R.

Canadian River

Red River

Note: Pawnee towns are shown at their 1842 locations.

The following case study examines elements of that destructive history. It focuses on Pawnee attempts to maintain cultural integrity by accommodating a foreign nation's increasingly suffocating policies. Divided into four chronological stages from 1833 to 1892, it illustrates how the Pawnee lost ground over time but without experiencing total cultural disintegration. It also shows how they used the logic of their culture to structure their resistance to the U.S. government's unconditional demands.

1833 TO 1847

In 1833, the four confederated bands of the Pawnee Nation, who called themselves the Chaui, Kitkahahki, Pitahawirata, and Skidi, claimed a vast central plains homeland encompassing much of what is now called Nebraska and Kansas. They lived a politically independent existence in accordance with a mandate given by their supreme deity, Tirawahut, to carry on their traditional beliefs, customs, and economic pursuits.

That October at a Chaui town near the Platte River the Pawnee hosted a U.S. treaty delegation. The chiefs and leading men from Pawnee towns on both sides of the Platte attended the treaty council to represent their peoples' interests. At this time, the nearest white American settlement was Bellevue, an outpost on the Missouri River near its confluence with the Platte, more than a hundred miles east of the Pawnee towns. The U.S. government maintained an agency there for surrounding Indians.[8]

Several years earlier, in a rush to push the Lenape (Delaware) Indians onto the central Plains to make more Indian lands available for white settlement, another U.S. treaty delegation had assigned them a strip of Pawnee hunting lands. When a Lenape party entered the area to hunt buffalo, a Pawnee force drove off the intruders, killing several of them. United States government officials opted to resolve the conflict they had created with a treaty that would accomplish two objectives. First, they would acquire title to a large tract of Pawnee territory and turn it into a common hunting ground for the Pawnee and Indians displaced by the federal removal policy. Second, they would subject the Pawnee to a civilization and religious conversion program.[9]

At least four factors severely disadvantaged the Pawnee in the resulting treaty dialogue. First, Pawnee leaders normally reached a consensus on important matters after lengthy deliberations, but now they were being called upon to respond quickly to a proposition that had far-reaching social, economic, and political implications. Second, they were vulnerable to manipulation because in 1831 a devastating smallpox epidemic had struck, reducing their population by about half, to approximately ten thousand people, and leaving them in a weakened state. Compounding matters, encroachments by white Americans and other Indian Tribes on Pawnee hunting lands were making it more difficult for them to consistently procure enough buffalo and hides to sustain them. Third, the Pawnee lacked not only legal advisors but also an understanding of the white man's concepts of land ownership, property values, and fairness. By 1833 the U.S. government had used coercion, bribery, deception, and manipulation to obtain Indian lands at a fraction of their real value.

Fourth, a language barrier, along with cultural differences, made the likelihood of misunderstandings and differing interpretations about the proposed treaty's terms

facing: Pawnee territory in the early nineteenth century, with shaded areas showing land ceded in the Treaties of 1833 and 1857; the Nebraska reservation from 1858 to 1876; and the reservation in Indian Territory to which the Pawnee were removed in the late 1870s. Map by Gene Thorp/ Cartographic Concepts, Inc. © Smithsonian Institution

Pawnee rattle used in the Star Dance, a Skidi Pawnee ceremony, ca. 1890. Oklahoma. Gourd, wood, hide, pigment. 27.9 × 10.6 cm. National Museum of the American Indian 21/3016

This rattle represents Tirawahut, the supreme being of the Pawnee. The inscribed stars identify the four sectors of the universe and the deities that preside over each.

very probable. No member of the treaty party spoke Pawnee and no Pawnee spoke English. But Louis LaChapelle, a Pawnee of mixed heritage who spoke the Pawnee and French languages and lived with his Kitkahahki relatives, served as the interpreter. The treaty party contained individuals fluent in English and French. Thus, the dialogue went through three conceptual filters, from English to French to Pawnee and from Pawnee to French to English.

On October 9 a treaty commissioner promised that his government would supply the Pawnee with trade goods (an annuity) each year for twelve years, white farmers to provide agricultural assistance, schools, blacksmiths, livestock, mills, firearms, and ammunition if they would cede their land lying south of the Platte River. According to the written version of the Treaty, they surrendered "all their right, interest, and title in and to" that territory, while retaining the right to hunt in common with other Indians within the ceded lands.[10] The agreement stipulated that the Pawnee "shall locate themselves in convenient agricultural districts and remain in these districts the whole year."[11] The Treaty did not state that they had to abandon the hunt and live solely by farming the land. A report of the negotiation, however, indicates that the U.S. representative told the Pawnee leaders that, with the buffalo becoming scarce, they must give up the chase and "cultivate the ground or starve." He added that they must stay in their new towns north of the Platte and protect the whites coming there to work.[12] Calculating the odds facing them and the potential benefits of the treaty, the chiefs accepted their understanding of its terms in hopes of gaining a measure of economic stability for their people without compromising their culture and sovereignty.

The Pawnee responded slowly and without a consensus to the Treaty's removal and civilization stipulations. Needing a secure food source, they continued to follow their customary pattern of hunting and planting as they dwelled in their towns on both sides of the Platte. Periodic poor hunts and harvests, however, left them destitute. In 1834, at the chiefs' invitation, John Dunbar and Samuel Allis, missionaries sent west by the American Board of Commissioners for Foreign Missions (ABCFM), joined them. In the winter of 1837–38, smallpox swept through the Pawnee towns once again, taking a quarter of their population. The death toll included hundreds of children who had been born following the previous epidemic. Warfare with encroaching Sioux, Cheyenne, and Arapaho, among others, was also becoming more intense and costly.[13]

In 1839 these conditions encouraged the Pawnee chiefs to request the assistance promised by the Treaty. The following year, U.S. Office of Indian Affairs officials refused to comply with the request until the Pawnee moved north of the Platte and stopped hunting for a year.[14] For the Pawnee, the choice was either to hunt or face starvation, malnutrition, and mass death. In a letter to his ABCFM supervisor, Dunbar took issue with the federal stance, writing

> To construe the treaty as I understand you say the Commissioner [of Indian Affairs] does, that the Pawnees shall at first all remain at their location for the whole year, or a whole year before any thing is done for them by the government, sounds too much like saying that for the improvement of the Pawnees, a big grave will be dug and, the whole tribe buried in it in the space of one year, instead of suffering them to diminish gradually as at the present.[15]

Soon thereafter, white officials dropped their unreasonable demand, but they retained the goal of assimilating the Pawnee within several years. The reversal paved the way for a joint U.S. government/ABCFM program to carry out a policy of ethnocide against the Pawnee. Dunbar and Allis, however, having lived among and been acquainted with them, astutely realized that few, if any, Pawnee would willingly surrender their way of life in exchange for another culture.[16]

Beginning in the spring of 1842 and continuing for a few years, about a thousand of them trickled into the area where Plum Creek (now Council Creek) and Willow Creek (now Cedar River) flow into the Loup River. The Skidi established a mud-lodge town near Plum Creek while Chaui, Kitkahahki, and Pitahawirata families built another one near the mouth of Willow Creek, about four miles west of the Skidi settlement. By then, the missionaries had constructed a permanent station, called the Pawnee Mission, near Willow Creek. A small number of other missionaries sent there by the ABCFM received appointments as U.S. government farmers. Most of the other Pawnee, numbering more than four thousand, refused to relocate and participate in the experiment, despite periodic U.S. Army threats to drive them to the Loup River sites.[17]

Pawnee culture was a spiritually endowed way of life. Its participants realized that accepting another religion and world view in any significant measure would turn their cultural world upside down. White American culture differed significantly from theirs. It idealized a life in which Christian men labored outdoors as farmers and mechanics, while their female counterparts cooked, baked, sewed, and took care of the children. Pawnee women and men also worked in separate spheres. In addition to handling domestic routines, women planted, cultivated, and harvested the crops. They planted the corn, bean, pumpkin, and squash seeds that their ancestors had received—along with instructions telling them what and how to plant—from the Sacred Deities. During the semiannual buffalo hunts, women tanned hides, pitched camp, and carried out other vital functions. Pawnee men hunted, defended the buffalo herds, guarded women working in the fields, and drove off intruders. They also raided enemy horse herds, engaged in trade relations with outsiders, and served as chiefs, doctors (medicine men), and priests. Their children learned societal roles, values, and beliefs through observation, role playing, storytelling, and participation. The adults assumed that the youth would grow, mature, and transmit their culture to unborn generations throughout time.[18]

Although they experienced deprivation from periodic poor hunts and harvests as well as pressure to abandon hunting in favor of white American agricultural methods, the Pawnee who moved near the Pawnee Mission continued to live in accordance with their customs. With the whites lacking the legal or physical mechanisms to induce them to surrender their culture, the Pawnee essentially remained independent. They made, however, several minor cultural modifications. In addition to growing crops in nearby ravines and river bottoms in accordance with custom, Pawnee women also began to plant seeds in fields broken for them by the white farmers, and they began to use metal hoes and axes. A few parents allowed their children to participate in the sparse educational activities provided by the whites. Hardly any of them showed more than a passing curiosity about Christianity.[19]

The Pawnee's first experiment with civilization quickly became mired in chaos, hunger, conflict, and violence. The whites associated with the endeavor divided into two factions, feuding amongst themselves over the most effective way to Americanize Pawnee culture. The U.S. government agent Daniel Miller, who maintained an office in Bellevue, believed that a physical approach would force Indians to become "civilize." Providing them food, he asserted, would encourage them to resist white attempts to control them. He did not want to give the Indians the impression that whites were their servants. His policy fostered a combustible environment. Farmer James Mathers and his son, Carolan, along with others, violently attacked Pawnee individuals and small groups, regardless of their gender or age, for transgressions ranging from insolence to theft. Conversely, Dunbar, Allis, and a few others advocated a gradual carrot-and-stick approach. Siding with the Pawnee mostly for humanitarian reasons, they disapproved of the farmers' tactics, pleading unsuccessfully for Miller to remove the white troublemakers from Pawnee land.[20]

During their reign of terror, the farmers shot Indian dogs and used their fists, whips, and firearms to punish, intimidate, and exert authority over Pawnees who crossed them and stole food. Following a scuffle during which a Pawnee struck James Mathers's wife in the head with a bow, the farmer, with a loaded firearm in hand and accompanied by his son, entered a Pawnee town intent on shooting the man. They left after learning that Indian authorities had already whipped him.[21] Hunger precipitated most of the conflict. On one occasion, Carolan Mathers beat several destitute women and children who had entered his field. On another, he shot a man in the back and severely beat a child for the same reason.[22]

The Pawnee retaliated by taking measures such as shooting arrows into livestock belonging to the offending whites, taking property, and confronting their attackers. The chiefs, however, prevented their people from spilling white blood. Apart from declaring that the whites must not whip any Pawnees, these leaders left it up to Miller to handle the troublemakers. During a public meeting, the chiefs expressed their discontent about the farmers' violent behavior and negative attitude toward working for the Pawnee. Miller responded angrily, denouncing the chiefs as thieves. After declaring that the farmers had authority to chasten the Indians for their misbehavior, he threatened that U.S. soldiers would punish all Pawnee if any of them harmed a white person. Miller did remove Carolan Mathers from Pawnee country, but without bringing him to justice for his crimes. He also discharged several government employees who opposed the Mathers faction, blaming them and the missionaries for poisoning the Indians' minds. In 1845, following an investigation, U.S. Indian Office personnel discharged Miller, but they allowed James Mathers to remain in Pawnee country.[23]

During late fall of that year, as the Pawnee were preparing for the winter hunt, Mathers struck Soldier Chief in the lower arm with an axe during a dispute over gunpowder that had been promised by the 1833 Treaty. Soldier Chief seized the weapon and mortally wounded Mathers's son. The chief died that evening. The chiefs shielded Mathers and his family from harm until their people departed on the hunt. With Miller's replacement declining to pursue criminal charges, James Mathers, along with his family, departed for California before the Pawnee hunters returned.[24]

Meanwhile, enemy encroachments worsened matters. On June 27, 1843, about five hundred Sioux struck the Pawnee town at Willow Creek, killing about seventy of its Pitahawirata, Kitkahahki, and Chaui inhabitants and burning twenty of their forty-one lodges. The whites living nearby at the Pawnee Mission witnessed with horror the bloody battle unfold. Following the fight, the Pawnee hastily buried their dead, went to a Pawnee town south of the Platte, and soon thereafter departed on the summer hunt.[25] The Pawnees subsequently referred to the town as the Burnt Village, which they never again occupied. Although they had lost more than forty men in the fight, the Sioux returned in June 1846, soon after the Pawnee had left to hunt. After burning the unoccupied Skidi town, they threatened to harm the whites at Pawnee Mission. Unnerved by the Sioux aggression, the missionaries and federal employees fled to Bellevue, taking about twenty Pawnee children with them. After that the ABCFM terminated the Pawnee Mission, and the following summer U.S. officials ended the troubled civilization program.[26]

By then, the Pawnee associated with the civilization program had rejoined their relatives south of the Platte River. During the early 1840s increasing numbers of white Americans en route to the Pacific Northwest and California had passed along the south bank of the Platte, destroying timber (a scarce resource on the barren plains), polluting the water, and trampling Pawnee crops. During the ensuing decade, the Pawnee faced severe hardships stemming from the westward-bound white emigrants, who scattered and slaughtered the diminishing buffalo herds, and from warfare with Indian enemies. In 1849, cholera struck, killing more than twelve hundred Pawnees. The newcomers demanded that their government rid the region of its Indian inhabitants.[27]

1857 TO 1869

Now with fewer than four thousand people and in a deplorable state, the Pawnee asked for another treaty. In September 1857 they relinquished their lands north of the Platte, except for a small reservation. The Treaty promised them an annuity in cash and trade goods, teachers, farmers, smiths, and laborers as well as manual labor schools, shops,

532

Pitaresaru waits for the Senate to ratify the 1857 Treaty, 1858. Washington, DC. Photo by McClees Studio. National Museum of the American Indian P02442

and mills. It also stipulated that the United States would protect the Pawnee from the Sioux. This time, however, the government did not limit the duration of the funding for the assimilation program, as it had in 1833.

The Pawnee had still not agreed to surrender their customary culture and adopt white American modes of life and worship, but the Treaty nonetheless contained two particularly coercive provisions. Article 3 required all Pawnee children between the ages of seven and eighteen to attend school for at least nine months a year. Article 8 stipulated that the Pawnee must surrender for punishment their people who violated U.S. laws, regulations, and treaties. To ensure compliance with these provisions, the government reserved the right to withhold funds from the promised annuity.[28]

In 1859 all Pawnee, complying with the terms of the new Treaty, grudgingly crossed the Platte to build and inhabit a sprawling town of mud lodges on the banks of the Loup near the town of Genoa, about seven miles east of the abandoned Pawnee Mission site. In 1862 a newly appointed U.S. agent found them mired "in a half-starved and nude state" and willing to learn agricultural and mechanical pursuits.[29] By then, Sioux bands had commenced raiding the reservation. Although the U.S. Army built a blockhouse and periodically stationed troops there, the federal government never fulfilled its promise to protect the reservation from Sioux incursions. Compounding matters, a climate of mutual distrust and tension existed between the Pawnee and white homesteaders who were occupying the ceded Pawnee land.[30]

Pawnee parents and guardians sent a handful of children, mostly orphans, to a small, dreary manual labor school that was established in 1862. School personnel forced the students to wear white American clothing and subjected the boys to the shame of wearing their hair in the white man's fashion. In addition to teaching the children a little spoken and written English as well as a smattering of other subjects, the instructors emphasized that the students must learn to work, think, and behave like whites. While the boys were assigned to work in the fields and in the mechanical arts, the girls received instruction in household tasks. Unhealthy conditions produced disease and death among the students. Although the agency expanded its educational facilities

and personnel, only about 20 percent of school-aged Pawnee children attended school in 1869.[31]

Meanwhile, the first Pawnee scout detachment saw duty in 1864 under white officers. This military alliance with the U.S. Army enabled the Pawnee to strike back at their more numerous enemies and solidify their policy of peaceful coexistence with the United States. The army claimed that military service would have a civilizing influence, but the men functioned for the most part according to traditional Pawnee war practices.[32] The scouts' sacrifices and valor failed to protect them, their Treaty, their culture, or their land from betrayal by their allies.

1869 TO 1876

Early in 1869 the United States turned the administration of reservations over to Christian denominations, a policy that, however well intentioned, effectively transformed Indian reservations into concentration camps. What happened on the reservations was no less than cultural genocide and ecocide, as defined today by international law.[33] The federal government now treated individual Indians as incompetent wards of the state and their governments as conquered entities, whether or not an actual conquest had

Scene of a Pawnee town, September 1871. Nebraska. Photo by William Henry Jackson. National Museum of the American Indian P01630

Aroosataka, or White Horse, a Pawnee scout, holds a pipe tomahawk and a revolver, 1868. Nebraska. Photo by Jackson Brothers Co. National Museum of the American Indian P20548

Yellow Sun, one of the accused murderers of white settler Edward McMurtry, ca. 1865. Nebraska. Photo by C. Griffin. National Museum of the American Indian P20576

occurred. The guardians' power was used in ways that violated treaties and human rights, and the United States waged war on those who rejected reservation life. Besides allowing starvation to weaken peoples' resolve, officials sanctioned hostage taking in some situations to force Indian compliance.

The Hicksite Quakers received control of the Pawnee reservation. Arriving in the spring of 1869, they devised measures to subject alleged Pawnee wrongdoers to white criminal jurisdiction, place children in school, restrict the people's free movement beyond the reservation, weaken the chiefs' authority, break up the communal way of life, and settle reservation inhabitants on allotted pieces of land scattered about the reservation. They also planned to end the hunts and transform Pawnee men into God-fearing farmers.[34]

The first test of their administrative capacity occurred upon their arrival. Several months earlier, unknown Indians had reportedly murdered a white settler near the reservation. Local white authorities felt that Pawnee chiefs had not cooperated with the investigation. The historical record indicates that few, if any, Pawnee knew the identity of the killer or killers. The Quakers nonetheless invoked the 1857 Treaty provision that allowed the U.S. government to withhold annuity goods until the Indians handed over the guilty parties. Prosecutors also seized the Pawnee chiefs and held them hostage in a failed attempt to force the suspects the Pawnee had eventually surrendered to admit their guilt. Later that fall an all-white jury convicted Yellow Sun, Horse Driver,

Young Pawnee women and girls at the Pawnee Reservation town near Genoa, Nebraska, 1871. Photo by William Henry Jackson. National Museum of the American Indian P02533

Blue Hawk, and Little Wolf of murder. Referring to the proceedings as a mockery of justice, the *Omaha Herald* declared that mob pressure had shaped the outcome of the trial. An appellate court subsequently decided that the U.S. courts lacked jurisdiction over the matter because the crime had occurred on state land and, therefore, Nebraska had jurisdiction. In 1871 a state court dropped charges against the defendants. Most of the men died soon after their release, perhaps from their incarceration in dungeonlike conditions.[35]

Meanwhile, the Quakers sought to fill the reservation schools with more students, to cultivate white versions of righteous thought and morality. In addition to threatening to withhold annuity goods and money from uncooperative families, they required leading men, called soldiers, to take children to the day schools. The men, however, did not always follow the agent's orders. In 1872 less than 20 percent of the 1,072 school-aged children attended school. Many of the older students felt they were being treated as servants.[36]

Although cognizant that the buffalo herds were rapidly disappearing, the chiefs insisted that they had a God-given right to hunt as long as the sacred animals existed. In 1871 Pitaresaru (Man Chief), the leading Chaui chief, stated, "We are afraid when we have no meat to offer the Great Spirit [Tirawahut], and he will be angry and pun-

Pawnee schoolchildren on the Pawnee Reservation, 1871. Nebraska. Photo by William Henry Jackson. National Museum of the American Indian P01058

ish us."[37] Protesting the slaughter of buffalo by whites, he declared, "Those Buffalo are mine, our Fathers owned both land and animals feeding on it. We sold the land, but reserved the Buffalo."[38] The following year, Tirawahutresaru (Sky Chief), a Kitkahahki chief, avowed his love for his people's way of life, adding that he did not want to lose it.[39]

Neither the U.S. government nor the Quaker representatives had viable ways of addressing the Pawnee's deteriorating situation. In 1873 they allowed about four hundred men, women, and children to hunt. On August 5 in southwestern Nebraska, a large Sioux force struck, killing Tirawahutresaru and more than seventy others in the party. This warfare ultimately delayed the plan to break up the Pawnee communal way of life. Yet the massacre encouraged the Quakers to abolish hunting, despite the chiefs' vehement opposition. The agent ordered the men to commence working full time in the fields, but the agency lacked funds to pay them for their labor. By then, some men, mostly Skidi, had begun to plow and plant in the white man's fashion, while a few others, mostly young adults who had been educated in the reservation schools, found employment at the agency. The U.S. government issued rations on a more regular basis, but hunger and malnutrition continued to proliferate among the Pawnee. Officials responded with the notion that the Pawnee should be removed southward to the dumping ground called Indian Territory (present-day Oklahoma).[40]

Five Pawnee men, including Tirawahutresaru, or Sky Chief, pose for a studio portrait, 1868. Nebraska. Photo by William Henry Jackson. National Museum of the American Indian P25801C

As the U.S. government prepared to relocate them to a new reservation, the Pawnee, now numbering twenty-eight hundred, were almost totally dependent on federal subsidies and subjected to U.S. domination.[41] Their condition would deteriorate dramatically following removal, but the United States continued to pursue the policy of forcing them to accept civilization.

Now removed to a small reservation in north-central Indian Territory, the Pawnee were plagued by suffering, sorrow, despair, and dramatic population decline. Within a year and a half of their arrival, more than eight hundred Pawnees perished from hunger and malaria. Negligent U.S. officials contributed to the situation by failing to supply them with provisions. Although allowed to conduct several hunts, the Pawnee found only a few buffalo, which were nearly extinct. Sickness and malnutrition left many of them too weak to work their fields. Starvation drove them to beg for food and money in white communities across the Indian Territory border, in southern Kansas. Some families tragically died altogether, while most others lost members. These conditions continued after the Quakers left government service, and the new reservation, in 1879.[42]

In 1876, following Custer's defeat at the Battle of the Little Bighorn in eastern Montana Territory, the U.S. Army called for the enlistment of a hundred Pawnees to help defeat the Sioux, Cheyenne, and Arapaho resisters. Later that summer Frank and Luther North, officers in the Pawnee scouts, reached the Pawnee Reservation and found them in a deplorable condition but eager to avenge the 1873 massacre and other deaths. Describing their poverty and poor health, Luther later wrote, "They were miserably poor, nearly all of them had ague, and many of them were dying. They were very much discouraged and many of them were longing to get back to Nebraska."[43] After participating in the army campaign, the discharged scouts returned the following year to their troubled reservation.

Meanwhile, the Pawnee tried to reestablish the integrity of their customary social organization. They built mud-lodge settlements, planted crops in the usual manner, and attempted to live and worship in accordance with Tirawahut's directives. Spiritual leaders carried out their annual round of religious ceremonies, in hopes of keeping conditions from worsening. Young men accepted apprenticeships and learned the sacred songs, dances, and knowledge necessary for carrying on their religion.

Pawnee leaders refused to surrender their authority, abandon their people, or allow their U.S. military service to be forgotten. In an April 1879 meeting with an agency employee concerning the extreme hunger overwhelming their people, Ter-re-re-cox complained that the "government took better care of wild Indians who killed white people than they did the peaceful Pawnees." Ti-re-re-ca-wah threatened to take his Pita-hawirata people away from the reservation, suggesting they might return to Nebraska. Frank White, a Chaui and former scout, reminded the employee that many Pawnee men had served in the U.S. Army.[44]

Although the U.S. government soon thereafter increased the reservation's food supply, its concern was short-lived. In 1881 it abruptly stopped providing rations in hopes of forcing the Pawnee to become self-sufficient farmers. Occurring when the Pawnee population was declining rapidly from disease and malnutrition, this coercive measure ensured that they would remain underfed and susceptible to sickness and premature death. In that year the population declined to 1,241.[45]

By then, a small but growing number of them, mostly Skidi, dressed either partially or fully in the white style of clothing, accepted individual land allotments, lived in log cabins, and planted crops in plowed fields. Some of them found employment at the agency, while others earned money as teamsters, transporting agency supplies from the railroad terminal in Coffeyville, Kansas.[46] Even if people wanted work, job opportunities were scarce. In 1885 a U.S. agent noted that the assimilation program had made "very moderate" progress among the Pawnees. He warned, "[I]f that pressure was withdrawn they would speedily relapse into utter idleness and barbarism."[47] By then, the population had declined to less than a thousand.[48]

During the 1880s more children gradually fell into the white system of education. Yet, the U.S. government failed to establish an adequate number of schools and a healthy educational environment. While some Pawnee children attended a boarding school on the reservation, others attended Hampton Institute in Virginia, Carlisle Indian Industrial School in Pennsylvania,

Ratakatsresaru, or Eagle Chief, January 21, 1904. Oklahoma. Photo by Thomas William Smillie. National Anthropological Archives, Smithsonian Institution NAA INV 06252800

Haskell Institute in Kansas, Chilocco Indian Agricultural School in northern Indian Territory, or Phoenix Indian School in Arizona. At all the institutions, the teachers and disciplinarians endeavored to eradicate Indian languages, beliefs, values, traditions, and religions. Operating the schools in the manner of military camps, they compelled the students to wear uniforms, march to and from classes, drill during holidays, work in the fields and school facilities, and respond to bells and bugles. Those children who dared to speak their own language, or who violated any of the numerous rules, ran the risk of corporal punishment. Schoolchildren often suffered and died from disease, homesickness, and malnutrition. In 1885, for example, twenty-one Pawnees went to Haskell. Of the ten students who died there in that year, four were Pawnee. More of them would die in schools both on and off the Pawnee Reservation.[49]

Meanwhile, federal policymakers intensified their efforts to wipe out traditional Indian cultures. Established in the 1880s, the civilization codes criminalized such practices as polygamy, ceremonial dancing, and feasting, while chipping away at traditional systems of governance and ways of living. To enforce the new laws, agents appointed influential chiefs and other men as judges to preside over newly formed Courts of Indian Offenses on the reservations.[50] This arrangement was designed to replace traditional governance structure and practices, and to enhance U.S. control over Indians.

On the Pawnee Reservation in 1890 an agent appointed Brave Chief, Sun Chief, and Eagle Chief as judges. They spoke no English, but, according to an agent, they used "their influence for the education of the children, live in comfortable log-houses, and

Eagle Chief's mud lodge on the Pawnee Reservation in Indian Territory, ca. 1899–1902. Oklahoma. Photo by George A. Dorsey. National Museum of the American Indian P22203

are of good character."[51] In addition to hearing a few civil and criminal cases dealing with divorce, probate, debt, arson, and drinking (which was becoming more common among the Pawnee), they also made laws for the reservation. An agent's report stated that by witnessing these court proceedings in action the Indians learned "how white men try their criminals, and they think it is a better way than to settle with clubs and butcher knives."[52] The U.S. agent also maintained a Pawnee police force, consisting of an officer and seven privates with authority among the people, to enforce U.S. regulations.[53]

The civilization codes had varied results. The custom of men having multiple wives diminished before vanishing in the early 1900s.[54] Yet Pawnee traditionalists continued to hold healing and sacred bundle ceremonies. In 1890, when the Indian police tried to disrupt a ritual, the practitioners justified their right to proceed by saying, "White men dance, and we dance."[55] With the death toll reducing each band's ability to maintain its separate ceremonies, however, surviving priests from the four bands joined together to hold communal rituals.[56] Increasingly, when the priests died, the sacred bundles were buried with them. Poverty and religious oppression drove some families to sell the sacred bundles and other cultural items to museum curators.[57]

The U.S. attack on Pawnee culture weakened the chiefs' authority. In 1893 the U.S. government ended the operations of the Pawnee court and police force in a scheme to further weaken the functionality of their traditional government structure. As anthropologist Alexander Lesser wrote, by the early 1890s "the Pawnee had been transformed from an independent self-determining nation into a group of families subjected to the rules of representatives of an alien race."[58] Among other things, this means that the

Kiskuhara, the annual Pawnee-Wichita visit, ca. 1900. Oklahoma. Photographer unknown. National Museum of the American Indian P20348

Pawnee leaders had lost their ability to make decisions regarding the future of their people. United States agents on the reservation progressively controlled most aspects of Pawnee life. Yet, white policymakers in Washington were still in the grip of their destructive obsession with civilization.

The Dawes Act, or General Allotment Act, of 1887 struck at the heart of the Pawnee's communal ways of living and owning land. When U.S. commissioners reached the Pawnee reservation in 1891, the Pawnees rejected the commissioners' plan for each family to settle on a parcel of allotted land and receive a payment for the sale of the remaining reservation land, which would then be opened for white American ownership and settlement. Sergeant Peters, a former scout, told the commissioners that they should defer to his chiefs.[59] After noting his willing army service and current impoverished state, he declared, "I get nothing from the government. You commissioners should listen to the chiefs." White Eagle, another former scout, added, "You should not try to scare us—talking about the western Indians. We *helped* put them on reservations. I am now nearly blind, I have no pension, but white soldiers do."[60] On November 23, 1892, under unrelenting pressure and threats, the Pawnee gave in and accepted allotments.[61] By 1894, U.S. agents had allotted reservation lands to the surviving 821 Pawnees. The remainder of the reservation was opened to settlement by non-Indians.[62]

Using coercion to obtain this agreement was one thing, but convincing the Pawnee to live on their allotments year round and follow the path of assimilation was another. As white homesteaders took up the so-called surplus reservation lands, many Pawnees defied government expectations by living in camps. These families, maintaining a nonmaterialistic world view, engaged only in enough farming to sustain themselves.

Leasing their allotted lands to white farmers and ranchers provided them with a small income that enabled them to maintain a degree of freedom from U.S. control. Within a few years, however, the federal government took charge of the leasing process and monies, forcing the Pawnee to ask the local agent for permission to buy such things as clothing, furniture, and other necessities of life.[63]

Not long before the Dawes commissioners' arrival, many Pawnees had become fervent Ghost Dance participants. This religious movement, inspired by the 1889 vision and teachings of Wovoka, a Paiute, was a spiritual response to the devastation and loss of freedom Indians had suffered as a result of white colonialism. The Pawnee had experienced dramatic population, land, and cultural losses since the 1833 Treaty. Frank White, an educated Kitkahahki who had learned the religion's tenets from the Arapaho, became the dance's prophet among the Pawnee. The Ghost Dance promised that if its adherents danced, sang, and behaved in a prescribed manner, the old ways, the buffalo, and their deceased loved ones would return, and a wind would sweep away the whites. Many of them became so involved with the new religion that they neglected to farm.[64]

On March 25, 1892, agent D. J. M. Wood sent a U.S. deputy marshal and Pawnee police to arrest White and transport him to a Guthrie, Oklahoma, jail for trial. A group of armed Pawnees went to the local train station to free White but found themselves facing U.S. soldiers who had come by rail at Wood's request. Outnumbered and outgunned, the Pawnees backed down. In April the chief Oklahoma territorial judge released White after he promised to no longer participate in the religion, to obey the U.S. agent, and to farm his allotment. The judge imposed the same conditions on the Pawnee chiefs who attended the trial, stating that the Pawnee would be punished for ghost dancing. As White's influence waned, other prophets took his place, and the Pawnee's resolve to ghost dance remained strong. They held the ceremonies in secret, and the U.S. overseers did little to forcibly suppress the religion, thinking it would soon die out.[65]

As the nineteenth century ended, many Pawnee continued to ghost dance, conduct other ceremonies, build mud lodges, and believe in Tirawahut. A variety of factors, however, including coercion and the indoctrinating influences of white teachers and missionaries, took a toll. More Pawnee turned to Christianity, engaged in wage labor, spoke English exclusively, and rejected traditions. Others joined the Native American Church, which involves the sacramental use of peyote and the acceptance of Jesus. Camp life gradually died out, as did the bundle ceremonies. Yet, to this day, many Pawnee retain a strong sense of their traditional identity, practice customary values, and participate in surviving ceremonies and dances.

CONCLUSION

This brief study shows that the U.S. government, driven by imperialistic impulses and a sense of racial superiority, used treaties and policy making as implements of social control, political domination, and cultural genocide. What happened to the Pawnee also happened to other Indian Peoples. Rather than working cooperatively with Native

LAST NIGHT OF FAMOUS COMPANY A. PAWNEE INDIAN SCOUTS. ALL HAVE SINCE
DIED SAVE THREE---RUSH ROBERTS, DOG CHIEF, AND ROBERT TAYLOR.Their Names

Left to right. Front row;--Wichita Blaine--To-too-ra-we-chat--High Eagle--
Se-ts-tis-tee--Robert Taylor--La-re-roo-la-chicks-se-wa-ra--and Billy Osborne.
Back row---Walking Sun--Se-te-roo-tiks-ta-we-ah---Leading Fox--La-he-rus-
        ka-wa-do--Rush Roberts--Le-ta-kuts-ka-ra-ha-roo---Dog Chief--
            (Simon Adams)--Cu-roox-la-le-sa-roo.   No.11
marion Tomblin photo   Pawnee. Oklahoma

Nations to find solutions based on the principles of fairness, justice, human dignity, and equitable treatment, U.S. policy makers plotted and implemented a course of action that left Indians on the brink of extinction, politically subjugated, impoverished, and struggling to maintain their identities and cultures.

The celebrated Pawnee scouts contributed to the growth of the United States, but their service failed to protect the Pawnee from harm intentionally inflicted by an untrustworthy ally. Despite the acts of betrayal, elements of Pawnee culture have survived the onslaught, and the Pawnee have remained loyal allies, sending soldiers to American wars in Europe, Asia, and the Middle East. For its part, the federal government has reformed its Indian policies and works with Indian Nations as they labor to overcome the effects of the civilization regulations. Still, we can readily understand why the Pawnee will long wonder about the steadfastness of their old ally.

Surviving Pawnee scouts, ca. 1927. Oklahoma. Photo by Marion Tomblin. National Museum of the American Indian P22216

Pawnee scouts Blue Herd (standing) and Coming Around the Herd, 1868. Nebraska. Photo by William Henry Jackson. National Museum of the American Indian P00842

American Indian Scouts

MARK G. HIRSCH

FIGHTING THE INDIAN TRIBES OF THE AMERICAN West was the primary mission of the U.S. Army after the Civil War. Engaging armed, mounted, and intrepid tribal warriors, determined to defend their traditional homelands against U.S. expansion, was daunting enough. But the thinning ranks of the post–Civil War army—which were reduced from fifty-seven thousand troops in 1867 to half that in 1877[1]—also challenged soldiers responsible for patrolling tribal territories dispersed across nearly half the continental United States.[2] To address the problem, Congress in 1866 authorized the army to enlist up to a thousand Indians to serve as scouts. Familiar with the vast terrain of the West, steeped in tribal cultures that celebrated bravery in warfare, and imbued with intimate knowledge of their own and rival tribes, American Indian scouts and auxiliaries became valuable allies in U.S. military operations during the Plains Indian Wars of the 1860s–80s.

Indian scouts typically served six-month tours of duty, with the option to reenlist, and received the same pay as white cavalry soldiers.[3] Scouts were issued infantry rifles—later replaced by Spencer repeating carbines—and partial or complete cavalry uniforms, including an elaborate dress hat that featured a feather, a tasseled cord, and crossed-saber insignia, the latter to enable white soldiers to distinguish the scouts from "hostiles." When the first Arikara scouts enlisted in 1868, they insisted on retaining their moccasins, and they furnished their own horses, for which they received forty cents a day.[4]

Valued for their ability to follow a trail and observe enemies without being detected, Indian scouts also played important roles in combat, serving "in virtually every theater and every Indian conflict in the trans-Mississippi West." Organized in all-Indian units, the scouts, according to one military historian, occasionally did the lion's share of the fighting, sometimes arriving just in time to save beleaguered cavalry soldiers.[5]

Although most Indian scout units were temporary organizations, some tribes, including the Pawnee, Crow, Wyoming Shoshone, Warm Springs of Oregon, and Tonkawa, maintained long relationships with the army.[6] Stationed near Fort Griffin, Texas, the Tonkawa served as scouts for some seventeen years; their commander in 1873–74 was Richard Pratt, who subsequently founded the Carlisle Indian Industrial School in Pennsylvania.[7]

Scouts hailed from a multitude of tribes. One Indian scout unit near Fort Sill, in Indian Territory, consisted of men from ten tribes, including the Wichita, Tehuacana, Waco, Keechi, Caddo, Delaware, Arapahoe, Shawnee, and Comanche.[8] Descendants of runaway slaves adopted by the Florida Seminole in the late eighteenth and early nineteenth centuries, African American Seminole scouts participated in expeditions against the Comanche and Apache along the Mexican border. Of the sixteen Indian scouts awarded the Medal of Honor, four were African-American Seminoles.[9]

Indian scouts often viewed army service as a way of getting even with tribal adversaries. Traditional targets of Lakota raids, Pawnee scouts assisted the army in campaigns against the Sioux and Cheyenne, and they guarded construction crews building the transcontinental railroad between Nebraska and southeastern Wyoming.[10] Surrounded by the numerically superior Sioux, Cheyenne, and Blackfeet Nations, the Crow had fought their traditional tribal rivals to maintain their homelands, which stretched across much of present-day Wyoming and Montana.[11] When alliance with the United States afforded them an opportunity for retribution, the Crow authorized 176 warriors, led by Chiefs Medicine Crow and Plenty Coups, to join General George Crook in his 1876 campaign against the Sioux and Cheyenne in the Montana Territory.[12] Crook's ranks including the Wyoming Shoshone under the leadership of Chief Washakie, a longtime U.S. ally, whose people had guarded white travelers moving west along the Oregon Trail.[13] Traditional intertribal enmity also encouraged the Klamath to serve as scouts in the 1872–73 American war against the Modocs in Northern California,[14] and the Bannock to join in General O. O. Howard's 1,400-mile, four-month pursuit of the Nez Perce across Oregon, Washington, Idaho, and Montana in 1877.[15]

Warriors who had once resisted the United States also were recruited as Indian scouts. After surrendering in 1883, Chato (Chiricahua Apache) became a first sergeant of scouts, and proved instrumental in tracking down and encouraging the surrender of still militant tribesmen. Other Chiricahua scouts convinced Geronimo to surrender.[16] The effectiveness of the Chiricauhua scouts was recognized by victors and vanquished alike. "We are not afraid of the Americans alone," Apache chief Cha-ut-lipan declared when he surrendered to General Crook. "But we cannot fight you and our own people together."[17]

It is easy to view the Native scouts as mercenaries who betrayed Indians for captured horses and army wages. Certainly some contemporary tribal people, such as Wooden Leg (Cheyenne), took a dim view of Indians who had joined forces with the United States to "kill friends." Doing so, Wooden Leg opined, "showed a bad heart."[18] Yet the scouts' motives for cooperating with Americans were varied and complex. Military service offered Native men an opportunity to maintain their tribal status and protect their people's homelands from rivals by continuing warrior traditions, which were viewed as "uncivilized" by white reformers and religious missionaries. Army service also provided a source of income for men confined to reservations, where poverty was pervasive.[19] Cooperation with the Americans also sprang from a strategic assessment of U.S. power. By 1870, many Native people had concluded that military resistance to the Americans was unfeasible, and that accommodation was the most viable strategy for survival. By enlisting in the army, the scouts not only made a strategic decision to obtain better treatment for themselves but also sought to prevent further bloodshed and assure a future for their people.

But the fruits of cooperation remained elusive for many Indian scouts. After years of service, the Tonkawa were removed in 1884 to Indian Territory, where their population dwindled to near extinction.[20] After Geronimo and his band surrendered in 1886, the United States shipped the Chiricahua Apache captives to internment camps in Florida and then Alabama. Among the exiles were the Apache scouts, including Chato, who had encouraged their people to surrender.[21] Despite their long association with the U.S. Army, the Pawnee lost their Nebraska homelands and accepted a reservation in Indian Territory, only to face allotment and the sale of their reservation lands in the 1890s.[22]

Alliance with the United States enabled the Wyoming Shoshone to retain a reservation in their tribal homelands, but when gold was discovered in the Wind River Mountains, they were pressured into ceding the southern portion of their territory. And in 1878, the army settled 938 Arapahos on the Eastern Shoshone Reservation, a move Chief Washakie protested to no avail.[23]

The Crow chief Plenty Coups never doubted the wisdom of allying with the United States. Those who had fought the whites, he recalled, wound up with little, whereas the Crow maintained a large reservation on their homelands. "When I think back my heart sings because we acted as we did," Plenty Coups recalled. "It was the only way open to us."[24]

"Civilization" and the Hupa Flower Dance Ceremony

LOIS J. RISLING

ON THE HOOPA INDIAN RESERVATION IN 2012, at the old town of Ta'kimiLding, on the Trinity River, a young woman is presented to the community as a woman of the Hoopa Tribe, continuing a tradition that the Hupa people have followed since time immemorial.[1] The K'iwinya'n-ya:n (Hupa people) were told to do a girl's adolescence ceremony—called ch'iLwa:l, which means They Beat Time with Sticks, or the Flower Dance—and instructed by the K'ixinay on how to perform the ceremony as the K'ixinay had.[2] The *kinahldung* (Flower Dance girl) is required to run long distances, fast, sing, pray, and learn, with the love and support of her family, community, and tribe. Women and men of the community come together to dance, sing, pray, and beat time with sticks over the kinahldung, performing ceremonial activities that come from the time of the animals. Since time immemorial the Hupa people have lived in their homeland, practicing the ceremonies and lifestyle the K'ixinay have given them. This dance is part of how the Hupa build and strengthen their community.

Euro-Americans intruded into Hoopa territory in the 1800s, determined to rid the land of the Hupa and take it for their own use. The plan was to exterminate the Indians of California and/or replace their traditions and customs with "habits and arts of civilization" based on Judeo-Christian, Anglo-American practices. Civilization represented an attack on the Hoopa culture, religion, language, family, and future generations. A letter issued in 1883 by the federal Commissioner of Indian Affairs to his agents nationwide outlined strict rules for Courts of Indian Offenses that were established on each reservation. Meant to suppress "evil practices,"

the rules outlawed ceremonies practiced by medicine men and women, traditional dances and feasts, reciprocal gift-giving, and funeral rites and customs. The rules remained in effect until the 1930s. The U.S. government built a boarding school on the Hoopa Reservation, but it also sent Hoopa children to off-reservation boarding schools such as Sherman Institute in Riverside, California; Chemawa Institute in Salem, Oregon; Stewart Indian School in Carson City, Nevada; and Carlisle Indian Industrial School in Carlisle, Pennsylvania. Designed to "kill the Indian and save the man," these institutions were created to separate Indian children from their families, homes, cultures, identities, and tribes.

The U.S. military also tried to stop the Hupa from practicing their ceremonies and beliefs. Indian people of northwestern California complained to army officials at Fort Gaston, in the Hoopa Valley, that miners and other white men in the area were kidnapping and stealing young women from their towns and villages. When the abductors were confronted, they often stated that it was all right to take the young women, because the Indians had a ceremony to make a girl a woman for the use of a man. With Christianity, the idea was introduced that women were "dirty" due to menstruation, that God had "cursed" women with menstrual bleeding, and that the Hoopa people believed that women were dirty because they isolated them during their periods in a menstrual hut. By the 1930s the Flower Dance Ceremony had gone underground, and for many years most Hupa people rarely practiced it.

Hupa people resisted, endured, and defended against the complete obliteration of the Flower Dance Ceremony. When I was a little girl, my uncle Ernest

175

Marshall Sr., taught me a women's Flower Dance song that had been handed down through his family. My paternal grandfather, David W. Risling Sr., taught me and my brothers (Baron, Gary, and Leslie Risling Jr.) and sister, Mary J. Risling, both men's and women's Flower Dance songs. He described how the ceremony was done and sang the songs to us, demonstrating the different timings of a heavy song and a light song. When I was a young girl, my aunties took me to see a semi-public Flower Dance that a family gave their daughter after years of not doing public or open Flower Dance Ceremonies. All I remember of this venture was that it was dark, men and women were dancing and singing, and the girl was covered. The singing was rich, strong, and beautiful.

I also remember when I started menstruating. I was at a public school about 150 miles from the Hoopa Reservation. The male teacher told me to see the school nurse because I was sick. The nurse sent me home. When I got home, only my grandfather—William O. Scott Sr., my mother's father—was there. He told me, "You are not sick. You are blessed. You can now give life. How wonderful!" My brothers walked into the house, and my grandfather handed them some money and told them to go to the store to buy me some sanitary napkins. The boys looked at each other blankly and hesitated. Grandpa said, "Is there a problem? You should be proud of your sister. She can give life. This is wonderful! There will be more Hupas. Go to the store." My brothers left, and Grandpa hugged me and sang a song over me. It wasn't a Flower Dance song, because this grandpa did not know one, but he knew what I call the "Hey Nunnie Song." This was a song he had made up and knew he should sing over me. It was in this moment that I went from being "sick" with menstruation to being wonderful and natural. The old Hoopa traditions and beliefs were strong, even 150 miles from the Hoopa Reservation. When a Flower Dance Ceremony was given for my grandniece, Dakota Carlson, the "Hey Nunnie Song" was sung over her.

I thank both my grandfathers, and my grandmothers, parents, aunties, uncles, brothers, sister, husband, children, community, and all Indian people who refused to accept, who refused to go along, and who defied. They stood firm to keep alive our culture, so that now I can plan the Flower Dance Ceremony of my granddaughter, Arya Yisuan Risling Baldy Mettier, and sing over her.

Hupa woman's skirt, ca. 1880. California.
Hide, abalone shell, haliotis shell, pine nuts,
bear grass, maidenhair fern stem. National
Museum of the American Indian 1045

Billy Frank Jr. (Nisqually) fishes the Nisqually River, 1973. Washington. Photo by Tom Thompson. Courtesy of the Northwest Indian Fisheries Commission, Olympia, Washington

During the 1960s, Frank's home became the epicenter of the fishing rights movement.

Rights Guaranteed by Solemn Treaties

FISHING IS CRITICAL TO THE SURVIVAL AND CULTURAL IDENTITY OF MANY Native Peoples. In the Treaties they negotiated with the federal government during the nineteenth century, Native Nations along the Puget Sound, the Columbia River, and the Great Lakes reserved their traditional rights to fish, hunt, and gather natural resources on lands ceded to the United States. In the twentieth century, however, states enacted laws that restricted tribal fishing, hunting, and gathering at age-old harvesting sites. When tribal fishermen attempted to exercise their treaty-guaranteed rights, they and their families were arrested and jailed by state game wardens.

In an effort to defend their treaty rights, Indian Peoples along the Puget Sound began in the 1960s to stage protests called fish-ins. Inspired by the civil rights movement and backed by Indian activists, celebrity supporters, and civil rights organizations, they argued that state game laws could not overturn federal treaties that guaranteed their right to fish. The U.S. Justice Department agreed and filed a lawsuit: *United States v. Washington*. The case landed in the hands of U.S. district court judge George H. Boldt, who in 1974 handed down a landmark decision in favor of the Indian Tribes. Reviewing the Treaties 120 years after they were negotiated, Boldt decreed that tribal fishing rights were "protected under the supreme law of the land," that state laws could not trump federal treaty guarantees, and that Indians were entitled to "take an equal share" of the salmon harvest.[1] "The mere passage of time," Boldt declared, "has not eroded, and cannot erode, the rights guaranteed by solemn treaties."

The decision sparked a firestorm of controversy. State officials asserted Washington State's right to conserve and manage natural resources by imposing on everyone licenses, seasons, catch limits, trespass laws, and other controls. Sport and commercial fishermen agreed, complaining that treaties gave Indians special rights no one else enjoyed—rights that would ultimately deplete the common supply of salmon. Despite the backlash, tribal fishing rights along the Puget Sound were upheld in 1979 by the U.S. Supreme Court.

A similar scenario played out along the Great Lakes. When Native Nations in Michigan, Wisconsin, and Minnesota invoked nineteenth-century treaties to secure their rights to fish, hunt, and gather wild rice, they were confronted by groups of angry non-Natives, who picketed the lake shores, chanted racist slogans, and derided treaties. Here, too, the stiff resistance failed to vanquish treaty rights. In 1983 the U.S. Court of Appeals for the Seventh Circuit upheld the claims of Wisconsin Ojibwe that their rights to fish, hunt, and gather on former tribal lands were guaranteed by the treaties their ancestors had signed with the United States. In 1999 the U.S. Supreme Court ruled that the Mille Lacs Band of Ojibwe in Minnesota retained fishing, hunting, and gathering rights on lands ceded in the Treaty of 1837.[2]

The Native Nations of the Pacific Northwest and the Great Lakes have come a long way since the fish-ins of the 1960s. Today, Puget Sound fisheries are managed by a cooperative system in which federal, tribal, and state governments share control. Tribes on the Columbia River and the Great Lakes also follow this model. Strong conservationists, tribal fishermen now work hand in glove with former treaty-rights opponents to stabilize habitat and ensure fish runs for future generations. For these environmental stewards, the struggle continues.

The Game and Fish Were Made for Us

Hunting and Fishing Rights in Native Nations' Treaties   HANK ADAMS

God created this Indian country and it was like He spread out a big blanket. He put the Indians on it. . . . Then God created fish in this river and put deer in these mountains and made laws through which has come the increase of fish and game. Then the Creator gave us Indians life; we awakened, and as soon as we saw the game and fish we knew that they were made for us. For the women God made roots and berries to gather, and the Indians grew and multiplied as a people. When we were created we were given our ground to live on, and from that time these were our rights.

MENINOCK (Yakama), 1915[1]

Through the treaties we reserved that which is most important to us as a people: The right to harvest salmon in our traditional fishing areas. But today the salmon is disappearing because the federal government is failing to protect salmon habitat. Without the salmon there is no treaty right. We kept our word when we ceded all of western Washington to the United States, and we expect the United States to keep its word.

BILLY FRANK JR. (Nisqually), July 14, 2011[2]

IN 1854–55, Governor Isaac Stevens of Washington Territory held a series of treaty councils with some seventeen thousand Indians in which tribal representatives reluctantly agreed to cede vast tracts of their homelands to the United States. But the leaders of these salmon-fishing peoples had the wisdom and moral courage to ensure that future generations would forever have access to the natural resources that defined their culture and lifeways. They insisted that the Treaties stipulate that their people would retain the rights to fish, hunt, and gather in their "usual and accustomed" places. A century later this treaty language would provide their descendants with a powerful weapon with which to defend those rights.

Twentieth-century treaty-rights activists drew strength not only from the language of the nineteenth-century treaties but also from treaty stories that tribal elders had passed down to them. Those stories echoed the words of tribal leaders captured in the handwritten minutes of the treaty council meetings.

In the sparse minutes and transcripts of these treaty councils, initially only Governor Stevens speaks of the pre-written provisions on fishing rights:

> For all time to come . . . the Great Father wishes you to have . . . fishing places.
> —Treaty of Medicine Creek, December 26, 1854

> You have your own glorious streams. We want to place you in homes where you can cultivate the soil, raising potatoes . . . and where you may be able to pass in canoes over the waters of the sound and catch fish, and [go?] back to the mountains to get roots and berries. The Great Father desires this.
> —Treaty of Point Elliott, January 22, 1855

Makah lidded basket with whaling scene, ca. 1900. Washington. Cedar bark, bear grass. 12 × 12 × 6.5 cm. National Museum of the American Indian 23/7272

The first quoted Indian statements come in the third treaty talks with the S'Klallam and Skokomish at Point No Point on January 25, 1855:[3]

> I wish to speak my mind as to selling the land, Great Chief: What shall we eat if we do so? Our only food is berries, deer and salmon—where then shall we find these? I don't want to sign away all my land. Take half of it, and let us keep the rest.
> —Ohe-lan-the-tat[?]

> I do not want to leave the mouth of the river. I do not want to leave my old home and my burying ground. I am afraid I shall die if I do.
> —S'hair-at-sehd-wk (Toanhooch)[?]

> [Mr. Frank Shaw, the Interpreter, explained to them that they were not called upon to give up their old modes of living and places of seeking food, but only to confine their homes to one spot.]

> I do not like the offers you make in the Treaty to us—you say you will give us land, but why should you give us the mouth of the river [which is ours]. . . . I don't want to sign away my right to the land. If it was myself alone that I signed for, I would do it. But we have women and children. Let us keep half of it and take the rest.
> —Hool-hole-tan, or Jim[?]

In the records of a pre-treaty meeting held on January 30, 1855, with Makah leaders at Neah Bay, comparable expressiveness is attributed to its Waatch, Tsoo-yess, Tatoosh (Stone House), and Ozette village leaders, who had resisted accepting "chief papers" because they believed that no one in their group should be ranked above any of the others.[4]

> *Kal-chote:* He thought he ou[gh?]t to have the right of fish and take whales and get food where he liked. He was afraid that if he could not take halibut where he wanted, he would become poor.

> *Koh-chook:* What Kal-chote had said was his wish. His country [should?] extend up to Nok-ho. He did not want to leave the salt water.

> Governor Stevens informed them that so far from wishing to stop their fisheries, he intended to send them oil, kettles and fishing apparatus.

> *Klah-pa-at-hoo:* He was willing to sell his land: all he wanted was the right of fishing.

> *Tse-heu-wrl:* He wanted the sea: What was his country if whales were killed and floated ashore[?] He wanted for his people the exclusive right of taking them.

> Governor Stevens replied that he wanted them to fish but that the whites should fish also. Whoever killed the whale was to have them if the [?] came ashore.

> *Ke-bach-sat:* My heart is not bad but I do not wish to leave all my land. I am willing you should have half, but I want the other half myself.

> *It-an-daha:* I do not wish to leave the salt water. I want to fish in common with the whites. I don't want to sell all the land. I want a part in common with the whites to plant potatoes on.

The next day, January 31, Governor Stevens addressed about six hundred Makahs who had gathered to hear him explain the treaty: "The Great Father wishes to give you your homes. He wants to buy your land . . . but [is] leaving you enough to live on and raise your potatoes. He knows what whalers

Gustav Sohon (1825–1903). *Coming for the Walla Walla Council*, May 18, 1855. Colored pencil, watercolor, and ink on laminated mat. Image 20.3 × 30.5 cm. National Anthropological Archives, Smithsonian Institution NAA INV 08602800

you are, how you go far to sea to take whales. He will send you barrels in which to put your oil, kettles to [try] it out, lines and implements to fish with."[5]

At the Walla Walla treaty council of May 28– June 11, 1855, in his efforts to persuade the Indian Nations of eastern Washington and Oregon, and northern Idaho, to accept reservations from cessions of all their lands, Governor Stevens noted that during his "four councils on Puget Sound," more Indians had accepted "one-fiftieth" as much land: "They take Salmon and catch whale and make oil. They ask for no more land. They think they have land enough." And, as he had during the other treaty negotiations, he told his listeners, "You will be allowed to go to the usual fishing places and fish in common with the whites, and to get roots and berries and to kill game on land not occupied by the whites; all this outside the Reservation."

Reflecting the promise that the Yakama could take produce and livestock down the Columbia River and to Puget Sound, their Treaty, which was one of three negotiated at the Walla Walla council, spec-

ified "rights of way . . . and access" as well as "the right, in common with citizens of the United States, to travel upon all public highways." Added to language included in the earlier Stevens Treaties was an express "exclusive right of taking fish in all the streams, where running through or bordering said reservation."

The Yakama chiefs Kamiakin, Owhi, Skloom, and Teias/Teayass had arrived late to the council. They expressed reluctance at proceeding while most their people were absent, being either at Nisqually or elsewhere in "the season for digging Roots and catching Salmon." By the second day (May 29), as on the last day (June 9), they were eager to return to their gardens.

Because Governor Stevens particularly sought to counter them, the following Indian statements of June 7 were of special significance:

Young Chief (Cayuse): I wonder if this ground has anything to say: I wonder if the ground is listening to what is said. I wonder if the ground would come to life and what is on it: though I hear what this

Gustav Sohon (1825–1903). *We-ah-te-na-tee-ma-ny: The Young Chief, Head Chief of the Cayuses*, June 8, 1855. Pencil on paper. 22.9 × 18.4 cm. Washington State Historical Society, Takoma 1918.114.9.48

Gustav Sohon (1825–1903). *Ou-hi, Chief of the Yakima Indians*, June 3, 1855. Pencil on paper. 22.9 × 18.1 cm. Washington State Historical Society, Takoma 1918.114.9.66

earth says, the earth says: God has placed me here. The Earth says that God tells me to take care of the Indians on this earth: the Earth says to the Indians that stop on the Earth, feed them right. God named the roots that he should feed the Indians on: the water speaks the same way: God says feed the Indians upon the earth: the grass says the same thing: feed the horses and cattle. The Earth and water and grass says God has given our names and we are told those names: neither the Indians or the Whites have a right to change those names: the Earth says God has placed me here to produce all that grows upon me, the trees, fruit, [etc.]. The same way the Earth says, it was from her man was made.

Owhi (Yakama): God gave us day and night, the night to rest in and the day to see—and that as long as the earth shall last, he gave us the morning with our breath; and so he takes care of us on this earth. . . . God was before the earth, the heavens were clear and good and all things in the heaven were good. God looked one way then the other

and named our lands for us to take care of . . . he made it to last forever. It is the earth that is our parent, or it is God [that] is our elder brother. This leads the Indian to ask where does this talk come from that you have been giving us. God made this earth, and it listens to him to know what he would decide. . . .

My friends, God made our bodies from the earth, as if they were different from the whites. What shall I do? Shall I give the lands that are part of my body and leave myself poor and destitute? Shall I say I will give you my lands? I cannot say. I am afraid of the Almighty.

At end of that day, Governor Stevens addressed reluctant and opposing speakers: "But Owhi is 'afraid lest God be angry at his selling his land.' Owhi, my brother, I do not think God will be angry if you do your best for yourself and your children. Ask yourself this question tonight: Will not God be angry with me if I neglect this opportunity to do them good? . . . I do not want to be ashamed of Owhi."[6]

The Treaty of Neah Bay with the Makah Indian Nation involved more than land cession and the right to harvest salmon. By the time its leaders signed the Treaty, the Makah were fully engaged in the commercial whaling industry, producing about thirty thousand gallons of whale oil annually. The Makah also processed seal oil and some fish oils. Relying on the 1855 Treaty, which guaranteed them "the right of taking fish and of whaling or sealing at usual and accustomed grounds and stations," the Makah soon joined in the new industry of harvesting fur seals, which developed shortly after the United States purchased Alaska in 1867.

At the outset the Pacific fur seal populations were comparable to those of the bison or buffalo on the Great Plains. The seals' annual migrations took them from California to island rookeries in the North Pacific and Bering Sea. Within two decades of the industry's rise in 1870, however, fur seal populations had been decimated from overharvesting and the waste inflicted by destructive harvest practices. The use of shotguns resulted in the loss of nearly 90 percent of all seals killed. Either they sank in the open waters or the puncture wounds rendered the hides of those recovered largely unusable. The pelagic kill took its highest toll upon feeding females, leaving their unfed pups on the shore to die, while the decks of sealing ships and adjacent waters turned white with mammary milk streaked red with blood.

To participate in the harvests, the Makah quickly purchased a fleet of schooners to sail to the Aleutian Islands and Bering Sea. Each schooner carried a minimum of five canoes in which the hunters would approach and spear the floating fur seals with appropriate harpoons. The Indian recovery rate of struck seals was higher than 90 percent, with virtually no waste of pelts or skins.

After issues of jurisdiction and fur seal preservation were presented to an international tribunal in Paris under the Treaty of Arbitration of 1892, the offshore Bering Sea sealing industry was closed down for most American and Canadian citizens. The United States made a request to Britain and Canada

Makah whalers, ca. 1920. Neah Bay, Washington. Photo by Asahel Curtis. National Museum of the American Indian P09485

that the nondestructive Makah treaty hunters be allowed to continue their pelagic seal harvests concurrent with onshore seal hunts in the Bering Sea. The request was denied on the basis that coastal Canadian Indians might perceive themselves to possess rights equivalent to those held by the Makah under their Treaty with the United States.[7] Oceanic seal hunting was prohibited by federal law in 1897.

The sealing loss was soon followed by the end of the Makah whaling harvests—also due to the depletion of populations by others. Among the last of the Makah's spring and autumn whale hunts was recorded by photographer Asahel Curtis.

The elk populations of the Olympic Peninsula likewise had been reduced to dangerously low levels. By 1905, when a state elk hunting ban was enacted, the size of the herd had declined to nine thousand animals, a fraction of those estimated to have ranged there fifty years earlier, at the time of the land cessions made under the Medicine Creek, Point Elliot, Point No Point, and Neah Bay Treaties with the United States.[8]

The Anti-Treaty Movement in the Pacific Northwest and the Great Lakes

SUZAN SHOWN HARJO

THE ANTI-TREATY MOVEMENT HAS EXISTED AS long as the United States and Native Nations have been making treaties; it was begun by those who favored warfare with and extermination of Indigenous Peoples, rather than treaty making and peaceful coexistence. That movement continued under the labels of states' rights and equal rights.

In the Pacific Northwest and the Great Lakes regions, the anti-treaty movement arose from a lack of recognition that Native Nations had in the nineteenth century negotiated and settled in treaties rights to fish, hunt, and gather in the ceded areas outside reservation borders. During the twentieth century, the movement led to virulent state and private efforts to stop Indians from exercising their treaty-guaranteed rights. Old fishermen such as David Sohappy (Yakama), who knew only one way of life and were fishing in their treaty-affirmed areas, were disrupted at their work and arrested by officials enforcing Washington state laws that challenged as invalid not only treaties but also federal and tribal laws. Sohappy almost died before being exonerated; prison left him a broken man.

Maiselle Bridges (Squaxin Island Tribe), the matriarch of Franks Landing Indian Community, a hub of treaty fishing activism, and her family were targeted by the state of Washington. Her brother, Billy Frank Jr. (Nisqually), who was arrested myriad times for fishing in the Nisqually River, said he was the "go-to-jail guy." Frank's counterpart in Michigan was Arthur Duhamel (Grand Traverse Band of Ottawa and Chippewa Indians), who was arrested hundreds of times, his boats and nets confiscated, until in 1979, Judge Noel Fox ruled for treaty fishing in the Great Lakes.

From the 1960s through the 1980s, in the Pacific Northwest and Great Lakes areas, it was common to see bumper stickers that reflected the racism of the time: Save a Salmon, Net an Indian; Save 2 Salmon, Kill a Pregnant Squaw; Save a Deer, Shoot an Indian; Spear Indians, Not Walleye. Native people were harassed when they were gathering berries, roots, seaweed, cedar, shellfish, and wild rice.

Federal district court judge George H. Boldt—whose 1974 landmark decision affirming treaty fishing rights was upheld by the Supreme Court in 1979—was hanged in effigy. He was so vilified that he personally interviewed all the hospital personnel who would have anything to do with his heart surgery to satisfy himself that they were not anti-Indian.

In the Great Lakes states, non-Natives stood on lake shores at night, throwing rocks at Native fishers on the water. Kids and adults alike bullied Native young people, even if they weren't from fishing or hunting families. Indian boys were even kicked out of a Boy Scout troop. When federal and tribal judges started receiving death threats, the National Congress of American Indians (NCAI), for which I served as executive director, and gaiashkibos (Lac Courte Oreilles Band of Lake Superior Ojibwe) served as first vice president, mobilized a national campaign.

Representative John Conyers (D-Michigan) and other House Judiciary Committee members convinced the Justice Department to investigate the threats and the anti-treaty movement. Groups with innocuous-sounding names organized under the Interstate Coalition for Equal Rights and Responsibilities and coordinated the anti-Indian, anti-treaty activities. One group in Wisconsin called Stop Treaty Abuse produced Treaty Beer. Representative

Treaty Beer can, ca. 1987. Aluminum, paint. 12.5 × 6 (diam.) cm. National Museum of the American Indian EP1036

In the 1980s, two Wisconsin businessmen marketed Treaty Beer to sport fishermen and hunters around the Great Lakes and Puget Sound as a protest against the fishing and hunting rights guaranteed to Native Nations by treaty.

An effigy of Judge George H. Boldt hangs on the fishing boat *Shenandoah*, September 1978. Seattle, Washington. Photo by Matt McVay, *Seattle Times*

Jim Sensenbrenner (R-Wisconsin) took an action that was not popular in his district—he joined us at an NCAI press conference in Green Bay, where we called for a boycott of Treaty Beer and poured it in a garbage can.

While the anti-treaty movement is in remission in states where it once dominated the news, it continues to roil with considerable intensity in New York State, where tribal land claims remain unresolved, and to a lesser extent elsewhere. Although the threats to treaty rights are not as immediate or targeted as were those in the Pacific Northwest and the Great Lakes, Native rights advocates remain watchful for signs that the anti-treaty movement could be growing again.

River by River: Treaty Rights in Washington State

An Interview with Susan Hvalsoe Komori

SUZAN SHOWN HARJO

SUZAN SHOWN HARJO: What were the human impacts of long-term attempts to exercise treaty rights, and what happened [during conflicts in the early 1970s on the Nisqually River in Washington State,] when oftentimes you were the person who took charge of the children?

SUSAN HVALSOE KOMORI: It's fishing season. The fish are coming up the river, and whole families gather as they have always done along the bank to help. The able-bodied men and women get their nets and go to their traditional fishing spots, or take their boats out. And, predictably, the game department—for the most part it was the Washington State Department of Game—would come swaggering down with their billy clubs, their macho holsters, and their lots-of-vehicles—they had boats, too—and they would go out, "get" the Indians, and they would haul them back to their vehicles. They would forcibly yank them out of the boats, often pulling the women into the water and then out by the hair. And then just beat them, put them in their police cars, and send them away to the jail. And the children, of course, are watching their mothers, their aunts, and their grandmothers be beaten with billy clubs and yanked out by their hair and hauled away [for] doing what they've learned since they were still in the cradle was the right of their people, the right of their community, the right of their family: to fish in that place, to take their fish there. So it's very damaging; when you see violence against a parent when you're that young, and the parent didn't do anything wrong, it's very, very hard. So you have children that grow up and hate the state government and don't trust non-Indians, because they've never seen anything to trust.

The children are watching their parents get arrested and go to jail and get out and go back on the river—and sometimes [the men] start drinking so that they won't feel the pain when they get beaten up the next time. Had there not been a Boldt decision, I think maybe the federal government eventually would have succeeded in destroying the structure of these Indian communities and families, through the loss of self-respect among the fishermen and the alcoholism that developed as a result.

When Judge Boldt made his decision, the state and the private non-Indian fishing groups appealed, and the ninth circuit court of appeals basically affirmed it. It then went up to the Supreme Court. In the meantime non-Indian fishermen and state regulatory agencies continued to fight the implementation of Indian fishing rights, continued to argue that Indians weren't entitled to those rights, and continued to feel that they didn't have to respect the treaties and court decisions. For some reason sport fishermen in particular felt that they were exempt from honoring Indian treaty rights because sport fishing must be a higher and better pursuit than Indian or commercial fishing, and therefore sport fishermen really, really fought it for many, many, many years—fought it individually in the rivers, fought it in the courts, and fought it in the implementation procedures. Almost every single fishery ended up being subjected to federal oversight concerning how the law got implemented, what the season would be, who got to go fishing, and what kind of fishing they got to do.

I think Judge Boldt recognized that his ruling couldn't be implemented voluntarily by the parties, and so he took over administration of the fisheries. Almost every regulatory decision by the state and

Norma McCloud Frank (Puyallup) is arrested and dragged from her boat on the Nisqually River for exercising her treaty fishing rights, 1969. Washington. Film still from Carol Burns, *As Long as the Rivers Run* (1971). Courtesy of the Northwest Indian Fisheries Commission, Olympia, Washington

by the tribes had to go through him. You had quasi-judicial bodies set up to try and mediate, and special masters set up to hear their arguments, river by river, fishery by fishery. It was an extraordinary process, and in this time, if non-Indian fishermen wanted to do something that wasn't part of what was agreed to or wasn't part of the court orders, they really thought nothing of ramming and firing shots at Indian boats, or at the U.S. Coast Guard boats that were enforcing the orders. And the sportsmen on the rivers were doing things to sabotage Indian fisheries and hurt Indians. It's still not entirely resolved, but certainly, after how many years—parties are getting more used to it. . . .

SUZAN SHOWN HARJO: Do you see the gathering rights being exercised in the same way, with the same ferocity, as the fishing and hunting rights?

SUSAN HVALSOE KOMORI: By the time the gathering issues really became big, there was a lot of violence on the fishing front. Indians were being told that they couldn't exercise their rights, that those rights were no longer valid because [the treaties] were too old. Or that the state didn't enter into the treaty, the federal government did; therefore the state isn't bound—all of the things that the Supreme Court has had to clear up.

As a result a lot of time was lost before non-Indians learned about important Indian practices. For example, a lot of times [Native people on the North Pacific Coast] took cedar bark from fallen trees, but if the tree wasn't already fallen, they made sure not to strip it all the way around because one didn't want to kill the tree. So there were certain protocols and ceremonies to be observed. Your first objective was to preserve the living heart of that item, and if the item fell, or if you truly needed it, like for a canoe or something, you performed a ceremony and you took it and used it honorably—and you used everything. The cedar tree was used for building homes, building canoes; it was your method of transportation, it was your clothing. You could make waterproof clothing out of cedar bark. It was light and it was pliable and, not to mention, it was also very beautiful.

Land and sea plants were gathered for virtually every aspect of life. How much of that, especially on the religious front or on the medicine front, Indians would ever be willing to share is a big question, and that's because of the way non-Indians have treated Indians. It's a matter of preserving what little is left. I think that one of the great tragedies here is that non-Indians who don't understand why we entered into the treaties have also lost so much. If they could be brought to understand that the treaties didn't just preserve something for the Indians—the treaties took a lot from them. But some of what they preserved for the Indians would also be a great benefit to non-Indians. Great pharmaceutical companies send researchers into aboriginal areas in South America, and also here, to try to learn more about medicines because of their commercial value. If we had confidence in each other, there might actually be some benefit to Indians sharing more of this knowledge. We've done so much to reduce that confidence by disrespecting the rights that we promised to American Indians. . . .

I think everybody should stand up and say, "We have a couple hundred years now of really bad history of implementing these treaties, but we entered into them, and it's time to start honoring them. Let's see if we can work together, so that both sides benefit from the resources, the culture, and the richness that it was the intention of the Indians to preserve.

From an interview that took place on April 18, 2013, at the Smithsonian's National Museum of the American Indian in Washington, DC.

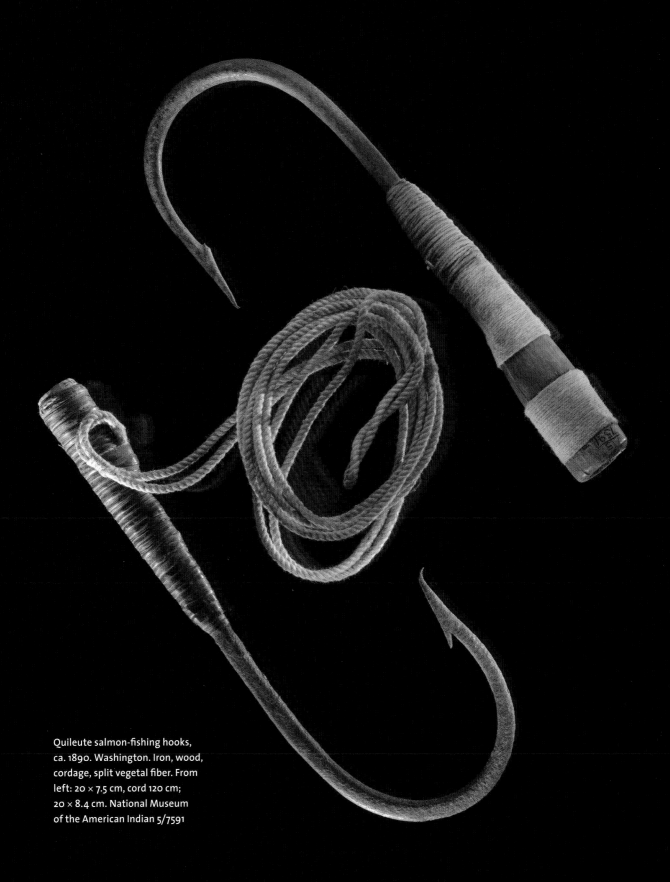

Quileute salmon-fishing hooks,
ca. 1890. Washington. Iron, wood,
cordage, split vegetal fiber. From
left: 20 × 7.5 cm, cord 120 cm;
20 × 8.4 cm. National Museum
of the American Indian 5/7591

"The Fish Helped to Bring People Together"

An Interview with Zoltán Grossman

ZOLTÁN GROSSMAN: My real background on treaty rights came as a community organizer in northern Wisconsin during the conflict of the late 1980s, early 1990s, after the federal courts reaffirmed Ojibwe treaty rights to harvest walleye, muskie, and other fish as well as deer and medicine plants outside the boundaries of the reservation. There was an immense backlash from white sport-fishing groups, from anti-treaty organizations like Protect Americans' Rights and Resources and Stop Treaty Abuse. They held protests at the boat landings and on the lakes in northern Wisconsin, at night, during the spring spearfishing season.

The Ojibwe were beginning to reinvigorate their culture and find again their cultural roots in harvesting these resources in seasonal cycles, as they had for millennia. And the white sport fishermen and other groups—and the media—didn't understand what this was about. They thought it would be the destruction of the resource. They thought that the tourist economy, the lifeblood of northern Wisconsin, would be destroyed by the tribes, even though the Ojibwe never took more than 3 percent of the walleye. Some of these groups started to organize very violent harassment of not only the spearfishers out on the water but also the families of the Ojibwe, right there at the boat landings.

I was part of an effort organized by the Midwest Treaty Network and Witness for Nonviolence, which trained about two thousand people, mainly non-Indians like myself, to go to the boat landings to monitor the harassment, try and deflect some of the violence, and try to show these groups for what they were. And also to open up dialogue with some of the people in northern Wisconsin . . . who had been misled by these groups into believing that the Ojibwe were going to threaten their livelihood and their rural culture. . . .

I remember one lake, Sand Lake. I believe it was April of '91. And it was a very hostile crowd, a mob of people were burning Native flags [and] throwing rocks, and I remember recording one remark from a mother who was talking to her two little kids—they couldn't have been more than six and seven. She saw that the boats were over by the shoreline of her lake, and she said, "Let's go over to Grandma's, they're over there, and let's get some rocks and let's throw some rocks at the Indians." So their public face was very much, "Oh we're concerned about the fish; we're concerned about the tourism," but [their hostility] was very evident [at] the boat landings [from] the violence that was being inflicted on the spearfishers and their families—pipe bombs, sniper fire, full beer cans, people being run off the road at night.

This is the type of thing that we put in the Witness for Nonviolence reports in the late eighties and early nineties. . . . So—by monitoring and exposing the racism of some of the leadership of these [anti-treaty] groups, and by getting a federal court injunction against anti-Indian harassment in northern Wisconsin, and by discrediting the lies that some of these groups had put forth—we began to reach some of the people who were following these movements, and they began to fall away.

At the same time, multinational mining companies started to come into the ceded territories of northern Wisconsin to open metallic sulfide mines along some of the same rivers and streams that were of concern to both the spearfishers and the anglers. And some of the anglers—Trout Unlimited, Walleyes for Tomorrow—actually began to realize that not only were the tribes not the enemy when it came to the fish population but also that, in fact, the tribes could end up—with their treaty rights standing in federal court, with their cultures reinvigorated, with their gaming—being some of the best allies in fighting these mining companies. So the same two groups, the tribes and the sport fishers, that had fought over the fish were by the mid-1990s actually coming together to protect the same fish from a common outside threat. And what I found is that it was some of the areas with the most intense conflicts over the natural resources that ended up having the strongest alliances between the former adversaries.

In the short run the tribes may have alienated some of their white neighbors, but they reached and educated more people through fighting and asserting their rights. In the areas where they asserted their rights the most strongly, they actually educated people on the history and culture of the area. They knocked a lot of non-Indian people off the fence and made them realize that tribal sovereign regulations were stronger than state regulations in fighting these mining companies. In particular, [to fight the proposed] Crandon Mine along the Wolf River—which is sacred to the Menominee—in an area where wild rice is harvested by the Ojibwe, the tribes built an alliance with the sport-fishing groups that were downstream. They ended up defeating the world's largest mining companies by 2003.

Not only did this very strong alliance of sport-fishing groups, environmentalists, and tribes defeat the mining companies, but two of the tribes, the Mole Lake Ojibwe and [the] Forest County Potawatomi, ended up actually purchasing the five thousand-acre mine site themselves, and they now own it, control it, and will determine its future. And many of the non-Indian people, the rural white neighbors, the retired folks, the cottage owners, the sport fisherman, are grateful that the tribes asserted their sovereignty to regulate the air and water around the reservation. That sovereign power is what gave the alliance the standing to fight the state government, which was going to allow the mining to take place. If it weren't for the tribes having fought for those treaty rights and on-reservation sovereign rights, that mine would almost certainly be going right now.

The white neighbors of the tribes went from hos-

David P. Bradley (Minnesota Chippewa, White Earth Ojibwe) b. 1954. *Anishinaabe Fishing Rights*. Canvas, wood, paint. 102 × 76.2 cm. National Museum of the American Indian 26/9269

tility to realizing that sovereignty was really the only thing between them and the destruction of their environment and their tourist economy. So the fish divided people at first, and in the end the fish helped to bring people together. And I think that they're building economic relationships, cultural relationships that never would have been possible before. This kind of cooperation, collaboration, which came from the grassroots—it came from the bottom up—is starting to bring some local and state officials along.

So I went from real despair to real hope, seeing how some of the tribes are using their sovereignty to build new models of ecological sustainability, new economic models to try to keep kids from leaving for the city or to draw people back to the reservation. I think a lot of the non-Indian communities are starting to learn from this. In a way, the reservations are becoming like greenhouses, places where new ways of relating to each other and new ways of relating to the land—which actually draw on very ancient traditions—are now beginning to flourish. And some of the white neighbors are starting to realize, if these people can do it, maybe we can, too.

From an interview that took place in September 2005 at The Evergreen State College in Olympia, Washington.

Arthur Duhamel

Treaty Fisherman

MATTHEW L. M. FLETCHER

ARTHUR DUHAMEL, THE LEADING FIGURE IN THE treaty fishing rights fight for the Grand Traverse Band of Ottawa and Chippewa Indians, once said, "I respect the law. That's why I broke it, you know."

In 1972, Art began fishing Grand Traverse Bay, which is at the center of the homeland of the Grand Traverse Band of Ottawa and Chippewa Indians. The Michigan Supreme Court had in 1971 recognized that tribal treaty rights to fish the Great Lakes had survived nearly 140 years of suppression by the state of Michigan. But the Michigan attorney general was fond of saying that the winner of that case, Al Jondreau, an Ojibwe man from the Keweenaw Bay Indian Community, was the only Indian allowed to fish in Michigan. In 1976, after an Upper Peninsula Ojibwe fisherman, Big Abe LeBanc, won a similar suit, the attorney general said that only Al and Big Abe could fish.

Geebo Sands, Arthur's father, encouraged him to start fishing, even though Arthur didn't know anything about fishing. For the next dozen years or so, until the 1985 federal consent decree that finally ended treaty rights litigation over fishing in Lake Michigan, state law-enforcement officers arrested Arthur hundreds of times for violation of state laws that conflicted with treaty rights. They confiscated his boats, his nets, and all his equipment. Sport and commercial fishermen physically threatened Arthur and vandalized his equipment. The state prosecuted him before Leelanau County judge Richard Benedict, who, famously, once asked the ethnohistorian Helen Hornbeck Tanner in open court what the treaties said about fishing and then—to the shock of everyone in the courtroom—immediately ordered her not to answer the question.

After 1979, when federal judge Noel Fox held in *United States v. Michigan* that the treaty right to fish on the Great Lakes survived, Arthur repeatedly testified in congressional hearings arguing against efforts by the state of Michigan to persuade Congress to abrogate the right. His tireless advocacy as both a treaty fisherman and a political advocate rallied the Grand Traverse Band, once a prominent Lake Michigan treaty tribe, from destitution, desperation, and poverty to become one of the most important political entities and economic engines in northwest lower Michigan.

Rights We Always Had

An Interview with Tina Kuckkahn

SUZAN SHOWN HARJO

TINA KUCKKAHN: The Ojibwe people in Wisconsin, Minnesota, Michigan, and North Dakota signed Treaties with the government in which our forefathers were wise enough to reserve for future generations the opportunity to hunt, fish, and gather on our lands, within the reservation boundaries and also within the ceded territories. That foresight ended up causing a huge amount of controversy in the 1970s, as our tribal members began to be arrested for exercising those rights.

In 1974 the Tribble brothers from the Lac Courte Oreilles Band of Lake Superior Ojibwe were arrested as they were exercising their right to spearfish on our lakes in northern Wisconsin. Fortunately, they were aware of their rights as members of an Indian Nation, and this began a series of cases that wound [their] way through the federal courts and affirmed the rights of our people.

The controversy came to a head in the 1990s. As the wintertime ended and the spring thaw came, as the ice began to thaw away from the lakes, our men would go out in their boats. Traditionally they went out in birchbark canoes, and they would hold torches of birchbark. The firelight would be reflected in the eyes of the walleye that were spawning along the beaches. That's how they had traditionally done it. Native people are always adapting, and so today you're as likely to see aluminum boats and men with hardhats that have headlights on the top, yet the idea is the same. The idea is that our people will continue to hunt, gather, and fish to provide for our community members, to provide for our elders.

As sport fishermen began to see what was happening in northern Wisconsin, there began to be a lot of protesting, and organizations were formed.

There [were] these very vigorous groups [that] were looking to call an end to the exercise of treaty rights by tribal members. They would inflame the public, they would inflame the media, by exclaiming about equal rights for everyone and asking, why do [these Indians] have special rights?

I was a student in law school at that time, and I'm always so proud that the Indigenous Law Student Association, the Black Law Student Association, and the Latino Law Student Association banded together in support of our treaty rights, that people stood together. It was very important to see how different people, disaffected groups historically, could come together to make important and powerful changes. And so our people began to spearfish, and the protesters would come, there were pipe bombs, there were rocks being thrown, there were bottles being thrown. People would go out in their powerful boats to try to make wakes to swamp our boats, yet our people persevered. They were lifted up, because we brought our drums, we had our cultural people present, and that sounding of the heartbeat had a way of helping calm even some of the most violent protesters. We had tribal leaders like Tom Maulson, who would walk right into a crowd of people who hated him, and he would talk about why our people were continuing to exercise their rights.

I would go and speak to different groups, and try to talk about the meaning of the Treaties, to explain that these are not ancient, historical documents that no longer have relevance today. If that is true, then the Constitution of the United States no longer has relevance. We would talk about how it's really a matter of contract law, so that if I, as a property owner, were to sell my home, I could write in the contract

Buck Chosa (Chippewa) fishes in Keweenaw Bay, 1971. Michigan. Photo by James L. Amos. © James L. Amos/Corbis

that I reserve the right to the minerals under the land. This is accepted contract law; people do it every day. In a very similar way, our forefathers were intelligent and thoughtful enough about the future generations to know that—in signing the Treaties that they didn't even want to sign in the first place—the best they could do was try to reserve for our people the rights to keep our traditional ways going. Our Treaties continue to be forceful documents asserting rights that we exercise each and every day, and they will continue to provide important rights and protections for our people into the future.

Some important groups of non-Native people came to stand as witnesses in protection of our rights: the Midwest Treaty Network and Witness for Nonviolence. Their cooperation and support helped us turn around the level of interaction at the boat landings. We were continuing to exercise our right in a dignified and respectful way, but it was very hard for people to maintain their composure while protesters were shouting really hateful and terri-

ble things at them, and at their children, and at our elders. Yet they maintained. It was difficult, and they were facing life-and-death situations, and yet other people came forward to support their work, the important foundational work for our future.

Two significant factors were very influential in stemming the tide of the racism and controversy surrounding the treaty rights. Native allies brought camcorders, tape recorders, and cameras, and they began to document the incidents of racism and harassment. When our tribal members began to pursue remedies through civil actions, we began to see results. It seemed as if, when the protesters realized that their mortgages and businesses were on the line, a lot of them backed off really quickly. The second major influence was that my tribe began to have a very successful casino venture. Suddenly historical enemies became financial partners, and so suddenly the chambers of commerce were working together. I'm hoping that as people come to our reservation, they will begin to interact with some of our people. That will also help with the educational aspect, the continuous informing that we need to do about contemporary Native people today. . . .

I graduated from law school in 1991. A few years after I moved out here to Washington State, the Makah began to exercise the right reserved in their Treaties to harvest whale. I work at The Evergreen State College. Many people here are environmentalists, and so there was a huge job in terms of educating people about the importance of the whale to Makah tribal culture. Once again, we were seeing very similar kinds of statements being made. Instead of [bumper stickers reading] Spear an Indian and Save a Walleye, it was Spear an Indian and Save a Whale. In fact they even tried to sell Treaty Beer, which initially had been a fundraising effort in northern Wisconsin that failed miserably, in part because the beer was terrible.

When the Makah were successful in harvesting their whale, they invited all nations to come to their community to witness and take part in their celebration of this rejuvenation of their culture. It was a huge celebration, because it had not been done in many, many years. Tribal people came in full support.

SUZAN HARJO: You referenced people who were questioning why Indians get these "special rights." Can you give your answer to that?

TINA KUCKKAHN: In my constitutional law class at the University of Wisconsin, the question was raised about special rights in relation to treaty rights, and how can that be when we have the equal protection clause. There is a very simple answer—and this has been established federal Indian law, beginning with the Marshall trilogy [of nineteenth-century Supreme Court cases]—which is that there is a unique relationship, a political relationship [between Native Nations and the U.S. government]. So we're not talking about distinguishing among races of people, we're talking about tribes as political entities, and their relationship to the federal government. That's what makes it different. These are not special rights that were given to tribal people, ever. These are rights that we always had. These are rights that our people were strong enough and had enough foresight to retain in the Treaties. They were not given to us. But our people wisely reserved them for our future generations.

From an interview that took place on September 24, 2005, at The Evergreen State College, Olympia, Washington.

THE RIGHT OF NATIVE PEOPLE TO MAINTAIN DISTINCT political and cultural communities was a foundational principle of early U.S.–Indian treaty making. In the late nineteenth and early twentieth centuries, that fundamental tenet withered under the weight of federal policies that weakened Indian cultures, eroded tribal land ownership, and promoted the imposition of unilateral government power over Native communities. Despite these challenges, American Indians never gave up on their treaties and struggled throughout the twentieth century to assert their right of tribal self-government, and to restore the principles of sovereign equality and nation-to-nation diplomacy that characterized the treaty-making era.

The principle of tribal self-government was bolstered by the Indian Reorganization Act of 1934, in which Congress recognized, for the first time in fifty years, that tribal governments were—and should be—the legitimate representatives of American Indian people.[1] But federal support of tribal authority would not last. In the 1940s, 1950s, and 1960s, Congress adopted a policy called termination, which advocated the dismantling of tribal governments, the dissolution of tribal lands, and the abolition of federal services to Native people.[2]

The threat of tribal termination promoted a surge of American Indian activism that laid the foundation for the emergence of modern Indian Nations. Inspired by the civil rights movement as well as the public's new openness toward human rights and social change, American Indians during the 1960s and 1970s increasingly invoked their treaties to assert their rights as citizens of Native Nations. They demanded the right of tribal self-determination, and they leveraged federal anti-poverty programs created under President Johnson's Great Society initiative to bypass the Bureau of Indian Affairs' heavy-handed supervision of day-to-day life on Indian reservations. Though rooted in urban communities, the red power movement of the 1960s and 1970s helped rejuvenate Indian Tribes by celebrating Indianness and tribal identity.[3]

Reforms in U.S. Indian policy reflected and shaped change in Indian Country. In his historic 1970 message to Congress, President Nixon rejected termination and called on legislators to make tribal self-determination federal policy. Intense lobbying by tribal leaders and Native organizations also persuaded Congress to pass more significant Indian legislation between 1970 and 1990 than during any comparable period in American history. At the same time, the U.S. Supreme Court handed down some sixty-five Indian law decisions,[4] which upheld the treaties as well as the sovereignty of Native Nations.

Today evidence of tribal self-determination and sovereignty pervades Indian Country. Native Nations manage their lands, pass laws and enforce them, regulate businesses, and provide services for tribal citizens. And the right of Indian people to maintain distinct political and cultural communities is now a fixed principle of U.S. policy. Nearly every president since 1970 has officially recognized Native Nations as sovereign entities and has pledged to respect and restore the consent-based, nation-to-nation relationship that existed between the United States and Indian Nations during the early years of treaty making.[5]

From Dislocation to Self-Determination

Native Nations and the United States in the Twentieth Century

BY THE EARLY TWENTIETH CENTURY THE IMPOSITION OF "CIVILIZATION" regulations and the implementation of the allotment policy led to the low point of American Indian relations with the U.S. government. Policies unilaterally imposed by the United States—ostensibly to help Indians become self-sufficient citizens—resulted in their near-absolute destitution and a deep dependence on federal services that persists today.

The losses were staggering. Under the allotment policy, in effect from 1887 to 1934, Indian land holdings—including much of the land that had been guaranteed to Indian Nations by treaty—were reduced by two-thirds.[6] Tribal self-government was quashed by a crushing array of laws imposed by the Department of the Interior, often without the benefit of any guidance or even authorization from Congress. Indians were arrested, tried, and punished for offenses created by Interior bureaucrats, not elected legislators. Remarkably, the federal courts turned a blind eye to the systematic taking of Indian property and ongoing deprivation of Indians' liberty. Native languages were forbidden at the federal schools that had been established for Indian children. Native religious events were prohibited by reservation superintendents, who held enormous power over Indians and their property.

Indians throughout the country and with few exceptions were desperately poor. Their educational achievement was extraordinarily low. Their health was bad, and infectious disease was rampant. Rarely, perhaps never, had policies intended to benefit a group of people—and that intent was sincere in many quarters—failed so completely and resulted in so much poverty, degradation, and death.[7]

Condemned Ojibwe (Chippewa) property ordered destroyed by U.S. Indian inspector Colonel Frank C. Churchill, 1906. Wild Rice River, Minnesota. Photo by Frank C. Churchill. National Museum of the American Indian N27557

In the 1920s a reform movement began to take shape. The small cohort of well-educated Native intellectuals, with support from sympathetic white people, began to find ways to address the poverty and accompanying social maladies that prevailed in Indian Country. A key event was the production of a report by Lewis Meriam and the Institute for Government Research on the conditions of Indian people on the reservations. The Meriam Report of 1928 catalogued in detail the impact of the civilization policy. The failure was evident, and the need for change extraordinarily clear.[8]

The Great Depression, the election of President Franklin D. Roosevelt, and the New Deal led to reform in Indian policy. John Collier and Felix Cohen, President Roosevelt's Commissioner of Indian Affairs and Interior Department Solicitor, respectively, had a very different vision of how Indian Nations might progress out of their dire circumstances. They had the Secretary of the Interior withdraw the "civilization regulations" that had suppressed Indian religions and traditional ways for fifty years. Native culture, Collier and Cohen believed, could serve to raise both the morale and economic fortunes of reservation Indians. Rather than suppress Indian self-government, Collier imagined that new governing institutions, likenesses of American governmental bodies, should be created by and for the Native Nations themselves. Further allotment of the reservations should cease, according to Collier, and federal efforts to support tribal economic advancement should begin. Tribal governments, said Collier, should assume authority over the service programs provided by the federal government on the reservations. Native culture, he thought, could raise both the morale and the economic fortunes of reservation Indians.[9]

Many of Collier and Cohen's ideas were enacted by Congress as part of the Indian

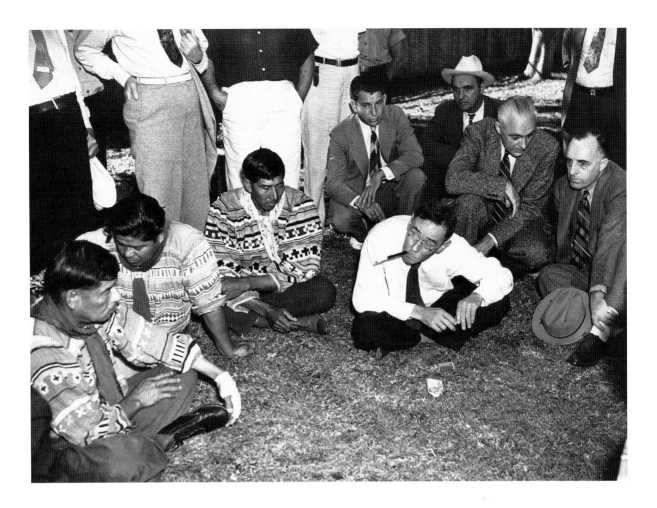

Reorganization Act of 1934 (IRA). The law authorized Indian Nations to forge constitutions, subject to federal approval, and establish corporations with federal charters to
conduct their business endeavors and develop the reservations. Programs were established to support reservation enterprises and encourage the production and sale of
Indian arts and crafts. Importantly, the Interior Department was empowered to add
land to the reservations and create new reservations. Native Nations and their citizens
also benefited from New Deal programs such as the Civilian Conservation Corps and
the Works Progress Administration.[10]

These initiatives relieved some of the poverty that had defined reservation life.
Many Indian Nations adopted constitutions under the IRA, and tribal governance
became real again, albeit in forms that scarcely resembled traditional institutions. Most
of the new governing systems involved elected tribal councils, which were empowered
to enact and enforce laws, and to conduct political relations with the United States.
Some of the new constitutions called for the establishment of courts and tribal execu-
tives. Criteria for tribal citizenship were established and the governments' territorial
authority defined. Virtually all the constitutions required federal approval of certain
actions of the new governments.

John Collier, Commissioner
of Indian Affairs, confers
with Seminole Indian leaders, January 5, 1940. Miami,
Florida. Associated Press
400105159

Henry Roe Cloud casts the first vote on the Winnebago Constitution, February 1936. Winnebago Agency, Nebraska. Photo by Charlotte Tuttle Westwood Lloyd Walkup. Yale Collection of Western Americana, Beinecke Rare Book and Manuscript Library, Yale University, New Haven, Connecticut 2014793

Many elements of the IRA were controversial among Indians as well as the non-Indian institutions that had long played major roles in governing the reservations. Collier was so certain of the law's benefits to Native Nations that its implementation often was manipulative, if not coercive, in achieving tribal compliance. Still, the IRA was a significant step toward the re-empowerment of Indian Nations. Even among the tribes that did not enact constitutions, the governing bodies of the Native Nations found ways to influence the federal policies that affected them.[11] While the IRA was no return to the principles of treaty making, it was an important repudiation of the idea that unilateral federal policy making was either desirable or effective.

The IRA might eventually have evolved into an equitable policy, giving Native Nations a greater voice in the matters that affected their well-being, but it was never completely implemented. Congress wavered in its support of the New Deal and the IRA, finding the expense of full implementation to be prohibitive. When World War II erupted, Indian policy, like many other domestic matters, fell out of the nation's priorities.

Indians participated in great numbers in the war effort. Some twenty-five thousand Native soldiers, sailors, and marines served in the armed forces, often distinguishing themselves in combat. Perhaps as many as fifty thousand Indians moved from the reservations to cities to work in the war industries or make new homes near family members.[12] Their participation did much to change attitudes about them. Given the chance, they showed themselves capable of full participation in American life, with no need of federal overseers.

Ironically, this show of capacity led to yet another federal policy initiative designed

to dissolve the Indian Nations. Immediately after the war the Truman administration began to consider how to reduce the size of the Indian affairs bureaucracy. The solution was to withdraw federal services and oversight from those nations that were deemed capable of managing their own affairs. Lists were drawn up of Indian tribes ready for "termination," those that would soon be ready, and those that would need more time to prepare.

When President Eisenhower took office in 1953, Congress urged the immediate implementation of the termination policy. The Eisenhower administration obliged, and over the coming years, Congress and the administration would withdraw federal

Navajo section hands Eddie Yazzie, Ta Bo Ho Nez, and Robert Long Salt work on the Southern Pacific Railroad, ca. 1942. Yuma, Arizona. Photo by Evans. Getty Images 3292417

acknowledgment of more than one hundred tribal governments, including some with treaty relationships with the United States. Once again, policy was being made unilaterally. While tribal governments were consulted, the process was largely pro forma, and the Indian Nations targeted for termination were not permitted to explore meaningful alternatives to the approach. Federal services were withdrawn, reservation lands were sold, and the proceeds were distributed to tribal citizens, who suddenly found themselves without the support of either their tribal governments or the United States.[13]

As the number of terminated tribes grew, so did tribal opposition to the policy. Tribal governments had not previously united politically, each contending with its own problems. But termination represented an existential threat to all Indian Tribes, and they found common purpose in fighting it.[14] They were helped in their opposition by the almost immediate and negative impacts of the policy. Stripped of their relationship with the federal government, and without the federal services upon which they had come to rely, the terminated tribes fell into disarray. Rather than prospering in the absence of federal supervision and tribal government support, Indians soon became burdens on the state and local governments that became responsible for their welfare. Formerly prosperous tribal enterprises began to fail. The Indian affairs bureaucracy was confronted with formidable tribal opposition, and it slowed implementation of the policy as the failures came into focus.

By 1960 the failure of termination was evident. Presidential candidates John F. Kennedy and Richard M. Nixon both indicated that they would seek a different approach to Indian policy. As the civil rights movement reached its peak, policy makers and the public began to understand the racial history of the country and its effects on all minorities, including Indian Peoples, who benefited from the civil rights legislation of the 1960s. Many Indians had long been attending colleges founded specifically for them, but as public schools began to desegregate, Indians attended mainstream colleges and universities in growing numbers. Discriminatory state voting laws, accompanied by Indian reluctance to participate in the political system that had treated them so badly, had suppressed voting by Indians in local, state, and national elections.[15] The new civil rights laws slowly changed that, and Indians gradually developed voting power in the western states where their populations were sufficient.

The emerging Indian rights movement, though, was different from the civil rights movement in a critical respect. Civil rights are personal rights belonging to individuals in a nation's body politic. Certainly Indian people wanted and were entitled to their individual rights as citizens of the United States. But they wanted something else as well: they wanted the rights of American Indian Nations to be honored. They wanted *group* rights as well as individual rights, and they based their claim for group rights on their inherent sovereignty and the Treaties that Indian Nations had made with the United States.[16]

Throughout the twentieth century, the United States had done much to deconstruct the idea of American Indian Nations, but it never quite finished the job. Federal courts throughout the 1900s upheld Indian water rights and hunting and fishing rights based on treaties. Though the Indian Nations' governmental authorities and institutions had been systematically suppressed, they had not been prohibited. Many tribes that had enacted Indian Reorganization Act constitutions had conditioned the exercise of their powers on federal approval, but no one doubted that it was *tribal* sovereign power that they were exercising. In reviewing their status, the federal courts determined that the Indian Nations retained those sovereign powers that had not been prohibited by Congress.[17] Thus, Indian Nations could not be sued without their consent.[18] Tribal citizens on their reservations held broad immunities from state laws.[19] Tribal governments could regulate the conduct of their citizens—and that of non-Indians in their interactions with tribal citizens on the reservations.[20]

Moreover, the treaties the United States had made with Indian Nations remained in effect, although some provisions had been changed by acts of Congress. The courts would not lightly find that a treaty promise had been repealed by Congress, requiring instead that Congress make clear its intention to violate treaty rights. And treaties and acts of Congress affecting Indian rights were interpreted liberally in favor of the Indians they were intended to benefit.[21] Thus, the principles of tribal sovereignty and the treaty relationship remained viable, notwithstanding the federal government's long and deliberate effort to dismantle them. The civil rights movement having redeemed the rights of American Indians as individuals, Native American activism focused on the rights and powers of American Indians as nations.

Tribal governments benefited from the Great Society programs of President Lyndon B. Johnson. Although most of the budget for services to Indians remained firmly in the hands of the federal Indian affairs bureaucracy, programs administered by the newly established Office of Economic Opportunity (OEO) did not carry the historical burden of the policy failures in Indian affairs. The OEO programs (community action programs, for example) placed funds directly with tribal governments, a precedent that would lead to a huge shift in the federal system of delivering services on the reservations.

By the mid-1960s the termination policy was dead, killed by good judgment and the activism of Native American leaders. The stage was set for a breakthrough. The termination policy arose not only from the federal government's desire to "get out of the Indian business" but also from the idea that federal support for Indian Nations necessarily brought with it a smothering superintendence that created a deep dependency and discouraged Native ambition. Native American leaders argued that there was no necessary relationship between services and support on the one hand and overbearing supervision on the other. Further, Native leaders argued that the federal government's fiduciary obligation to protect Indian resources meant that the Indians and their tribal nations, the putative beneficiaries of the relationship, should control the management of their resources.

The Native Nations were urging a return to the relationship envisioned in the early treaties between the United States and Indian Nations, one of friendship and alliance in which the tribal nations were self-governing and under the *protection,* not the *control,* of the United States. It was an audacious assertion in some respects. Much had happened since the early treaty days. The United States had prospered, becoming a global superpower and the richest nation in the world. Indian Nations, on the other hand, were a pale reflection of what they once had been, due in no small part to their systematic dispossession, exploitation, and despoliation by the United States. Indians were poor, unhealthy, and undereducated. But they had survived and were still insisting on their right to nationhood.

Although their treaties and agreements with the United States had been grossly violated, they insisted that as much of the treaties as could still be honored should be honored. Few Americans thought much about the treaties, and fewer still imagined that the Indian Nations could benefit from treaty promises in the same manner as the

Protestors in a multi-leveled prison cellblock on Alcatraz Island, 1969. San Francisco Bay, California. Photo by Art Kane. National Museum of the American Indian P28162

world's nation-states. But the country was reassessing its racial past; there was a sense that a just nation should do something for those who had been treated unjustly.

The popular culture began contributing to the public mood. Indians, who had long been portrayed as villainous, hapless, or both in Hollywood westerns, became the gallant but victimized heroes in a series of revisionist movies in the 1960s and 1970s. The protest music of the 1960s often made sympathetic reference to Indians: Johnny Cash released a concept album protesting the treatment of Indians, and Cree singer-songwriter Buffy Sainte-Marie found an enthusiastic audience for her heartfelt works. Kiowa writer N. Scott Momaday received a Pulitzer Prize for his novel *House Made of Dawn* (1968). Vine Deloria Jr. (Standing Rock Sioux) wrote the best-selling *Custer Died for Your Sins: An Indian Manifesto* (1969). Historian Dee Brown wrote *Bury My Heart at Wounded Knee: An Indian History of the American West* (1971), a sympathetic treatment of the late nineteenth-century Plains Indian Wars. Luiseño painter Fritz Scholder, Kiowa-Caddo artist T. C. Cannon, and other Native artists gained international attention with their innovative works.

The social unrest of the 1960s also included Indians. Native activists protested

President Nixon and other government officials meet at the White House with Taos Pueblo leaders before Nixon's message on Indian affairs is sent to Congress, July 8, 1970. Washington, DC. From left: James Mirabal, senior councilman of the tribe; Secretary of the Interior Walter J. Hickel; Quirino Romero, governor of Taos Pueblo; President Nixon; and Paul Bernal, Taos Pueblo tribal council secretary. Associated Press 700708064

various issues in a array of public settings. Tribal people and their supporters defied state fish and game laws in the Pacific Northwest to assert their treaty fishing rights. Activists seized and occupied Alcatraz Island in San Francisco Bay. Styling themselves the United Indians of All Tribes, the activists held the island for nineteen months, demanding that the United States give it to Indians for the establishment of a Native university and museum.

But none of this was directly aimed at specific policy issues. That work would be left to tribal officials and other advocates, who worked in Congress and through the executive agencies to advance reforms in Indian policy. In 1970 the breakthrough came without drama or cheering crowds—in the form of a "Special Message to the Congress on Indian Affairs" from President Richard Nixon. In an opening startling for its candor and sympathy, the president wrote:

> The first Americans—the Indians—are the most deprived and most isolated minority group in our nation. On virtually every scale of measurement—employment, income, education, health—the condition of the Indian people ranks at the bottom.
>
> This condition is the heritage of centuries of injustice. From the time of their first contact with European settlers, the American Indians have been oppressed and brutalized, deprived of their ancestral lands and denied the opportunity to control their own destiny.[22]

This opening was notable for its adoption of the Indian point of view of the long arc of relations between the United States and the Indian Nations. Directly blaming the historic treatment of Indians for their poor current conditions was a bold move for the president, one made possible by the transition in popular discourse about the history of the United States and American Indians. Having established responsibility for the situation, the president then posed the issue of what should be done and who should decide:

> Both as a matter of justice and as a matter of enlightened social policy, we must begin to act on the basis of what the Indians themselves have long been telling us. The time has come to break decisively with the past and to create the condi-

tions for a new era in which the Indian future is determined by Indian acts and Indian decisions.

The president then firmly repudiated the policy of termination. Carefully dismantling the reasoning behind the policy, he noted that treaties, not federal largesse, were the foundation of the relationship:

> Termination implies that the Federal government has taken on a trusteeship responsibility for Indian communities as an act of generosity toward a disadvantaged people and that it can therefore discontinue this responsibility on a unilateral basis whenever it sees fit. But . . . [t]he special relationship between Indians and the Federal government is the result instead of solemn obligations which have been entered into by the United States Government. Down through the years, through written treaties and through formal and informal agreements, our government has made specific commitments to the Indian people. For their part, the Indians have often surrendered claims to vast tracts of land and have accepted life on government reservations. In exchange, the government has agreed to provide community services such as health, education and public safety, services which would presumably allow Indian communities to enjoy a standard of living comparable to that of other Americans.

This long history—the failure of the United States to meet its obligations, and the special status of the Indian Nations—meant that, "to terminate this relationship would be no more appropriate than to terminate the citizenship rights of any other American."

Further, said the president, the policy had failed to produce the desired results, noting that the tribes' "economic and social condition has often been worse after termination than it was before." The policy also had the effect of creating "a great deal of apprehension among Indian groups and this apprehension, in turn, has had a blighting effect on tribal progress." Indians, the president argued, were all the more reluctant to take charge of finding solutions to their problems for fear that "it will only bring them closer to the day when the Federal government will disavow its responsibility and cut them adrift."

President Nixon rejected the false choice between federal support and federal control and laid out a new direction for Indian policy:

President Nixon signing a bill to return the sacred Blue Lake to the Taos Pueblo. Looking on are, from left, Paul Bernal and Juan de Jesus Romero, December 15, 1970. Washington, DC. White House Photo Office Collection (Nixon Administration) 1/20/1969–8/9/1974, National Archives and Records Administration, Washington, DC

Federal termination errs in one direction; Federal paternalism errs in the other. Only by clearly rejecting both of these extremes can we achieve a policy which truly serves the best interests of the Indian people. Self-determination among the Indian people can and must be encouraged without the threat of eventual termination. In my view, in fact, that is the only way that self-determination can effectively be fostered.

This, then, must be the goal of any new national policy toward the Indian people: to strengthen the Indian's sense of autonomy without threatening his sense of community. We must assure the Indian that he can assume control of his own life without being separated involuntarily from the tribal group. And we must make it clear that Indians can become independent of Federal control without being cut off from Federal concern and Federal support.

The statement goes on to list a number of specific recommendations, several of which would soon become law. One of the most important was the return of Blue Lake to Taos Pueblo. The pueblo had long requested the return of the lake and its surrounds, pointing out its importance in the Taos religion. President Nixon argued that "No government policy toward Indians can be fully effective unless there is a relationship of trust and confidence between the Federal government and the Indian people. . . . [W]e can contribute significantly to such a relationship by responding to just grievances which are especially important to the Indian people." Returning Blue Lake was a matter critical to Taos Pueblo and would send an important message to all Indian Nations that the United States wished to address past wrongs. Legislation returning to Taos the lake and forty-eight thousand acres of land surrounding it was approved in late 1970.[23]

The president also called for an improved and expanded program of financing for Indian economic enterprises. Congress responded with the Indian Financing Act of 1974. A lack of access to credit had long discouraged economic development on Indian reservations. While not as expansive as the president's proposed legislation, the Indian Financing Act has in fact provided crucial financing for many Indian-owned enterprises.

The most important of President Nixon's proposals concerned tribal control of service programs theretofore administered by federal agencies in the Department of the Interior and the Department of Health, Education and Welfare (HEW, now the Department of Health and Human Services). The president said that these programs should be administered by tribal governments rather than federal agencies, and he recommended legislation that would allow tribal governments to contract with Interior and HEW to administer directly such programs as the tribes might choose. In 1975, Congress enacted the Indian Self-Determination and Education Assistance Act, authorizing Indian Nations to take over the administration of most federal programs administered by the Bureau of Indian Affairs and the Indian Health Service. In the years since passage of the act, tribal governments have contracted to administer the majority of eligible programs, putting billions of dollars annually into the hands of Indian Nations to provide services on the reservations.

Specifics aside, the approach enunciated by President Nixon has in many ways transformed federal government interaction with Indian Nations. Every president since Nixon has endorsed the policy and carried it out.[24] While the details and level of enthusiasm vary by presidential administration, the policy has stood the test of time and enjoys bipartisan support, both presidential and congressional.

Equally significant was the process by which the policy evolved. The Nixon administration listened to and negotiated with Native leaders to produce proposals that advanced both federal and tribal interests. In the legislative process that followed, Indian Nations again participated in the conversation and greatly influenced the outcome. No longer was the policy affecting Indians being made unilaterally. Indeed, it is not too much to say that the modern process of making Indian policy strongly resembles treaty making. Rarely today does Congress or the executive branch make laws affecting Indians without considerable consultation with Indian Nations. The specifics of these laws are routinely negotiated and clarified in discussions among federal and tribal representatives. Compromise is frequent, and the two sides rarely find perfect agreement. They have, however, found sufficient common ground to make the last forty years the most productive in the history of federal Indian policy making.[25]

This reformed process was adopted by Congress as well. In 1975, Congress established an American Indian Policy Review Commission to examine Indian policy and make recommendations to Congress for how to improve the laws affecting Native Americans and the impact of federal programs for Indians. The commission—composed of six members of Congress and five Native people—held dozens of hearings in Indian Country to receive the complaints and recommendations of Native leaders. In 1977 it produced

Forrest J. Gerard (Blackfeet) with Senator Henry M. "Scoop" Jackson (left), 1976. Washington, DC. Photographer unknown. Courtesy of the estate of Forrest J. Gerard

As a staffer on Capitol Hill, Gerard formed a friendship with influential Senator Jackson that changed Jackson's position on Indian issues. In 1977, President Carter nominated Gerard as the first Assistant Secretary for Indian Affairs.

a report containing hundreds of proposals for reform.[26] Many, perhaps most, of these ideas came directly from Native leaders.

To give the commission's recommendations the careful consideration they required, the Senate established the Select Committee on Indian Affairs. The select committee later became a permanent standing committee of the Senate.[27] The House of Representatives chose to handle Indian policy issues in its Interior Committee and, later, in its Resources Committee. In both the House and the Senate, committee members and staff work closely with representatives of the Indian Nations on legislation affecting Indians. It is fair to call the Indian affairs legislative process a negotiation. While Congress holds the ultimate authority, it is unusual for that authority to be used in the absence of support from affected Indian Nations.[28]

Executive branch processes also have changed, and so has the structure of the Indian affairs bureaucracy. In 1977, President Jimmy Carter established in the Interior Department the Office of the Assistant Secretary–Indian Affairs (as President Nixon had recommended in his 1970 special message). Forrest J. Gerard, a Blackfeet citizen, became the first Assistant Secretary of Indian Affairs that same year. Since then, eleven other tribal citizens have received the presidential appointment. In 1994, President Bill Clinton issued an executive memorandum requiring all federal agencies to establish procedures for consulting with Indian Nations on relevant matters.[29] Presidents George W. Bush and Barack Obama restated and elaborated on the consultation requirement. Thus, in both the legislative and executive branches, policy affecting Indian Nations is now made with the advice and participation of Native leaders.

The results of this new way—or, perhaps, this return to the old way—of making policy have been most impressive. Since the early 1970s, a spate of legislation has been

directed toward clearing the wreckage of past policy failures and ameliorating their
contemporary effects on Indian Nations. Vine Deloria Jr. referred to this series of laws
as "treaty adjustments," which, given the manner of their enactment, seems a fair char-
acterization. Congress has passed legislation restoring many of the terminated Indian
tribes, including the largest of them: the Menominee Indian Tribe and the Klamath
Tribes. Congress also has approved land-claim settlements negotiated by Native
Nations whose homelands were taken by the states of Rhode Island, Maine, Connecticut, Massachusetts, and South Carolina in illegal treaties during the eighteenth and
nineteenth centuries.[30] The Carter administration negotiated the first of these settlements with the Indian Nations of Rhode Island and Maine. The settlements—as well
as agreements that were later struck with Native Nations in Connecticut, Massachusetts, and South Carolina—were, in effect, modern Treaties ratified by both houses of
Congress.

The federal government's social service programs for Indians have been the subjects
of constant attention for the last forty years. In addition to a number of laws meant to
improve education services to Indian students, Congress has enacted and periodically
updated laws regarding Indian health care, tribal community colleges and universities,
law enforcement on the reservations, and housing programs that serve Native Americans. Congress also has tried to address the injuries to Indian Nations and their cultures caused by the civilization regulations and the termination policy. It passed the
American Indian Religious Freedom Act in 1978, the National Museum of the American Indian Act in 1989, and the Native American Graves Protection and Repatriation
Act and Native American Languages Act in 1990.

To assist in the economic development of the reservations and improve the manage-

Walter R. Echo-Hawk (Pawnee) in front of Native American Rights Fund (NARF) sign, n.d. Washington, DC. Photographer unknown. As a senior attorney at NARF during most of the 1970s, 1980s, and 1990s, Echo-Hawk played a key role in developing the Native American Graves Protection and Repatriation Act (1990) and the American Indian Religious Freedom Act amendments (1994). Courtesy of the Native American Rights Fund, Washington, DC

ment of tribal resources, Congress has passed the Indian Financing Act, the Indian Tribal Governmental Tax Status Act, the Indian Land Consolidation Act, the Indian Gaming Regulatory Act, the American Indian Trust Fund Management Reform Act, and the Indian Mineral Development Act, among others. To better ensure environmental quality on reservations, Congress enacted amendments to the Safe Drinking Water Act, the Clean Water Act, and the Clean Air Act to allow tribes to participate in these regulatory programs in the same manner as state governments. To provide financial support to tribal regulatory programs, Congress passed the Indian Environmental General Assistance Program Act.

The net effect of these many laws has been to bring the governments of Indian Nations more fully into the social service and regulatory structures of modern American federalism. These matters had long been the exclusive province of federal and state governments, but American federalism has been redefined in many areas to include Indian tribal governments as full partners in protecting and advancing the welfare of the American people. Many of the laws listed above not only are the product of negotiations among tribal, state, and federal governments but also require ongoing consultation and cooperation among these governments and their agencies.

Little more than fifty years ago, the objective of federal Indian policy was literally the end of relations between the United States and the Indian Nations. But Indian Nations rejected U.S. unilateralism, dusted off their treaties, and demanded that they be honored and that the bilateral relationship they enunciated be fulfilled. To its credit, the United States ultimately agreed. It is no coincidence that the economic and social conditions of Native Nations have steadily improved in the years since the Indian self-determination policy was adopted, and though there is more to be done, the merits of bilateral policy-making have been established beyond doubt. We cannot know what lies ahead in the federal-tribal relationship, but it again seems possible that the friendship can be a permanent one, and that the United States and Indian Nations can prosper together.

facing: President Clinton listening to tribal drumming and singing at the Pine Ridge Reservation, as Oglala Sioux tribal president Harold Dean Salway looks on, 1999. Pine Ridge Reservation, South Dakota. Photo by Dirck Halstead. Time & Life Pictures/Getty Images 5913039

The Treaty with the Lower Klamath, Upper Klamath, and Trinity River Indians—and Who We Are Today

LOIS J. RISLING

FOR MANY YEARS I HEARD, TRAVELED, AND LIVED the history of the Indian Peoples of the Klamath and Trinity Rivers in northwestern California. My grandfather often spoke of our family history and our tribes' treaty history. In many ways, the two histories are intertwined. The written documents serve as reminders of not only a painful past but also the continuing strength and survival of California Indian Peoples, whom many thought would one day be extinct.

The treaty of October 6, 1851, was made and concluded at Camp Klamath, at the junction of the Klamath and Trinity Rivers. The Treaty with the Lower Klamath, Upper Klamath, and Trinity River Indians was a "treaty of peace and friendship" between the U.S. government and various Indian Nations in Northern California. The bands of Indian Peoples represented in this Treaty include the Poh-lik, or Lower Klamath; the Peh-tsick, or Upper Klamath; and the Hoo-pah, or Trinity River Indians.

My grandfather told me of the men in his family who signed the Treaty:

My great-granduncle and his two brothers told us that one of the soldiers held and guided their hands to make an X on a piece of paper. This was done in front of a line of armed soldiers. If they refused to obey their orders, all of our Indians in the area would be exterminated, and this is what the government calls a treaty. The Treaty made by the federal government was to force us Indians to give up our country to them. However, here in California, the government Treaties were never ratified, because gold was discovered at that time. Every nature of freedom was allowed to the miners to take up mining claims. The Treaty was hidden away by the white men and, after about sixty years, the treaties for California were found. The Treaty is not ratified, and we found that we still own California and all its resources by immemorial rights.

In 1851 a United States treaty commission made eighteen Treaties with the Native Nations in California. When these Treaties reached Washington and were submitted to the Senate, the California senators prevented ratification, and the Treaties were hidden away. In 1905 the Treaties were found.

I learned about the men who signed the Treaty first as family members and then as leaders and historical figures. Sa-von-ra, Up-pa-grah, and Ex-fin-e-pah signed the Treaty for the Sa-von-ra Tribe. Kee-chap and Red Cap, also known as Mik-ku-ree, signed for the Up-pa-goines, who lived near Red Cap's Bar, on the Klamath River. By the 1890s, when my grandfather was a boy, his great-granduncle was one of the oldest persons living. The white man named him Chet-Gus, but his name was Up-pa-grah, and he was a medicine man. I remember my grandfather telling me, "Up-pa-grah had many bullet wounds in his body from the white soldiers' guns. He was about forty years old when he saw the first white man with a wide hat that came to his area. About 1895, Up-pa-grah was then almost a hundred years old, and I was about seven years old. We both could not speak the English language."

My grandfather, SuWorhrom David W. Risling Sr., was a member of the Hoopa Valley Tribe. His ancestors were the Karuk. He was born in 1887, in an old Indian house (a house made of cedar or redwood slabs, dug into the ground) at SuWorhrom, a village in Karuk territory. David lived with his grandfather, SuWorhrom Charlie, and his grandfather's uncle,

216

Up-pa-grah. His great-grandmother lived in the village of Woo-pum, also called Red Cap's Bar. Their homes and cemeteries were mined into the river. David said, "The white people killed my ancestors like they were animals and called it war."

David's great-granduncle, Up-pa-grah; his two brothers, Sa-von-ra (SuWorhrom) and Ethop-tom; and Mik-ku-ree, from Woo-pum, who was married to David's great-grandmother, were Treaty signers as well as political and spiritual leaders. Great-uncle Up-pa-grah died of starvation. He helped take care of David until he was about ten years old. Ethop-tom and his brother Sa-von-ra were killed in a canoe while fishing for food from the river. These two men and David's great-grandmother's husband from Red Cap Village, Mik-ku-ree, put their mark on the Treaty on October 6, 1851.

Grandpa took me to the places where the men who signed the Treaty lived and fought for our land and where they did our ceremonies and prayers. He also took me to their graves, located in the heart of Karuk country. As a young child, at the graveyard of the SuWorhrom people, I remember thinking, why would someone bury their people in this place? The small cemetery was located on a steep mountainside between a state highway and the Klamath River. When we went there, my grandfather would tell the history of how his mother, grandfather, great-uncles, and other relatives came to be on a small flat on a steep mountainside away from the original village of SuWorhrom. He kept telling me that I must learn all this, as he had learned it from his ancestors. I had to teach it, not only to my children and my grandchildren but also to all the Indian people from this place.

The white miners had come to the Klamath River looking for gold. They mined the villages and the cemeteries into the Klamath River. The SuWorhrom people had moved the dead once before, and the second time they moved them up the steep mountain to a flat where they wouldn't be disturbed. Eventually, the construction of a state highway threatened the SuWorhrom people again. My grandfather said no—the highway would have to bypass the cemetery. The people remained, and now, he said, my job was to make sure that my grandchildren and their grandchildren knew about this place and how to care for it. This was a part of the lasting legacy of the men who signed our Treaty. We were now responsible for caring for them, for remembering where they were from and how hard they fought for us, our land, and our future.

My grandfather, David W. Risling Sr., said: "I am from SuWorhrom, a [village of the] Karuk people who lived along the Klamath River. The area where we lived . . . was rich in gold, and the miners by the hundreds came during the gold rush days. As a result, our villages, cemeteries, religious ceremonial grounds, and many other places of importance were mined into the river and our people were killed, starved, and driven from their lands."

These Treaty signers left a legacy of survival and strength. They fought to protect their ancestors, culture, beliefs, practices, and lifestyle. They were successful. We see this each time the graves on the mountainside are tended, when the White Deerskin Dance and the Brush Dance are held, and when one of the members of the tribe or a descendant of the Treaty signers sings a family song, eats salmon, prepares acorns, does a prayer, or continues in any other way to live in their culture.

Their legacy carries on through our family. My grandfather, David W. Risling Sr., helped start a public school, serving on the first board of trustees. He served on the Hoopa tribal council. He was one of the first people in California to assert Treaty land claims against the federal government. He helped pass legislation to secure fishing rights for the Karuk at the Ishi Pishi Falls on the Klamath River. David Risling Jr., was a college professor and political leader. SuWorhrom David Milton Risling Baldy is an artist and singer-songwriter. He continues to sing the "oldest Karuk song" that David W. Risling Sr., learned from his grandfather and great-uncle.

One-year-old David Warren Risling-Eagle Speaker is carried in a baby basket, in the same way Up-pa-grah and David W. Risling Sr., were carried. Viola E. Risling Evans Ryerson gave a Brush Dance Ceremony for her great-niece, Mary G. Risling, at Orleans, California. Gary B. Risling, a captain for a wildfire unit, helps organize the Brush Dance and White Deerskin Dance Ceremonies. Mary Jane Risling, the senior attorney for the Hoopa Valley Tribe, gave her granddaughter a Flower Dance Ceremony.

Cutcha Risling Baldy, a PhD student in Native American Studies, sat with her daughter Arya in the Brush Dance House for A Ceremony, which is thousands of years old. I, Lois J. Risling, a Hoopa tribal member, make the medicine for the Brush Dances at Panamnik, where descendants of SuWorhrom and Woo-pum Peoples participate. This ceremony is done by descendants of the men who signed the Treaty of October 6, 1851. The treaty signers made it possible for their descendants to be lawyers, artists, basket weavers, boat makers, nurses, teachers, politicians, tribal council members, tribal council chairpersons, mothers, fathers, grandparents, and Karuks, Yuroks, and Hupas.

Treaties and the United Nations Declaration on the Rights of Indigenous Peoples

ARWEN NUTTALL

IN 2010, AFTER BEING ONE OF FOUR MEMBER states originally opposed to the 2007 passage of the United Nations Declaration on the Rights of Indigenous Peoples, the United States endorsed it. Following that endorsement, James Anaya, who was the United Nations Special Rapporteur on the Rights of Indigenous Peoples, conducted an official visit to the United States to assess "how the standards of the Declaration are reflected in United States law, policy, and programs at both the state and federal levels, and to identify needed reforms as well as good practices." This was the first visit of its kind to be conducted within the United States. From April 23 to May 4, 2012, Anaya visited with Native residents in Washington, DC, Arizona, Oregon, Alaska, South Dakota, and Oklahoma to see and hear firsthand their stories of struggle and survival, and to expose the issues that demanded the most immediate redress.

Some of the leading concerns among Native Nations are the restoration of land, and the protection of sacred places and natural resources. The special rapporteur's report to the United Nations states, "In nearly all cases the loss of land meant the substantial and complete undermining of indigenous peoples' own economic foundations and means of subsistence, as well as cultural loss, given the centrality of land to cultural and related social patterns." The report goes on to say, "Securing [the] rights of indigenous peoples to their lands is of central importance to indigenous peoples' socio-economic development, self-determination, and cultural integrity." The protection of what remains of these lands from destructive activities such as mining, logging, and drilling is also of crucial impor-

tance. Not only are natural resources damaged by and millions of acres lost to these extractive projects, which are often undertaken in violation of treaties, but Native Peoples' access to sacred lands also is disrupted. In addition, the development projects place the sacred sites themselves in jeopardy and constitute a defilement of sacred space. Anaya notes, "The desecration and lack of access to sacred places inflicts permanent harm on indigenous peoples, for whom these places are essential parts of identity."[1]

Anaya points to the case of the Black Hills as an example of treaty violation and the detrimental impacts of land loss. Following the discovery of gold in the Black Hills, the U.S. government claimed ownership of these ancestral lands, which had been promised to what was then known as the Great Sioux Nation under the 1868 Fort Laramie Treaty. Losing control of a traditional land base containing some of their most sacred areas has had a direct bearing on the economic well-being of the Lakota. The residents of the Rosebud and Pine Ridge Reservations exist in some of the poorest living conditions in the United States. Despite their dire economic situation, they still refuse to accept the payment outlined by a 1980 Supreme Court ruling because of the Black Hills' sanctity. They continue to hold out for the return of the traditional lands promised to them by the 1868 treaty.

To redress concerns about land loss and the protection of sacred places, the report of the special rapporteur recommends strengthening current federal initiatives to return lands taken in violation of treaties. Anaya views this as a critical step that the U.S. government could take toward true reconciliation with Native Peoples. According to Anaya, the declaration affirms respect for treaties as well as an awareness of treaties as instruments for defining relations between Native people and the federal government.

> The Declaration . . . points towards a method of developing relations between Indigenous Peoples and the broader society of governments that really amounts to treaty-making by advocating for arrangements and decisions based on agreement or consent with Indigenous Peoples. That really is paving the way toward treaty-making, toward the future—a different kind of relationship than has occurred in the past; one that is not the imposition of government decision-making on indigenous people.[2]

Anaya believes the situation with the Black Hills is an "example where returning land taken by the U.S. government could improve a tribe's fortunes as well as contribute to a 'process of reconciliation.'"[3] Anaya also cites as a move toward reconciliation a recent agreement between the Department of the Interior and the Oglala Lakota to establish control over traditional lands in the form of an Oglala-run national park. In his mind, such land restorations do not undermine the U.S. government, nor are they damaging to the general populace. He believes in a process of land return that is "not divisive but restorative. That's the idea behind reconciliation."[4] Anaya also recognizes that the United States still has a long way to go in accepting responsibility and making reparations to Native Peoples. However, now that the federal government has endorsed the U.N. Declaration on the Rights of Indigenous Peoples, it can be used as a guide for improving upon as well as developing new processes for addressing the needs of Native people. The restoration of lands and protection of sacred places and natural resources will be a major step toward a reconciliation that redresses the historical wrongs of cultural and political suppression, land theft, racism, and discrimination.

Modern Treaties

An Interview with Ben Nighthorse Campbell   SUZAN SHOWN HARJO

BEN NIGHTHORSE CAMPBELL: Treaties are promises between . . . two nations. And whether they are going to be valid or not, and whether they are going to last or not, is based on the heart and the belief of the people that are participating. As most Indian people look at treaties, there's a real need for clarification on what treaties ought to be doing.

Now, we do a lot of things by compacting or contracting . . . and in fact, [compacts] are a form of a treaty. We just use different words for them now. We still do a lot of contractual agreements that can only be fulfilled if the parties on both sides of the agreement have good intentions and they are willing to commit themselves to making sure it works right.

SUZAN SHOWN HARJO: Vine Deloria Jr. [said] that laws of general applicability, of the kind that you've sponsored so many times, are really modern treaties made for everyone, even if the people never had treaties, and that they're the modern version of peace and friendship. As sponsor of some of these modern treaties, could you address some of that?

BEN NIGHTHORSE CAMPBELL: The problem with modern treaties, i.e., agreements between the federal government and tribes, is that the people who put them together, validate them, and have them signed into law or approved by the administration or by the Senate are rarely, if ever, the people who are going to administer them. So there's a huge disconnect between the intent of the treaty, the intent of the agreement, and how it actually gets implemented.

The end result is that, very often, after they have negotiated some kind of agreement, Indian people think it is going to be fulfilled based on [its] intent. [But] it doesn't always work out that way. . . . It seems to disintegrate in the process of being implemented.

SUZAN SHOWN HARJO: You've served as both a lawmaker for the United States and as a chief for the Cheyenne. Could you talk about any differences, however subtle, between the two kinds of leaders and explain any differences in approach to treaties?

BEN NIGHTHORSE CAMPBELL: Since the Indian Reorganization Act of 1934, the [legal] power to validate and sign treaties rests in the hands of an elective body, which is generally the tribal council. But the old folks, the seniors, the elders, the spiritual people, many of them still believe in the old ways, in which the clans or the chief[s] or the societies should have a major voice in the direction the tribe should take. Many times, there's not very good communication between those two different bodies. Unfortunately, under the Indian Reorganization Act, the old forms of governance have no valid power. Some tribes still keep the chief and the society system alive, but they don't have any legal authority within the tribe. They're in an advisory capacity . . . but I've always thought the system of societies was a very important part of keeping the old traditions alive.

From an interview that took place on August 16, 2010, at Acoma Pueblo, New Mexico.

Kaw calumet, ca. 1870. Oklahoma. Wood, pigment, woodpecker beak, wool, silk fabric, dye, cotton twine, eagle and owl feathers, mallard duck head and feathers, horsehair. 106 × 50 cm. National Museum of the American Indian 2/7126

Calumets with eagle feathers represent a sacred badge of friendship. Used by some Indian leaders in the opening ceremonies of treaty meetings, these ceremonial pipes marked the solemnity of the occasion.

Treaties and Contemporary American Indian Cultures

W. RICHARD WEST, JR.

I CAME TO THE SUBJECTS OF TREATIES, "MODERN treaties," and "treaty adjustments" early in my professional life. In 1971, I had just graduated from Stanford Law School and was joining the American Indian Law Department in the Washington, DC, office of Fried, Frank, Harris, Shriver & Kampelman.

I had appreciated from a young age the unique status of Native communities and people in the United States, but an Indian law course at Stanford had schooled me in its specific history and conceptual tenets. However distant treaties dating back to the eighteenth century seem, they remain in a constant state of renegotiation and "adjustment."

My legal practice at Fried, Frank during the 1970s and 1980s quickly moved the discussion of treaties from the historical and theoretical to the current and applied. The law firm represented a number of Native communities and tribes before Congress; the executive branch of the federal government; and federal, state, and tribal courts.

Almost all the issues I addressed were based directly or indirectly on treaties or on federal statutes and administrative orders of the president of the United States relating to treaties. Many of the court cases I worked on revolved around treaty provisions that recognized and confirmed the rights of Native communities inherent in their constitutionally based political sovereignty.

The scope of the cases was diverse, and the issues they covered included water rights, fishing rights, and tribal civil jurisdiction. The positions taken in the litigation always derived from original provisions in treaties between Native governments and the United States. The cases represented a contemporary invocation of judicial force and sanction to uphold promises that had been made by the United States a century or more before.

In addition to twentieth-century court rulings, treaty adjustments, or modern treaties, also have taken the form of congressional legislation linked directly to treaty provisions or to the concepts of tribal self-government and political autonomy that treaties confirmed. The 1970s and 1980s were especially active, as the law firm, in collaboration with others, lobbied in support of numerous pieces of major legislation on subjects addressed repeatedly over time by various treaties. These enactments included, among others, the Indian Self-Determination and Education Assistance Act, the Indian Education Act, the Indian Health Care Improvement Act, the Indian Child Welfare Act, Indian Tribal Governmental Tax Status Act, the American Indian Religious Freedom Act, and many others.

In the late 1980s my professional journey in Indian Country took a turn that in retrospect seems quite logical but at the time was something of a personal epiphany. Throughout the 1970s and 1980s, my lens for analyzing the impact of treaties in Native communities had been primarily legal and political. Since I was trained as a lawyer and had practiced American Indian law for the better part of two decades, the focus made sense.

What occurred to me with increasing clarity as the years of legal practice passed, however, was the ultimate outcome of it all in contemporary, living Native communities. The real, practical import of legal work—upholding the political rights and prerogatives of tribal governments—ultimately was cultural in nature. Treaties, at their center, were a confirmation of the status of American Indian Tribes as polities in the American constitutional fabric. But their enduring relevance and power was in protecting ways of life and the cultural self-determination of Native Peoples.

Thus began my transition in 1990 from lawyer to director of the Smithsonian Institution's National Museum of the American Indian—a position I held for almost two decades. The very authorizing legislation of the museum represented, in cultural terms, a treaty adjustment of the most profound nature.

The legislation contained two quite discrete but related sets of provisions that spoke to the "adjustment" that was occurring. First, it was the first piece of federal legislation that at long last, after years of petition by Native representatives, addressed the matter of repatriating human remains, funerary materials, sacred objects, and cultural patrimony. Under a process defined by the legislation, these objects were to be returned by the Smithsonian Institution, upon application, to the originating Native communities. This 1989 legislation was extended in 1990 by the Native American Graves Protection and Repatriation Act to cover virtually all museums in the United States holding Native collections.

Second, the 1989 act also created the Smithsonian Institution's National Museum of the American Indian. But the provisions in the congressional enactment, as well as the legislative history supporting them, made clear that the museum would be anything but business as usual. It was not to be an exercise in colonial ethnography but rather something quite different. The National Museum of the American Indian was to be a place where Native cultural authority and voice were assumed, and Native perspective was evident and respected. Ultimately made real through policies generated by its board of trustees and the practices of its staff, the museum became in substance an international institution of living Native cultures. Thus, in this place at the head of the National Mall in the nation's capital, the guiding principles of the historic treaties that are the bedrock of Native America were given new cultural life and impact for the future.

NOTES

FOREWORD [pp. xi–xiii]   *Kevin Gover*

1   Black concluded his dissent with these words in the Supreme Court case *Federal Power Commission v. Tuscarora Indian Nation* (1960).

2   Senator Daniel K. Inouye, foreword to *Documents of American Indian Diplomacy: Treaties, Agreements, and Conventions, 1775–1979,* ed. Vine Deloria Jr. and Raymond J. DeMallie (Norman: University of Oklahoma Press, 1999), 1:ix.

INTRODUCTION [pp. 1–11]
Suzan Shown Harjo

1   N. Scott Momaday, interview by Suzan Shown Harjo, August 15, 2005, School of Advanced Research, Santa Fe, New Mexico, film transcript, *Treaties Project—Great Nations in Their Own Words*, National Museum of the American Indian, Washington, DC.

2   Vine Deloria Jr., telephone participation in the first planning meeting of the Treaties Project advisors, National Museum of the American Indian Cultural Resources Center, Suitland, Maryland, July 14, 2005.

3   Redick McKee to U.S. Commissioner of Indian Affairs, 1851, Records of the Bureau of Indian Affairs, RG 75, National Archives and Records Administration.

4   Senate *Journal,* 32nd. Cong., 1st. sess., June 1852.

5   Carey N. Vicenti, interview by Suzan Shown Harjo, August 15, 2005, School of Advanced Research, Santa Fe, New Mexico, film transcript, *Treaties Project.*

6   Commissioner of Indian Affairs to Indian agents, "Rules Governing the Court of Indian Offenses," March 30, 1883, Interior Solicitor's Library, U.S. Department of the Interior.

7   Circular No. 1665, "Indian Dancing," 26 April 1921; Supplement to Circular No. 1665, February 14, 1923, Records of the Bureau of Indian Affairs, RG 75, National Archives and Records Administration.

8   U.S. Department of the Interior, *Civilization: Regulations of the Indian Department, Revised by the Indian Bureau* (Washington, DC: Government Printing Office, 1884).

9   U.S. Department of the Interior, *Civilization: Regulations of the Indian Department, Revised by the Indian Bureau* (Washington, DC: Government Printing Office, 1894).

10   Commissioner of Indian Affairs to Indian agents, "Long Hair Prohibited," January 13, 1902, in *Annual Reports of the Department of the Interior for the Fiscal Year Ended June 30, 1902, Indian Affairs. Part 1. Report of the Commissioner, and Appendixes* (Washington: Government Printing Office, 1903), 13–15.

11   Richard Henry Pratt, *Battlefield and Classroom: Four Decades with the American Indian, 1867–1904* (1964, repr. Norman: University of Oklahoma Press, 2003), 335.

12   United States Board of Indian Commissioners, *Annual Report of Indian Commissioners to the Secretary of the Interior,* vol. 22 (Washington, DC: Government Printing Office, 1891), 170.

13   Richard Leiby, "Bury My Heart at RFK," *Washington Post,* November 6, 1994.

TREATIES WITH NATIVE NATIONS [pp. 14–33]   *Robert N. Clinton*

1   Vine Deloria Jr. and Raymond J. DeMallie, Documents of American Indian Diplomacy: Treaties, Agreements, and Conventions, 1775–1979 (1999); Francis Paul Prucha, American Indian Treaties: History of a Political Anomaly (1997); Jill St. Germain, Indian Treaty-Making Policy in the United States and Canada, 1867–1877 (2001); Francis Jennings The Invasion of America: Indians, Colonialism and the Cant of Conquest (1976); Francis Jennings et al., The History and Culture of Iroquois Diplomacy (1995); Francis Jennings, Empire of Fortune: Crowns, Colonies and Tribes in the Seven Years War in America (1988); Francis Jennings, The Ambiguous Iroquois Empire (1984); Robert A. Williams Jr., Linking Arms Together: American Indian Treaty Visions of Law and Peace, 1600–1800 (1997); Robert N. Clinton, *The Proclamation of 1763: Colonial Prelude to Two Centuries of Federal-State Conflict Over the Management of Indian Affairs,* 69 B.U.L. Rev 329–85 (1989); Robert N. Clinton, *There Is No Federal Supremacy Clause for Indian Tribes,* 34 Az. St. L. J. 113–260 (2002).

2   21 U.S. (8 Wheat.) 543 (1823).

3   Eric A. Kades, *The Dark Side of Efficiency: Johnson v. M'Intosh and the Expropriation of Amerindian Lands,* 148 U. Pa. L. Rev. 1065 (2000) and Eric A. Kades, *History and Interpretation of the Great Case of* Johnson v. M'Intosh,

19 Law & Hist. Rev. 67 (2001); *see generally,* Robert J. Miller, Discovering Indigenous Lands: The Doctrine of Discovery in the English Colonies (Oxford University Press 2010).

4 *E.g.,* Treaty with the Menominee Tribe, March 30, 1817, 17 Stat. 153; Treaty with the Winnebago Tribe, June 3, 1816, 17 Stat. 144.

5 *E.g.,* Treaty with the Menominee Tribe, Feb. 8, 1831, 7 Stat. 342.

6 The most thorough description and collection of sources relative to *Mohegan Indians v. Connecticut* is found in Joseph Henry Smith, Appeals to the Privy Council from the American Plantations 422–42 (1950). *See also* John William DeForest, History of the Indians in Connecticut from the Earliest Known Period to 1850, 303–42, 447–64 (1852); Trumbull, 1 History of Connecticut, 412, 421–27 (1818); Beardsley, The Mohegan Land Controversy, 3 Papers of the New Haven Colony Historical Society, 205–25.

7 Felix S. Cohen, *Original Indian Title,* 32 Minn. L. Rev. 28 (1947).

8 In *Arizona v. California,* 373 U.S. 546 (1963), the Supreme Court held that tribal water rights were not exclusively dependent on treaties and that Indian Tribes whose reservations were created by executive order, rather than by treaty, had the same right to water as treaty tribes.

9 *See generally,* Peter Wraxall, An Abridgement of the Indian Affairs Contained in Four Folio Volumes, Transacted in the Colony of New York, from the Year 1678 to the Year 1751 (Charles H. McIlwain ed., 1915).

10 Francis Jennings, The Ambiguous Iroquois Empire (1984). On the wampum belt tradition, *see* Robert A. Williams Jr., Linking Arms Together: American Indian Treaty Visions of Law & Peace 1600–1800, 51–54 (1997).

11 *Minutes of the Provincial Council of Pennsylvania* 211–12 (Samuel Hazard ed. 1838–53), *quoted in* Francis Jennings, Empire of Fortune: Crowns, Colonies & Tribes in the Seven Years War in America 399–400 (1988) (emphasis added).

12 7 Stat. 18.

13 7 Stat. 135.

14 7 Stat. 160.

15 31 U.S. (6 Pet.) 551, 582 (1832)

16 *E.g.,* Washington v. Washington State Commercial Passenger Fishing Vessel Ass'n, 443 U.S. 858 (1979) and Minnesota v. Mille Lacs Band of Chippewa Indians, 526 U.S. 172 (1999).

17 *E.g.,* Winters v. United States, 207 U.S. 564 (1908).

18 While most Indian languages only became transliterated or were otherwise captured in written form only after the treaty-making period ended, Cherokee became a written language in the 1820s, when an innovative Cherokee man named Sequoyah, or George Gist, produced a Cherokee syllabary of eighty-six characters, which almost overnight rendered literate large portions of the Cherokee Nation. Sequoyah's syllabary became official when it was adopted by the Cherokee Nation in 1825. By the end of the decade the Cherokee national newspaper, the *Cherokee Phoenix,* regularly was being published in both English and Cherokee. Given this fact, it is surprising that the Cherokee never demanded that their later Treaties, such as the Treaty of New Echota of December 29, 1835, 7 Stat. 478, or the Treaty of Washington of July 19, 1866, 14 Stat. 799, be memorialized simultaneously in both English and Cherokee.

19 "The Meaning of the Treaty," Waitangi Tribunal, www.justice.govt.nz/tribunals/waitangi-tribunal/the-meaning-of-the-treaty.

20 7 Stat. 13 (emphasis added).

21 Act of May 28, 1830, 4 Stat. 411 (emphasis added).

22 In *Minnesota v. Mille Lacs Band of Chippewa Indians,* 526 U.S. 172 (1999), the requirement of formal treaty consent for removal proved critical to invalidating an executive order purporting to extinguish tribal off-reservation treaty fishing rights as part of a removal initiative by the president to which the tribe had not consented.

23 Treaty of Dancing Rabbit Creek, Sept. 27, 1830, with the Choctaw Nation, 7 Stat. 333; Treaty of Pontitock Creek, Oct. 20, 1832, with the Chickasaw Nation, 7 Stat. 381; Treaty of Washington, March 24, 1832, with the Creek (Muscogee) Nation, 7 Stat. 366; Treaty of Payne's Landing, May 9, 1832, with the Seminole Nation, 7 Stat. 368; Treaty of New Echota, Dec. 29, 1835, with the Cherokee Nation, 7 Stat. 478.

24 15 Stat. 635.

25 15 Stat. 667.

26 Act of Mar. 3, 1871, ch. 120, 16 Stat. 544, 566, codified as amended at 25 U.S.C. § 71 (emphasis added).

27 Act of Mar. 29, 1867, § 6, 15 Stat. 7 (emphasis added).

28 Act of July 20, 1867, 15 Stat. 18.

29 The congressional debate over the 1871 statute ending Indian treaty making is set forth and well described in Deloria and DeMallie, *supra* note 1.

30 *Congressional Globe,* 41st Cong., 3rd Sess. 1154 (1871) (emphasis added).

31 *E.g.,* Robert N. Clinton, *There Is No Federal Supremacy Clause for Indian Tribes,* 34 Az. St. L. J. 113, 168–69 (2002); Phillip M. Kannan, *Reinstating Treaty-Making with Native American Tribes,* 16 Wm & Mary Bill of Rts. J. 809, 809–18 (2008).

32 For example, as the United States Supreme Court recognized in *DeCoteau v. District Court,* 420 U.S. 425 (1975), the Act of March 3, 1891, c. 543, 26 Stat. 1035, ratified an 1889 agreement made with Sisseton and Wahpeton bands of Sioux Indians that had facilitated the allotment of the Lake Traverse Reservation, together with the sale of the so-called surplus lands and their return to the public domain. This type

of specific allotment agreement was common during the late nineteenth and early twentieth centuries as a prelude to implementing the Dawes General Allotment Act of 1887 on any reservation.

33   187 U.S. 553 (1903).

34   Sioux Nation of Indians v. United States, 601 F.2d 1157, 1173 (Ct. C1. 1979) (Nichols, J.)

35   While Congress or the executive branch certainly had resorted to federal fiat before *Lone Wolf,* most notably in establishing and implementing Indian boarding schools and in creating the Code of Indian Offenses, which was enforced by the Indian Police and the Courts of Indian Offenses, after *Lone Wolf* the federal government virtually abandoned negotiating any kind of agreements with Indian Tribes as part of its Indian policy formation or implementation.

36   H.R. 7902, 73d Cong. 2d. Sess, § 4i.

37   Pub. L. No. 93-638, 88 Stat. 2203 (1975), codified as amended at 25 U.S.C. §§ 450f–450n, 455–458e.

38   Salazar v. Ramah Navajo Chapter, 132 (S.Ct. 2181. 2012); Cherokee Nation of Oklahoma v. Leavitt, 543 U.S. 631 (2005); *see generally,* Robert McCarthy, *The Bureau of Indian Affairs and the Federal Trust Obligation to American Indians,* 19 B.Y.U.J. Pub. L. 1, 133–141 (2004).

39   25 U.S.C. § 2510(d).

40   *See* Matthew L. M. Fletcher, *The Power to Tax, the Power to Destroy, and the Michigan Tribal-State Tax Agreements,* 82 U. Det. Mercy L. Rev. 1, 5 n.29 (2004) (providing a listing of the then-existing Michigan tribal tax agreements); *see also,* State of Oklahoma Indian Affairs Commission, Tobacco Compacts, https://www.sos.ok.gov/tribal.aspx.

41   25 U.S.C. § 1919.

42   Deloria and DeMallie, *supra* note 1.

LINKING ARMS AND BRIGHTENING THE CHAIN [pp. 36–58]   *Richard W. Hill, Sr.*

1   Alan Taylor, *The Divided Ground: Indians, Settlers, and the Northern Borderland of the American Revolution* (New York: Alfred A. Knopf, 2006), 4, 6, 118.

2   Vine Deloria Jr. and Raymond J. DeMallie, eds., *Documents of American Indian Diplomacy: Treaties, Agreements, and Conventions, 1775–1979* (Norman: University of Oklahoma Press, 1999), 1:38.

3   Ibid.

4   Ibid.

5   Henry Knox to President George Washington, May 23, 1789, *American State Papers: Indian Affairs,* 1:8.

6   James H. Merrell, "'I desire all that I have said . . . may be taken down aright': Revisiting Teedyuscung's 1756 Treaty Council Speeches," *William and Mary Quarterly* 63, 3rd ser., no. 4 (October 2006): 783 and *passim.*

7   Jonathan Evans, comp., *A Journal of the Life, Travels, and Religious Labours of William Savery, Late of Philadelphia, A Minister of the Gospel of Christ in the Society of Friends.* (London, 1844), 53–98.

8   Quoted in Michigan Pioneer and Historical Society, "The Haldimand Papers," Historical Collections of the Pioneer and Historical Society, vol. 20 (1892), 178.

9   Joseph Brant, "Message to Governor of Quebec, Frederick Haldimand, 1783," in Michael P. Johnson, ed., *Reading the American Past: Selected Historical Documents, Volume 1: To 1877,* 5th ed. (Boston: Bedford/St. Martin's, 2012), 140.

10   George Clinton, Speech to the Oneidas and Tuscaroras, Ft. Schuyler [Stanwix], New York, September 10, 1784, in Frederick B. Hough, ed., *Proceedings of the Commissioners of Indian Affairs Appointed by Law for the Extinguishment of Indian Titles in the State of New York* (Albany, 1861), 59.

11   "Treaty of Fort Stanwix, in 1784," in Neville B. Craig, ed., *The Olden Time* (Cincinnati, 1876), 2:418–19.

12   Barbara Graymont, "New York State Indian Policy after the Revolution," *New York History* 57 (October 1976): 438–74.

13   Alan Taylor, *The Divided Ground: Indians, Settlers, and the Northern Borderland of the American Revolution* (New York: Alfred A. Knopf, 2006), 4, 118; Timothy J. Shannon, *Iroquois Diplomacy on the Early American Frontier* (New York: Penguin, 2008), 198; Jack Campisi, "From Stanwix to Canandaigua: National Policy, States' Rights and Indian Land," in *Iroquois Land Claims,* ed. Christopher Vecsey and William A. Starna (Syracuse, NY: Syracuse University Press, 1988), 58; J. David Lehman, "The End of the Iroquois Mystique: The Oneida Land Cession Treaties of the 1780s," *William and Mary Quarterly* 47, no. 4 (October 1990): 528.

14   *An ordinance for the government of the territory of the United States, Northwest of the river Ohio,* July 17, 1787, *Journals of the Continental Congress,* 32: 334–43, http://hdl.loc.gov/loc.rbc/bdsdcc.22501.

15   George Washington to the Commissioners Negotiating a Treaty with the Southern Indians, August 29, 1789, in *The Writings of George Washington,* John C. Fitzpatrick, ed. (Washington, DC: Government Printing Office, 1931–44), 30:392.

16   Lehman, "The End of the Iroquois Mystique," 525; Graymont, "New York State Indian Policy after the Revolution," 451–52.

17   Henry Knox, Report to the President of the United States, relative to the Northwestern Indians, June 15, 1789, *American State Papers: Indian Affairs,* 1:13.

18   Ibid.

19   George Washington, Special Message to the Senate, 17 September 1789, in James D. Richardson, ed., *A Compilation of the Messages and Papers of the Presidents,* (1897), vol. 1, part 1, http://www.gutenberg.org/files/11314/11314.txt.

20 George Washington, reply to December 1, 1790, address of Cornplanter, Halftown, and the Great Tree, December 29, 1790, in Dorothy Twohig, ed., *The Papers of George Washington,* Presidential Series: September 1788–March 1797 (Charlottesville: University of Virginia Press, 1998), 7:147.

21 Quoted in Barnet Schecter, *George Washington's America: A Biography through His Maps* (New York: Walker, 2010), 233.

22 Frederick Hoxie, "A Brief History of Congressional Investigations and American Indian Affairs from 1789 to 1989," U.S. Senate, Senate Committee on Indian Affairs, A Report of the Special Committee on Investigations, Final Report and Legislative Recommendations, 101st Congress, 1st Session, Report 101–216 (1989), 31.

23 Henry Knox, instructions to Arthur St. Clair, March 21, 1791, *American State Papers: Indian Affairs,* 1:171.

24 George Washington to James Duane, September 7, 1783, in Francis Paul Prucha, ed., *Documents of United States Indian Policy,* 3rd ed. (Lincoln: University of Nebraska Press, 2000), 1.

25 Quoted in Granville Carter, ed., *The Collected Speeches of Sagoyewatha, or Red Jacket* (Syracuse, NY: Syracuse University Press, 2006), 64–65.

26 Francis Paul Prucha, *The American Indian Treaties: History of a Political Anomaly* (Berkeley: University of California Press, 1994), 96; Alan Taylor, *The Divided Ground: Indians, Settlers, and the Northern Borderland of the American Revolution* (New York: Alfred A. Knopf, 2006), 291.

27 Richard W. Hill, Sr. "Six Nations Participation in the War of 1812," Six Nations Legacy Consortium, http://sixnationslegacy.org/history/six-nations-participation-in-the-war-of-1812/.

28 "The Covenant Chain, the Two Row Wampum, and the Canada/Six Nations Relationship: A Federal Perspective," June 3, 2009, quoted in "The Unresolved Peace" on the Six Nations Legacy Consortium website, http://sixnationslegacy.org/the-unresolved-peace/.

THE TWO-ROW WAMPUM BELT
[pp. 59-60] *Mark G. Hirsch*

1 Two Row Wampum Renewal Campaign, "Native Peoples and Allies Plan Campaign to Renew the Two Row Wampum," press release, January 14, 2013, http://www.honorthetworow.org.

2 Oren Lyons, "Indian Self-Government in the Haudenosaunee Constitution," *Nordic Journal of International Law* 121 (1986), 119, cited on the Two Row Wampum Renewal Campaign, http://www.honorthetworow.org. See also National Museum of the American Indian interview with Richard W. Hill, Sr. and Oren Lyons, November 1, 2007, Tape 3, Line 885–7.

3 Paul Otto and Jaap Jacobs, "Introduction: Historians and the Public Debate about the Past," *Journal of Early American History* 2 (2013): 1-2.

4 Charles Gehring, William Starna, and William Fenton, "The Tawagonshi Treaty of 1613: The Final Chapter," *New York History* 68, no. 4 (October 1987): 373–93.

5 Charles Gehring and William Starna, "Revisiting the Fake Tawagonshi Treaty of 1613," *New York History* 93 (Winter 2012): 95, 101.

6 Jon Parmenter, "The Meaning of the Kaswentha and the Two Row Wampum Belt in Haudenosaunee (Iroquois) History: Can Indigenous Oral Tradition be Reconciled with the Documentary Record?" *Journal of Early American History* 2 (2013), 88.

7 Katsitsionni Fox, "Two Row Wampum Renewal Campaign Completes Journey to United Nations," *Indian Time Haudenosaunee News,* August 22, 2013, http://www.indiantime.net/issue/08_22_2013.

8 Richard W. Hill, Sr., "Talking Points on History and Meaning of the Two Row Wampum Belt," March 2013, Two Row Wampum Renewal Campaign: http://www.honorthetworow.org.

ILLEGAL STATE TREATIES [pp. 66-67]
Mark G. Hirsch

1 Francis Paul Prucha, *The Great Father: The United States Government and the American Indians* (Lincoln: University of Nebraska Press, 1984), 1:90; Kevin Gover, "Statutes as Sources of Modern Indian Rights: Child Welfare, Gaming, and Repatriation: A Statutory History of Federal Indian Policy," in *Treaties with American Indians: An Encyclopedia of Rights, Conflicts, and Sovereignty,* ed. Donald L. Fixico (Santa Barbara: ABC-CLIO, 2007), 1:109; Nell Jessup Newton, "Federal Power of Indians: Its Sources, Scope, and Limitations," *University of Pennsylvania Law Review,* 132, no. 2 (January 1984): 200-201; Robert N. Clinton and Margaret Tobey Hotopp, "Judicial Enforcement of the Federal Restraints on Alienation of Indian Lands: The Origins of the Eastern Land Claims," *Maine Law Review* 31, no. 17 (1979): 29.

2 Arrell Morgan Gibson, "Philosophical, Legal, and Social Rationales for Appropriating the Tribal Estate, 1607-1980," *American Indian Law Review* 12 (1984): 34.

3 R. David Edmunds, Frederick E. Hoxie, and Neal Salisbury, *The People: A History of Native America* (Boston: Houghton Mifflin, 2007), 330; Helen Vanderhoop Manning, "Wampanoag," in *Encyclopedia of North American Indians,* ed. Frederick E. Hoxie (Chicago: Houghton Mifflin Harcourt, 1996), 661.

4 Arrell Morgan Gibson, "Philosophical, Legal, and Social Rationales for Appropriating the Tribal Estate, 1607–1980," *American Indian Law Review* 12 (1984): 31; Clinton and Hotopp, "Judicial Enforcement," 49.

5 Linda S. Parker, *Native American Estate: The Struggle Over Indian and Hawaiian Lands* (Honolulu, HI: University of Hawaii Press, 1989), 151.

6 *Christian Science Monitor,* quoted in Linda S. Parker, *Native American Estate,* 150; Charles Wilkinson, *Blood*

Struggle: The Rise of Modern Indian Nations (New York: W. W. Norton, 2005), 231.

7 David Ghere, "Passamaquoddy/ Penobscot," in Hoxie, *Encyclopedia of North American Indians*, 471; Tim Vollman, "A Survey of Eastern Indian Land Claims, 1970–1979," *Maine Law Review* 31, no. 5 (1979): 6.

8 Judith Royster, "Indian Land Claims," in *Handbook of North American Indians: Indians in Contemporary Society*, ed. Garrick Bailey (Washington, DC: Smithsonian Institution Scholarly Press, 2008), 2:36.

9 Anne F. Boxberger Flaherty, "American Indian Land Rights, Rich Indian Racism, and Newspaper Coverage in New York State, 1988–2008," *American Indian Culture and Research Journal* 37, no. 4 (2013): 65–66; Christopher Vecsey, "Introduction: The Issues Underlying Iroquois Land Claims," in *Iroquois Land Claims*, ed. Christopher Vecsey and William A. Starna (Syracuse, NY: Syracuse University Press, 1988), 3–5; Philip Harnden, "Whose Land? An Introduction to the Iroquois Land Claims in New York State," report prepared for the American Friends Service Committee, Syracuse, NY, 2000, 5; Tim Vollman, "A Survey of Eastern Indian Land Claims, 1970–1979," *Maine Law Review* 31, no. 5 (1979): 6; Barbara Graymont, "New York State Indian Policy after the Revolution," *New York History* 57 (October 1976): 460–70.

10 Patrick W. Wandres, "Indian Land Claims: Sherrill and the Impending Legacy of the Doctrine of Laches," *American Indian Law Review* 31, no. 1 (2006–7): 133, 135; Kathryn Fort, "Disruption and Impossibility: The Unfortunate Resolution of the Iroquois Land Claims in Federal Courts," *Wyoming Law Review* 11, no. 2 (2011): 376, 379, 383, 387, 391, 393, 395–96.

11 Paul C. Rosier, *Native American Issues,* Contemporary American Ethnic Issues (Westport, CT: Greenwood Press, 2003), 77.

12 Wilkinson, *Blood Struggle,* 229, 443; Arrell Morgan Gibson, "Philosophical, Legal, and Social Rationales for Appropriating the Tribal Estate, 1607–1980," *American Indian Law Review* 12 (1984): 34; James H. Merrell, "Catawba," in Hoxie, *Encyclopedia of North American Indians,* 102; Parker, *Native American Estate,* 151; Edmunds et al, *The People,* 439; Manning, "Wampanoag," 661.

UNINTENDED CONSEQUENCES
[pp. 68–84] *Lindsay G. Robertson*

1 Colin G. Calloway, *Pen and Ink Witchcraft: Treaties and Treaty-Making in American Indian History* (New York: Oxford University Press, 2013), 4.

2 Stuart Banner, *How the Indians Lost Their Land: Law and Power on the Frontier* (Boston: Belknap Press, 2005), 10–48; Walter R. Echo-Hawk, *In the Courts of the Conqueror: The 10 Worst Indian Law Cases Ever Decided* (Golden, CO: Fulcrum Press, 2012), 58.

3 Lindsay G. Robertson, *Conquest by Law: How the Discovery of America Dispossessed Indigenous Peoples of Their Lands* (New York: Oxford University Press, 2005).

4 William T. Hagan, "'To Correct Certain Evils: The Indian Land Claims Cases," in *Iroquois Land Claims*, ed. Christopher Vecsey and William A. Starna (Syracuse, NY: Syracuse University Press. 1988), 17.

5 Robertson, *Conquest by Law*, 143; Eric Foner, review of Banner, *How the Indians Lost Their Land* in *London Review of Books*, February 9, 2006, http://www.ericfoner.com/reviews/020906lrb.html.

6 For additional information about the Illinois and Wabash Land Companies, see the companies' papers at digital.libraries.ou.edu/IWLC. The papers were preserved by the family of the companies' last secretary, John Hill Brinton, and entrusted to the University of Oklahoma College of Law by his great-great-great-grandson, Jasper Brinton. Had it not been for the Brinton family, the history of the *Johnson v. M'Intosh* litigation would never have been known.

7 Marshall to Frelinghuysen, May 22, 1830, ALS, Collection of Samuel L. Lawton, Jr., Highland Park, Illinois, TS at The Papers of John Marshall, College of William & Mary, Williamsburg, Virginia; Marshall to Everett, June 5, 1830, ALS, Everett Papers, Mass. Hist. Society, TS at The Papers of John Marshall.

8 Ibid.

9 *Richmond Enquirer,* 11 January 1831, 2.

10 Ibid.

11 U.S. Constitution, art. 3, sec. 2.

12 Cherokee Nation v. Georgia, 30 U.S. (5 Peters) 1, 17.

13 Ibid., 20.

14 Charles J. Kappler, ed., *Indian Affairs: Laws and Treaties*, vol. 2, *Treaties* (Washington, DC: Government Printing Office, 1904), 310–11.

15 Ibid., 311 (emphasis added).

16 Grant Foreman, *Indian Removal* (Norman, Oklahoma: University of Oklahoma Press, 1953), 29.

17 Kappler, *Indian Affairs: Laws and Treaties,* 2:325–41.

18 Worcester v. Georgia, 31 U.S. (6 Peters) 515, 528–33 (1832).

19 Ibid., 562–63, 597.

20 Ibid., 544.

21 Ibid., 546 (emphasis added). John Marshall here made clear that he intended that the rule be construed pursuant to the rule of construction *expressio unius est exclusio alterius,* "to include one is to exclude the other." It is also worth considering that the section in *Worcester* overruling the fee title portion of the *Johnson* formulation of the discovery doctrine does not once mention *Johnson* overtly. Marshall, superintending a Supreme Court that was still fragile, never expressly overruled himself. *Worcester* was intended to *erase* the former opinion, by making the new rule, as was Marshall's wont, appear self-evident.

22 See generally, Joseph C. Burke, "The Cherokee Cases: A Study in Law, Politics, and Morality," *Stanford Law Review* 21 (February 1969): 500; Jill Norgren, *The Cherokee Cases: The Confrontation of Law and Politics* (New York: McGraw-Hill, 1996).

23 Richard E. Ellis, *The Union at Risk: Jacksonian Democracy, States' Rights, and the Nullification Crisis* (New York: Oxford University Press, 1987), 75-76, seriatim.

24 Carl Brent Swisher, *The Taney Period, 1836-64,* vol. 5 of *The Oliver Wendell Holmes Devise History of the Supreme Court of the United States* (New York: Macmillan, 1974), 53-54.

25 Alexander A. Lawrence, *James Moore Wayne, Southern Unionist* (Chapel Hill: University of North Carolina Press, 1943), 61-62. Duvall's replacement, Jackson appointee Philip P. Barbour, would not join the court until 1837.

26 Joseph Story to Fay, March 2, 1835, *The Life and Letters of Joseph Story,* ed. William Wetmore Story (Boston, 1851), 2:192, quoted in Warren, *The Supreme Court in United States History,* 1:803.

27 Of the thirty-nine opinions reported that term, Marshall delivered only fifteen. Story delivered ten, McLean seven, Thompson five, and Baldwin and Wayne each one.

28 Mitchel v. United States, 34 U.S. (9 Peters) 711, 746 (1835).

29 United States v. Fernandez, 35 U.S. (10 Peters) 303, 304 (1836).

30 Catron was confirmed four days into the Van Buren administration. Henry J. Abraham, *Justices and Presidents: A Political History of Appointments to the Supreme Court,* 2nd ed. (New York: Oxford University Press, 1985), 101, 103.

31 Swisher, *The Taney Period,* 61, citing, *inter alia,* Catron to Martin Van Buren, December 12, 1835, Martin Van Buren Papers, Library of Congress and Georgia Historical Society, Savannah. *Foreman,* like *Tassells,* involved the application to an Indian of state criminal laws. Catron's opinion constituted a twenty-three-page declaration that, as far as discovery was concerned, *Worcester* was wrong and *Johnson* was right. State v. Foreman, 16 Tenn. (8 Yerger) 256 (1835).

32 Abraham, *Justices and Presidents,* 103.

33 Clark v. Smith, 38 U.S. (13 Peters) 195, 201 (1839).

34 Mitchel v. United States, 40 U.S. (15 Peters) 52, 89 (1841).

35 Martin v. Lessee of Waddell, 41 U.S. (16 Peters) 367, 409 (1842).

THE GREAT TREATY COUNCIL AT HORSE CREEK [pp. 88-111] *Raymond J. DeMallie*

1 The term *Sioux* includes three large groups of tribes: the Eastern, or Santee, Sioux of Minnesota, the Middle, or Yankton and Yanktonai, Sioux who lived on the prairies of North and South Dakota east of the Missouri River, and the Teton, or Western, Sioux who lived on the high plains west of the Missouri. The Eastern and Middle groups called themselves Dakota, while the Western group called themselves Lakota. They all spoke dialects of the same language. See Raymond J. DeMallie, "Sioux Until 1850," in *Plains,* ed. Raymond J. DeMallie, vol. 13, *Handbook of North American Indians,* ed. William C. Sturtevant (Washington, DC: Smithsonian Institution), 718-60.

2 Francis Paul Prucha, *American Indian Treaties: The History of a Political Anomaly* (Berkeley: University of California Press, 1994), 238.

3 Colin G. Calloway, *Pen and Ink Witchcraft: Treaties and Treaty Making in American Indian History* (New York: Oxford University Press, 2013), 174-75; Calculated from data in Campbell Gibson, "Population of the 100 Largest Cities and Other Urban Places in the United States: 1790–1990," U.S. Census Bureau, Population Division Working Paper No. 27 (June 1998), Table 8, http://www.census.gov/population/www/documentation/twps0027/twps0027.html.

4 Loretta Fowler, "The Great Plains from the Arrival of the Horse to 1885," in *North America*, ed. Bruce G. Trigger and Wilcomb E. Washburn, vol. 1, part 2, *The Cambridge History of the Native Peoples of the Americas* (New York: Cambridge University Press, 1996), 32; Richard White, "The Winning of the West: The Expansion of the Western Sioux in the Eighteenth and Nineteenth Centuries," *Journal of American History* 65, no. 2 (September, 1978): 340.

5 Paul Vandevelder, *Savages and Scoundrels: The Untold Story of America's Road to Empire through Indian Territory* (New Haven: Yale University Press, 2009), 216–17; R. David Edmunds, Frederick E. Hoxie, and Neal Salisbury, *The People: A History of Native America* (Boston: Houghton Mifflin Company, 2007), 289; Calloway, *Pen and Ink Witchcraft*, 176.

6 Red Cloud, "The Great Chief: Red Cloud Meets His White Brethren at Cooper Institute," *New York Times,* June 17, 1870.

7 For a general overview of Plains Indians, see DeMallie, "Introduction," in *Plains,* 5–12.

8 See, for example, the 1815 Treaty with the Teton in Charles J. Kappler, ed., *Indian Affairs: Laws and Treaties,* vol. 2, *Treaties* (Washington, DC: Government Printing Office, 1904), 112–13.

9 For a historical overview see William R. Swagerty, "History of the United States Plains Until 1850," in DeMallie, *Plains,* 256–79.

10 See Raymond J. DeMallie, "Touching the Pen: Plains Indian Treaty Councils in Ethnohistorical Perspective," in *Ethnicity on the Great Plains,* ed. Frederick C. Luebke (Lincoln: University of Nebraska Press), 38–53.

11 For a good description, see the report of Pierre-Antoine Tabeau, an early nineteenth-century trader who lived with the Arikara, in *Tabeau's Narrative of Loisel's Expedition to the Upper Missouri*, ed. Annie Heloise Abel

(Norman: University of Oklahoma Press, 1939), 130–33.

12 Thomas H. Harvey, superintendent, St. Louis Superintendency, to Commissioner of Indian Affairs William Medill, May 6, 1846, enclosing petition from the Brule and Oglala Lakota chiefs forwarded by Indian agent Andrew Dripps, Letters received by the Commissioner of Indian Affairs, Upper Missouri Agency, M234, roll 884, document 1846-H2279, National Archives and Records Administration.

13 9 Stat. 570, 572.

14 For biographical sketches, see Ray H. Mattison, "David Dawson Mitchell," in *The Mountain Men and Fur Trade of the Far West,* ed. LeRoy R. Hafen (Glendale, CA: Arthur H. Clark, 1965), 2:241–46, and LeRoy R. Hafen and Ann W. Hafen, "Thomas Fitzpatrick," ibid. (1969), 7:87–106.

15 Thomas Fitzpatrick to Commissioner of Indian Affairs Luke Lea, November 24, 1851, *Annual Report of the Commissioner of Indian Affairs,* 1851, 70–75.

16 George Wilkins Kendall, *New Orleans Picayune,* "Editorial Correspondence," October 11, 1851. Kendall, one of the paper's editors, accompanied Wharton's return expedition to the Pawnee.

17 For a biography of De Smet and a detailed account of his activities involving the 1851 Treaty, see John J. Killoren, S. J.,*"Come, Blackrobe": De Smet and the Indian Tragedy* (Norman: University of Oklahoma Press, 1994).

18 The experiences of the commissioners in traveling to Fort Laramie are reported in the *Missouri Republican,* August 25 and October 6, 1851.

19 Report of Commissioner of Indian Affairs Luke Lea, November 27, 1851, in *Annual Report of the Commissioner of Indian Affairs,* 1851, 272.

20 If there was an official record of the treaty council proceedings, it has been lost. The commission's activities on September 1 are reported in the *Missouri Republican,* September 26, 1851.

21 *Missouri Republican,* October 6, 1851.

22 The events of Saturday and Sunday, September 6 and 7, are reported in the *Missouri Republican,* October 6 and 24, 1851.

23 The events of Monday, September 8, are reported in the *Missouri Republican,* October 6, 24, and 28, 1851.

24 Called Gros Ventres in the treaty proceedings and in the Treaty itself. During the nineteenth century the Siouan-speaking Hidatsa were sometimes called Gros Ventre of the Missouri to differentiate them from the Algonquian-speaking Gros Ventre of the Plains (also called Atsina).

25 An experienced fur trader, Mitchell would have understood the importance of beginning the council with a Pipe Ceremony. Smoking the pipe ceremonially was ubiquitous among Plains Indians. Lakota religious leader George Sword commented in 1896, "The Lakota should smoke the pipe first when considering any matter of importance." He explained, "The spirit in the smoke will soothe the spirits of all who thus smoke together and all will be as friends and all think alike." James R. Walker, *Lakota Belief and Ritual,* ed. Raymond J. DeMallie and Elaine A. Jahner (Lincoln: University of Nebraska Press, 1980), 83.

26 Raymond J. DeMallie, "The Lakota Ghost Dance: An Ethnohistorical Account," *Pacific Historical Review* 51, no. 4 (1982): 385–405.

27 Reported in the *Missouri Republican,* October 29, 1851.

28 The events of September 9 and 10 are reported in the *Missouri Republican,* November 2, 1851.

29 The chief's name is Mathó sap'íc'iye, or Bear That Paints Itself Black, more commonly translated as Smutty Bear.

30 The events of September 11–14 are reported in the *Missouri Republican,* November 9, 1851.

31 Killoren, *"Come, Blackrobe,"* 177–78.

32 The events of September 15 are reported in the *Missouri Republican,* November 23, 1851.

33 The events of September 17–23 are reported in the *Missouri Republican,* November 30, 1851.

34 See, for example, the winter count entries from American Horse, Cloud Shield, Battiste Good, and No Ears in *The Year the Stars Fell: Lakota Winter Counts at the Smithsonian,* ed. Candace S. Greene and Russell Thornton (Lincoln: University of Nebraska Press, 2007), 230–31.

35 For the delegation see Killoren, *"Come, Blackrobe,"* 170–73, 188–90, and reports in the (Washington) *National Intelligencer,* "Indian Interview with the President," November 19, 1851; "Indian Visit," December 12, 1851; and "Indian Visit to the Navy Yard," December 13, 1851.

36 See Harry H. Anderson, "The Controversial Sioux Amendment to the Fort Laramie Treaty of 1851," *Nebraska History* 37 (1956): 201–20.

NAAL TSOOS SANÍ [pp. 116–31]
Jennifer Nez Denetdale

1 Stuart Banner, *How the Indians Lost Their Land: Law and Power on the Frontier* (Cambridge: Belknap Press, 2007), 228–90.

2 Peter Iverson, *Diné: A History of the Navajos* (Albuquerque: University of New Mexico Press, 2002), 59; John L. Kessell, "General Sherman and the Navajo Treaty of 1868: A Basic and Expedient Misunderstanding," *Western Historical Quarterly* 12, no. 3 (July 1981): 263.

3 Peter Iverson, *The Navajos* (New York: Chelsea House, 1990), 46.

4 R. David Edmunds, Frederick E. Hoxie, and Neal Salisbury, *The People: A History of Native America* (Boston: Houghton Mifflin, 2007), 286; Richard White, *The Roots of Dependency: Subsistence, Environment, and Social Change among the Choctaws, Pawnees, and Navajos* (Lincoln: University of Nebraska Press, 1983), 215, 219–20, 222.

5 White, *Roots of Dependency,* 219.

6 Ibid., 216.

7 Robert Roessel, Jr., "Navajo History, 1850–1923," in *Southwest,* ed. Alfonso

Ortiz, vol. 10, *Handbook of North American Indians*, ed. William C. Sturtevant (Washington, DC: Smithsonian Institution, 1983), 519–20.

8 Navajo Area Office, Indian Health Service website, http://www.ihs.gov/navajo/index.cfm?module=nao_navajo_nation; U.S. Department of Interior, Bureau of Indian Affairs, http://www.bia.gov/FAQs/index.htm.

9 Iverson, *Diné,* 70, 73; Iverson, *Navajos,* 47.

10 The names Diné and Navajo are used interchangeably throughout this essay, because both refer to who we are.

11 William A. Keleher, *Turmoil in New Mexico, 1846–1868* (Santa Fe: Rydal Press, 1952), 277, cited in Crawford R. Buell, "The Navajo 'Long Walk': Recollections by Navajos" in *The Changing Ways of Southwestern Indians: A Historic Perspective*, ed. Albert Schroeder (Glorieta, NM: Rio Grande Press, 1971), 183.

12 Cherokee Nation v. Georgia, 30 U.S. (5 Peters) 1, 17.

13 Joanne Barker, "For Whom Sovereignty Matters," in *Sovereignty Matters: Locations of Contestation and Possibility in Indigenous Struggles for Self-Determination* (Lincoln: University of Nebraska Press, 2005), 18.

14 David E. Wilkins, *The Navajo Political Experience* (Tsaile, AZ: Diné College Press, 1999), 20–23, 210, 211.

15 Robert M. Utley, *The Indian Frontier of the American West, 1846–1890* (Albuquerque: University of New Mexico Press, 1984).

16 James Carleton to Thompson, September 19, 1863, in Lawrence C. Kelly, *Navajo Roundup: Selected Correspondence of Kit Carson's Expedition Against the Navajos, 1863–1865* (Boulder, CO: Pruett Publishing, 1970), 56, 57.

17 Neal Ackerly, "A Navajo Diaspora: The Long Walk to Hwéeldi" (Silver City, NM: Dio Rios Consultants, 1998), http://bloodhound.tripod.com/longwalk.htm.

18 Howard W. Gorman, in *Navajo Stories of the Long Walk Period*, ed. Broderick H. Johnson (Tsaile, AZ: Navajo Community College Press, 1973), 23–42.

19 Kayah David, quoted in Buell, "Navajo 'Long Walk,'" 171.

20 John Daw, testimony before the Land Claims Commission, 1951, in Buell, "Navajo 'Long Walk,'" 177.

21 Ackerly, "Navajo Diaspora."

22 Ethnic cleansing is the deliberate and systematic removal of a racial, political, or cultural group from a specific geographical area. The 1993 United Nations Commission defined it more specifically as "the planned deliberate removal from a specific territory, persons of a particular ethnic group, by force or intimidation, in order to render that area ethnically homogenous." U.S. Legal Definitions, http://definitions.uslegal.com/e/ethnic-cleansing.

23 Quoted in Gerald Thompson, *The Army and the Navajo* (Tucson: University of Arizona Press, 1976), 36.

24 Thompson, *Army and the Navajo*, 67.

25 Quoted in Fred Descheene, in Johnson, *Navajo Stories*, 212.

26 See Johnson, *Navajo Stories* for Navajo perspectives on the Long Walk.

27 Quoted in ibid., 2-4.

28 Quoted in Martin Link, ed. *The Navajo Treaty—1868: Treaty Between the United States of America and the Navajo Tribe of Indians / with a Record of Discussions That Led to Its Signing* (Las Vegas, NV: KC Publications, 1968).

29 Pete Price, interview, n.d., Fort Defiance, Arizona. Newberry Library, Ayer Modern MS, Box, 24, Folder 231, Chicago, Illinois.

30 Quoted in ibid., 4.

31 John L. Kessell, "General Sherman and the Navajo Treaty of 1868: A Basic and Expedient Misunderstanding," *Western Historical Quarterly* 12, no. 3 (1981): 259.

32 Quoted in ibid., 5, 6.

33 Kessell, "General Sherman."

34 Wallace Coffey and Rebecca Tsosie, "Rethinking the Tribal Sovereignty Doctrine: Tribal Sovereignty and the Collective Future of Indian Nations," *Stanford Law and Policy Review* 12, no. 2 (2001): 194.

35 Joanne Barker, *Native Acts: Law, Recognition, and Cultural Authenticity* (Durham, NC: Duke University Press, 2011). Barker argues that as Native Peoples we should appreciate the deplorable conditions under which our leaders agreed to treaty terms with the United States.

36 Scott Richard Lyons, *X-Marks: Native Signatures of Assent* (Minneapolis: University of Minnesota Press, 2010), 32, 33.

37 Wilkins, *Navajo Political Experience,* 22.

38 Ibid., 23-25.

39 Ibid., 16, 17.

40 Quoted in Jennifer Nez Denetdale, *Reclaiming Diné History: The Legacies of Navajo Chief Manuelito and Juanita* (Tucson: University of Arizona Press, 2007), 82-84.

41 Ibid.

42 Wilkins, *Navajo Political Experience.*

43 Bethany R. Berger, "Williams v. Lee and the Debate Over Indian Equality," *Michigan Law Review* 109 (June 2011): 1463–528.

44 Ibid.

45 Gregory Scott Smith, "A Concern for the Future," *El Palacio* 108 (Winter 2003): 19. See also Jennifer Nez Denetdale, *The Long Walk: The Forced Navajo Exile* (New York: Chelsea House, 2007), 112–13.

46 Lloyd L. Lee, "Reclaiming Indigenous Intellectual, Political, and Geographical Space: A Path for Navajo Nationhood," *American Indian Quarterly* 32, no. 1 (Winter 2008): 96-110.

47 Ibid., 107.

48 See the Navajo Nation Human Rights Commission's website at http://www.nnhrc.navajo-nsn.gov. The commission is charged with several responsibilities, including the need to have a presence at the United Nations.

TREATIES MY ANCESTORS MADE FOR ME
[pp. 132–51] *Suzan Shown Harjo*

1 Colin G. Calloway, *Pen and Ink Witchcraft: Treaties and Treaty Making in American Indian History* (New York: Oxford University Press, 2013) 2, 11; Alexandra Harmon, "Indian Treaty Rights: A Subject for Agile Minds," *Oregon Historical Quarterly* 106, no. 3 (Fall 2005): 361.

2 Arlene Hirschfelder and Martha Kreipe de Montaño, "Treaties," in *The Native American Almanac: A Portrait of Native America Today* (New York: Macmillan, 1993), 54.

3 W. Richard West, Jr., and Kevin Gover, "The Struggle for Indian Civil Rights," in *Indians in American History: An Introduction,* ed. Frederick E. Hoxie and Peter Iverson (Wheeling, IL: Harlan Davidson, 1997), 218, 231.

4 Cited in George White, *Historical Collections of Georgia: Containing the Most Interesting Facts, Traditions, Biographical Sketches, Anecdotes, Etc. . . . From Its First Settlement to the Present Time* (New York: Pudney and Russell, 1855), 156.

5 John Trumbull, *Autobiography, Reminiscences and Letters of John Trumbull, From 1756 to 1841* (New York, 1841), 164–65.

6 Act to regulate trade and intercourse with the Indian tribes, Pub. L. No. 1-33, § 4, 1 Stat. 137, 138 (July 22, 1790).

7 The Reply of the President of the United States to the Speech of the Cornplanter, Half-Town, and Great-Tree, Chiefs and Councillors of the Seneca Nation of Indians, December 29, 1790, *American State Papers: Indian Affairs*, 1:142

8 Charles J. Kappler, ed., in *Indian Affairs: Laws and Treaties*, vol. 2, *Treaties* (Washington, DC: Government Printing Office, 1904), 25–29.

9 Henry Knox to George Washington, 7 August 1790, in *Papers of George Washington: Presidential Series*, ed. Mark A. Mastromarino, vol. 6, *1 July 1790–30 November 1790* (Charlottesville: University Press of Virginia, 1996), 206–12, http://founders.archives.gov/documents/Washington/05-06-02-0094, ver. 2014-02-12.

10 Kappler, *Treaties*, 107–10.

11 Treaty of Peace and Amity between His Britannic Majesty and the United States of America, December 24, 1814, in *Treaties and Other International Acts of the United States of America*, ed. Hunter Miller, vol. 2, *Documents 1–40: 1776–1818* (Washington, DC: Government Printing Office, 1931), http://avalon.law.yale.edu/19th_century/ghent.asp.

12 *Washington Daily Morning Chronicle*, March 28, 1863.

13 Abraham Lincoln, *Collected Works of Abraham Lincoln*, ed. Roy P. Basler (Springfield, IL: Abraham Lincoln Association and Rutgers University Press, 1953), 6:152–53, http://name.umdl.umich.edu/lincoln6.

14 Herman J. Viola, *Diplomats in Buckskins: A History of Indian Delegations in Washington City* (1981; repr. Bluffton, SC: Rivilo Books, 1995), 99–102.

15 Robert M. Utley, *Indian Frontier of the American West 1846–1890* (Albuquerque: University of New Mexico Press, 1985), 89.

16 Kappler, *Treaties*, 984–89.

17 Ibid., 1012–15.

18 Dee Brown, *Bury My Heart at Wounded Knee* (New York: Holt, Rinehart and Winston, 1970), 169.

19 Ibid., 265; General Philip H. Sheridan, *Personal Memoirs of P. H. Sheridan*, (New York: Charles L. Webster, 1888), 2:297.

THE BETRAYAL OF "CIVILIZATION" IN UNITED STATES–NATIVE NATIONS DIPLOMACY [pp. 152–71] *James Riding In*

1 Eric Foner, *Reconstruction: America's Unfinished Revolution, 1863–1877* (New York: Harper & Row, 1988), 29–30, 463; Eric Foner, *The Fiery Trial: Abraham Lincoln and American Slavery* (New York: W. W. Norton, 2010), 262.

2 Frederick E. Hoxie, *A Final Promise: The Campaign to Assimilate the Indi-ans, 1880–1920* (Lincoln: University of Nebraska Press, 2001), passim.

3 David Wallace Adams, *Education for Extinction: American Indians and the Boarding School Experience, 1875–1928* (Lawrence, KS: University Press of Kansas, 1995), 335.

4 Frederick E. Hoxie, ed., *Talking Back to Civilization: Indian Voices from the Progressive Era* (Boston: Bedford/St. Martin's, 2001), 9–10.

5 Ibid., vii, 6.

6 Francis Paul Prucha, "America's Indians and the Federal Government, 1900 to 2000: A Prominent Historian of Indian Relations and Policy Reviews a Century of Tumult and Hope," *Wisconsin Magazine of History* 84, no. 2 (Winter 2000–2001): 26–37.

7 Hoxie, *Talking Back to Civilization*, viii, ix, 4, 6-7; Charles F. Wilkinson, *Blood Struggle: The Rise of Modern Indian Nations* (New York: W. W. Norton, 2006), 352–82.

8 For a description of the treaty party's experiences, see John Irving Treat Jr., *Indian Sketches Taken during an Expedition to the Pawnee Tribes*, ed. John Francis McDermott (Norman: University of Oklahoma Press, 1955).

9 Edward A. Ellsworth, "Council with the Pawnee Nation (of the Platte River)," Ratified Treaty No. 190, Documents Relating to the Negotiation of the Treaty of October 9, 1833, with the Pawnee Indians (October 9, 1833), 4–10, http://digicoll.library.wisc.edu/cgi-bin/History/History-idx?type=turn&entity=History.IT1833no190.p0001&id=History.IT1833no190&isize=M.

10 Treaty with the Pawnee, 1833, in Charles J. Kappler, comp. and ed., *Indian Treaties, 1778–1883* (New York: Interland Publishing, 1972), 416-18.

11 Ibid.

12 Ellsworth, "Council with the Pawnee Nation," 5.

13 John Dunbar to David Greene, June 1, 1838, in Richard E. Jensen, ed., *The Pawnee Mission Letters, 1834–1851* (Lincoln: University of Nebraska

Press, 2010), 219–21; Dunbar to Major Hamilton, October 1, 1839, 246–47. Hereafter all letters and depositions cited refer to this volume.

14 T. Hartley Crawford to Rev. David Greene, February 6, 1840, 254; Samuel Allis to Greene, October 12, 1840, 268; D. D. Mitchell, Superintendent of Indian Affairs, St. Louis, to T. Hartley Crawford, Commissioner of Indian Affairs, May 7, 1842, Letters Received, Office of Indian Affairs, RG 75, Council Bluff Agency, Roll 215, National Archives and Records Adminstration [hereafter NARA].

15 Dunbar to Greene, July 13, 1840, 262.

16 Dunbar to Greene, June 4, 1836, 190; Allis to Greene, July 14, 1836, 176; T. Hartley Crawford, Commissioner of Indian Affairs, to Rev. David Greene, February 6, 1840, 254; Greene to Crawford, February 13, 1840, 255–57; George B. Gaston to Green, April 19, 1842, 294.

17 Dunbar to Greene, July 31, 1841, 279–81; Allis to Greene, September 1, 1841, 281–84. Also see Josiah E. Stevens's deposition, 467. The Pawnee asserted the land cession aspect of the 1833 treaty was fraudulent; see Charles Augustus Murray, *Travels in North America during the Years 1834, 1835, and 1836 . . .* (New York, 1839), 1:179.

18 For discussions of nineteenth-century Pawnee culture, see, Martha Royce Blaine, *Pawnee Passage: 1870-1875* (Norman: University of Oklahoma Press, 1990); and James R. Murie, *Ceremonies of the Pawnee*, ed. Douglas R. Parks (Washington: Smithsonian Institution Press, 1981). For a depiction of Skidi culture in the 1860s, see Gene Weltfish, *The Lost Universe: Pawnee Life and Culture* (Lincoln: University of Nebraska Press and Basic Books, 1965).

19 Allis to Greene, October 14, 1844, 396–97.

20 Dunbar to Greene, April 24, 1844, 361–64; Allis to Greene, October 14, 1844, 393–95; Daniel Miller, Indian Agent, to Thomas H. Harvey, Superin-tendent of Indian Affairs, October 18, 1844, 409.

21 Allis to Greene, October 14, 1844, 393–95; see also James Mathers's deposition, 425-26.

22 Allis to Greene, October 14, 1844, 394–95.

23 Miller to Harvey, October 18, 1844, 403–10; Allis to Greene, October 9 and 14, 1844, 388–93, 404-5; see also Peter A. Sarpy's deposition, 239–43; Timothy E. Ramsey to Greene, October 9, 1844, 381–83.

24 Dunbar to Greene, April 15, 1846, 534-35.

25 Allis to Greene, July 21, 1843, 337-40.

26 Dunbar to Greene, June 30, 1846, 541–42; R. B. Mitchell, Indian Sub-agent, to Harvey, June 28, 1846, 545–46; Allis to Greene, January 16, 1849, 574–76.

27 Captain Wharton described the Pawnees as being in a "wretched condition." See H. M. Wharton to George A. Manypenny, Commissioner of Indian Affairs, January 21, 1854, Letters Received, Office of Indian Affairs, RG 75, Microfilm 234, Council Bluff Agency, Roll 218, NARA; Allis to Greene, January 16, 1849, 574–76; Report of Joseph V. Hamilton, October 1, 1849, *Annual Report of the Commissioner of Indian Affairs*, 1849-1850 (Washington, 1850), 318–19.

28 Treaty with the Pawnee, 1857, Kappler, *Indian Treaties*, 764-67.

29 B. F. Lushbaugh, Indian Agent, to Charles E. Mix, Commissioner of Indian Affairs, September 15, 1862, *Annual Report of the Commissioner of Indian Affairs*, 1862, 122.

30 James Riding In, "The United States v. Yellow Sun et al. (The Pawnee People): A Case Study of Institutional and Societal Racism and U.S. Justice in Nebraska from the 1850s to 1870s," *Wicazo Sa Review* 17 (Spring 2002): 13-16.

31 Blaine, *Pawnee Passage,* 166.

32 For glorified accounts of the white leaders of the Pawnee scouts, generally see, George Bird Grinnell, *Two Great Scouts and their Pawnee Battalion: The Experiences of Frank J. North and Luther H. North* (Cleveland: Arthur H. Clark, 1928); and Donald F. Danker, ed., *Man of the Plains: Recollections of Luther North . . .* (Lincoln: University of Nebraska Press, 1961). For a more balanced account, see Mark Van De Logt, *War Party in Blue: Pawnee Scouts in the U.S. Army* (Norman: University of Oklahoma Press, 2010).

33 For a discussion of genocide, see Walter R. Echo-Hawk, *In the Courts of the Conqueror: The 10 Worst Indian Law Cases Ever Decided* (Golden, CO: Fulcrum Publishing, 2010), 399-420.

34 See generally, Martha Royce Blaine, *Some Things Are Not Forgotten: A Pawnee Family Remembers* (Lincoln: University of Nebraska Press, 1997); and Clyde A. Milner II, *With Good Intentions: Quaker Work among the Pawnees, Otos, and Omahas in the 1870s* (Lincoln: University of Nebraska Press, 1982).

35 Riding In, "United States v. Yellow Sun," 13-41.

36 Blaine, *Pawnee Passage,* 166–69; William Burgess, U.S. Agent, to Barclay White, Superintendent of Indian Affairs, September 20, 1873, *Annual Report of the Commissioner of Indian Affairs*, 1873, 193.

37 Quoted in Blaine, *Pawnee Passage,* 66.

38 Barclay White, Superintendent of Indian Affairs, to H. R. Clum, Acting Commissioner of Indian Affairs, February 22, 1873, RG 75, Microcopy 234, Office of Indian Affairs, Pawnee Agency, Letters Received, Reel 662, NARA.

39 "Pawnee Agency Council Minutes," Indian Archives Division, Oklahoma State Historical Society, Oklahoma City, 53.

40 For a Pawnee account of the massacre, see Garland James Blaine and Martha Royce Blaine, "Pa-Re-Su A-Ri-Ra-Ke: The Hunters That Were Massacred," *Nebraska History* 58 (1977): 342-58.

41 Wm. Burgess, Indian Agent, to Edward P. Smith, October 21, 1874, Let-

ters Received, Office of Indian Affairs, RG 75, Microfilm 234, Pawnee Agency, Roll 663, NARA.

42 Burgess to Wm. Nicholson, Superintendent of Indian Affairs, August 12, 1876, *Annual Report of the Commissioner of Indian Affairs,* 1876, 56; Blaine, *Pawnee Passage,* 214ff.

43 Quoted in Van De Logt, *War Party in Blue,* 190.

44 Ibid., 25, 26.

45 Blaine, *Some Things Are Not Forgotten,* 18.

46 Ibid., 28–33.

47 Report of John W. Scott, Agent, August 20, 1885, *Annual Report of the Commissioner of Indian Affairs,* 1885, 92.

48 Blaine, *Some Things Are Not Forgotten,* 18.

49 *Annual Report of the Commissioner of Indian Affairs,* 1885, 230.

50 *Annual Report of the Commissioner of Indian Affairs,* 1890, 197.

51 Ibid, 198.

52 Cited in ibid.

53 Ibid.

54 Ibid., 197.

55 Quoted in ibid.

56 Blaine, *Some Things Are Not Forgotten,* 16–25.

57 Ibid., 182.

58 Alexander Lesser, *The Pawnee Ghost Dance Hand Game: Ghost Dance Revival and Ethnic Identity* (Lincoln: University of Nebraska Press, 1996), 49.

59 Quoted in Blaine, *Some Things Are Not Forgotten,* 43.

60 Ibid., 43–44.

61 Ibid., 28–50.

62 *Annual Report of the Commissioner of Indian Affairs,* 1893, 33.

63 Blaine, *Some Things Are Not Forgotten,* 43.

64 Ibid., 51–68.

65 Ibid., 60–79.

AMERICAN INDIAN SCOUTS [pp. 172–74]
Mark G. Hirsch

1 Herman Viola, *Warriors in Uniform* (Washington, DC: National Geographic, 2007), 37.

2 Thomas W. Dunlay, *Wolves for the Blue Soldiers: Indian Scouts and Auxiliaries with the United States Army, 1860–90* (Lincoln: University of Nebraska Press, 1982), 50; Viola, *Warriors in Uniform,* 37, 57.

3 Trevor K. Plante, "Lead the Way: Researching U.S. Army Indian Scouts, 1866–1914," *Prologue* 41, no. 2 (Summer 2009): 52–60.

4 Dunlay, *Wolves for the Blue Soldiers,* 49.

5 Ibid., 200.

6 Herman Viola, *Warriors in Uniform,* 39.

7 Dunlay, *Wolves for the Blue Soldiers,* 106.

8 Ibid., 117.

9 Ibid., 8, 105.

10 Loretta Fowler, "The Great Plains from the Arrival of the Horse to 1885," in *North America,* ed. Bruce C. Trigger and Wilcomb Washburn, vol. 1, part 2, *The Cambridge History of the Native Peoples of the Americas* (New York: Cambridge University Press, 1996), 26; Dunlay, *Wolves for the Blue Soldiers,* 156.

11 Viola, *Warriors in Uniform,* 39.

12 Ibid.

13 Ibid., 42; Clifford Trafzer, ed., *American Indians/American Presidents: A History* (New York: HarperCollins, 2009), 104; Dunlay, *Wolves for the Blue Soldiers,* 115.

14 Tom Holm, "Scouts," in *The Encyclopedia of North American Indians,* ed. Frederick Hoxie (New York: Houghton Mifflin, 1996), 573–74.

15 Dunlay, *Wolves for the Blue Soldiers,* 120.

16 James Riding In, "Geronimo," in Hoxie, *Encyclopedia of North American Indians,* 222; Eve Ball, "The Apache Scouts: A Chiricauhua Appraisal," *Arizona and the West* 7, no. 4 (Winter, 1965): 323, 326.

17 Quoted in Dunlay, *Wolves for the Blue Soldiers,* 88.

18 Ibid., 144.

19 Martha Royce Blaine, *The Pawnees: A Critical Bibliography* (Bloomington: Indiana University Press, 1980), 21–22.

20 Dunlay, *Wolves for the Blue Soldiers,* 119.

21 Riding In, "Geronimo," 222.

22 Martha Royce Blaine, "Pawnee," in Hoxie, *Encyclopedia of North American Indians,* 473.

23 Larry G. Murray, "Shoshone," in Hoxie, *Encyclopedia of North American Indians,* 588.

24 Quoted in Dunlay, *Wolves for the Blue Soldiers,* 114, 205.

"CIVILIZATION" AND THE HUPA FLOWER DANCE CEREMONY [pp. 175–77]
Lois J. Risling

1 Hupa refers to the people, and Hoopa refers to the place. The official spelling of the federally recognized tribe is Hoopa.

2 K'ixinay are the immortal spirits, the beings who inhabited this world before human beings arrived. They did not know death. They now live in a world across the ocean and inhabit things on this earth. K'ixinay means literally, "the ones who escape, the ones who are safe."

RIGHTS GUARANTEED BY SOLEMN TREATIES [pp. 178–80]

1 Quoted in Colin G. Calloway, *Pen and Ink Witchcraft: Treaties and Treaty Making in American Indian History* (New York: Oxford University Press, 2013), 240.

2 Ibid.

THE GAME AND FISH WERE MADE FOR US [pp. 181–85] Hank Adams

1 John Bailey, "A Century on Earth and a Lifetime Together," *Tacoma News Tribune,* January 13, 1979; Francis A. Garrecht, "An Indian Chief," *Washington Historical Quarterly* 19, no. 4 (October 1928), 165–80; "Chiefs Meninock and Wallahee (Yakama), Testimony During a 1915 Trial for Violating a Washington State Code on Salmon Fishing," in *Great Documents in American Indian History,* ed. Charles Van Doren and

Wayne Moquin (1973; repr., New York: Da Capo Press, 1995), 297–300.

2 Northwest Indian Fisheries Commission, "Treaty Rights at Risk: Habitat Loss, the Decline of the Salmon Resource, and Recommendations for Change" (Olympia, WA: Northwest Indian Fisheries Commission, 2011), 6.

3 Record of Council Proceedings, January 24–26, 1855, Ratified Treaty no. 284, Documents Relating to the Negotiation of the Treaty of January 26, 1855, with the S'Klallam, Skokomish, Toanhooch, and Chimakum Indians, Documents Relating to the Negotiation of Ratified and Unratified Treaties with Various Indian Tribes, 1801–1869, http://digital.library.wisc.edu/1711.dl/History.IT1855no284.

4 Record of Council Proceedings, January 30, 1855, Ratified treaty no. 286, Documents Relating to the Negotiation of the Treaty of January 31, 1855, with Makah Indians, Documents Relating to the Negotiation of Ratified and Unratified Treaties with Various Indian Tribes, 1801–1869, http://digital.library.wisc.edu/1711.dl/History.IT1855no286

5 Ibid.

6 "Certified Copy of the Original Minutes of the Official Proceedings at the Council in Walla Walla Valley, Which Culminated in the Stevens Treaty of 1855," 1953, Bureau of Indian Affairs, Portland Area Office, Portland, Oregon, http://www.lib.uidaho.edu/mcbeth/governmentdoc/1855council.htm.

7 Bering Sea Tribunal of Arbitration, "Proceedings of the Tribunal of Arbitration, Convened at Paris, under the Treaty between the United States . . . and Great Britain, concluded at Washington, February 29, 1892, for the Determination of Questions Between the Two Governments Concerning the Jurisdictional Rights of the United States in the Waters of Bering Sea" (Washington, DC, 1895).

8 Washington Department of Fish and Wildlife, "Olympic Elk Herd Plan," 2004, 6–7.

FROM DISLOCATION TO SELF-DETERMINATION [pp. 198–215]
Kevin Gover

1 W. Richard West, Jr., and Kevin Gover, "The Struggle for Indian Civil Rights," in *Indians in American History: An Introduction,* ed. Frederick E. Hoxie and Peter Iverson (Indianapolis: Wiley-Blackwell, 1997), 223.

2 Ibid., 224; Charles Wilkinson, *Blood Struggle: The Rise of Modern Indian Nations* (New York: W. W. Norton, 2005), 81.

3 William T. Hagan, "Tribalism Rejuvenated: The Native American Since the Era of Termination," *Western Historical Quarterly* 12, no. 1 (January 1981): 8, 15.

4 R. David Edmunds, Frederick E. Hoxie, and Neal Salisbury, *The People: A History of Native America* (Boston: Houghton Mifflin, 2007), 435.

5 Clifford Trafzer, ed., *American Indians/American Presidents: A History* (New York: HarperCollins, 2009), 30.

6 West, Jr., and Gover, "The Struggle for Indian Civil Rights," 221; Charles Wilkinson, *Blood Struggle,* 43.

7 Francis Paul Prucha, *The Great Father: The United States Government and the American Indians*, vols. 1 and 2, unabridged (Lincoln: University of Nebraska Press, 1984), 562–606, 611–916.

8 Institute for Government Research Studies in Administration, *The Problem of Indian Administration* (Baltimore: Johns Hopkins Press, 1928).

9 Kenneth Philip, *John Collier's Crusade for Indian Reform 1920–1954* (Tucson: University of Arizona Press, 1977); Edmunds et al., *The People*, 375–79; John Collier, *From Every Zenith: A Memoir—And Some Essays on Life and Thought* (New York: Sage Books, 1963), 159–236.

10 Edmunds et al., *The People*, 379–82; Vine Deloria Jr. and David Wilkins, *Tribes, Treaties, and Constitutional Tribulations* (Austin: University of Texas Press, 2000), 36.

11 Frederick E. Hoxie, "The Reservation Period, 1880–1960," in *The Cambridge History of the Native Peoples of the Americas*, vol. 1, part 2, *North America*, ed. Bruce G. Trigger and Wilcomb Washburn (Cambridge: Cambridge University Press, 1996), 230–31.

12 Hoxie, "Reservation Period, 1880–1960," 236.

13 Wilkinson, *Blood Struggle*, 81.

14 Charles F. Wilkinson and Eric R. Biggs, "The Evolution of the Termination Policy," *American Indian Law Review* 5, no. 1 (1977): 159.

15 Peter Iverson, "American Indian Voting Rights, 1884–1965," in Susan Cianci Salvatore, *Civil Rights in America: Racial Voting Rights: A National Historic Landmarks Theme Study* (Washington, DC: National Park Service, U.S. Department of the Interior, 2009), 82–83; Edmunds et al., *People*, 405.

16 West, Jr., and Gover, "Struggle for Indian Civil Rights," 218, 225, 229–31.

17 Worcester v. Georgia, 31 U.S. (6 Peters) 515, 551–61 (1832); Santa Clara Pueblo v. Martinez, 436 U.S. 49 (1978); See also, Felix S. Cohen, *Handbook of Federal Indian Law* (Ann Arbor: University of Michigan Library, 1942), 122.

18 Three Affiliated Tribes of the Fort Berthold Reservation v. Wold, 476 U.S. 877 (1986).

19 Williams v. Lee, 358 U.S. 217 (1959); Warren Trading Post v. Arizona State Tax Commission, 380 U.S. 685 (1965); McClanahan v. State Tax Commission of Arizona, 411 U.S. 164, 174–75 (1973); Fisher v. District Court, 424 U.S. 382 (1976).

20 U.S. v. Wheeler, 435 US 313 (1978); Montana v. U.S., 450 U.S. 544 (1981).

21 Charles F. Wilkinson and John M. Volkman, "Judicial Review of Indian Treaty Abrogation: As Long as Water Flows, or Grass Grows upon the Earth—How Long a Time Is That?" *California Law Review* 63, no. 3 (1975): 606–7, 617.

22 This and the following passages from Nixon's message are from Richard M. Nixon, "Special Message to the Congress on Indian Affairs," July 8, 1970,

in Gerhard Peters and John T. Woolley, *The American Presidency Project*, http://www.presidency.ucsb.edu/ws/?pid=2573.

23 Peter Iverson, *"We Are Still Here": American Indians in the Twentieth Century* (Wheeling, IN: Harlan Davidson, 1998), 139–41.

24 Troy Johnson, "The Era of Self-Determination: 1975–Today," in *American Indians/American Presidents: A History,* ed. Clifford Trafzer (New York: HarperCollins, 2009), 185–86.

25 Edmunds et al., *People*, 435.

26 American Indian Policy Review Commission, *Final Report*, 2 vols. (Washington, DC: Government Printing Office, 1977).

27 Kevin Gover, "Statutes as Sources of Modern Indian Rights: Child Welfare, Gaming, and Repatriation—A Statutory History of Federal Indian Policy," in *Treaties with American Indians: An Encyclopedia of Rights, Conflicts, and Sovereignty*, ed. Donald L. Fixico (Santa Barbara: ABC-CLIO, 2007), 115.

28 Ibid., 127.

29 William J. Clinton, "Memorandum on Government-to-Government Relations with Native American Tribal Governments," April 29, 1994, in Peters and Woolley, *American Presidency Project*, http://www.presidency.ucsb.edu/ws/?pid=50064.

30 Clara Sue Kidwell, "Ada Deer, Menominee," in *The New Warriors: Native American Leaders Since 1990*, ed. R. David Edmunds (Lincoln: University of Nebraska Press, 2001), 246–51; Iverson, *"We Are Still Here,"* 142–44; Wilkinson, *Blood Struggle*, 220–31.

HANK ADAMS (Assiniboine-Sioux) is an iconic figure in the American Indian civil rights movement. As a member of the National Indian Youth Council and later with the Survival of American Indians Association—an organization he founded and still directs—Adams strategized and coordinated the first protests and "fish-ins" during the Northwest Coast tribes' struggle to secure their inherent fishing rights. This resistance led to the landmark Boldt decision in 1974 and the beginning of organized protests by Native people across the country to reclaim their sovereign rights.

ROBERT N. CLINTON is the Foundation Professor of Law at the Sandra Day O'Connor College of Law at Arizona State University (ASU) and an affiliated faculty member of the ASU American Indian Studies Program. He is also a faculty fellow at the Center for Law, Science and Innovation. He has served on the courts of several tribes in addition to teaching and writing about tribal law, Native American history, federal courts, cyberspace law, copyright, and civil procedure. His publications include numerous articles on federal Indian law and policy, constitutional law, and federal jurisdiction.

PHILIP J. DELORIA (Standing Rock Sioux) is the Carroll Smith-Rosenberg Collegiate Professor of history, American studies, and Native American studies at the University of Michigan. He is the author of *Playing Indian* (1998) and *Indians in Unexpected Places* (2004) as well as numerous other writings. Deloria is the past president of the American Studies Association and a trustee of the National Museum of the American Indian.

RAYMOND J. DEMALLIE is a Chancellor's Professor of Anthropology and American Studies and codirector of the American Indian Studies Research Institute at Indiana University. He has worked extensively with the Sioux and Assiniboine in North and South Dakota and Montana, with a focus on kinship and social organization, religion, and oral traditions. His numerous publications include *Documents of American Indian Diplomacy* (compiled with Vine Deloria Jr.) and the *Plains* volume of the Smithsonian Institution's *Handbook of North American Indians*.

JENNIFER NEZ DENETDALE (Diné [Navajo]) is the first citizen of the Navajo Nation to earn a doctorate in history, and is a commissioner on the Navajo Nation Human Rights Commission. She is an associate professor of American studies at the University of New Mexico, specializing in Navajo history and culture; Native American women, gender, and feminism; and Indigenous Nations, colonialism, and decolonization. Denetdale has authored *Reclaiming Diné History: The Legacies of Navajo Chief Manuelito and Juanita* and two books on Navajo history for young adults.

MATTHEW L. M. FLETCHER (Grand Traverse Band of Ottawa and Chippewa Indians) is a professor of law at Michigan State University College of Law and the director of the university's Indigenous Law and Policy Center. He is the chief justice of the Poarch Band of Creek Indians Supreme Court and an appellate judge for various tribes. He has published articles with numerous law journals and has authored several books, including *American Indian Tribal Law*, the first casebook for law students on tribal law.

KEVIN GOVER (Pawnee) is the director of the Smithsonian's National Museum of the American Indian and a former professor of law at the Sandra Day O'Connor College of Law at Arizona State University (ASU). He served on the faculty of the university's Indian Legal Program and was co–executive director of ASU's American Indian

Policy Institute. From 1997 to 2001 Gover was the assistant secretary for Indian Affairs in the U.S. Department of the Interior. His tenure in that position is perhaps best known for his apology to Native American people for the historical conduct of the Bureau of Indian Affairs.

ZOLTÁN GROSSMAN is a professor of geography and Native studies at The Evergreen State College in Olympia, Washington, with his PhD from the University of Wisconsin. His focus of study includes interethnic relations, social movements, and environmental and climate justice. He is a coeditor of *Asserting Native Resilience: Pacific Rim Indigenous Nations Face the Climate Crisis*, and a coauthor of *Wisconsin's Past and Present: A Historical Atlas*. He is working on a book for the University of Washington Press on treaty conflicts and environmental "unlikely alliances" between Native and white rural neighbors.

SUZAN SHOWN HARJO (Cheyenne and Hodulgee Muscogee), president of The Morning Star Institute, a national Indian rights organization founded in 1984, is a writer, curator, and policy advocate who has helped Native Nations recover sacred places and more than one million acres of land. Since 1975 she has developed key federal Indian law, including the most important national policy advances in the modern era for the protection of Native American ancestors, arts, cultures, languages, and religious freedom. A poet and an award-winning columnist, her work appears in numerous publications, and she received the Institute of American Indian Arts' first honorary doctorate of humanities awarded to a woman. Dr. Harjo is a founder of the National Museum of the American Indian and has served as a guest curator and editor of this and various museum projects.

RICHARD W. HILL, SR. (Tuscarora) is an artist, writer, curator, and professor, and teaches at the First Nations Technical Institute in Tyendinaga Mohawk Territory, Ontario. From 1992 to 1995, Hill served as the assistant director for Public Programs and as the special assistant to the director at the National Museum of the American Indian. He has lectured and written extensively on placing Native American art history, history, and culture in its proper context, as well as on museum-history issues such as tribal consultation, repatriation, stereotyping, and cross-cultural education.

MARK G. HIRSCH is a historian and writer at the National Museum of the American Indian. Coauthor of *The American Presidency: A Glorious Burden* and a regular contributor to *American Indian* magazine and other museum publications, he has edited numerous books on American and Native American history.

SUSAN HVALSOE KOMORI became a lawyer because of what she witnessed during fishing rights battles of the 1970s at Franks Landing, on the Columbia River, and at other Pacific Northwest Indian fishing grounds. A political appointee in the Carter administration, she represented the United States in international negotiations and other efforts to protect Indian treaty rights, and in efforts to protect salmon, bowhead whale, and other species and their habitats. After serving as special assistant in the Office of the Secretary of the Interior, she went into private practice and has represented Franks Landing, the Hoh, and other Northwest Native Nations in treaty rights and other matters.

TINA KUCKKAHN (Lac du Flambeau Ojibwe) is the founding director of the Longhouse Education and Cultural Center at The Evergreen State College in Olympia, Washington. As an adjunct member of the faculty at Evergreen, she also serves as the planning unit coordinator for Native American academic and public service programs at the college. Kuckkahn is the author of *Hiteemlkiliiksix: Within the Circle of the Rim*.

N. SCOTT MOMADAY (Kiowa) is a scholar and pioneer of modern Native American literature. His 1969 novel, *House Made of Dawn,* was awarded the Pulitzer Prize for fiction. He is the author of thirteen books, including novels, poetry collections, literary criticism, and works on Native American culture. He is also a founding trustee of the National Museum of the American Indian, a Regents Professor of English Emeritus at the University of Arizona, and a member of the Kiowa Gourd Clan. Momaday was awarded the National Medal of Arts by President George W. Bush in 2007.

BEN NIGHTHORSE CAMPBELL (Northern Cheyenne) served as a U.S. senator from Colorado from 1993 to 2005 and as a member of the House of Representatives from 1987 to 1993. During his tenure as the chairman of the Senate Committee on Indian Affairs, Nighthorse

Campbell worked to pass legislation that benefited Indian Country in areas such as health care, education, transportation, energy, and water. The president of the lobbying firm Ben Nighthorse Consultants, he resides in Colorado, where he is an award-winning contemporary jewelry maker. He serves on the Council of Forty-Four Chiefs of the Northern Cheyenne and is a trustee of the National Museum of the American Indian.

ARWEN NUTTALL (Cherokee) is a writer and editor in the Publications Office at the National Museum of the American Indian and has worked on numerous projects, including *indiVisible: African-Native American Lives in the Americas, Up Where We Belong: Native Musicians in Popular Culture, Glittering World: Navajo Jewelry and the Yazzie Family Legacy,* and the new imagiNATIONS Activity Center. Before taking her position in publications she was a researcher for the museum's *Our Lives* permanent gallery.

JAMES RIDING IN (Pawnee) is an associate professor of American Indian studies at Arizona State University. He is the editor of *Wicazo Sa Review: A Journal of Native American Studies* and the coeditor of *Native Historians Write Back: Decolonizing American Indian History.* His research about repatriation, as well as historical and contemporary Indian issues, has appeared in numerous books and scholarly journals.

LOIS J. RISLING (Hupa/Yurok/Karuk) is an educator and the land specialist for the Hoopa Valley Tribe. She served as director of the Center for Indian Community Development at Humboldt State University.

LINDSAY G. ROBERTSON is a law professor and the faculty director of the Center for the Study of American Indian Law and Policy at the University of Oklahoma. He teaches courses in federal Indian law, comparative Indigenous Peoples law, constitutional law, and legal history. Robertson previously taught federal Indian law at the University of Virginia School of Law and the George Washington University National Law Center. He serves as special justice on the Supreme Court of the Cheyenne and Arapaho Tribes and is the author of the award-winning *Conquest by Law: How the Discovery of America Dispossessed Indigenous Peoples of Their Lands.*

CAREY N. VICENTI (Jicarilla Apache) is an assistant professor of sociology at Fort Lewis College in Durango, Colorado, and a former chief judge of the Jicarilla Apache tribal court. He has served as a president of the Native American Bar Association and as an assistant to the head of the Bureau of Indian Affairs. Vicenti is an advocate of building legal institutions based upon tribal tradition, and he has written on the use of traditional concepts of justice in the development of a new and emerging tribal jurisprudence.

W. RICHARD WEST, JR., a citizen of the Cheyenne and Arapaho Tribes of Oklahoma and a Peace Chief of the Southern Cheyenne, is the president and CEO of the Autry National Center of the American West and founding director and director emeritus of the National Museum of the American Indian. As general counsel and special counsel to numerous American Indian tribes, communities, and organizations, he represented clients before federal, state, and tribal courts, various federal government departments, and Congress.

Myriad brilliant and talented people contributed to this publication and the related exhibition. I am privileged to have worked with and learned from them, and their contributions to the Treaties Project, now titled *Nation to Nation,* are highly prized and deeply appreciated.

The Morning Star Institute developed the Treaties Project for the National Museum of the American Indian (NMAI) from 2003 to the present with Vine Deloria Jr. (Standing Rock Sioux), who served as co-curator until his passing in 2005. The project was shaped and structured by many advisors and writers, including Hank Adams (Assiniboine-Sioux), Ben Nighthorse Campbell (Northern Cheyenne), Robert N. Clinton, Jennifer Nez Denetdale (Diné), Philip J. Deloria (Standing Rock Sioux), Raymond J. DeMallie, Matthew L. M. Fletcher (Grand Traverse Band of Ottawa and Chippewa Indians), Richard W. Hill Sr. (Tuscarora), Susan Hvalsoe Komori, Oren Lyons (Onondaga), the late John Mohawk (Seneca), Wilson K. Pipestem (Otoe-Missouria), James Riding In (Pawnee), Lois J. Risling (Hupa/Yurok/Karuk), Lindsay G. Robertson, Robert W. Trepp (Creek & Cherokee), Carey N. Vicenti (Jicarilla Apache), and David E. Wilkins (Lumbee). Many of their words grace these pages and NMAI exhibit spaces.

The Treaties Project was informed by recorded interviews with Native and non-Native treaty and sovereignty experts, including most of the writers and advisors listed above. These video and audio recordings are part of the NMAI Archives and are an inestimable resource for students, scholars, and other researchers. Among the interviewees were Herman Agoyo (Ohkay Owingeh), the late Keith Basso, Manley A. Begay Jr. (Diné), Maiselle Bridges (Squaxin Island), W. Roger Buffalohead (Ponca), John E. Echohawk (Pawnee), Walter R. Echo-Hawk Jr. (Pawnee), the late Billy Frank Jr. (Nisqually), Jodi Gillette (Standing Rock Sioux), Mario Gonzalez (Oglala Sioux), Zoltan Grossman, G. Peter Jemison (Seneca), Maurice John Sr. (Seneca), Tina Kuckkahn Miller (Lac du Flambeau Ojibwe), N. Scott Momaday (Kiowa), Alan R. Parker (Chippewa Cree), Anthony F. C. Wallace, and Peterson Zah (Diné).

In June 2012 the NMAI convened and recorded a roundtable discussion of heritage language speakers from each of the Native Nations that signed the Horse Creek Treaty of 1851—Arapaho, Arikara, Assiniboine, Cheyenne, Hidatsa, Mandan, and Sioux—which was the first time since the signing of the Treaty that all the languages had been spoken in the same place. In October 2010 we filmed interviews at the Bosque Redondo Memorial, New Mexico, with Diné descendants of those who endured confinement and the Long Walk but who made the U.S.–Navajo Nation Treaty of 1868, which guaranteed that the Navajo People could return to the safety of their homelands within their sacred mountains.

The Treaties Project documented the historic 2007 signing of the Treaty of Indigenous Nations at Lummi Nation in Washington State as well as the landing of nearly a hundred canoes on Lummi shores in the Northwest Native Nations' annual exercise of sovereignty on the waters. We interviewed Native and non-Native people on the importance of their written and unwritten treaties at a 2005 gathering at Evergreen State College's Longhouse Education and Cultural Center in Olympia, Washington; at a 2010 annual commemoration of the Canandaigua Treaty of 1794 in Canandaigua, New York; and at a 2010 NMAI board meeting at Acoma Pueblo, New Mexico. Special thanks to Jason Ordaz of the School of Advanced Research; Kelly Nitushi Byars (Choctaw/Chickasaw) and Ramona Emerson (Diné) of Reel Indian Pictures; and Gwendolen Cates, Steve Robinson, and Mark Trahant (Shoshone/Bannock) for documenting many of these interviews and events.

Artists also energized the project with both presentation ideas and their views on treaties. Their participation in consultations is greatly appreciated, and we regret that space limitations did not permit the use of contemporary art in the manner and to the extent that we hoped. Among the artists were Marcus Amerman (Choctaw), Shonto Begay (Diné), David P. Bradley (Minnesota Chippewa, White Earth Ojibwe), Kelly Church (Grand Traverse Band of Ottawa and Chippewa Indians), Melissa Cody (Diné), Anita Fields (Osage), Shan Goshorn (Eastern Band of Cherokee), Bob Haozous (Chiricahua Apache), Edgar Heap of Birds (Cheyenne/Arapaho), Jean LaMarr (Pit River/Paiute), Linda Lomahaftewa (Hopi/Choctaw), America Meredith (Cherokee), Raymond Nordwall (Pawnee/Cherokee/Ojibwe), Diego Romero (Cochiti Pueblo), Mateo Romero (Cochiti Pueblo), Preston Singletary (Tlingit), Roxanne Swentzel (Santa Clara Pueblo), and Richard Ray Whitman (Yuchi/Muscogee Creek).

Special acknowledgement must be made of Peter J. Powell, Francis Paul Prucha, Thomas N. Tureen, and the other, innumerable Native treaty experts whose conversations were invaluable; and of David Hurst Thomas, Allen V, Pinkham Sr. (Nez Perce), the late Barber B. Conable Jr., the late Daniel K. Inouye, Thomas R. White (Gila River Maricopa), Norbert S. Hill Jr. (Oneida),

Clara Sue Kidwell (Choctaw/Chippewa), Phyllis Young (Standing Rock Lakota/Dakota), the late Helen Maynor Scheirbeck (Lumbee), and other NMAI board and staff members, who were early and steadfast supporters of the Treaties Project. I am especially indebted to NMAI directors W. Richard West, Jr. (Southern Cheyenne), and Kevin Gover (Pawnee), whose expertise, leadership, and collegiality guided the Treaties Project as an NMAI priority. No one could have asked for better allies.

I am most grateful to the Smithsonian and NMAI researchers, writers, editors, photographers, designers, mapmakers, conservators, collections specialists, and other staff who contributed to the Treaties exhibition and publication. Among many others deserving of special appreciation for their contributions are the museum's media specialists as well as NMAI communications, public programming, development, education, outreach, management, and administrative staff members for their continuing work on the Treaties Project.

Aho! Mvto!

SUZAN SHOWN HARJO
General Editor and Guest Curator

Banner, Stuart. *How the Indians Lost Their Land: Law and Power on the Frontier.* Boston: Belknap Press, 2005.

Blaine, Martha Royce. *Pawnee Passage: 1870–1875.* Norman: University of Oklahoma Press, 1990.

Buell, Crawford R. "The Navajo 'Long Walk': Recollections by Navajos." In *The Changing Ways of Southwestern Indians: A Historic Perspective.* Edited by Albert Schroeder. Glorieta, NM: Rio Grande Press, 1971.

Calloway, Colin G. *Pen and Ink Witchcraft: Treaties and Treaty-Making in American Indian History.* New York: Oxford University Press, 2013.

Deloria, Vine, Jr., and Raymond J. DeMallie, eds. *Documents of American Indian Diplomacy: Treaties, Agreements, and Conventions, 1775–1979.* 2 vols. Norman: University of Oklahoma Press, 1999.

DeMallie, Raymond J., "Touching the Pen: Plains Indian Treaty Councils in Ethnohistorical Perspective." In *Ethnicity on the Great Plains.* Edited by Frederick C. Luebke. Lincoln: University of Nebraska Press, 1980.

Denetdale, Jennifer Nez. *The Long Walk: The Forced Navajo Exile.* New York: Chelsea House, 2007.

Gover, Kevin. "Statutes as Sources of Modern Indian Rights: Child Welfare, Gaming, and Repatriation: A Statutory History of Federal Indian Policy." In vol. 1 of *Treaties with American Indians: An Encyclopedia of Rights, Conflicts, and Sovereignty.* Edited by Donald L. Fixico. Santa Barbara: ABC-CLIO, 2007.

Hoxie, Frederick E. *A Final Promise: The Campaign to Assimilate the Indians, 1880–1920.* Lincoln: University of Nebraska Press, 2001.

Kappler, Charles J., ed. *Treaties.* Vol. 2 of *Indian Affairs: Laws and Treaties.* Washington, DC: Government Printing Office, 1904.

Kessell, John L. "General Sherman and the Navajo Treaty of 1868: A Basic and Expedient Misunderstanding." *Western Historical Quarterly* 12, no. 3 (July 1981).

Merrell, James H. "'I desire all that I have said . . . may be taken down aright': Revisiting Teedyuscung's 1756 Treaty Council Speeches," *William and Mary Quarterly* 3rd ser., 63, no. 4 (October 2006).

Norgren, Jill. *The Cherokee Cases: The Confrontation of Law and Politics.* New York: McGraw-Hill, 1996.

Parmenter, Jon. "The Meaning of the Kaswentha and the Two Row Wampum Belt in Haudenosaunee (Iroquois) History: Can Indigenous Oral Tradition Be Reconciled with the Documentary Record?" *Journal of Early American History* 2 (2013).

Powless, Irving, G. Peter Jemison, and Anna M. Schein, eds. *Treaty of Canandaigua 1794: 200 Years of Treaty Relations Between the Iroquois Confederacy and the United States.* Santa Fe, New Mexico: Clear Light Publishers, 2000.

Prucha, Francis Paul. *American Indian Treaties: History of a Political Anomaly.* Berkeley: University of California Press, 1997.

Prucha, Francis Paul. *The Great Father: The United States Government and the American Indians.* 2 vols. Lincoln: University of Nebraska Press, 1984.

Robertson, Lindsay G. *Conquest by Law: How the Discovery of America Dispossessed Indigenous Peoples of their Lands.* New York: Oxford University Press, 2005.

Shannon, Timothy J. *Iroquois Diplomacy on the Early American Frontier.* New York: Viking Press, 2008.

Vandevelder, Paul. *Savages and Scoundrels: The Untold Story of America's Road to Empire through Indian Territory.* New Haven: Yale University Press, 2009.

Viola, Herman J. *Diplomats in Buckskins: A History of Indian Delegations in Washington City.* Bluffton, SC: Rivilo Books, 1995. First published 1981 by Smithsonian Institution Press.

West, W. Richard, Jr., and Kevin Gover. "The Struggle for Indian Civil Rights." In *Indians in American History: An Introduction.* Edited by Frederick E. Hoxie and Peter Iverson. Wheeling, IL: Harlan Davidson, 1997.

Wilkinson, Charles. *Blood Struggle: The Rise of Modern Indian Nations.* New York: W. W. Norton, 2005.

Wilkinson, Charles. *Messages from Frank's Landing: A Story of Salmon, Treaties, and the Indian Way.* Seattle: University of Washington Press, 2000.

Williams, Robert A., Jr. *Linking Arms Together: American Indian Treaty Visions of Law and Peace, 1600–1800.* New York: Oxford University Press, 1997.

Wright, J. Leitch, Jr., "Creek-American Treaty of 1790: Alexander McGillivray and the Diplomacy of the Old Southwest." *Georgia Historical Quarterly* 51, no. 4 (December 1967).

© American Museum of Natural History, New York, Denis Finnin: ii–iii, 99 (photo of Hidatsa pipe bag)

Ernest Amoroso, NMAI: i, ii–iii (composite photo), x, 38, 39 top, 40, 41, 43–45, 62, 99, 109 bottom left and right, 131, 141, 144, 156, 182, 191, 222

Reproduced with the permission of David P. Bradley: 2, 193

Katherine Fogden (Akwesasne Mohawk), NMAI: 177

David Heald, NMAI: 22, 118

Donald E. Hurlbert, Smithsonian Institution: front cover, 129

Walter Larrimore, NMAI: iv–v, 39 bottom

Courtesy of J. J. Prats, HMdb.org: 61

Peter Siegel, Pillar Digital Imaging, LLC: 53

R.A.Whiteside, NMAI: 65

Captions for Images on Pages i–vii

page i, top: Chippewa wampum belt, detail, ca. 1807. Great Lakes region. 125.7 × 8.3 cm. Whelk shell, quahog shell, bast fiber yarn. National Museum of the American Indian 1/4004.

page i, bottom: Lenape (Delaware) "Penn" wampum belt, detail, ca. 1682. Pennsylvania. Whelk shell, quahog shell, hide, bast fiber yarn, ocher. 103 × 13.5 cm. National Museum of the American Indian 5/3150

pages ii–iii: Pipes and pipe bags representing the nine Native Nations present at the 1851 Horse Creek treaty council. Counter-clockwise from top (pipes to the left of each bag originated in the same Native Nation): Assiniboine, Minitari (Hidatsa), Numakiki (Mandan), Shoshone, Apsáalooke (Crow), Tsistsistas (Cheyenne), Sahnish (Arikara), Northern Inunaina (Arapaho), Yankton Sioux bag and Lakota Sioux pipe, ca. 1851–80. Bags: Hide, glass beads, porcupine quills, dye, pigment sinew, horsehair, cotton thread, wool yarn, wool cloth, metal cones, copper alloy disks, feathers, tobacco. Pipes: wood, pipestone, stone, lead, lead alloy, feathers, horsehair, porcupine quills, dye, cotton yarn, bird skin. Lengths: pipe bowls 8.4 to 24.2 cm; pipe stems 30.9 to 73.2 cm; pipe bags 58 to 106.7 cm. National Museum of the American Indian (bags) 12/7393, 8/8088, 2/3294, 14/828, 8/8037, 20/1400, 23/1176, 16/7255; (pipes) 11/392, 11/393, 8/8030, 20/3667, 1/2599, 11/3150, 14/5105, 1/389, 8/8028. Hidatsa pipe bag courtesy of the Division of Anthropology, American Museum of Natural History, New York 50.1/5350B

pages iv–v: Franklin Pierce peace medal and pouch, 1853–1900. Keshena, Menominee Reservation, Wisconsin. Silver medal (1853), deerhide, satin ribbon, glass beads. 13 × 10 cm. National Museum of the American Indian 24/1210

page vii: Vine Deloria Jr. at his home, January 2, 2005. Tucson, Arizona. Photo by Chris Richards, *Indian Country Today*

A

Adams, John Quincy, 64
Alabama, 46, 66, 73, 139, 140, 174
Alabama Nation, 133
Alcatraz Island protestors (1969), 207–8, **207**
Algonquian language, 113
Alights on a Cloud, **108, 145**
alliances
  among Native Nations, 2, 42, 91, 133–34, 140
  kinship alliances, 17, 19, 21
  military alliances, 44, 140
  See also Covenant Chain of Peace; *specifically listed Native Nation confederacies*
Allis, Samuel, 156
allotment, 13, 28–29, 30, **31**, 127, 167, 169–70, 199, 226–27n32
  See also General Allotment Act (1887)
American Board of Commissioners for Foreign Missions (ABCFM), 156, 157
American Civil War, 145
  and the Treaty of 1863, 145–47
American Fur Company, 95
American Indian Policy Review Commission, 211–12
Anaya, James, 219–20
Anishinaabe, 2
Anishinaabe Fishing Rights (David P. Bradley), **193**
anti-treaty movement, in the Pacific Northwest and the Great Lakes, 179–80, 186–89, 192, 194–197
Apache Nation (Plains Apache), 89, 91, 145, 151
  Chiricauhua Apache, 174
  Kiowa Apache, 94
  Mescalero Apache, 128
Arapaho Nation, 89, 95, 96, 97, 112, 114, 143, 145, 151, 166
  alliance with the Cheyenne, 91

land reserved for in the Treaty of 1851, 144
  language of, 113
  resettlement of on the Eastern Shoshone Reservation, 174
Arikara Nation, 89, 91, 97, 98, 112, 143
Arizona v. California (1963), 226n8
Armstrong, William, 28
Arra-tu-resash (or Big Robber), 104, 108
Articles of Confederation, 46
Asdzáá Tł'ógi (or Juanita), **128, 129**
  weaving of on a loom, **129**
Aspenall, Nellie, 7, 8
Assiniboine Nation, 89, 97, 98, 112, 143
Authon-ish-ah, 104
Awoninahku (or Lean Bear, Starving Bear), 145, 146, **147**
  murder of, 147

B

bags
  bandolier bag, Muscogee (Creek), **141**
  pipe bag, Tsistsistas/Suhtai (Cheyenne), **144**
  pipe bags representing the nine Native Nations present at the Horse Creek treaty council, **99**
  shoulder bag pouch, Lenape (Delaware), **22**
Baldwin, Henry, 75, 80, 81
Baldy, Cutcha Risling, 218
Baldy, SuWorhrom David Milton Risling, 218
Bannock Nation, 174
Barboncito, 123, **123**, 125
Barbour, Philip P., 81, 230n25
Bark (or The Bear's Feather), 104
baskets
  lidded basket, Makah, **182**
  Pieced Treaty: Spider's Web Treaty Basket (Shan Goshorn), **x**
Battle of Fallen Timbers, 51
Battle of Horseshoe Bend, 140

Battle of the Little Bighorn, 66, 88, 151, 166
Battle of New Orleans, 140
Battle of the Wabash, 50
Bear That Paints Itself Black (or Mathó sap'íc'iye, Painted Bear, Smutty Bear), 103, **103**, 231n29
Bear's Feather (or Bark), 104
Beka-chebotha (or Cut Nose), 104
Benedict, Richard, 194
Bernal, Paul, **208, 209**
Biah-at-sah-ah-kah-che (or Little Owl), 104
Big Robber (or Arra-tu-resash), 104, 108
Black, Hugo, xi
Black Hawk, 107
Black Hills (Paha Sapa), 151
  U.S. confiscation of, 29, 219
Black Kettle, 147, 148, 151
Blue Earth, 97, 101, 103
Blue Hawk, 163
Blue Jacket, 50
boarding schools, 4, 35, 152, 154, 167, 175
  Carlisle Indian Industrial School, 5–6, 8, 127, 167, 173, 175
  Chemawa Institute, 175
  Chilocco Indian Agricultural School, 9, 11, 167
  efforts to obliterate Native languages and cultures in, 8–9, 11, 152, 167, 175
  Euchee Indian School, 8–9
  Hampton Institute, 167
  Haskell Institute, 167
  Phoenix Indian School, 167
  Sherman Institute, 175
  Stewart Indian School, 175
Boldt, George H., 179, 186, 188
  effigy of, **187**
Bosque Redondo (Navajo reservation at Fort Sumner), 25, 116, 121, 125, 128
  poor conditions at, 122–23
Bosque Redondo Memorial, 128
Brant, Joseph, 44, 45

Brave Chief, 167
Bridger, Bobby, 96
Bridger, Jim, 96, **96,** 105
Bridges, Maiselle, 186
Brown, Benjamin Gratz, 95
Brown, Dee, 207
Brown Owl Woman, 113
Brush Dance Ceremony, 218
buffalo/buffalo hunting, **90,** 91, 94 101,
    107, 108, 151, 163–64
Buffalo Bear (or Bull Bear), 8, 145, 148, 151
Buffalo Wallow, 8, 151
Bull Bear (or Buffalo Bear), 8, 145, 148,
    151
Bull Bear, Oscar, 6, **7, 9**
Bureau of Indian Affairs, 32, 198
    See also U.S. Office of Indian Affairs
*Bury My Heart at Wounded Knee: An
    Indian History of the American West*
    (Brown), 207
Bush, George W., 34, 212
Butler, Elizur, 77, 79, 80

C

Caddo Nation, 145, 173
California, 91
    admission of to the Union, 94
    dishonor by the U.S. government in
        regard to its treaties in, 3, 216
    gold rush in, 3, 91, 216
California Trail, 91
calumets, 222, **222**
Camden-Yorke opinion (1772), 69, **71**
Campbell, Ben Nighthorse, 221
Canada, 57, 58, 89, 185
Cannon, T. C., 207
Carleton, James H., 120, 123
Carlson, Dakota, 176
Carr, Dabney, 73
Carroll, Charles, 71
Carson, Kit, 25, 120–21
Carter, Jimmy, 212, 213, **213**
Cash, Johnny, 207
Cass, Lewis, 86, 87
Catawba Nation, 66, 67
Catholicism, conversion to among Native
    people, 86, 87
Catron, John, 81, 230nn30–31
Cayuga Nation, 17, 36, 46
    See also Haudenosaunee Nations
Cayuse (or Young Chief), 183–84
cedar trees/bark, 189–90
Chambers, A. B., 95, 96, 104
Charles II (king of England), 61

Chato, 174
Chaui Band (Pawnee), 155, 157
Cha-ut-lipan, 174
Cherokee Constitution (1827), 77
Cherokee Nation, 19, 23, 73–75, 134, 140
    written language of, 226n18
    See also *Worcester v. Georgia* (1832)
Cherokee Nation v. Georgia (1831), 75, 77
Cherokee Phoenix, **76,** 77, 226n18
Cheyenne Nation, 89, 95, 96, 98, 102, 112,
    114, 166
    alliance with the Arapaho, 91
    language of, 113
    treaties with other Native Nations, 143
    treaties with the United States, 133,
        143–48, 151
    Treaty of 1825, 143
    Treaty of 1851, 143–44. *See also*
        Great Horse Creek Treaty (1851)
    Treaty of 1863, 145–46
    Treaty of 1867 (Medicine Lodge
        Creek Treaty), 8, 29, 30, 148, 151
    Treaty of 1868 (Fort Laramie
        Treaty), 23, 25, 29, 148, 151, 219
Chickasaw Nation, 23, 73, 134, 140
Chilton, Roger, 95
Chippewa, 19, 194
Chivington, John M., 147
Choctaw Nation, 23, 73, 77, 85, 134, 140
Christian Science Monitor, 66
Christianity, 107, 158
Civilization Fund, 4
civilization regulations, 4, 9, 11, 13, 152,
    153, 166–69, 171, 175, 199, 200, 213
    See also cultural assimilation of Native
        Nations, program of; Pawnee
        Nation, attempts to impose civili-
        zation regulations on
Clark, William, 97
Clark v. Smith (1838), 81, 83
Claus, William (or Kora Shotsitsyowanen),
    39, 57
Clinton, Bill, 212, **215**
Clinton, George, 46
clothing and accoutrements
    concho belt, Diné (Navajo), **131**
    knife and sheath, Lenni Lenape (Dela-
        ware), **65**
    serape, Diné (Navajo), **118**
    shirt (man's), Tsistsistas/Suhai (Chey-
        enne), **150**
    skirt (woman's), Hupa, **177**
Clouding Woman, 6
Coffee, John, 77

Coffey, Wallace, 126
Cohen, Felix, 200
Collier, John, 32, 200, **201**
Colorado, 143, 144
Colorado Volunteers, 146, 148
Comanche Nation, 89, 91, 94, 145, 151, 173
Committee on Indian Affairs, Continen-
    tal Congress, 37
"Concessions to the Province of Pennsyl-
    vania" (Penn), 62
Conestoga Nation, 61
Connecticut, 16, 66, 213
Conyers, John, 186
Courts of Indian Offenses, 167–68, 175
Covenant Chain of Friendship/Peace,
    18–19, 40–41, 42, 51, 53, 58
    links of (respect, trust, and friend-
        ship), 40
    Native intent of, 41
    "polishing" of, 18, 40, 51, 53
Crazy Horse, 145
Creek Nation. *See* Muscogee Confederacy/
    Alliance (Creek Nations)
Crook, George, 174
Crow Nation (Apsáalooke), 89, 91, 97, 102,
    104, 108, 111, 112, 143, 173–74
Culbertson, Alexander, 95, 97, 104
cultural assimilation of Native Nations,
    program of, 14, 35, 122, 152, 153, 157,
    160, 167–69
    of the Navajo, 126–27
    of the Pawnee, 166–67
    See also civilization regulations
Curtis, Asahel, 185
Custer, George Armstrong, 5, 148, 151,
    166
*Custer Died for Your Sins: An Indian
    Manifesto* (Deloria), 207
Cut Nose (or Beka-chebotha), 104

D

Dakota, 143
    See also Sioux Nations
Davis, Elsie (or Wah-stah), 6, 8
Davis, Richard (or Thunderbird, Nono-
    ma'ohtsevhahtse), 6, **6,** 7, 8, **9**
Daw, John, 122
Dawes Act (1887). *See* General Allotment
    Act (1887)
De Smet, Pierre-Jean, **95,** 95, 96, 97, 105,
    107
De Vos, Rob, 60
DeCoteau v. District Court (1975),
    226–27n32

Delaware Nation. *See* Lenni Lenape (Delaware) Nation
Deloria, Vine, Jr., 3, 33, 207, 213, 221
DeMallie, Raymond J., 33, 112, 113
Descheene, Fred, 123
Diné Nation. *See* Navajo Nation
Diné Bikéyah, 120, 125
Dinétah, 25, 118
discovery doctrine. *See* Doctrine of Discovery
disease, spread of among Native Nations by white people, 3, 91, 94, 155, 156
    See also smallpox
Doctrine of Discovery, 15–16, 68, 69
    incorporation of into U.S. law in *Johnson v. M'Intosh* decision, 68, 69, 72–73
    recognition of "aboriginal title" in, 15
    reformulation of by Chief Justice Marshall in *Worcester v. Georgia,* 77–79
    restoration of the *Johnson v. M'Intosh* formulation of, 80–81, 83, 84
Dog Men Society. *See* Hotamétaneo'o (Dog Men Society)
Douglas, Freeland Edward, 8–9, **10,** 11
Douglas, Susie Eades, **10,** 11
Duhamel, Arthur, 186, 194
Dunbar, John, 156, 157
Duvall, Gabriel, 80, 81

E
Eagle Chief (or Ratakatsresaru), 167, **167**
    mud lodge of, **168**
Eagle Head, 151
Eaton, John, 77
Echo-Hawk, Walter R., 214, **214**
Edwards, Jake, 59
elk hunting, 185
Elliott, W. L., 98
ethnocide, 4–6, 35, 122, 153, 157, 161–62, 166–67, 168–71
    See also cultural assimilation of Native Nations, program of
Euchee Nation, 133
Everett, Edward, 73
Ex-fin-e-pah, 216

F
fishing, **178,** 194
    critical nature of to the survival and culture of Native Nations, 179, 182
    fishhooks, Quileute, **191**
    fish-ins, 179

rights and alliances of the Wisconsin Ojibwe, 192–93, 195–96
    spearfishing, 192, 195
    sport fishing, 179, 188, 189, 192, 193, 194, 195
    See also anti-treaty movement; Native Nations, hunting and fishing rights of
Fitzpatrick, Thomas, 94, **94,** 96, 97, 98, 107
Florida, 174
Flower Dance. *See* Hupa Flower Dance (ch'iLwa:l) ceremony
Fort Defiance, 120, 121
Fort Gaston, 175
Fort John (later Fort Laramie), 94
Fort Laramie, 95
Fort Laramie Treaty (1868), 23, **24,** 148, 151, 219
    article 16, 25–26
    terms of, 29
Fort Leavenworth, 95
Fort Marion, 6
Fort Sill, 173
Fort Stanwix Treaty (1784), 48, 49, 50, 53
    terms of, 48
Fort Sumner, 121
Fort Union, 95
Fort Wingate, 121
Forty-Fifth Infantry "Thunderbirds" Division, **10,** 11
Fox, Noel, 186, 194
Fox Nation, 19
Frank, Billy, Jr., **178,** 181, 186
Franklin, Benjamin, 46
Franks Landing Indian Community, 178, 186
Frelinghuysen, Theodore, 73
French and Indian War, 36, 64
Frightening Bear (or Mah-toe-wah-yu-whey), 88, 107

G
gaiashkibos, 186
Gawanese Nation, 61
Gehring, Charles, 59
General Allotment Act (1887), 28–29, 30, 169–70, 226–27n32
    See also allotment
George III (king of England), 69
Georgia, 73, 80, 137, 139, 140
    See also *Worcester v. Georgia* (1832)
Gerard, Forrest J., 212, **212**
Geronimo, 174
Ghost Dance religion, 170

Gilmer, George, 75
Gist, George (or Sequoyah), 226n18
Good Buffalo Road, 151
Gover, Kevin, 112
Grahame, Thomas, 72
Grand River Haudenosaunee, 57–58
Grand Traverse Band of Ottawa and Chippewa Indians, 194
Grattan, John Lawrence, 88
"Grattan Fight," the, as prelude to decades of war against the Plains Nations, 88
Gray Beard, 151
Great Britain, 16, 46, 57, 78, 140, 185
    treaty relationships with Native Nations on the American borderlands, 46
    See also War of 1812
Great Depression, the, 200
Great Father, 88, 100, 101, 102, 104, 107, 111, 181, 182
Great Horse Creek Treaty (1851), 88, 89–91, 94–98, 100–105, **106,** 107–8, 111, 231n20
    amount of Native land covered by, 143–44
    arrival of delegations at, 96, 97, 98, 102
    authorization of by Congress, 94
    chief selection for each Native nation at, 100, 102, 104, 107
    delineation of territorial boundaries at, 100, 104–5, **105,** 107
    land loss following, 144
    language and world view of the Native Nations during, 101–2, 112–13
    mixed reception by Native Nations of invitations to, 94–95
    organization of, 94, 97–98
    presents distributed to Native Nations at the conclusion of, 108
    sign language at, 97, 113, 144
    smoking ceremony at, 98, 100, 143, 231n25
    terms of, 100–101, 143–44
    translation problems encountered at, 101–2, 112–13, 144
    treaty details, 143–44
    upper Missouri nations represented at, 97
    winter count images of, 108, **109**
Great Law of Peace (Kayahnerenhkowah), 17, 42, 44
Great Smoke, the, 143, 144
    See also Great Horse Creek Treaty

Great Treaty. *See* Treaty of Amity and Friendship (1682 [Penn Treaty])

Gros Ventre Nation, 231n24

Grossman, Zoltán, 192–93

Guerin v. The Queen (Canada [1984]), 83

H

Harmar, Josiah, 50

Harmar's Defeat (1790), 50

Harper, Robert Goodloe, **70**, 70–72

Harrison, William Henry, 71

Haudenosaunee Confederacy, 17, 18, 36, 46

chiefs of (1871), **57**

and the Tree of Peace, 37, 57

Haudenosaunee Nations (Six Nations, Iroquois), 2, 21, 37, 46, 48, 49, 50, 51, 61, 66, 134

culture of treaty making, 39–45, 47, 59–60

land claim lawsuits of, 67, 187

support for the British, 46, 48, 57

See also Grand River Haudenosaunee; *specifically listed Haudenosaunee Nations*

Henry, Joseph, 146

Hickory Ground (Oce Vpofv), 140

Hidatsa Nation, 89, 91, 97, 98, 112, 143, 231n24

language of, 113

Hill, Aaron (or Kenwendeshon), 48

Hill, Richard W., Sr., 60

Hill, Sid, **56, 60**

Hool-hole-tan (or Jim), 182

Hoopa/Hupa Nation, 175–76, 218, 235n1

Horse Creek Treaty. *See* Great Horse Creek Treaty (1851)

Horse Driver, 162

Hotamétaneo'o (Dog Men Society), 8, 148

House Made of Dawn (Momaday), 207

Howard, O. O., 174

hunting. *See* Native Nations, hunting and fishing rights of; *specifically listed names of animals hunted*

Hupa Flower Dance (ch'iLwa:l) ceremony, 175–76, 218

federal attempts to stop, 175

requirements of the *kinahldung* (Flower Dance girl) during, 175

role of the K'ixinay in, 175, 235n2

songs of, 176

I

Illinois, 46, 49

Illinois Nation, 69

Indian Gaming Regulatory Act (IGRA) (1988), 32

Indian Health Service, 32

Indian Helper (Carlisle Indian Industrial School), 8

Indian Removal Act (1830), 23, 73, 75, 77, 86, 87

development of, 140

Indian Reorganization Act (IRA [1934]), 13, 32, 198, 200–201, 205, 221

controversial elements of, 202

Indian Self-Determination and Education Assistance Act (1975), 32, 210, 223

Indian Territory. *See* Oklahoma

Indian Trade and Intercourse Act (1790), 66, 13

Indiana, 46, 49, 87

Inouye, Daniel K., xi–xii

interpreters. *See* treaty making, role of interpreters in

Iroquois. *See* Haudenosaunee Nations (Six Nations, Iroquois)

Iroquois Confederacy. *See* Haudenosaunee Confederacy

It-an-daha, 182

J

Jackson, Andrew, 73, 77, 79, 80, 81, 85

cruelty of at the Battle of Horseshoe Bend, 140

fracturing of the Muscogee Confederacy by, 140, 143

Jefferson, Thomas, 73, 85

Johnson, Andrew, **xiv**, 27

Johnson, Joshua, 72

Johnson, Lyndon, 198, 206

Johnson, William, 73

Johnson v. M'Intosh (1823), 15, 68, 72, 74, 229n6

effect of on related Supreme Court decisions, 83–84

legal details of, 69–73, 75, 77–81

and the discovery doctrine, 68, 69, 80–81, 83, 84

opinion of Chief Justice Marshall in, 68, 73

origins of, 69–70

plaintiffs in, 72

troubling history of the litigation of, 70–71

use of the ruling in to oust the Cherokee from lands in Georgia, 73

Jondreau, Al, 194

Juanita (or Asdzáá Tł'ógi), **128, 129,** 131

weaving of on a loom, **129**

K

Kal-chote, 182

Kamiakin, 183

Kappler, Charles J., 33

compilation of treaty texts, 33

Karuk Nation, 218

Kayahnerenhkowah (Great Law of Peace), 17, 42

relation of to treaty making, 44

Ke-bach-sat, 182

Kee-chap, 216

Keechi Nation, 173

Kennedy, John F., 205

Kentucky, 46, 73

Kenwendeshon (or Aaron Hill), 48

Kerr McGee Corp. v. Navajo Tribe of Indians (1985), 127–28

Kessell, John, 125

Ki-moon, Ban, 60

Kiowa Nation, 89, 91, 94, 145, 151

Kiowa Apache, 94

Kitkahahki Band (Pawnee), 155, 157

K'iwinya'n-ya:n (Hupa people), 175–76, 218, 235n1

Kiyashuta, 18

Klah-pa-at-hoo, 182

Klamath Nation, 174, 213

treaties with the United States (1851), 216–18

Klamath River, 216–218

Knox, Henry, 42, 49, **49**, 50, 136, 137

Koasati Nation, 133

Koh-chook, 182

Komori, Susan Hvalsoe, 188–90

Kuckkahn, Tina, 195–97

Kora Shotsitsyowanen (or William Claus), 39, 57

L

Lac Courte Oreilles Band of Lake Superior Ojibwe, 195

LaChapelle, Louis, 156

Lakota, 26, 29, 91, 94, 112, 113, 143, 145, 151, 173, 219, 220, 230n1, 231n25

Brule Lakota, 94

Hunkpapa Lakota, 145

Oglala Lakota, 94, 107, 145, 220

See also Sioux Nations, Teton Sioux

land claims, of Native Nations, 30, 66–67, 213

land loss (land cession), by Native Nations, xii, 13, 14, 30, 48–49, 75, 152, 185, 199, 234n17

of Choctaw lands, 77

of Lakota lands, 29
of Mohegan lands, 16
proposal to redress, 219–20
treaties as the primary means of, 15–16,
46, 49, 66
Land Ordinance (1785), 13
language, misunderstandings of in treaty
negotiations, 3, 20, 112–13, 114, 155–56,
226n18
Lean Bear (or Starving Bear, Awoni-
nahku), 145, 146, **147**
murder of, 147
LeBanc, Abe, 194
Lee, Lloyd, 131
Leiby, Richard, 9
Lenni Lenape (Delaware) Nation, 2, 19, 21,
61, 62, 64, 155, 173
Life of George Washington (Marshall),
73, 78
Lincoln, Abraham, **146**
treaty negotiations of with southern
Plains Nations, 145–48
Little Chief, **108, 145**
Little Owl (or Biah-at-sah-ah-kah-che),
104
Little Turtle, 50
Little Wolf (Cheyenne), 151
Little Wolf (Pawnee), 163
Logan, James, 63
Lone Wolf v. Hitchcock (1903), 30, 227n35
"Long Hair Prohibited" (Commissioner
of Indian Affairs), 5
Loup River, 157, 160
Louisiana, 66
Lumpkin, Wilson, 80
Lyons, Oren, **56,** 59

M

Mabo v. Queensland (1988 [Australia]),
83–84
Mah-toe-wah-yu-whey (or Frightening
Bear), 88, 107
Ma'ii' Bizéé'nast'á, 125
Maine, 66, 213
Maine Indian Claims Settlement Act
(1980), 66
Makah Nation, 182–83, 197
seal hunting of, 185
whalers/whaling industry of, 185,
185
Maliseet Nation, 66
Man Chief (or Pitaresaru), **160,** 163
Mandan Nation, 89, 91, 97, 98, 112, 143
Manuelito, 117, 123, 127, **128,** 131

Many Magpies, 151
Māori Nation, ceding of sovereignty to
the British, 20–21
Marshall, Ernest, Sr., 175–76
Marshall, John, 20, 21, 64, 72, 77, **79,** 80,
81, 230n27
distress of over the disingenuous
use of his opinion in *Johnson v.
M'Intosh,* 73–74
opinion of in *Cherokee Nation v. Geor-
gia* (1831), 75
opinion of in *Johnson v. M'Intosh*
(1823), 68, 73
reformulation of the discovery doc-
trine by in *Worcester v. Georgia,*
77–79, 229–30n21
Martin v. Lessee of Waddell (1842), 83
Massachusetts, 66, 67, 213
Matches, 6
Mathers, Carolan, 158, 159
Mathers, James, 158, 159
Mathó sap'íc'iye (or Bear That Paints
Itself Black, Painted Bear, Smutty
Bear), 103, **103,** 231n29
McGillivray, Alexander, 134, 136
on dealing with American negotiators
during treaty negotiations, 134
McLean, John, 75, 80
medicinal plants, 190, 192
Medicine Crow, 174
Medicine Creek Treaty (1854). *See* Treaty
of Medicine Creek (1854)
Medicine Lodge Creek Treaty (1867), 8,
29, 30, 148, **149,** 151
medicine men/women, 4, 125, 143, 157,
175, 216
Meninock, 181
Menominee (Potawatomi leader), 87
Menominee Nation, 193, 213
signing ceremony restoring tribal sta-
tus to, **211**
Meriam Report (1928), 200
Merrell, James H., 227n6
Mexico, 91, 118
Miami Nation, 50, 71
Eel River Miami, 71
Miccosukee Nation, 134
Michigan, 46, 49, 86, 87, 180, 194, 195
Mik-ku-ree (or Red Cap), 216
Mille Lacs Band of Ojibwe, 180
See also *Minnesota v. Mille Lacs Band
of Chippewa Indians* (1999)
Miller, Daniel, 158–59
Minnesota, 49, 180, 195

*Minnesota v. Mille Lacs Band of Chippewa
Indians* (1999), 226n22
See also Mille Lacs Band of Ojibwe
M'Intosh, Lydia, 71
M'Intosh, William, 71–72
missionaries, 20, 153, 156, 157
as interpreters, 144
Mississippi (river), removal of Native
Nations west of, 23, 77, **82,** 86
Mississippi (state), 46, 73, 139
Mississippi Choctaw, 85
Missouri Republican, 96, 231n20
Mitchel v. United States (Mitchel I [1835]),
80–81, 83
Mitchel v. United States (Mitchel II [1841]),
83
Mitchell, David Dawson, 94, 96–97, 98, **101,**
104, 107, 231n25
opening speech of at the Horse Creek
treaty council, 100
Modoc Nation, 174
Mohawk Nation, 17, 36, 57
See also Haudenosaunee Nations; Grand
River Haudenosaunee
Mohegan Nation, 16
Mohegan Indians v. Connecticut (1703–73),
16
Mole Lake Ojibwe, 193
Momaday, N. Scott, 3, 114–15, 207
Montana, 143
Mormons, 91
Murray, Henry, 72
Muscogee Confederacy/Alliance (Creek
Nations), 2, 23, 73, 133–34, 143
actions of in the War of 1812 (for both
Britain and the United States), 139–40
capital of (Hickory Ground [Oce
Vpofv]), 140
fracturing of by Andrew Jackson, 140,
143
new capital of (Okmulgee), 143
removal of to Oklahoma, 85, 140–43
Red Stick warriors, 140
treaties of with the United States, 133–37,
139, 143, 151
See also Treaty of Fort Jackson (1814);
Treaty of New York (1790)

N

Narragansett Nation, 66
Native American Graves Protection and
Repatriation Act (1989), 213, 224
National Congress of American Indians
(NCAI), 186

National Museum of the American Indian (NMAI [Smithsonian Institution]), xii, 112, 224

Native American scouts, 173–74
    African American Seminole scouts, 173
    effectiveness of Chiricauhua scouts, 174
    Pawnee scouts, 166, 169, 171, **171, 172,** 173
    motives for becoming, 173–74
    value of to the U.S. Army, 173

Native confederacies, 2
    Founding Fathers' admiration of, 2
    See also *specifically listed confederacies*

Native Nations
    European view of, 3
    political organization of, 17, 19
    population decimation of, 152, 166
    See also Native Nations, hunting and fishing rights of; Native Nations, and the United States in the twentieth century; *specifically listed Native Nations*; treaties, between Native Nations and the United States

Native Nations, hunting and fishing rights of, 181–85
    and the anti-treaty movement, 179–80, 186–89, 192, 194–197
    guaranteed treaty rights upheld by courts, 179–80, 186, 188–89, 194–97
    specific treaties guaranteeing fishing rights, 181–83, 185
    treaty rights in Washington State, 179–83, 185, 188–90
    See also anti-treaty movement; fishing

Native Nations, and the United States in the twentieth century, 198–214 *passim*
    benefits of the Great Society programs to Native Americans, 206
    changing public perception of Native Americans, 206
    changing structure of federal Indian affairs bureaucracy, 212–13
    crushing of tribal self-government by federal laws, 199
    emergence of the Indian rights movement, 205
    Native activism in the 1960s, 207–8
    origins of the reform movement to better Native living conditions, 200–201
    New Deal programs benefiting Native Nations, 201

participation of Native Americans in World War II, **10,** 11, 202–3, **203**
    poverty of Native Nations due to U.S. Indian policy and loss of land, 199
    social and economic programs enacted by Congress for Native Americans, 213–14
    transformation of federal Indian policy under Nixon, 208–11

Navajo (Diné) Nation, 25
    "civilization" of, 120, 122
    determination of to return to their homeland, 125–26
    establishment of Fort Defiance in Navajo territory, 120
    "ethnic cleansing" of, 122, 232n22
    imprisonment of at Bosque Redondo, **121,** 122, **122,** 123–24, **124,** 125
    Kit Carson's military campaign against, 120–21
    leaders of the Navajo resistance, 123
    Long Walk, 121–23
    origins of, 118, 120
    philosophy of, 118, 120, 131
    resistance of to colonial power, 117–18
    the return home from Bosque Redondo, 125–26
    transformations of Navajo life due to foreign invasions, 120
    treaties with Spain and Mexico recognizing Navajo territorial sovereignty, 118
    See also Treaty of Fort Sumner (1868)

Navajo Nation Human Rights Commission, 131, 232n48

Navajo Treaty (1868). *See* Treaty of Fort Sumner (1868 [Treaty with the Navajo])

Navajo Treaty Day, 131

Nebraska, 8, 34, 88, 94, 95, 143, 155, 163, 164, 166, 173, 174

New Deal programs, 201, 202

New York State, 59, 67
    agreements of with individual Haudenosaunee Nations, 48
    attempts to extinguish Haudenosaunee land titles, 48
    and the state-federal struggle for treaty-making authority, 46, 48

New Zealand, 20–21

Nez Perce, 174

Nixon, Richard M., 198, 205, **208, 209**
    "Special Message to the Congress on Indian Affairs," 208–11

Nonoma'ohtsevehahtse (or Thunderbird, Richard Davis), 6, **6, 7,** 8, **9**

North, Frank, 166

North, Luther, 166

North Carolina, 81

North Dakota, 143, 195

Northwest Ordinance (1787), 13, 48

Nuyakv/Nuyakv Ground, 139–40, 143

O

Obama, Barack, 42, 212

Odawa Nation, 2, 19

Ohe-lan-the-tat, 182

Ohio, 46, 49

Ojibwe
    Lac Courte Oreilles Band of Lake Superior Ojibwe, 195
    Mille Lacs Band of, 180
    Mole Lake Ojibwe, 193
    property ordered to be destroyed (1906), **200**
    Wisconsin Ojibwe, 180
        disputes with mining companies, 193
        fishing rights and alliances of, 192–93, 195–96

Oklahoma (Indian Territory), 8, 11, 30, 133, 144, 148, 151, 167, 170, 173, 174, 219
    removal of Native Nations to, 73, 85, 116, 125, 140–43, 164–66

Old Northwest, the Indian war in, 49, 50
    treaty violations as the cause of, 50

Oneida Nation, 17, 36, 46
    See also Haudenosaunee Nations

Onondaga Nation, 17, 36, 46
    partnership of with non-Native supporters of Haudenosaunee treaty rights, 59
    See also Haudenosaunee Nations

Oregon Trail, 90–91, 97, 174

Ottawa Nation, 77
    See also Grand Traverse Band of Ottawa and Chippewa Indians

Oweneco, 16

Owhi, 183, 184, **184**

P

Painted Bear (or Mathó sap'íc'iye, Bear That Paints Itself Black, Smutty Bear), 103, **103,** 231n29

Palo Duro Canyon, 151

Parmenter, Jon, 60

Passamaquoddy Nation, 66

Pawnee Mission, 157, 158, 160
Pawnee Nation, 89, 95, 174, 234n27
　confederated bands of, 155
　culture and spirituality of, 157–58
　effects of white migration to the West
　　on, 159
　ethnocide attempted against, 157, 161–
　　62, 166–67, 168–71
　kiskuhara (annual Pawnee-Wichita
　　visit) (ca. 1900), **169**
　military alliance of with the United
　　States, 152, 153, 161, 171
　participation in the Ghost Dance reli-
　　gion, 170
　schoolchildren, Pawnee Reservation,
　　Nebraska (1871), **164**
　scouts, 166, 169, 171, **171, 172,** 173
　Sioux attack on, 164
　treaty negotiations in 1833, 156–57
　　disadvantages faced by the Pawnee
　　　during, 155–56
　　removal and civilization stipula-
　　　tions of, 156
Pawnee Nation, attempts to "civilize,"
　　153, 155, 170–71
　from 1833 to 1847 (Treaty of 1833),
　　155–59
　　chaos/violence as a result of treaty
　　　regulations, 158–59
　　lack of Pawnee interest in Christi-
　　　anity, 158
　　terms of, 156
　from 1857 to 1869 (Treaty of 1857),
　　159–61, 162
　　establishment of manual labor
　　　school for Pawnee children,
　　　160–61
　　relinquishment of Pawnee lands
　　　north of the Platte River, 159
　　terms of, 159–60
　from 1869 to 1876, 161–65
　　attendance of children at reserva-
　　　tion schools, 163
　　deteriorating conditions on the
　　　reservation, 164–65
　　Hicksite Quaker control of the
　　　reservation, 162–63
　　incident of a settler murder, 162–63
　　insistence of the Pawnee on the
　　　right to hunt buffalo, 163–64
　from 1876 to 1892, 166–70
　　attempts by the Pawnee to reestab-
　　　lish their social organization,
　　　166

　　cultural assimilation of the Paw-
　　　nee, 166–67
　　effects of the General Allotment
　　　Act (1887) on Pawnee commu-
　　　nal ways, 169–70
　　effects of the white educational sys-
　　　tem on Pawnee children, 167
　　establishment of the Courts of
　　　Indian Offenses, 167–68
　　removal to Indian Territory,
　　　165–66
　　starvation and population decline,
　　　166
　　weakening of the chiefs' authority,
　　　168–69
peace medals, **iv,** 51, **52, 53,** 145, 147
Peace of Westphalia (1648), 19
Penn, John, 63
Penn, Thomas, 63
Penn, William, 61–64, **61**
　"holy experiment" of, 62
Penn Treaty. *See* Treaty of Amity and
　Friendship (1682)
Penobscot Nation, 66
Pequot Nation, 66
　Mashantucket Pequot, 67
Piankashaw Nation, 69
Pickering, Timothy, **51**
　respectful dealings of with the Haude-
　　nosaunee, 50
　as Washington's envoy at the Canan-
　　daigua treaty council, 51, 53
Pieced Treaty: Spider's Web Treaty Basket
　(Shan Goshorn), **x**
Pike's Peak gold rush (1858), 144
Pipe Woman, 151
Pitahawirata Band (Pawnee), 155, 156
Pitaresaru (or Man Chief), **160,** 163
Plains Indian Wars (1860s–80s), 173
Plains Nations, 90, 91, 112
　oratory of and use of sign language, 97
　relations with whites, 91, 94
　understanding of the content of trea-
　　ties by, 91
Platte River, 25, 88, 91, 94, 97, 105, 108, 112,
　143, 155, 156, 157, 159, 160
Plenary Power Doctrine, 30
　attenuation of, 32–33
Plenty Coups, 174
Pokagon, Leopold, 86
polygamy, 168, 169
Potawatomi Nation, 2, 19, 71, 86, 111
　avoidance of removal by Pokagon
　　Band, 86–87

Forest County Potawatomi, 193
Pokegnek Bodewadmik community
　of, 86
Pratt, Richard Henry, 5–6, 8, 173
Preparing a Warrior, 121
Price, Pete, 125
Proclamation of 1763, 12, 69, 72
Protect Americans' Rights and Resources,
　192
Public Law 638. *See* Indian Self-
　Determination and Education
　Assistance Act (1975)
Puget Sound, 179, 180, 183

Q
Quakers/Quakerism, 2, 62, 63
　Hicksite Quaker control of the Pawnee
　　reservation, 162–63
　as witnesses of treaty negotiations, 44

R
racism, 186, 192, 196, 197
railroads, 94, 144, 173
Ransom, Epaphroditus, 87
Ratakatsresaru (or Eagle Chief), 167, **167**
　mud lodge of, **168**
Red Cap (or Mik-ku-ree), 216
Red Cloud, 23, 88
Red Jacket, 53, **53**
Red River War (1874–75), 6, 151
removal, xii, 14, 16, 23, 46, 68, 73, 75, 77,
　79–80, 81, **82,** 83, 117, 120–22, 123,
　125, 140, 143, 153, 155, 156, 164, 165–
　66, 174, 232n22
　removal treaties, 85–87, 226n22
　See also Indian Removal Act (1830)
reservations, 3, 4, 12, 13, 30, 68, 116, 127,
　128, 132, 143, 148, 151, 152, 159, 165–
　66, 167–68, 169, 174, 175, 176, 183, 195,
　198, 200–202, 204, 205, 206, 209,
　210, 213, 226n8
　administration of by Christian
　　denominations, 161–62
"Revisiting the Fake Tawagonshi Treaty
　of 1613" (Starna and Gehring), 59
Rhode Island, 66, 213
Richard, Gabriel, 86
Risling, David W., Sr., 176, 216–18
Risling, Gary B., 218
Risling, Lois J., 218
Risling, Mary G., 218
Risling, Mary Jane, 176, 218
Risling-Eagle Speaker, David Warren,
　218

Roman Nose, 6
Roosevelt, Franklin D., 200
Ross, John, 75, **75**, 85
R & W Campbell, 94
Ryerson, Viola E. Risling Evans, 218

S

Sagoyewatha (Red Jacket), 51, 53
Sainte-Marie, Buffy, 207
Sand Creek Massacre, 88, 148
Sands, Geebo, 194
Santa Fe, 91
Santa Fe Trail, 94
Sargent, Harry, 8
Saswe, 12
Sa-von-ra, 216, 217
Scholder, Fritz, 207
Scott, William O., Sr., 176
scouts. *See* Native American scouts
seal hunting, 185
self-determination, xi, xii–xiii, 2, 198, 210,
    214, 219
    cultural self-determination, 224
    Navajo formulations of, 117–18, 131
Seminole Nation, 23, 85, 173
Senate Select Committee on Indian
    Affairs, 212
Seneca Nation, 17, 19, 50, 53, 77, 136
    See also Haudenosaunee Nations
Sensenbrenner, Jim, 187
Sequoyah (or George Gist), 226n18
Sergeant, John, 75
Shackamaxon elm tree, 61–64, **63**
    treaty chair made from, **64**
S'hair-at-sehd-wk (or Toanhooch), 182
Shawnee (Shawnese) Nation, 19, 50, 61, 77,
    134, 173
Sheridan, Philip H., 5, 148, 151
Sherman, William Tecumseh, **25**, 125, **125**
    serape owned by, 118, **118**
Shoshone Nation, 89, 91, 96, 98, 102, 108,
    112, 274
Sioux Nations, 23, 88, 90, 91, 94, 95, 96,
    112, 143, 166, 220, 230n1
    Brule (Lakota), 94
    Dakota, 143
    Hunkpapa (Lakota), 145
    Oglala (Lakota), 94, 220
    Sisseton and Wahpeton Bands of,
        226–27n32
    Teton (Lakota), 88, 91
    Yankton, 95
Sitting Bear, 114
Sitting Bull, 145

Six Nations. *See* Haudenosaunee Nations
    (Six Nations, Iroquois)
Six Nations Confederacy. *See* Hau-
    denosaunee Confederacy
Skidi Band (Pawnee), 155, 156, 164
    adoption of the white style of clothing
        by, 166–67
S'Klallam Nation, 182
Skloom, 183
Skokomish Nation, 182
Sky Chief (or Tirawahutresaru), 164, **165**
smallpox, 3, 91, 95, 155, 156
Smith, Gregory Scott, 128
Smutty Bear (or Mathó sap'íc'iye, Painted
    Bear, Bear That Paints Itself Black),
    103, **103**, 231n29
Society of Friends. *See* Quakers/
    Quakerism
Sohappy, David, 186
Soldier Chief, 159
South Carolina, 66, 67, 213
South Dakota, 143–44
sovereignty, of Native Nations, xi, xii,
    34–35, 13, 50, 66, 77, 78, 79, 101, 152–
    53, 193, 198, 205–6
    ceding of Māori sovereignty to the
        British, 20–21
    cultural sovereignty issues inherent in
        the Treaty of Fort Sumner, 128
    territorial sovereignty issues inher-
        ent in the Treaty of Fort Sumner,
        126–27
    treaties with Spain and Mexico
        recognizing Navajo territorial sov-
        ereignty, 118
St. Clair, Arthur, 50
St. Mary's (mission school for the
    Potawatomi), 111
Starna, William, 59
Starving Bear (or Lean Bear), 145, 146, **147**
    murder of, 147
State v. Foreman (1835), 81
Stevens, Isaac, 181
    at Medicine Creek treaty council, 181
    at Neah Bay treaty council, 182–83
    at Treaty of Point Elliot council, 181
    at Walla Walla treaty council, 183–84
Stone Calf, 151
Stop Treaty Abuse, 186, 192
Story, Joseph, 80
Sullivan-Clinton Expedition (1779), 46
Sun Chief, 167
Sun Dance, 8
    banning of, 4, 89

SuWorhrom, 216, 217
Sweet Medicine, 144
Sword, George, 231n25
Syracuse (New York) *Post-Standard,* 59

T

Tamanend, 61, 62
    statue of, **61**
Tanner, Helen Hornbeck, 194
Tappan, Samuel F., **25**, 125
Tassel, George, 75
Teedyuscung, 18
Tehuacana Nation, 173
Teias/Teayass, 183
Ten Bears, 145
"termination" policy, 198, 203–5, 213
    failure of, 205, 206
    repudiation of, 209–10
Teton Sioux, 29
    See also Lakota, Sioux Nations
Texas, 66
Thompson, Smith, 80
Thomson, Gerald, 123
Thunderbird (or Nonoma'ohtsevhahtse,
    Richard Davis), 6, **6, 7,** 8, **9**
Tirawahut (Great Spirit), 155, 163, 166
Tirawahutresaru (or Sky Chief), 164,
    165
Toanhooch (or S'hair-at-sehd-wk), 182
Tokaaion, 18
Tonkawa Nation, 173
Topinabee, 86
trappers/fur traders, 90–91
treaties, between Native Nations and the
    United States, xi–xiii, 1–2, 15–33
    passim, 77, 206–7
    and American intent during 1780s,
        46–49
    changing of by acts of Congress,
        29, 206
    clauses in treaties as Washington-
        drafted boilerplate texts, 24, 25
    congressional procedure for approval
        of, 26–29
    and contemporary Native American
        cultures, 223–24
    and differences between Western and
        Native political organization and
        thinking at the time of first con-
        tact, 17–19
    illegal treaties, 48, 63, 234n17
        illegal state treaties, 66–67, 213
    as legally binding and still in effect,
        xi, 2

modern treaties, 32–33, 221, 223
necessity of full congressional
    approval for the enactment of,
    28–29, 127
oral tradition concerning, 59
and the recognition of tribes as nations,
    xi, 12, 14, 30, 34–35, 132, 198, 224
and the relinquishment of Native
    homelands, 132
removal treaties, 85–87, 132, 226n22
    See also Indian Removal Act
    (1830)
and the rights to tribal
    self-determination and self-
    government, 198
signing of, 19
treaties making peace in 1815, 56–58
    at Burlington Heights, 57–58
"treaty adjustments," 213, 223
treaty relationships undermined by
    "civilization," 4–11
tribal reverence/veneration of, 16, 21,
    30, 132
and the United Nations Declaration
    on the Rights of Indigenous Peo-
    ples (2007), 219–20
written, English versions of, 3, 20, 113,
    114
    See also Covenant Chain of Peace; spe-
    cifically listed individual treaties;
    treaty councils
Treaty of 1851. *See* Great Horse Creek
    Treaty (1851)
Treaty of Amity and Friendship (1682
    [Penn Treaty]), 2, 61–64
    terms of, 62
Treaty Beer, 186, **187,** 197
    boycott of, 187
Treaty of Canandaigua (1794), **54–55**
    and the annual delivery of treaty cloth
    by the U.S. government, 58
    background of, 50–51
    terms of, 53, 56
Treaty of Chicago (1833), 86, 87
treaty councils, 44, 181
    and interpreters, 42, 44
    rhetoric of, 41
    See also Great Horse Creek Treaty
    (1851); Walla Walla treaty council
    (May 28–June 11, 1855)
Treaty of Dancing Rabbit Creek (1830),
    77, 85
Treaty Dollar (David P. Bradley), **2**
Treaty of Fort Jackson (1814), 140

Treaty of Fort Pitt (1778), 21–23, 34
    article 4, 22
    article 6, 23
Treaty of Fort Sumner (1868 [Treaty with
    the Navajo]), 23, **24,** 25–26, 34, 123,
    126–31, **127**
    cultural sovereignty issues inherent
    in, 128
    Navajo rights protected by, 127–28
    terms of, 127
    territorial sovereignty issues inherent
    in, 126–27
Treaty of Ft. Meigs (1817), 19
Treaty of Ghent (1815), 56, 140
Treaty of Guadalupe Hidalgo (1848), 120
Treaty of Hopewell (1785), 19, 34
Treaty of Long Meadows. *See* Great Horse
    Creek Treaty (1851)
treaty making, 198
    and the federal-state struggle for
    treaty-making authority, 46, 48,
    66–67
    fundamental tenets of early treaty
    making, xiii
    Haudenosaunee culture of, 39–44
    Indian Nations' view of early treaties,
    17, 30, 112–13, 114–15
    language misunderstandings during,
    3, 20, 112–13, 114, 155–56, 226n18
    misunderstandings in, 3, 101, 102, 112–14
    modern treaty-making, 32–33, 221
    origins of, 37–38
    role of interpreters in, 2, 42, 44, 96–97,
    98, 100, 107, **108,** 113
    missionary interpreters, 144
    roots of American treaty making, 15,
    37–42, 62, 66, 68
    roots of Native treaty making, 42,
    133–34, 143
    style of oratory in early treaties, 2
Treaty of Medicine Creek (1854), 181, 185
Treaty of Neah Bay (1855), 182–83, 185
Treaty of New Echota (1835), 226n18
Treaty of New York (1790), **138, 139,** 143
    goals of the United States in, 135–36
    secret provision of, 137
    terms of, 136–37
Treaty of Paris (1783), 50
Treaty of Pensacola (1784), 134
Treaty of Point Elliott (1855), 181, 185
Treaty of Point No Point (1855), 185
Treaty of Portage des Sioux (1815), 19
Treaty of Waitangi (1840), 20–21
Treaty of Washington (1866), 226n18

Treaty with the Cheyenne and Arapaho.
    See Medicine Lodge Creek Treaty (1867)
Tree of Peace symbol, 37, 57
Trinity River, 175, 216
Trumbull, John, 51, 135
Tse-heu-wrl, 182
Tséyi' (Canyon de Chelly), 121
Tsistsistas. *See* Cheyenne Nation
Tsoodził (Mount Taylor), 120, 126
Tsosie, Rebecca, 126
Tuscarora Nation, 36
    See also Haudenosaunee Nations
Tvpafkv (or Heart of the Fire), 139
Two Row Renewal Campaign, 59–60
Two Row Treaty (1613), controversy con-
    cerning the "forgery" of, 59–60
Two-Row Wampum Belt. *See* wampum
    belts, Two-Row Wampum Belt
    (Guswenta)

U

Uncas, 16
United Illinois and Wabash Land Compa-
    nies, 69, 70, 71, 72, 229n6
United Nations Declaration on the Rights
    of Indigenous Peoples (2007), 84
    and Native Nation treaties with the
    United States, 219–20
United States, 16, 152, 153
    defeat of by united Indian Nations in
    the Old Northwest, 50
    enactment of the first federal law
    regarding Native Nations (P.L.
    1-33), 136
    following of British treaty-making
    protocols by, 48–49
    modernization of, 152
    principles on which U.S. relations with
    Native Nations should be con-
    ducted, 49
    tensions with Great Britain, 46
    See also Native Nations, and the United
    States in the twentieth century;
    treaties, between Native Nations
    and the United States; War of 1812
United States Code, 25 U.S.C. § 71, 26,
    28–29
    history of its adoption, 26–28
United States Constitution, 195
    article 2, section 2, 26
    article 6, 34
    article 6, clause 2, 1
    Fifth Amendment takings clause of, 30
    Supremacy Clause of, 77, 78